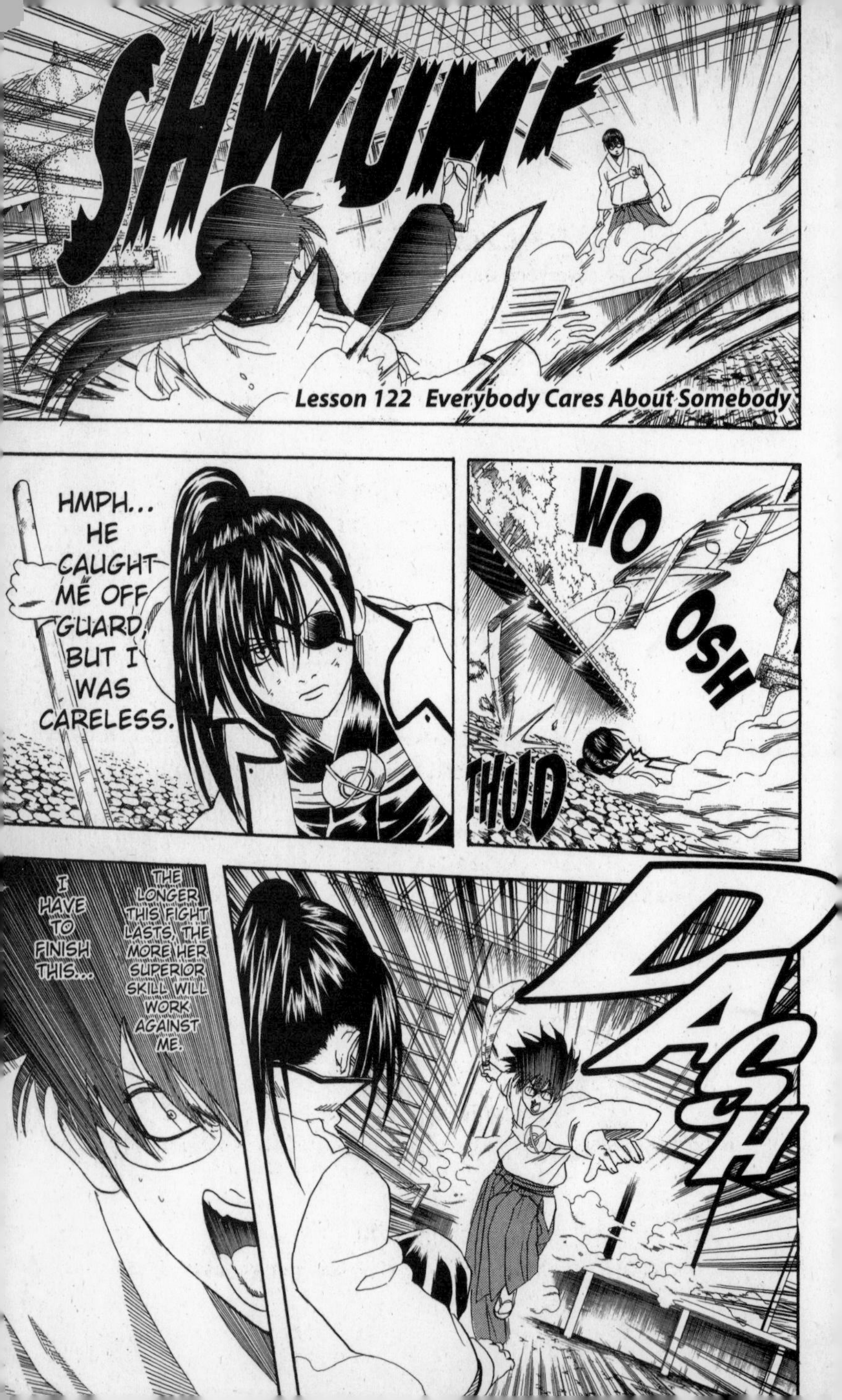
SHWUMF
Lesson 122 Everybody Cares About Somebody
WOOSH
THUD
HMPH... HE CAUGHT ME OFF GUARD, BUT I WAS CARELESS.
DASH
THE LONGER THIS FIGHT LASTS, THE MORE HER SUPERIOR SKILL WILL WORK AGAINST ME.
I HAVE TO FINISH THIS...

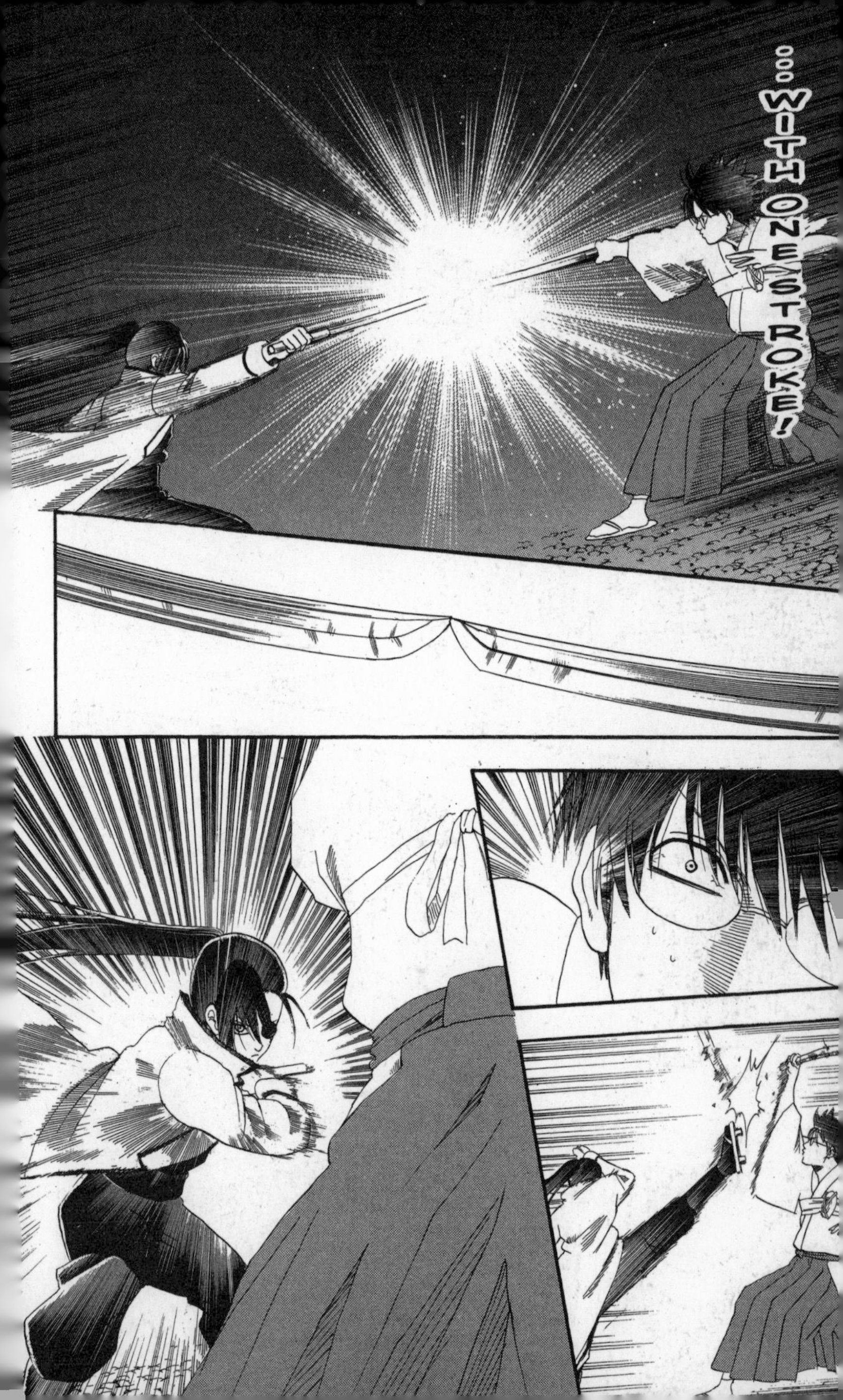
...WITH ONE STROKE!

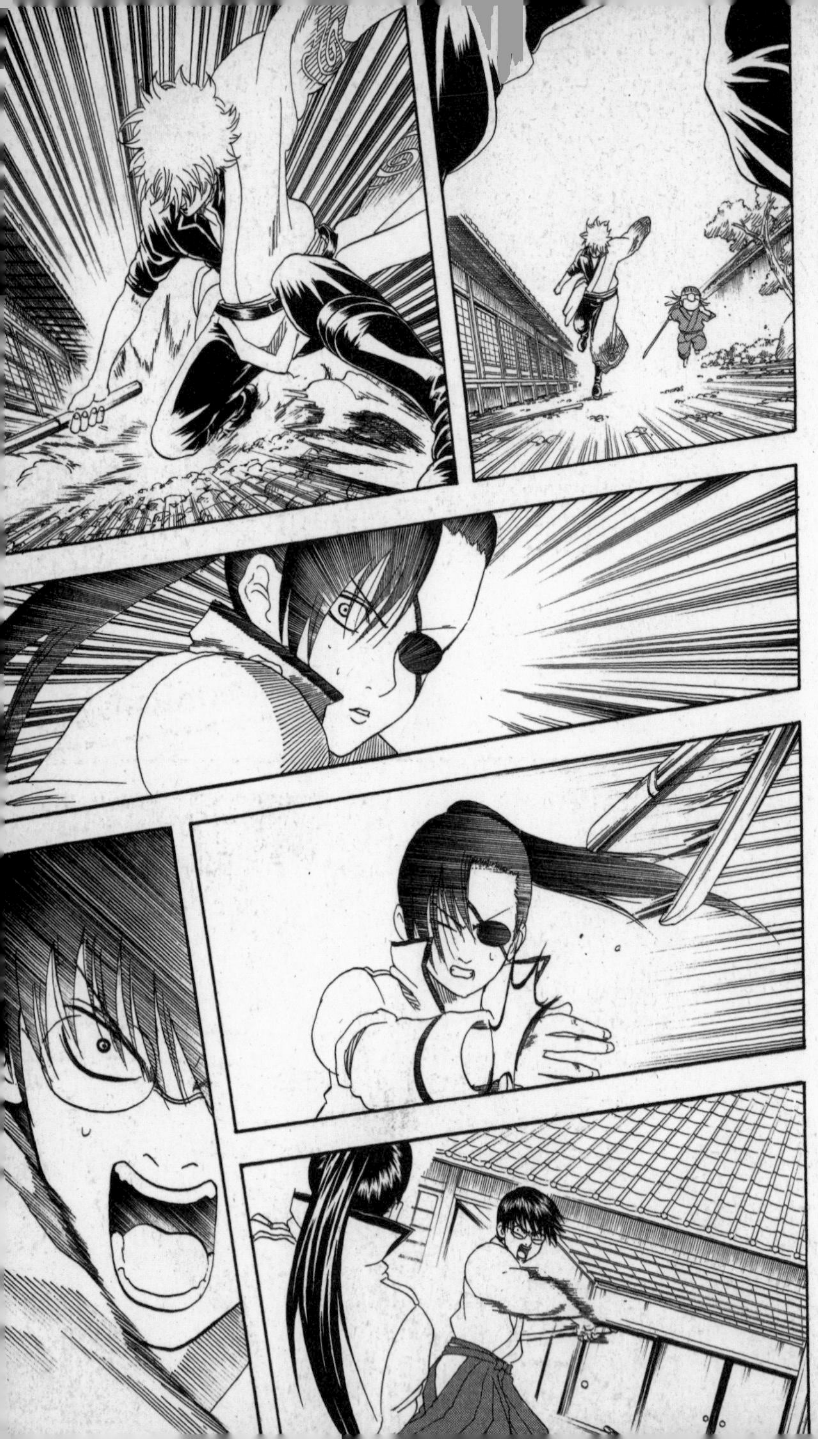

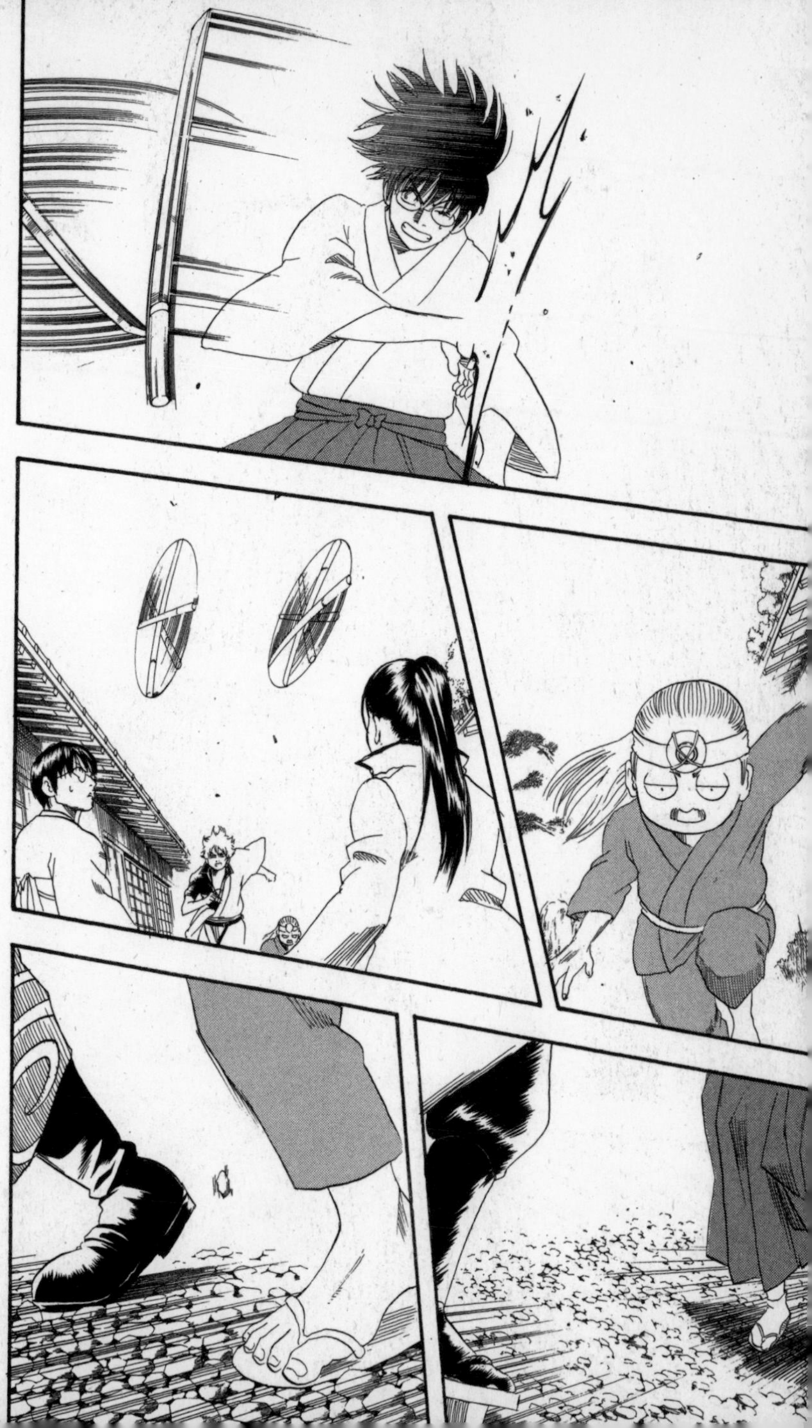

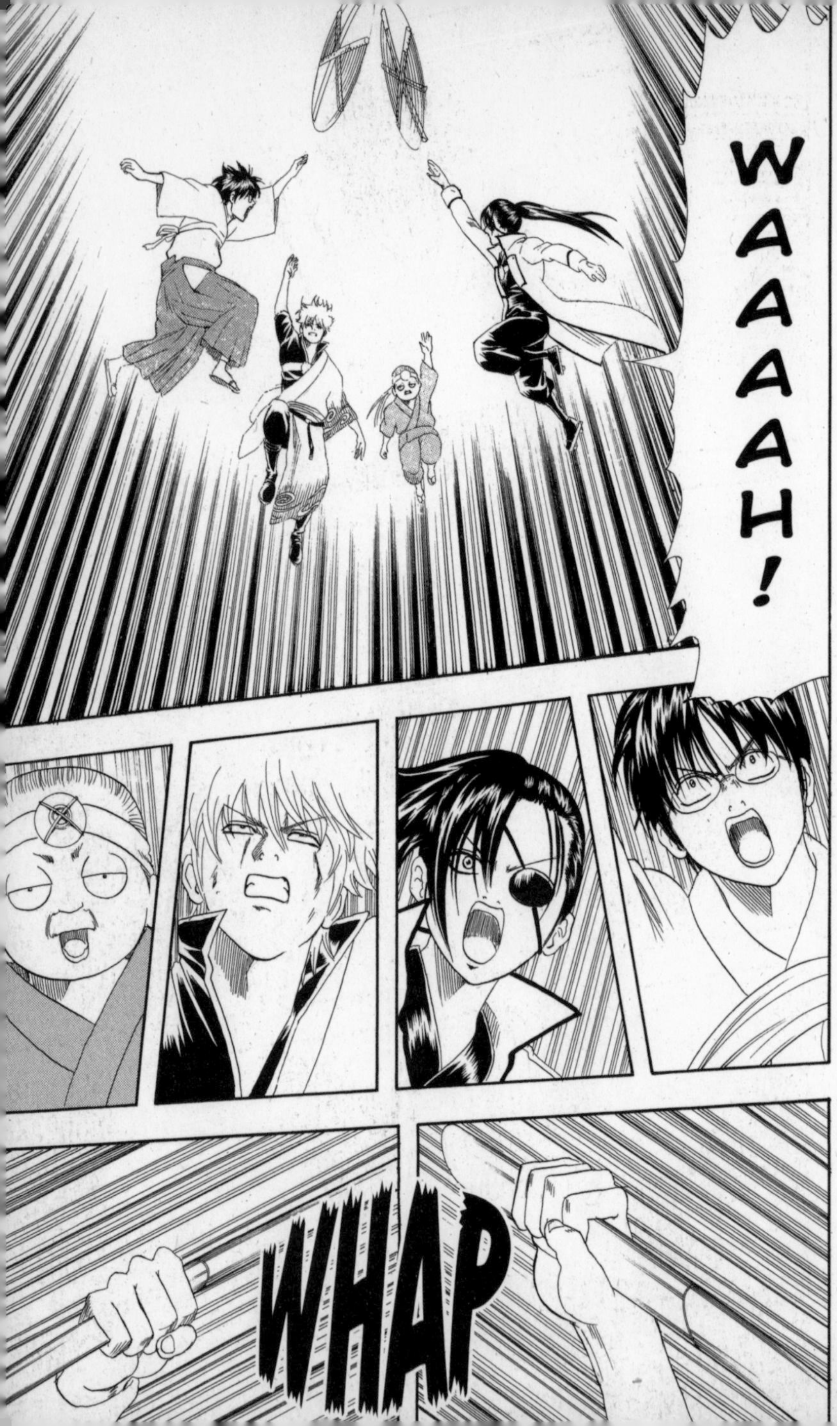
WAAAAH!
WHAP

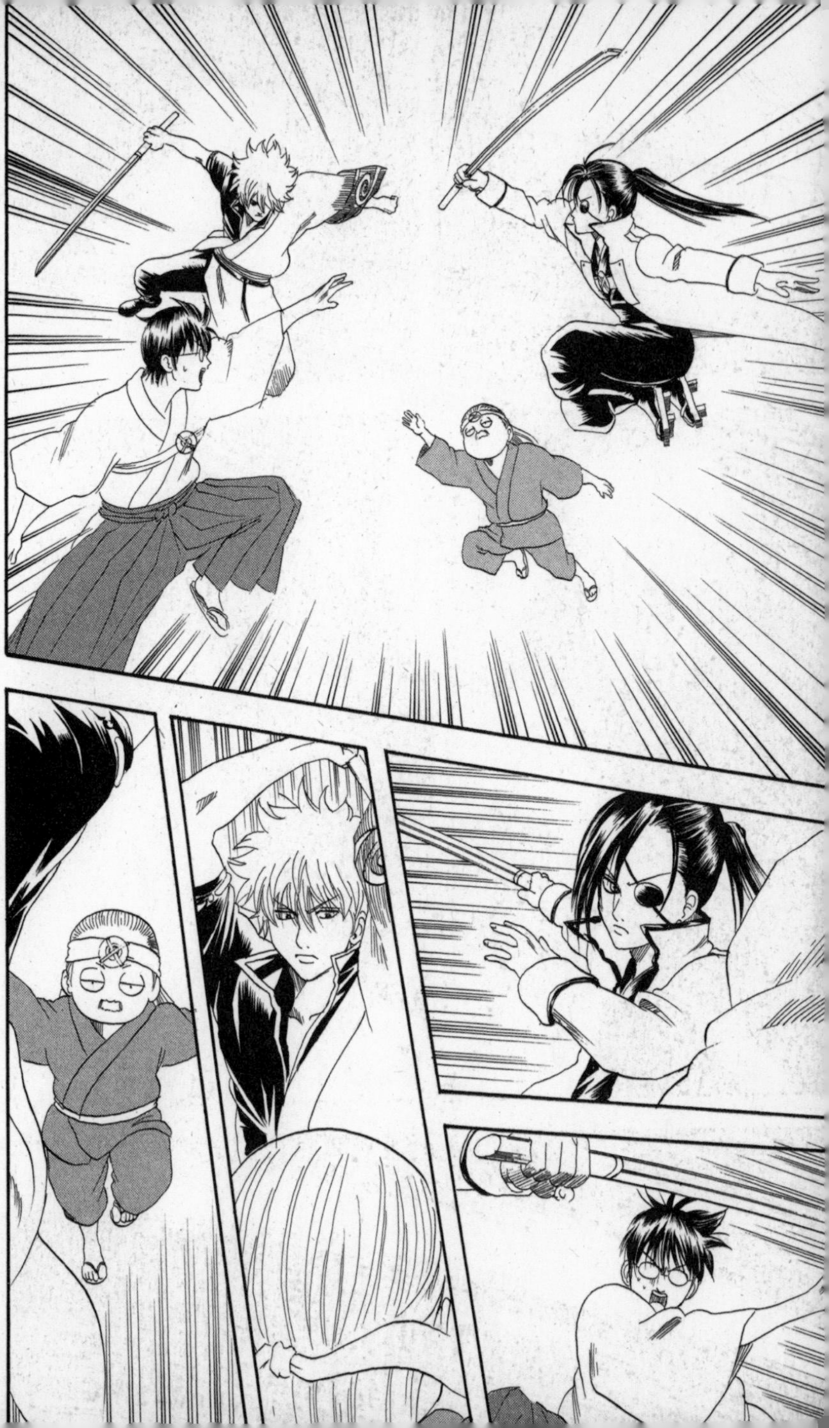

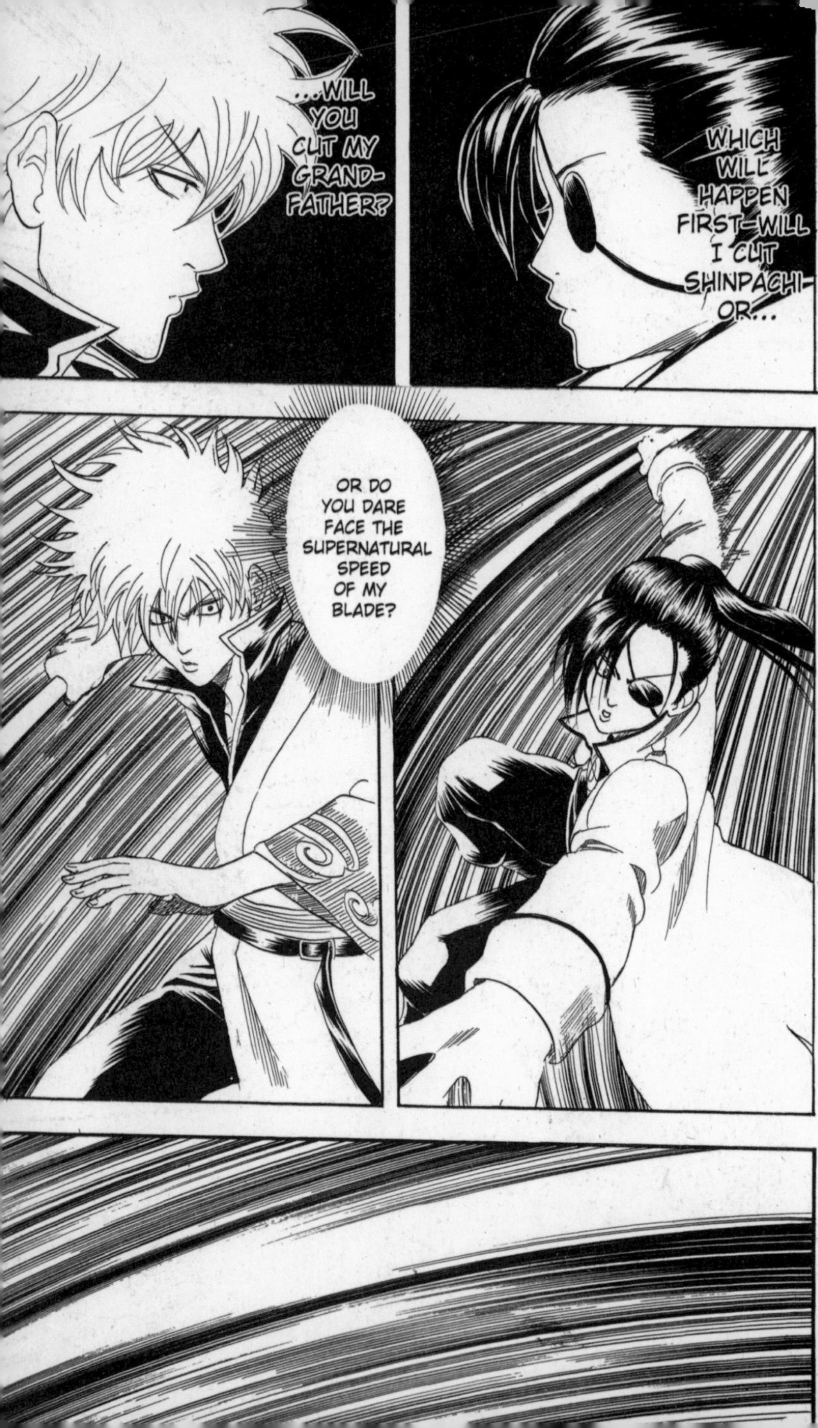
WHICH WILL HAPPEN FIRST—WILL I CUT SHINPACHI OR...
...WILL YOU CUT MY GRAND-FATHER?
OR DO YOU DARE FACE THE SUPERNATURAL SPEED OF MY BLADE?

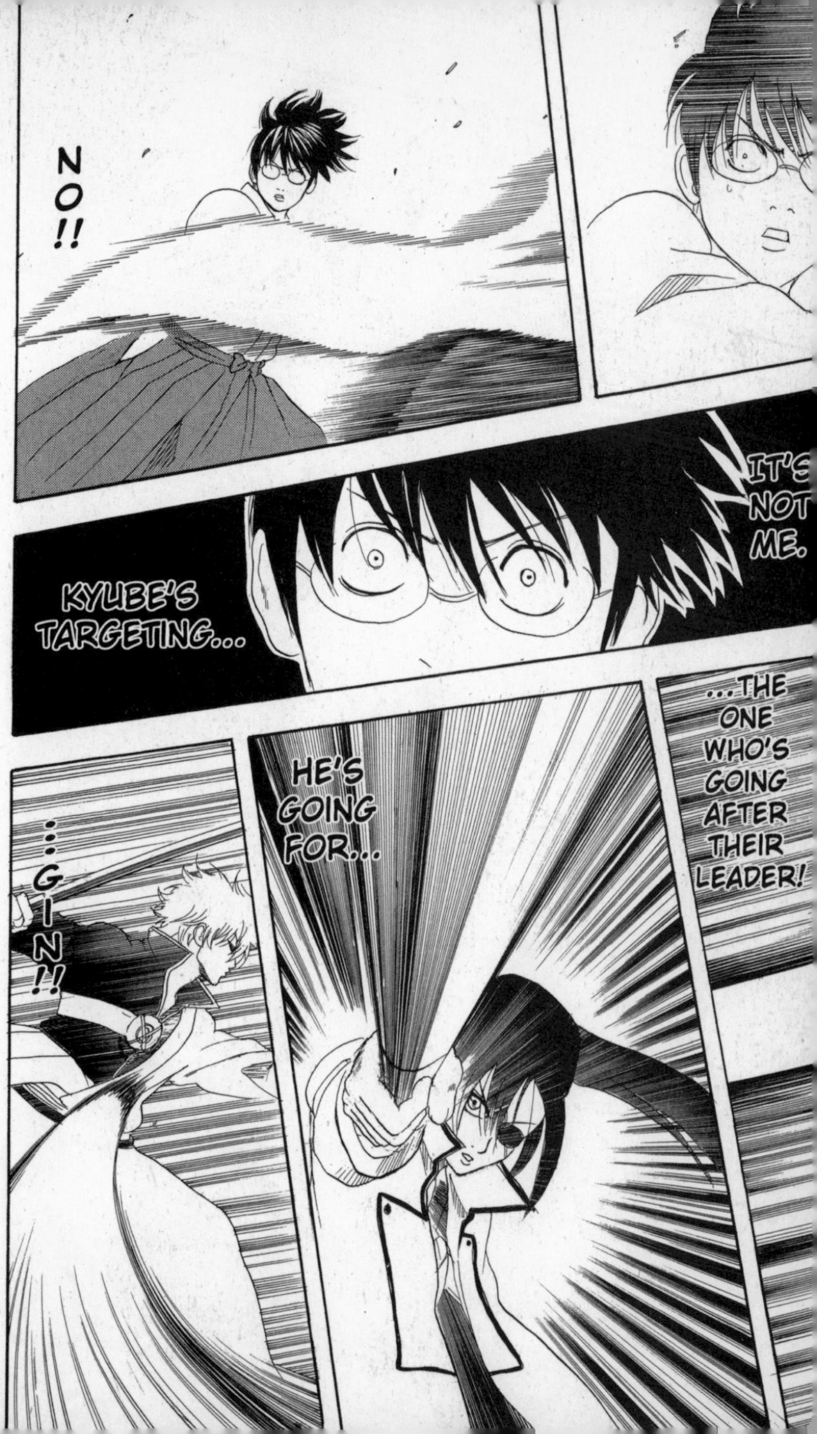
NO!!
IT'S NOT ME.
KYUBE'S TARGETING...
...THE ONE WHO'S GOING AFTER THEIR LEADER!
HE'S GOING FOR...
...GIN!!

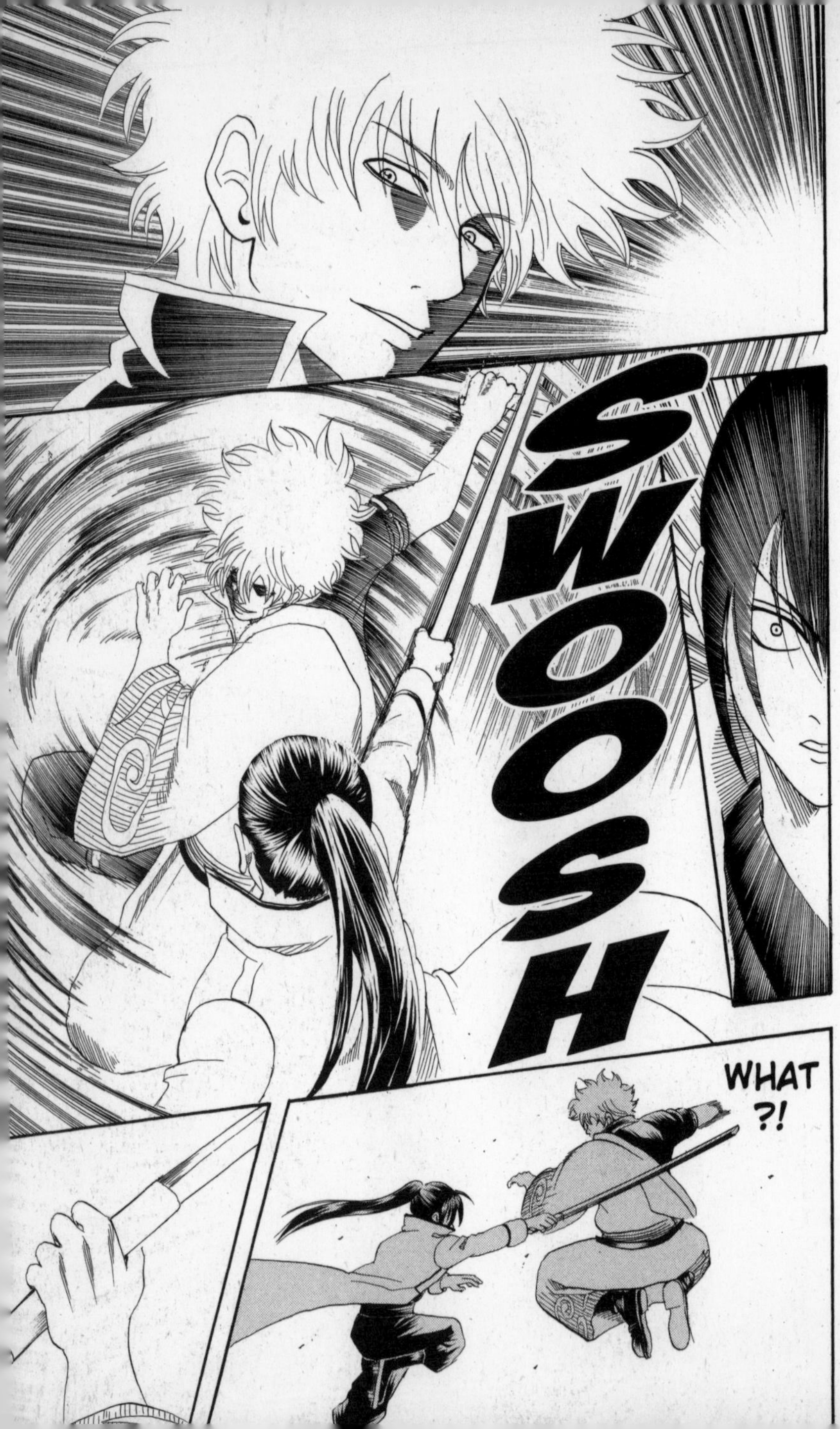
SWOSH
WHAT ?!

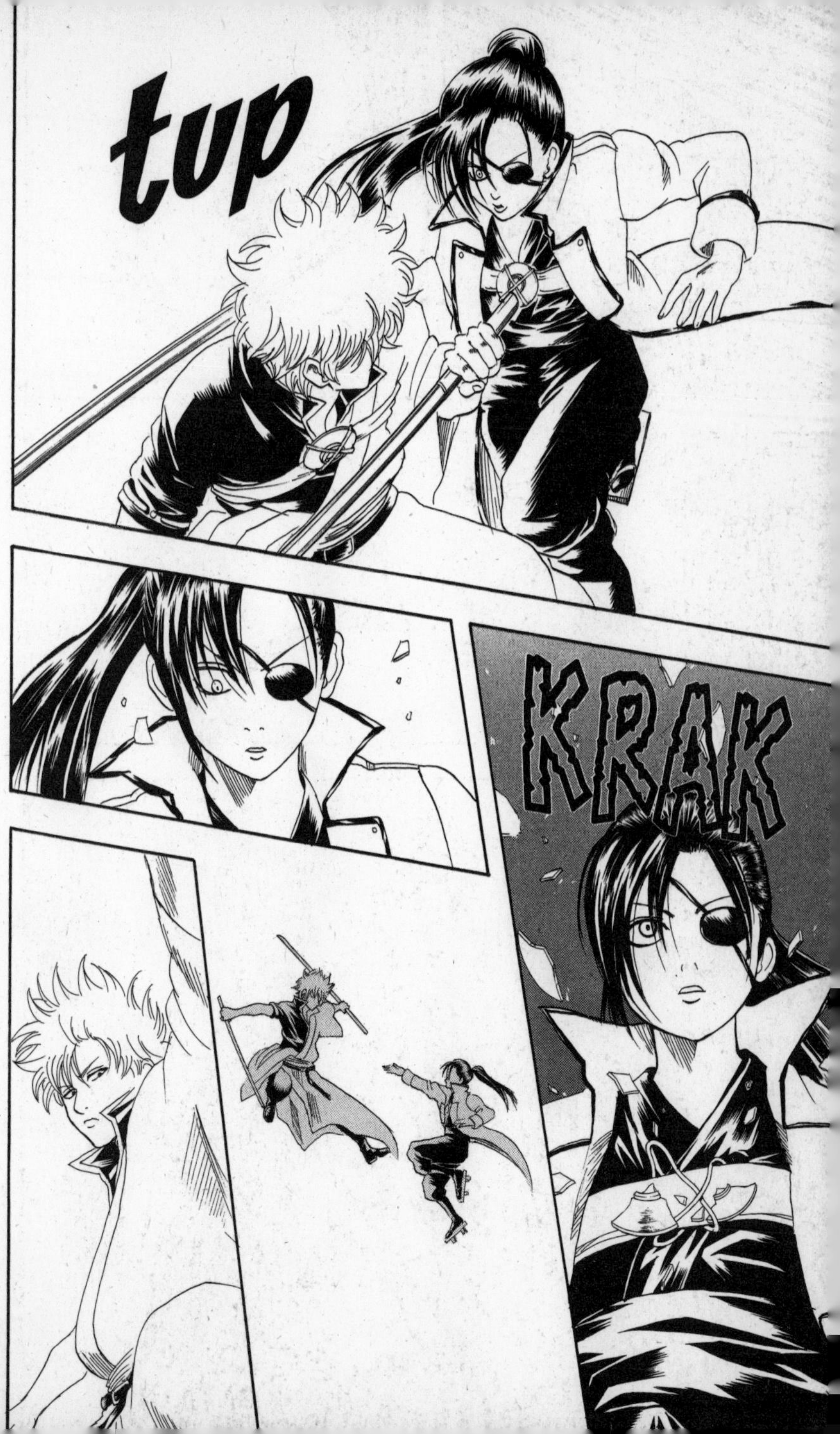
tup
KRAK

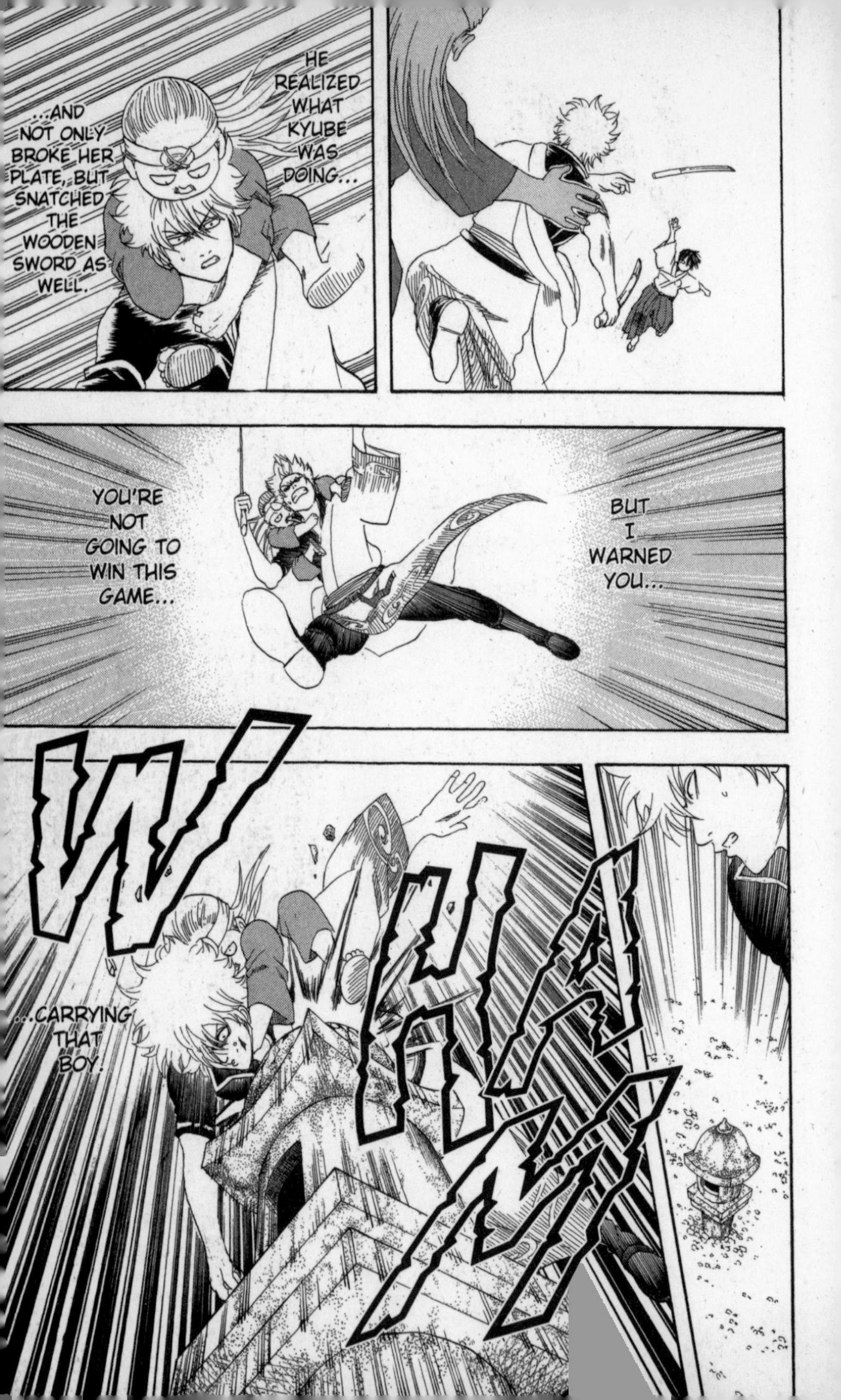
HE REALIZED WHAT KYUBE WAS DOING...
...AND NOT ONLY BROKE HER PLATE, BUT SNATCHED THE WOODEN SWORD AS WELL.
BUT I WARNED YOU...
YOU'RE NOT GOING TO WIN THIS GAME...
WHAM
...CARRYING THAT BOY.

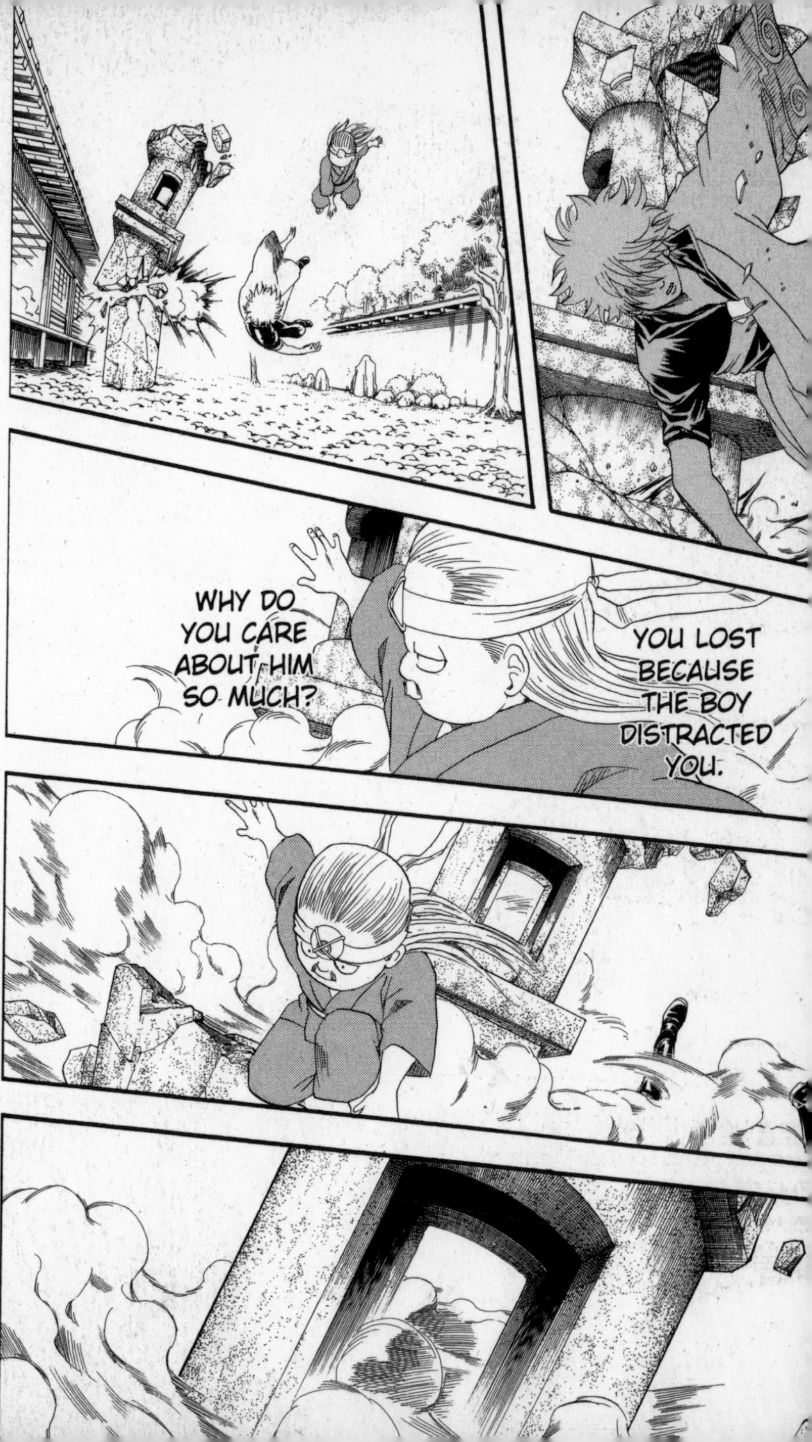
YOU LOST BECAUSE THE BOY DISTRACTED YOU.
WHY DO YOU CARE ABOUT HIM SO MUCH?

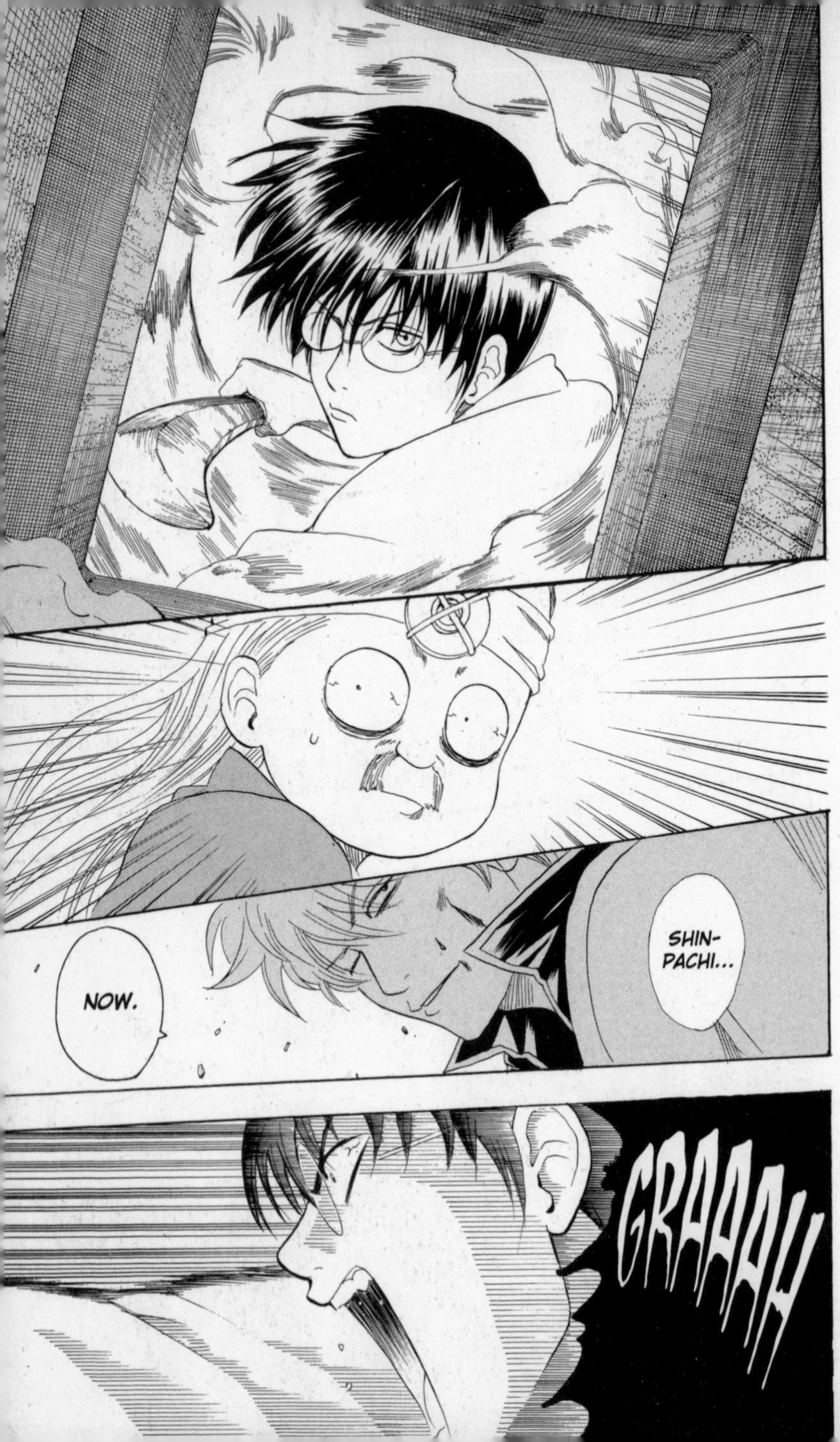
SHIN-PACHI...
NOW.
GRAAAH

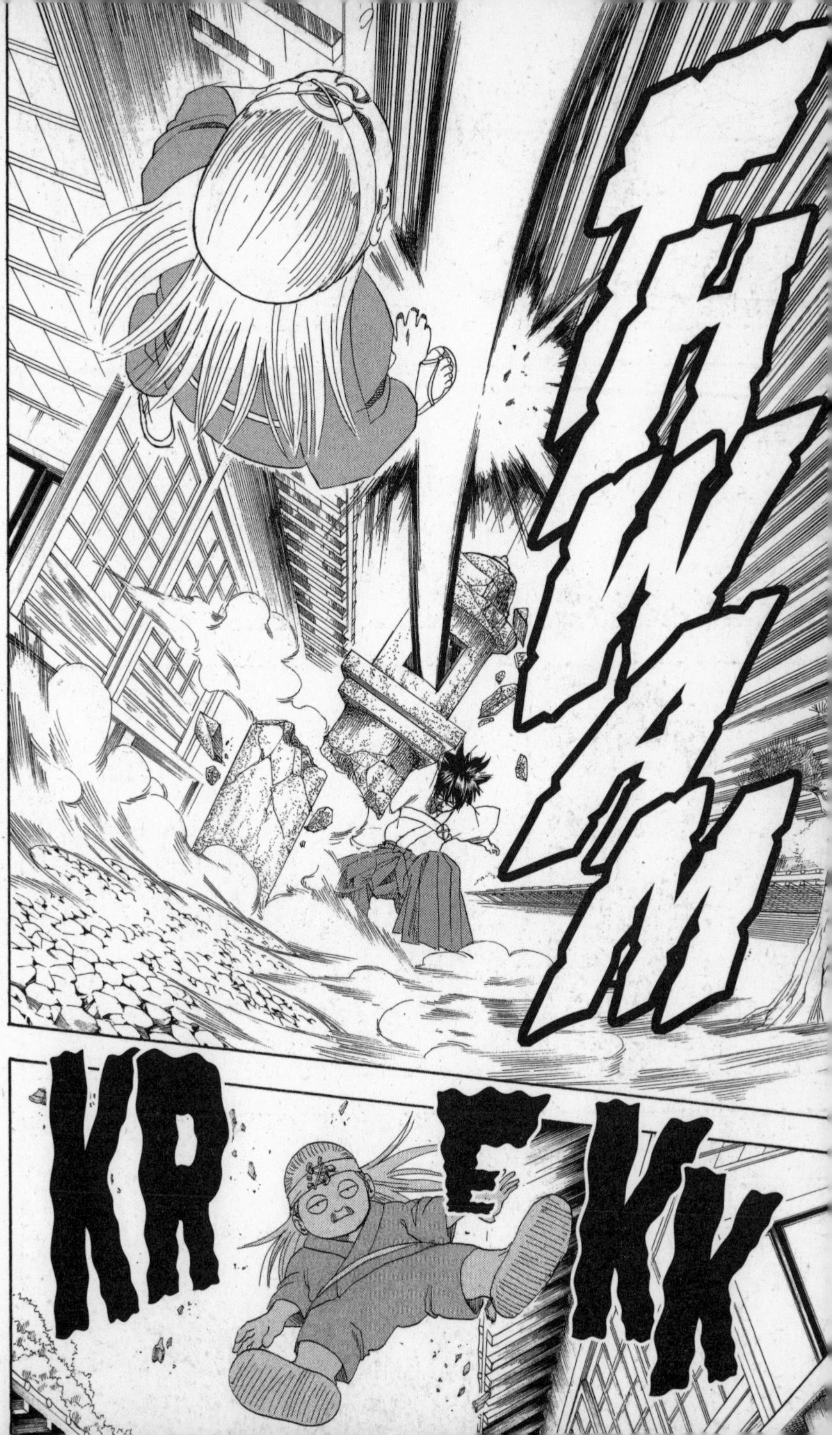
KREKK

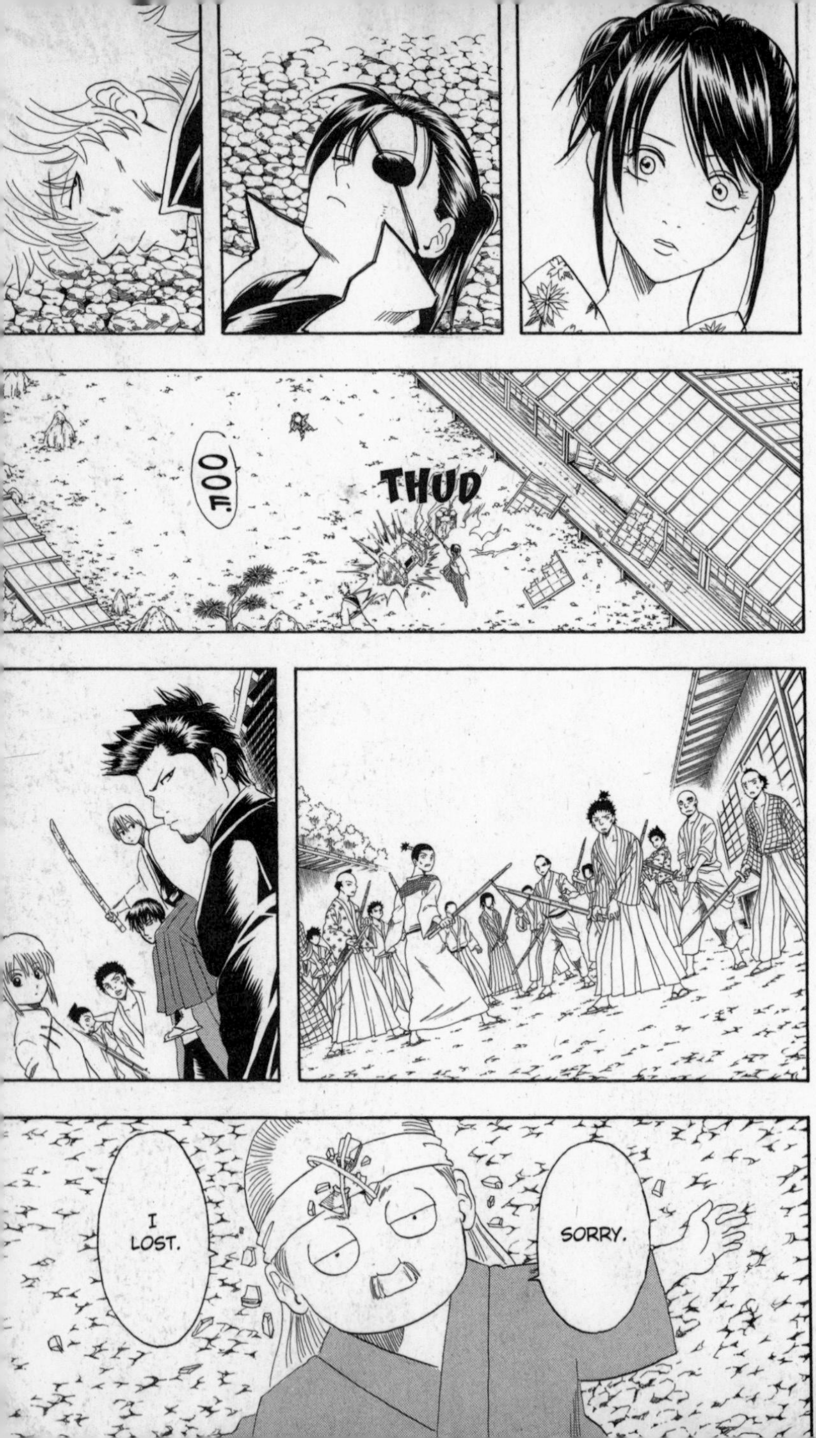
THUD
OOF.
SORRY.
I LOST.

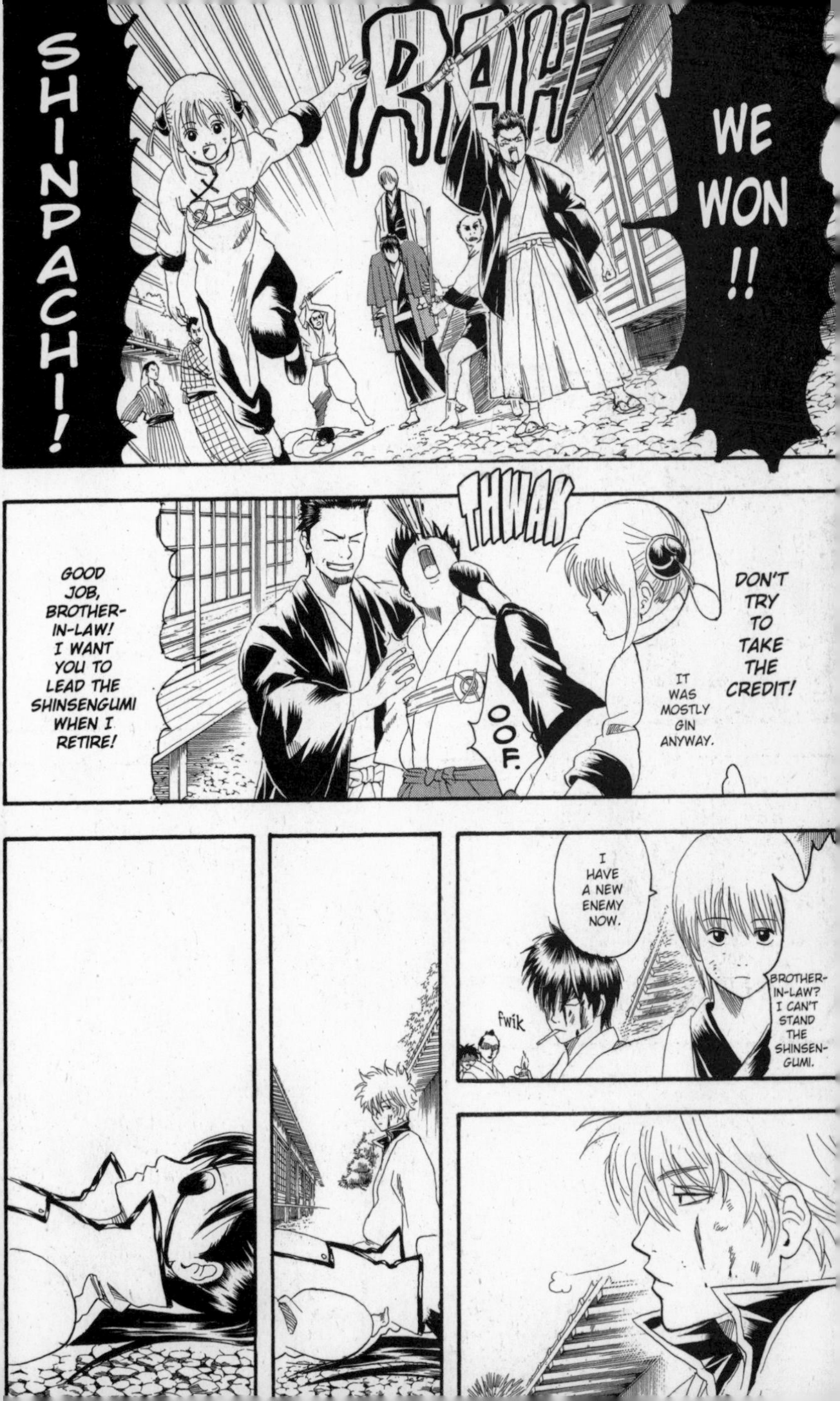
WE WON!!
RAH
SHINPACHI!
DON'T TRY TO TAKE THE CREDIT!
IT WAS MOSTLY GIN ANYWAY.
THWAK
OOF.
GOOD JOB, BROTHER-IN-LAW! I WANT YOU TO LEAD THE SHINSENGUMI WHEN I RETIRE!
BROTHER-IN-LAW? I CAN'T STAND THE SHINSEN-GUMI.
I HAVE A NEW ENEMY NOW.
fwik

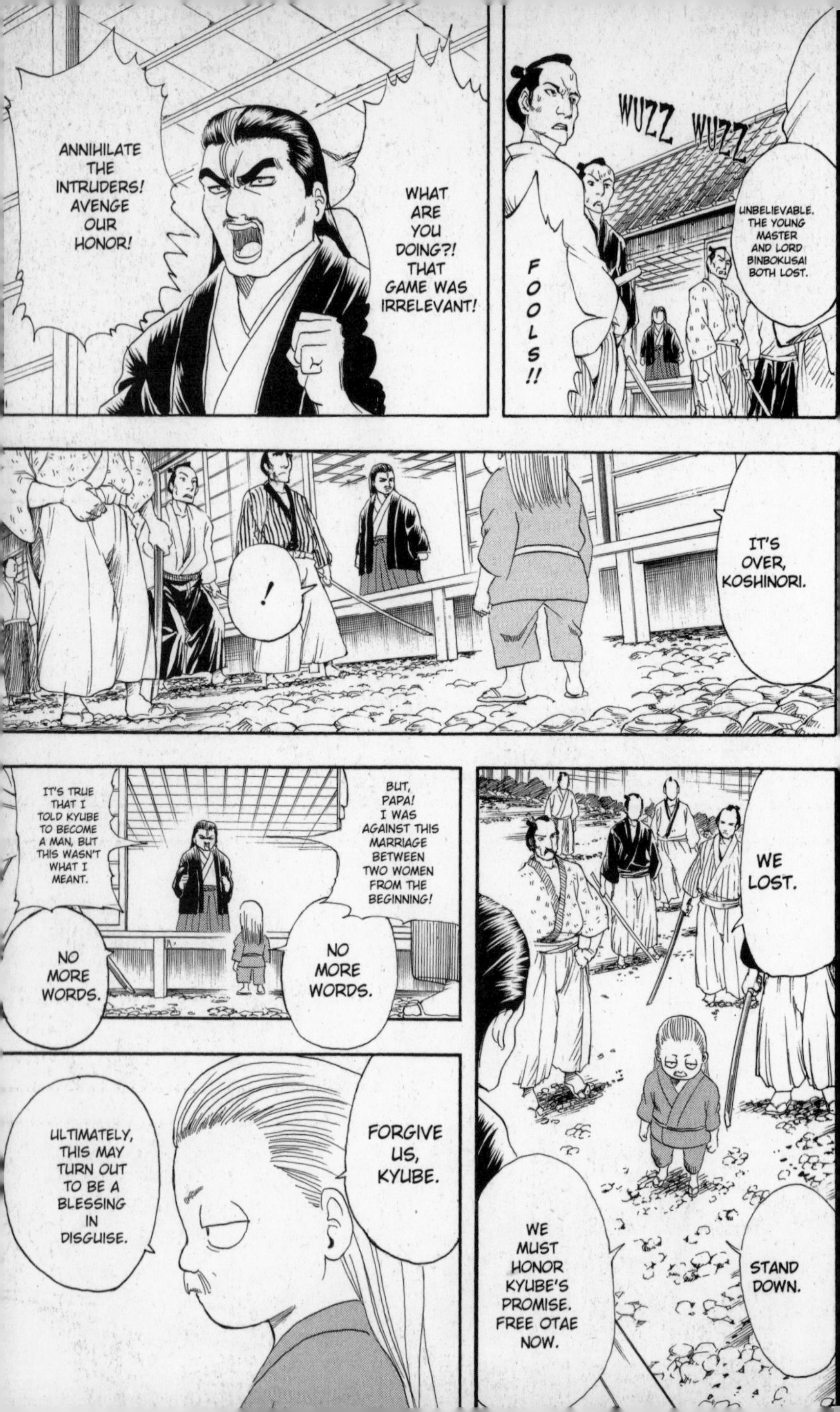
WUZZ WUZZ
UNBELIEVABLE. THE YOUNG MASTER AND LORD BINBOKUSAI BOTH LOST.
FOOLS!!
WHAT ARE YOU DOING?! THAT GAME WAS IRRELEVANT!
ANNIHILATE THE INTRUDERS! AVENGE OUR HONOR!
IT'S OVER, KOSHINORI.
!
WE LOST.
STAND DOWN.
WE MUST HONOR KYUBE'S PROMISE. FREE OTAE NOW.
BUT, PAPA! I WAS AGAINST THIS MARRIAGE BETWEEN TWO WOMEN FROM THE BEGINNING!
IT'S TRUE THAT I TOLD KYUBE TO BECOME A MAN, BUT THIS WASN'T WHAT I MEANT.
NO MORE WORDS.
NO MORE WORDS.
FORGIVE US, KYUBE.
ULTIMATELY, THIS MAY TURN OUT TO BE A BLESSING IN DISGUISE.

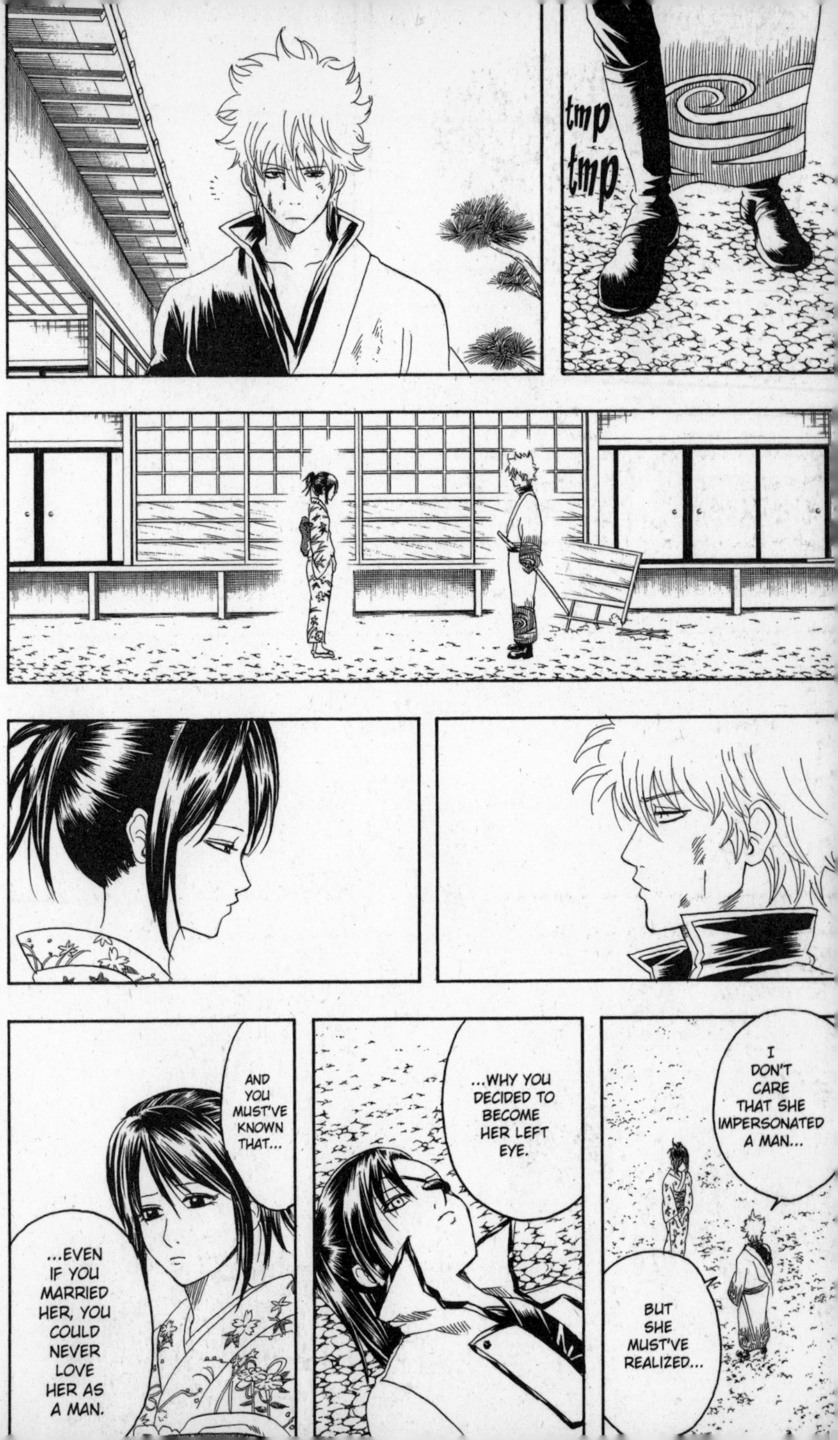
tmp
tmp
I DON'T CARE THAT SHE IMPERSONATED A MAN...
BUT SHE MUST'VE REALIZED...
...WHY YOU DECIDED TO BECOME HER LEFT EYE.
AND YOU MUST'VE KNOWN THAT...
...EVEN IF YOU MARRIED HER, YOU COULD NEVER LOVE HER AS A MAN.

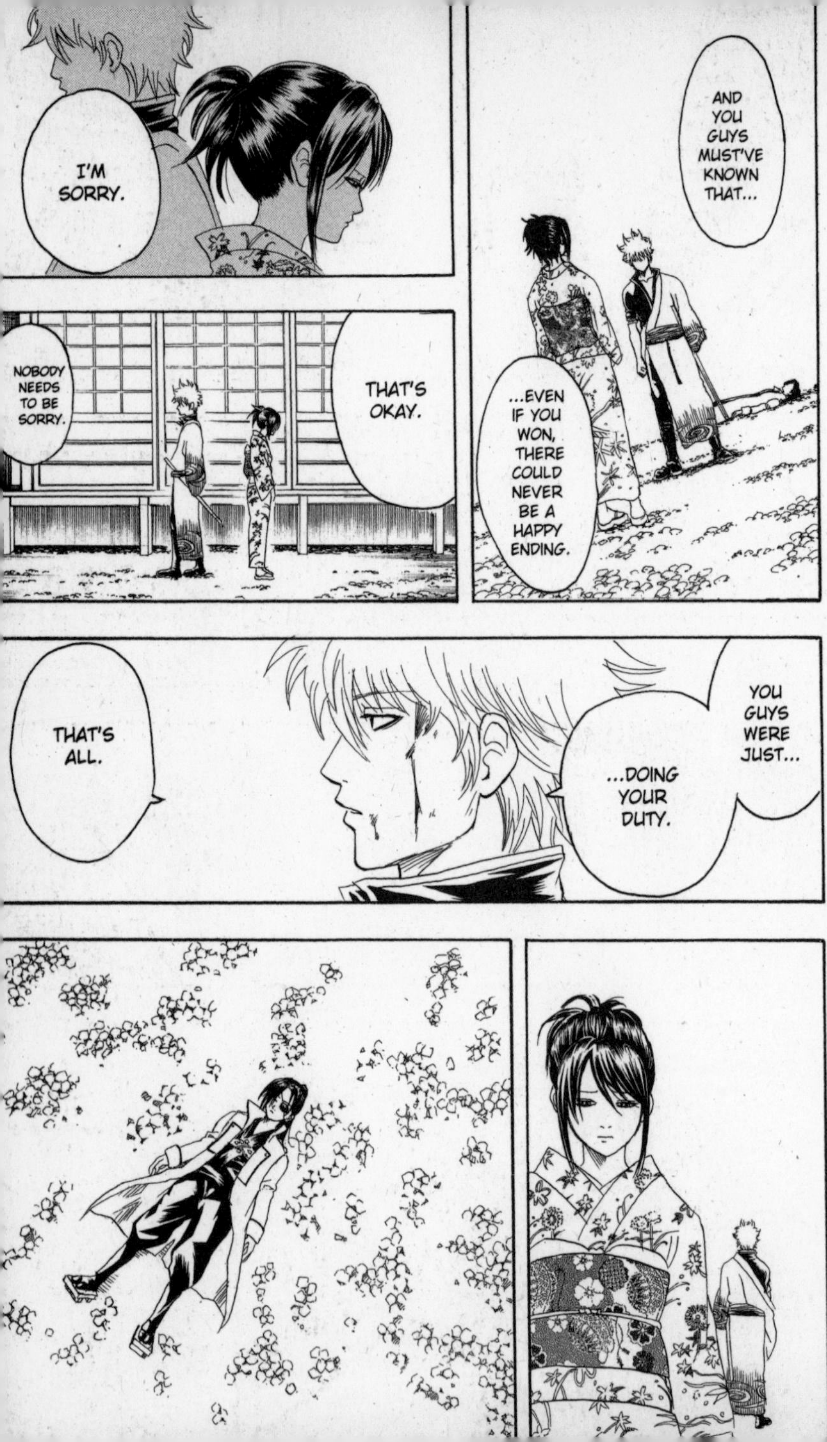
AND YOU GUYS MUST'VE KNOWN THAT...
...EVEN IF YOU WON, THERE COULD NEVER BE A HAPPY ENDING.
I'M SORRY.
THAT'S OKAY.
NOBODY NEEDS TO BE SORRY.
YOU GUYS WERE JUST...
...DOING YOUR DUTY.
THAT'S ALL.

● Published in *Weekly Shonen JUMP*, 2006 as the
cover illustration of Volume 36 & 37 joint issue

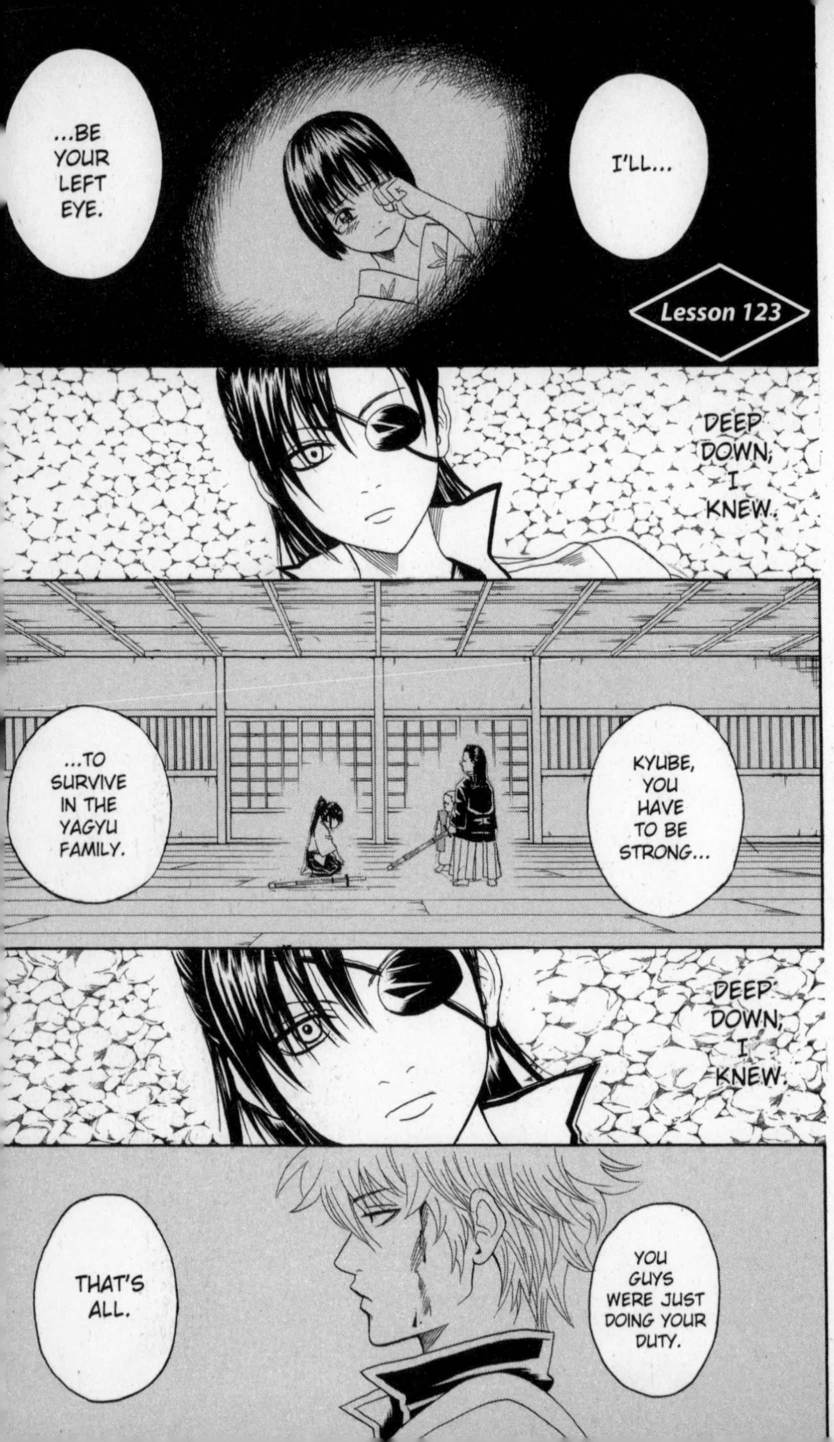
I'LL...
...BE YOUR LEFT EYE.
Lesson 123
DEEP DOWN, I KNEW.
KYUBE, YOU HAVE TO BE STRONG...
...TO SURVIVE IN THE YAGYU FAMILY.
DEEP DOWN, I KNEW.
YOU GUYS WERE JUST DOING YOUR DUTY.
THAT'S ALL.

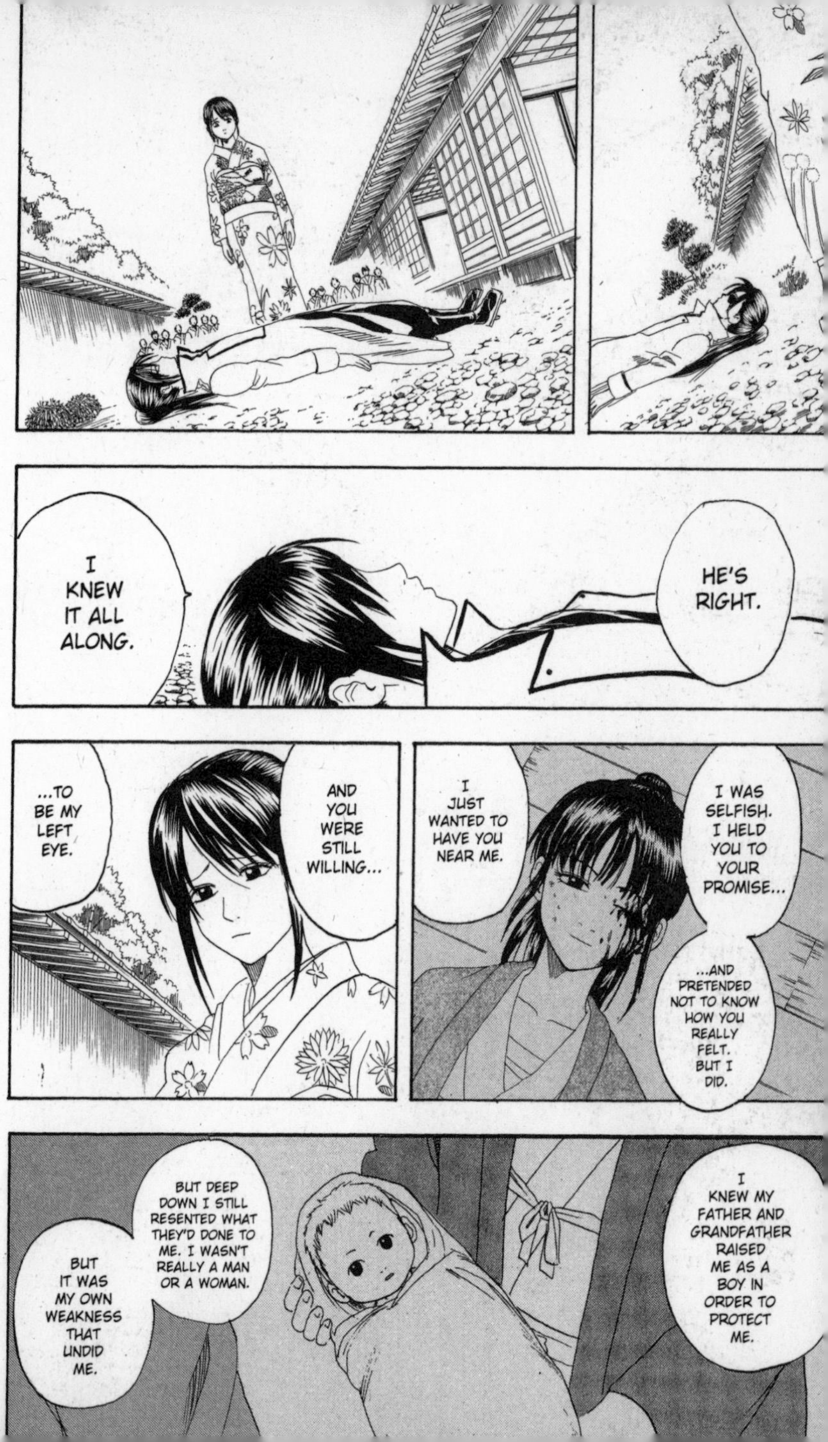
HE'S RIGHT.
I KNEW IT ALL ALONG.
I WAS SELFISH. I HELD YOU TO YOUR PROMISE...
...AND PRETENDED NOT TO KNOW HOW YOU REALLY FELT. BUT I DID.
I JUST WANTED TO HAVE YOU NEAR ME.
AND YOU WERE STILL WILLING...
...TO BE MY LEFT EYE.
I KNEW MY FATHER AND GRANDFATHER RAISED ME AS A BOY IN ORDER TO PROTECT ME.
BUT DEEP DOWN I STILL RESENTED WHAT THEY'D DONE TO ME. I WASN'T REALLY A MAN OR A WOMAN.
BUT IT WAS MY OWN WEAKNESS THAT UNDID ME.

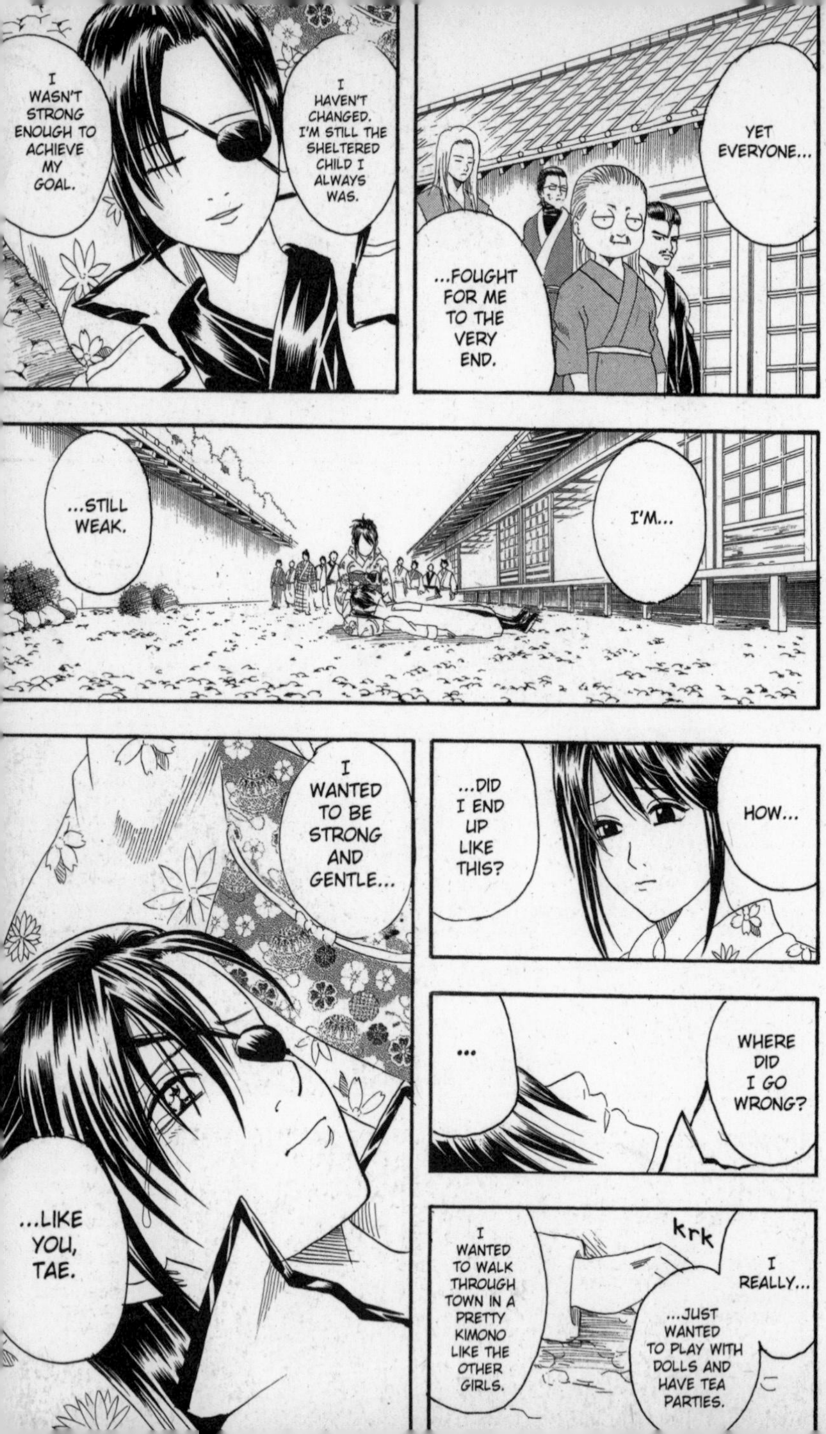
YET EVERYONE...
...FOUGHT FOR ME TO THE VERY END.
I HAVEN'T CHANGED. I'M STILL THE SHELTERED CHILD I ALWAYS WAS.
I WASN'T STRONG ENOUGH TO ACHIEVE MY GOAL.
I'M...
...STILL WEAK.
HOW...
...DID I END UP LIKE THIS?
WHERE DID I GO WRONG?
...
krk
I REALLY...
...JUST WANTED TO PLAY WITH DOLLS AND HAVE TEA PARTIES.
I WANTED TO WALK THROUGH TOWN IN A PRETTY KIMONO LIKE THE OTHER GIRLS.
I WANTED TO BE STRONG AND GENTLE...
...LIKE YOU, TAE.

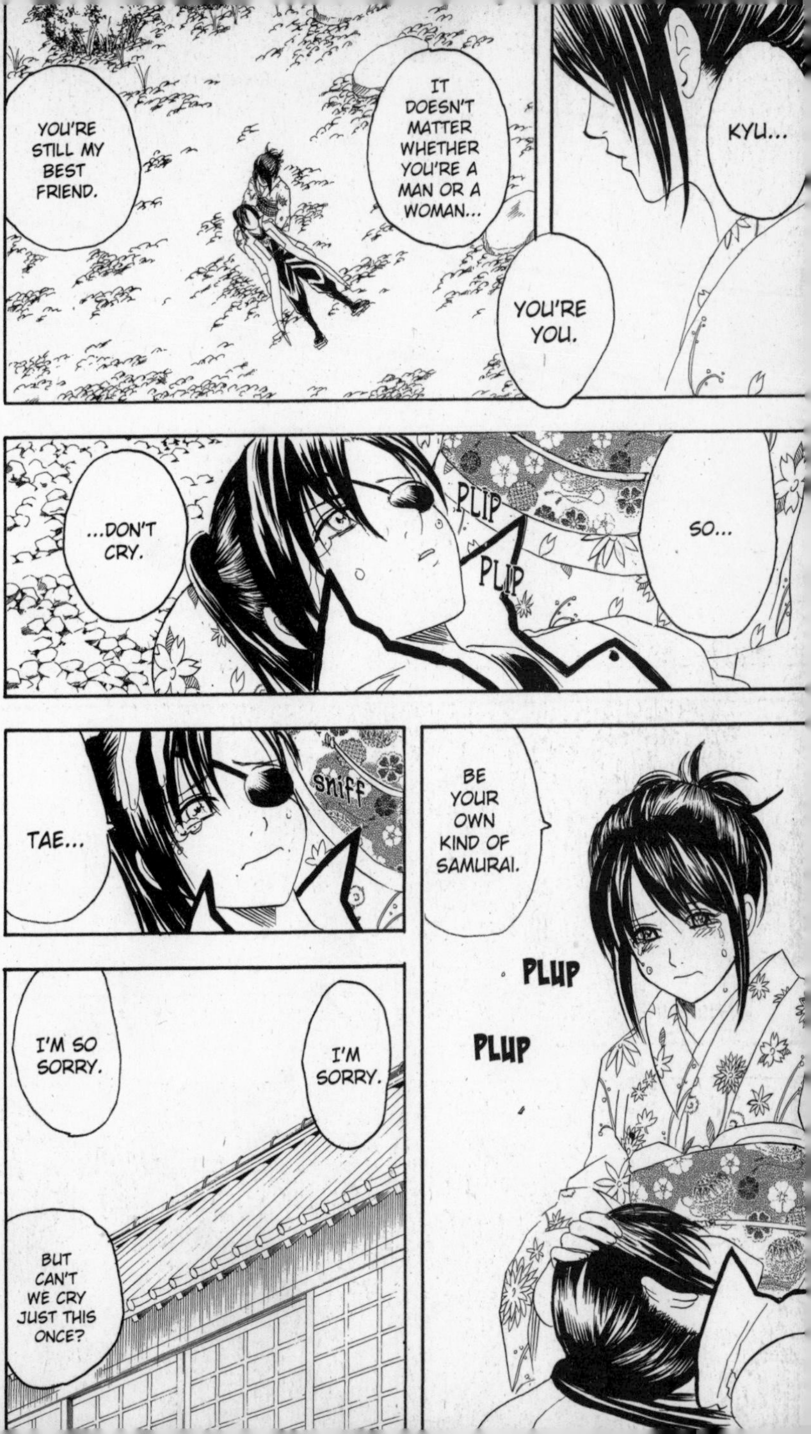
KYU...
IT DOESN'T MATTER WHETHER YOU'RE A MAN OR A WOMAN...
YOU'RE YOU.
YOU'RE STILL MY BEST FRIEND.
SO...
PLIP
PLIP
...DON'T CRY.
BE YOUR OWN KIND OF SAMURAI.
PLUP
PLUP
sniff
TAE...
I'M SORRY.
I'M SO SORRY.
BUT CAN'T WE CRY JUST THIS ONCE?

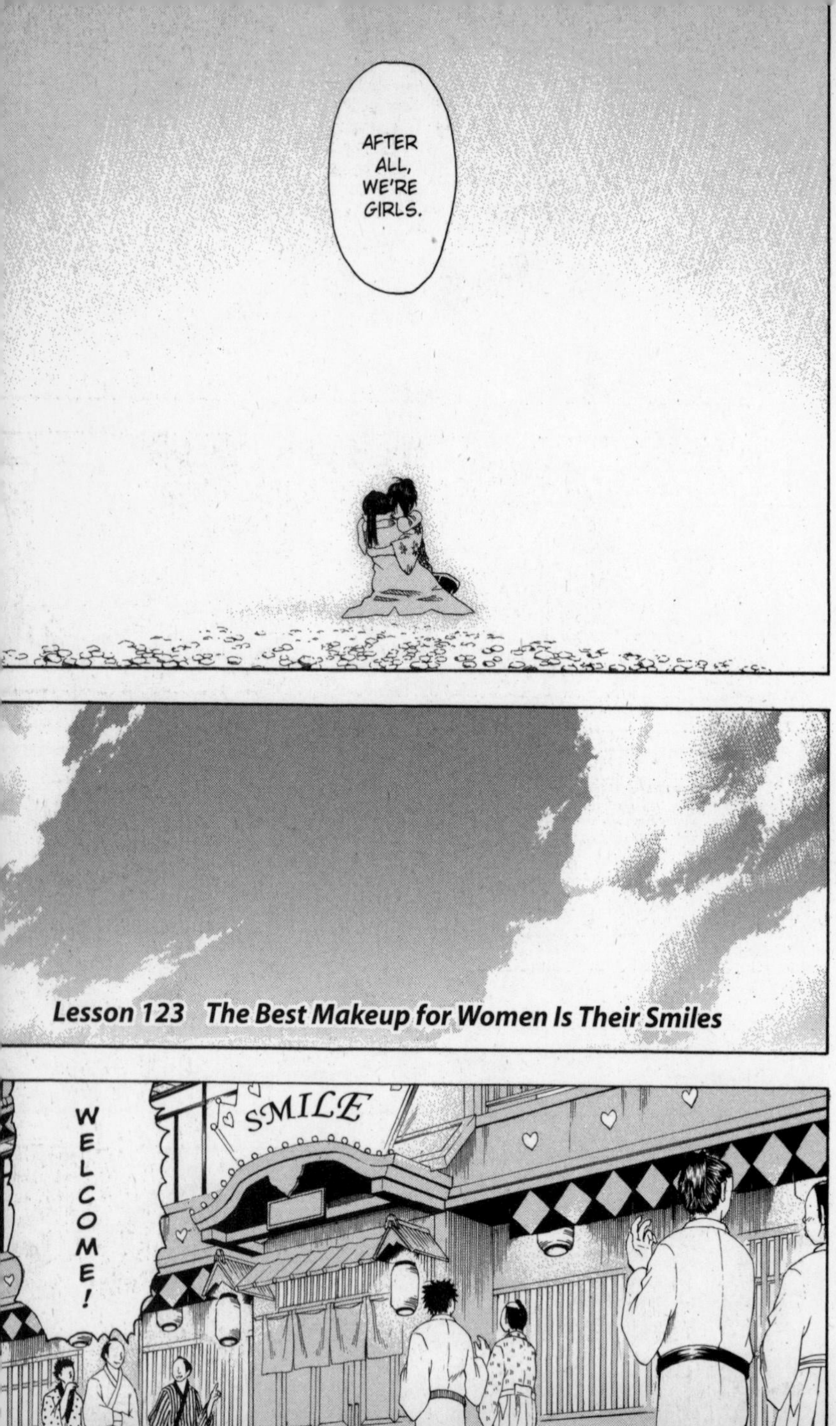
AFTER ALL, WE'RE GIRLS.
Lesson 123 The Best Makeup for Women Is Their Smiles
SMILE
WELCOME!

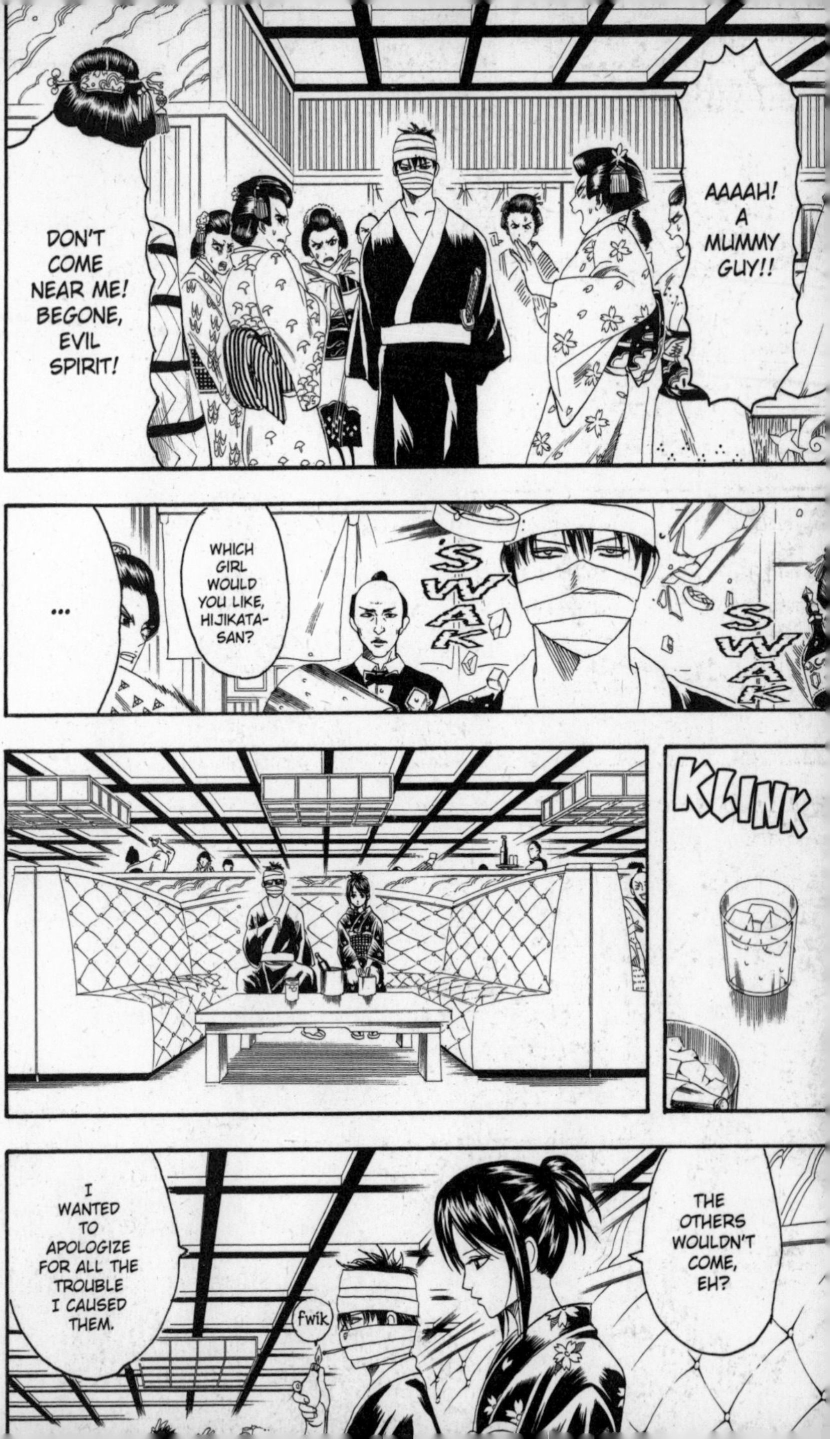
AAAAH! A MUMMY GUY!!
DON'T COME NEAR ME! BEGONE, EVIL SPIRIT!
SWAK
SWAK
WHICH GIRL WOULD YOU LIKE, HIJIKATA-SAN?
...
KLINK
THE OTHERS WOULDN'T COME, EH?
fwik
I WANTED TO APOLOGIZE FOR ALL THE TROUBLE I CAUSED THEM.

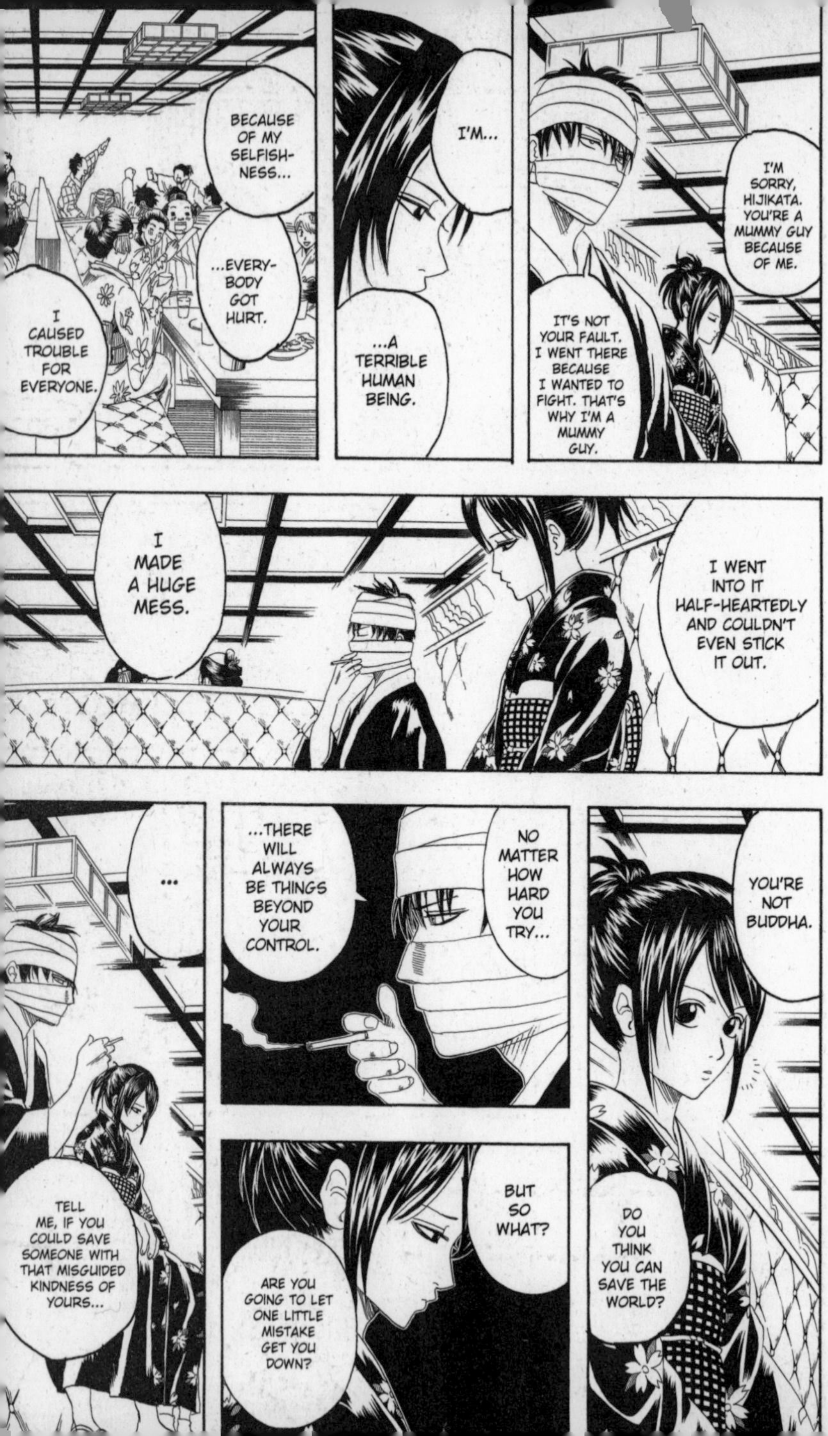
I'M SORRY, HIJIKATA. YOU'RE A MUMMY GUY BECAUSE OF ME.
IT'S NOT YOUR FAULT. I WENT THERE BECAUSE I WANTED TO FIGHT. THAT'S WHY I'M A MUMMY GUY.
I'M...
...A TERRIBLE HUMAN BEING.
BECAUSE OF MY SELFISH-NESS...
...EVERY-BODY GOT HURT.
I CAUSED TROUBLE FOR EVERYONE.
I WENT INTO IT HALF-HEARTEDLY AND COULDN'T EVEN STICK IT OUT.
I MADE A HUGE MESS.
YOU'RE NOT BUDDHA.
DO YOU THINK YOU CAN SAVE THE WORLD?
NO MATTER HOW HARD YOU TRY...
...THERE WILL ALWAYS BE THINGS BEYOND YOUR CONTROL.
BUT SO WHAT?
ARE YOU GOING TO LET ONE LITTLE MISTAKE GET YOU DOWN?
...
TELL ME, IF YOU COULD SAVE SOMEONE WITH THAT MISGUIDED KINDNESS OF YOURS...

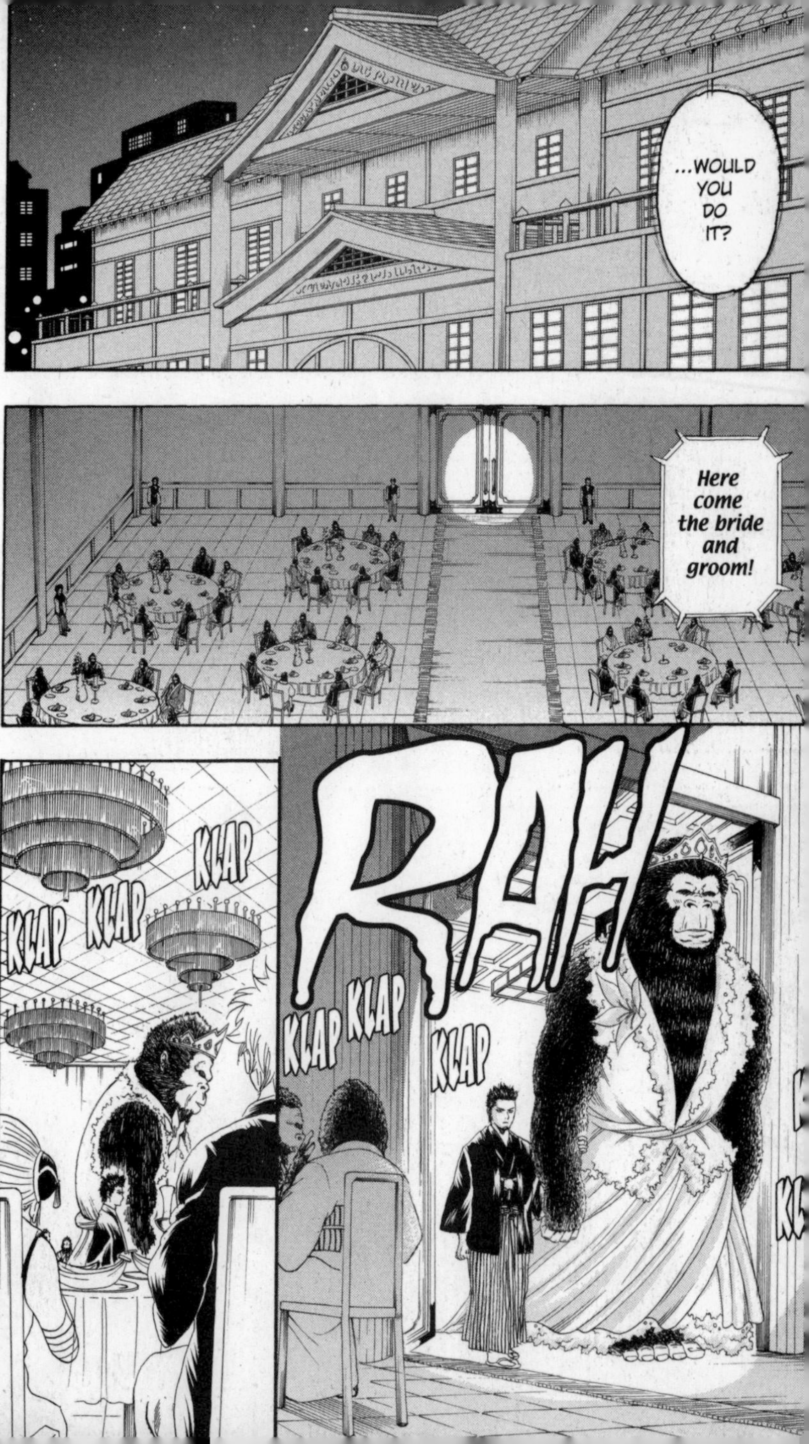
...WOULD YOU DO IT?
Here come the bride and groom!
RAH
KLAP
KLAP KLAP
KLAP
KLAP
KLAP

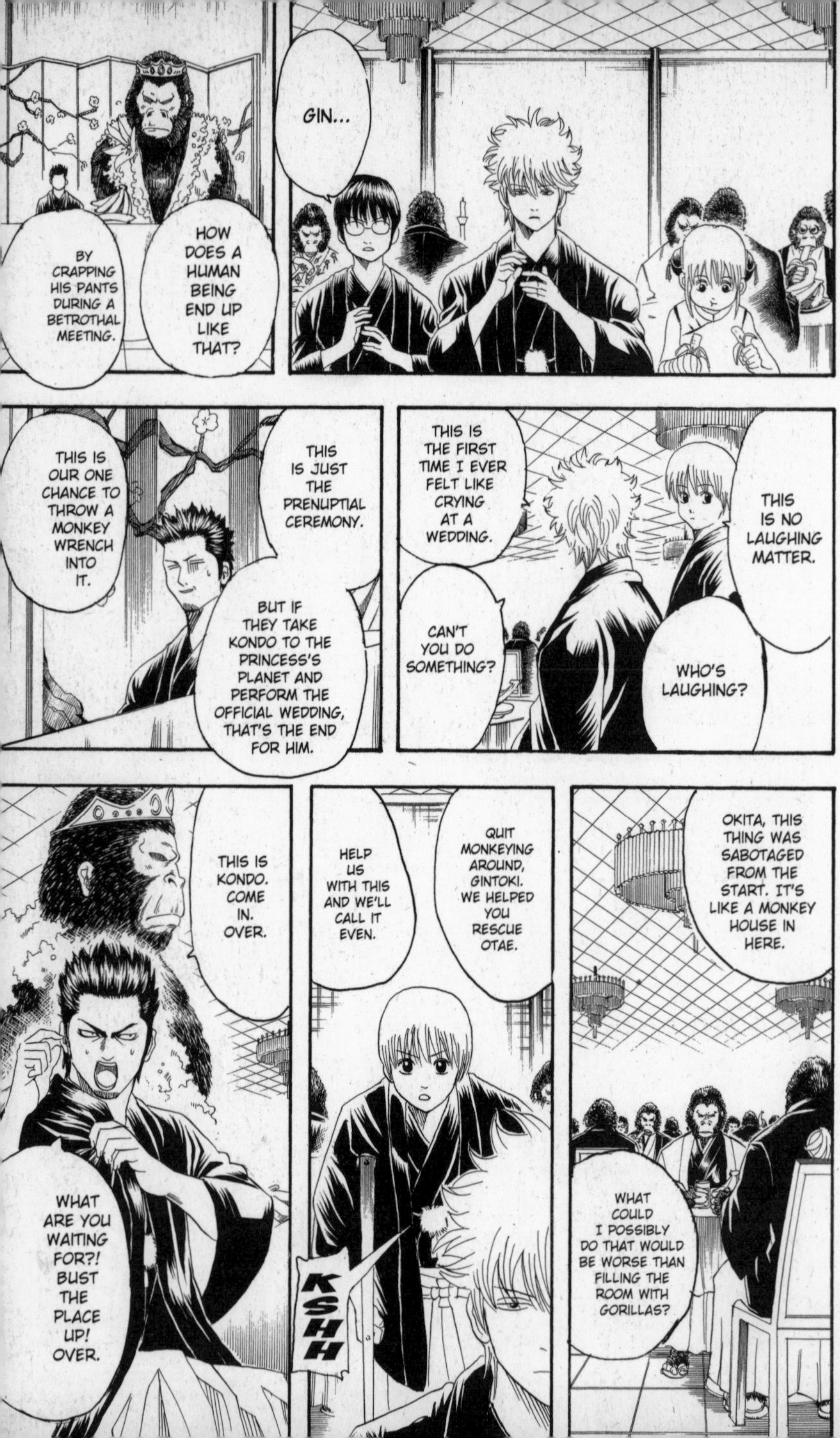
GIN...
HOW DOES A HUMAN BEING END UP LIKE THAT?
BY CRAPPING HIS PANTS DURING A BETROTHAL MEETING.
THIS IS NO LAUGHING MATTER.
THIS IS THE FIRST TIME I EVER FELT LIKE CRYING AT A WEDDING.
WHO'S LAUGHING?
CAN'T YOU DO SOMETHING?
THIS IS JUST THE PRENUPTIAL CEREMONY.
BUT IF THEY TAKE KONDO TO THE PRINCESS'S PLANET AND PERFORM THE OFFICIAL WEDDING, THAT'S THE END FOR HIM.
THIS IS OUR ONE CHANCE TO THROW A MONKEY WRENCH INTO IT.
OKITA, THIS THING WAS SABOTAGED FROM THE START. IT'S LIKE A MONKEY HOUSE IN HERE.
WHAT COULD I POSSIBLY DO THAT WOULD BE WORSE THAN FILLING THE ROOM WITH GORILLAS?
QUIT MONKEYING AROUND, GINTOKI. WE HELPED YOU RESCUE OTAE.
HELP US WITH THIS AND WE'LL CALL IT EVEN.
KSHH
THIS IS KONDO. COME IN. OVER.
WHAT ARE YOU WAITING FOR?! BUST THE PLACE UP! OVER.

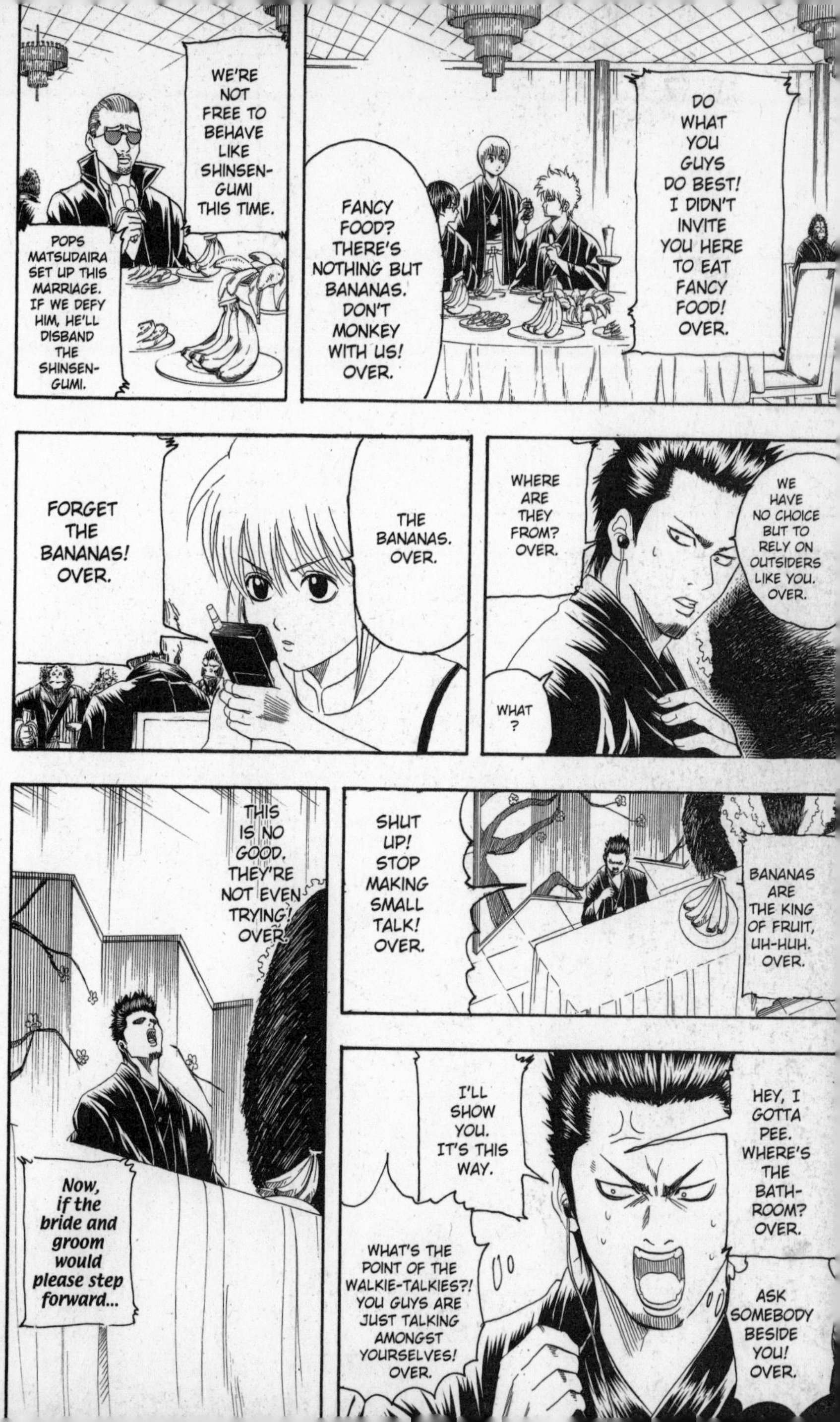
DO WHAT YOU GUYS DO BEST! I DIDN'T INVITE YOU HERE TO EAT FANCY FOOD! OVER.
FANCY FOOD? THERE'S NOTHING BUT BANANAS. DON'T MONKEY WITH US! OVER.
WE'RE NOT FREE TO BEHAVE LIKE SHINSEN-GUMI THIS TIME.
POPS MATSUDAIRA SET UP THIS MARRIAGE. IF WE DEFY HIM, HE'LL DISBAND THE SHINSEN-GUMI.
WE HAVE NO CHOICE BUT TO RELY ON OUTSIDERS LIKE YOU. OVER.
WHERE ARE THEY FROM? OVER.
WHAT?
THE BANANAS. OVER.
FORGET THE BANANAS! OVER.
BANANAS ARE THE KING OF FRUIT, UH-HUH. OVER.
SHUT UP! STOP MAKING SMALL TALK! OVER.
HEY, I GOTTA PEE. WHERE'S THE BATH-ROOM? OVER.
I'LL SHOW YOU. IT'S THIS WAY.
ASK SOMEBODY BESIDE YOU! OVER.
WHAT'S THE POINT OF THE WALKIE-TALKIES?! YOU GUYS ARE JUST TALKING AMONGST YOURSELVES! OVER.
THIS IS NO GOOD. THEY'RE NOT EVEN TRYING! OVER.
Now, if the bride and groom would please step forward...

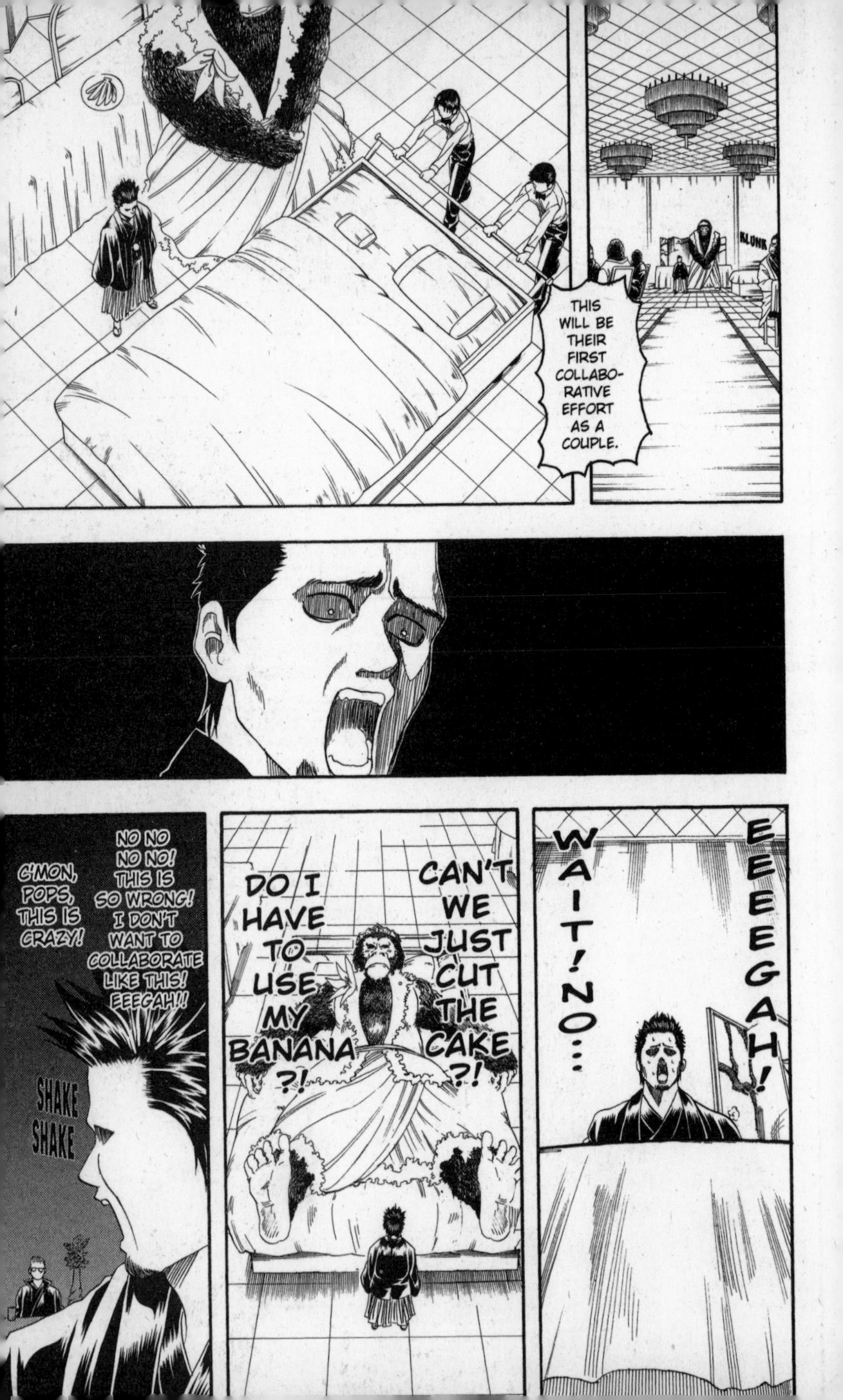
KLUNK
THIS WILL BE THEIR FIRST COLLABORATIVE EFFORT AS A COUPLE.
EEEEGAH!
WAIT! NO...
CAN'T WE JUST CUT THE CAKE?!
DO I HAVE TO USE MY BANANA?!
NO NO NO NO! THIS IS SO WRONG! I DON'T WANT TO COLLABORATE LIKE THIS! EEEGAH!!
C'MON, POPS, THIS IS CRAZY!
SHAKE SHAKE

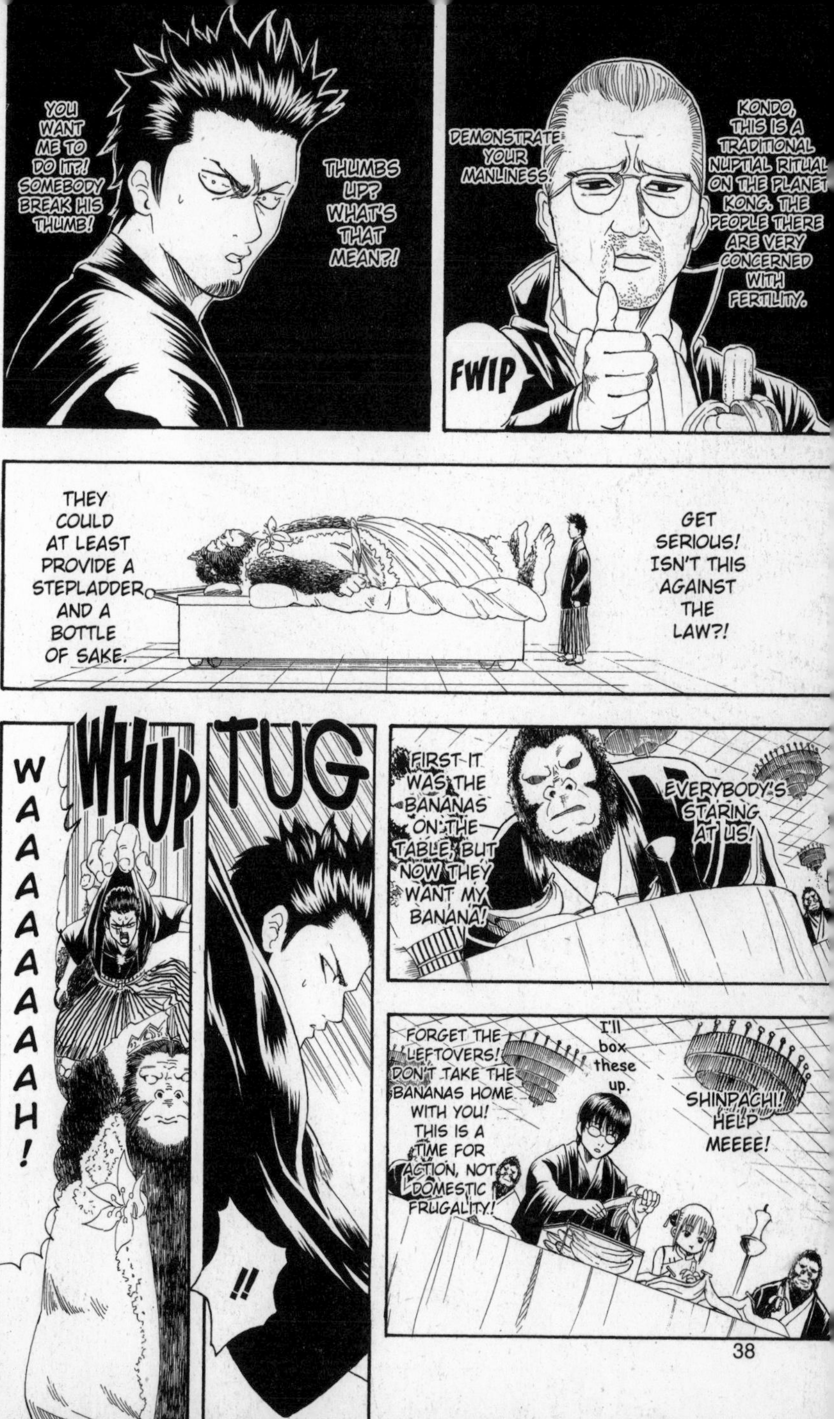

KONDO, THIS IS A TRADITIONAL NUPTIAL RITUAL ON THE PLANET KONG. THE PEOPLE THERE ARE VERY CONCERNED WITH FERTILITY.
DEMONSTRATE YOUR MANLINESS.
FWIP
THUMBS UP? WHAT'S THAT MEAN?!
YOU WANT ME TO DO IT?! SOMEBODY BREAK HIS THUMB!
GET SERIOUS! ISN'T THIS AGAINST THE LAW?!
THEY COULD AT LEAST PROVIDE A STEPLADDER AND A BOTTLE OF SAKE.
EVERYBODY'S STARING AT US!
FIRST IT WAS THE BANANAS ON THE TABLE, BUT NOW THEY WANT MY BANANA!
SHINPACHI! HELP MEEEE!
I'll box these up.
FORGET THE LEFTOVERS! DON'T TAKE THE BANANAS HOME WITH YOU! THIS IS A TIME FOR ACTION, NOT DOMESTIC FRUGALITY!
TUG
!!
WHUP
WAAAAAAAAAAH!

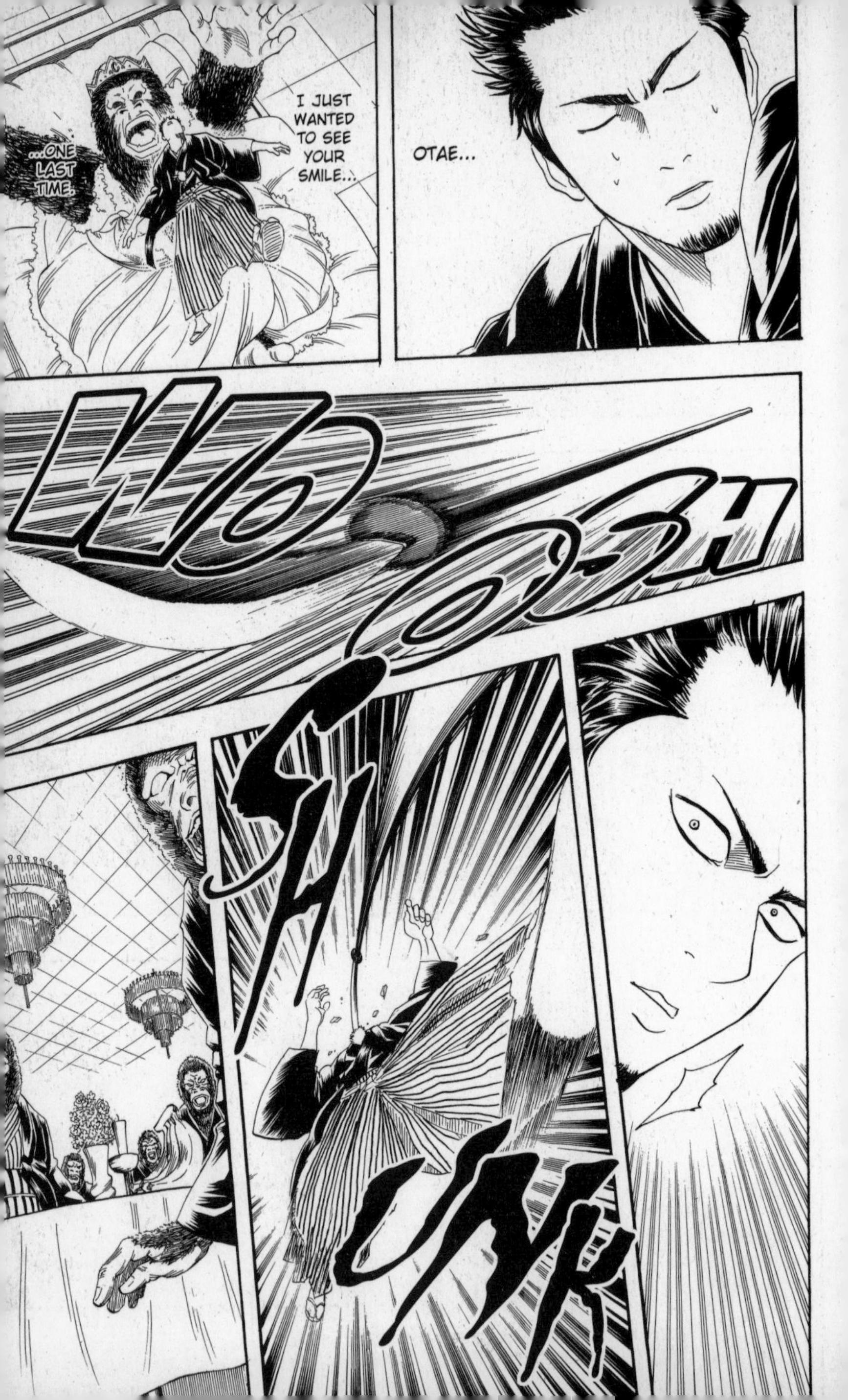
OTAE...
I JUST WANTED TO SEE YOUR SMILE...
...ONE LAST TIME.
WHOOSH

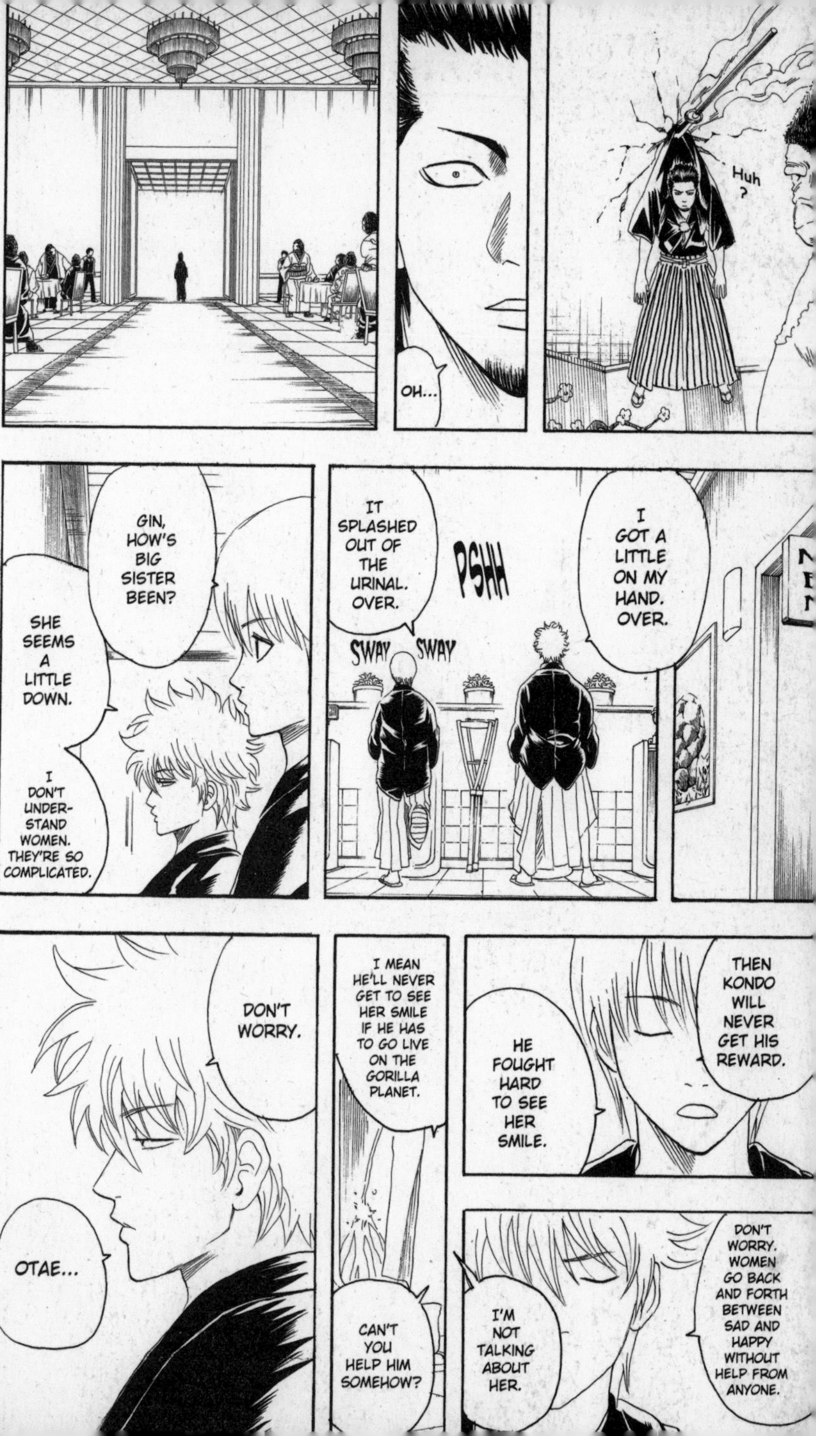
Huh ?
OH...
I GOT A LITTLE ON MY HAND. OVER.
IT SPLASHED OUT OF THE URINAL. OVER.
PSHH
SWAY SWAY
GIN, HOW'S BIG SISTER BEEN?
SHE SEEMS A LITTLE DOWN.
I DON'T UNDER-STAND WOMEN. THEY'RE SO COMPLICATED.
THEN KONDO WILL NEVER GET HIS REWARD.
HE FOUGHT HARD TO SEE HER SMILE.
DON'T WORRY. WOMEN GO BACK AND FORTH BETWEEN SAD AND HAPPY WITHOUT HELP FROM ANYONE.
I'M NOT TALKING ABOUT HER.
I MEAN HE'LL NEVER GET TO SEE HER SMILE IF HE HAS TO GO LIVE ON THE GORILLA PLANET.
CAN'T YOU HELP HIM SOMEHOW?
DON'T WORRY.
OTAE...

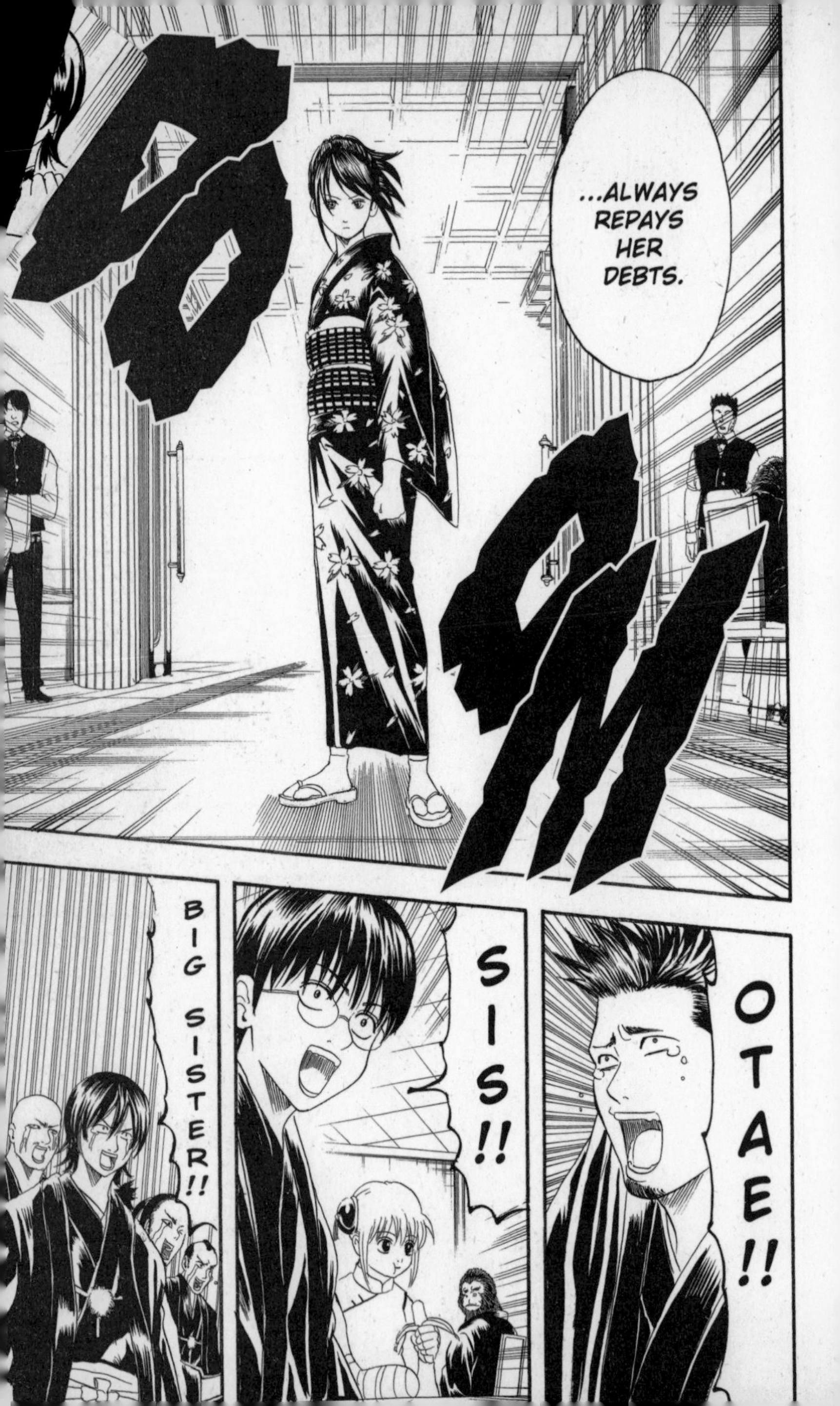
...ALWAYS REPAYS HER DEBTS.
OTAE!!
SIS!!
BIG SISTER!!

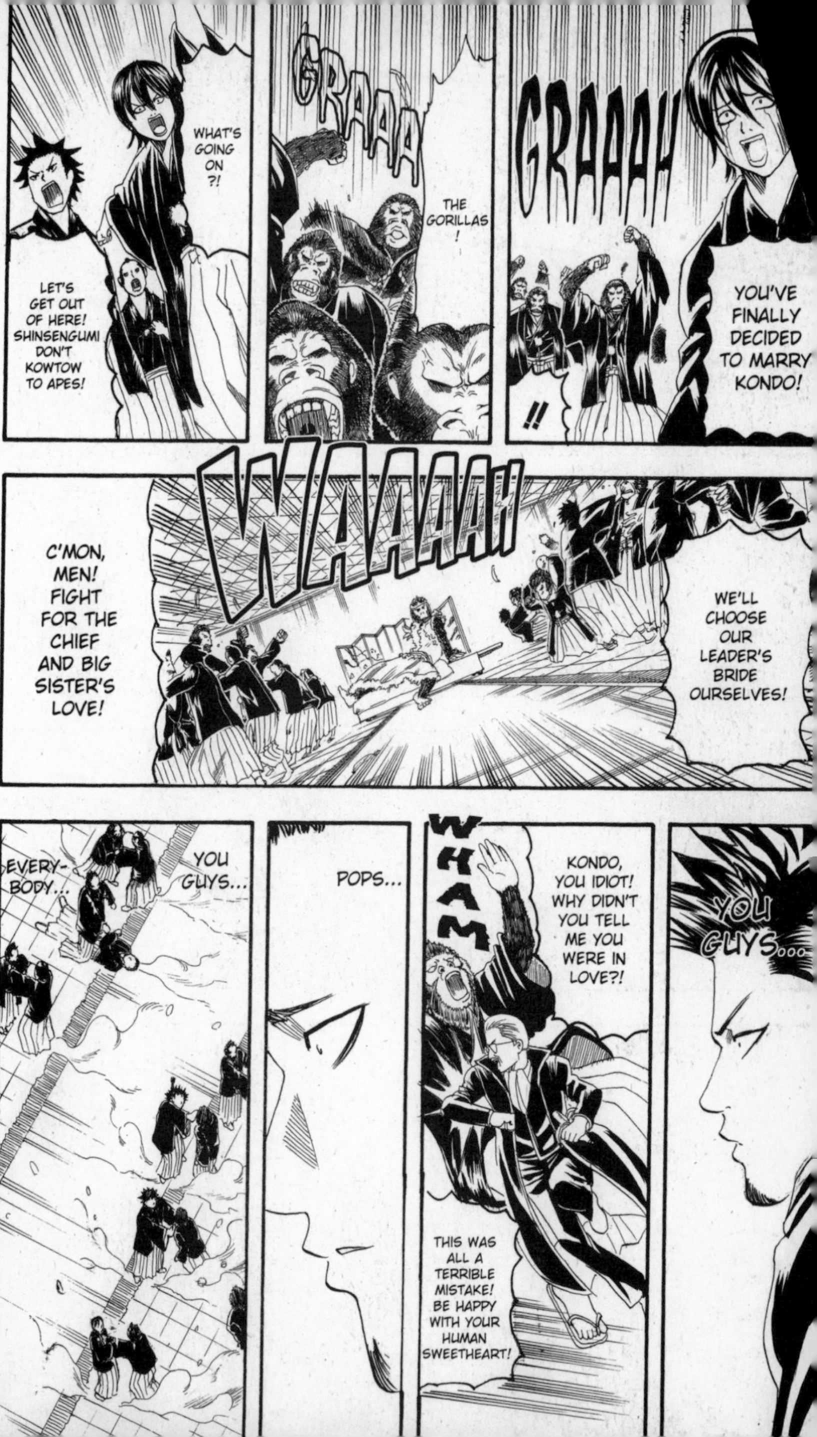
YOU'VE FINALLY DECIDED TO MARRY KONDO!
GRAAAH
!!
GRAAA
THE GORILLAS!
WHAT'S GOING ON?!
LET'S GET OUT OF HERE! SHINSENGUMI DON'T KOWTOW TO APES!
WAAAAAH
WE'LL CHOOSE OUR LEADER'S BRIDE OURSELVES!
C'MON, MEN! FIGHT FOR THE CHIEF AND BIG SISTER'S LOVE!
YOU GUYS...
WHAM
KONDO, YOU IDIOT! WHY DIDN'T YOU TELL ME YOU WERE IN LOVE?!
THIS WAS ALL A TERRIBLE MISTAKE! BE HAPPY WITH YOUR HUMAN SWEETHEART!
POPS...
YOU GUYS...
EVERY-BODY...

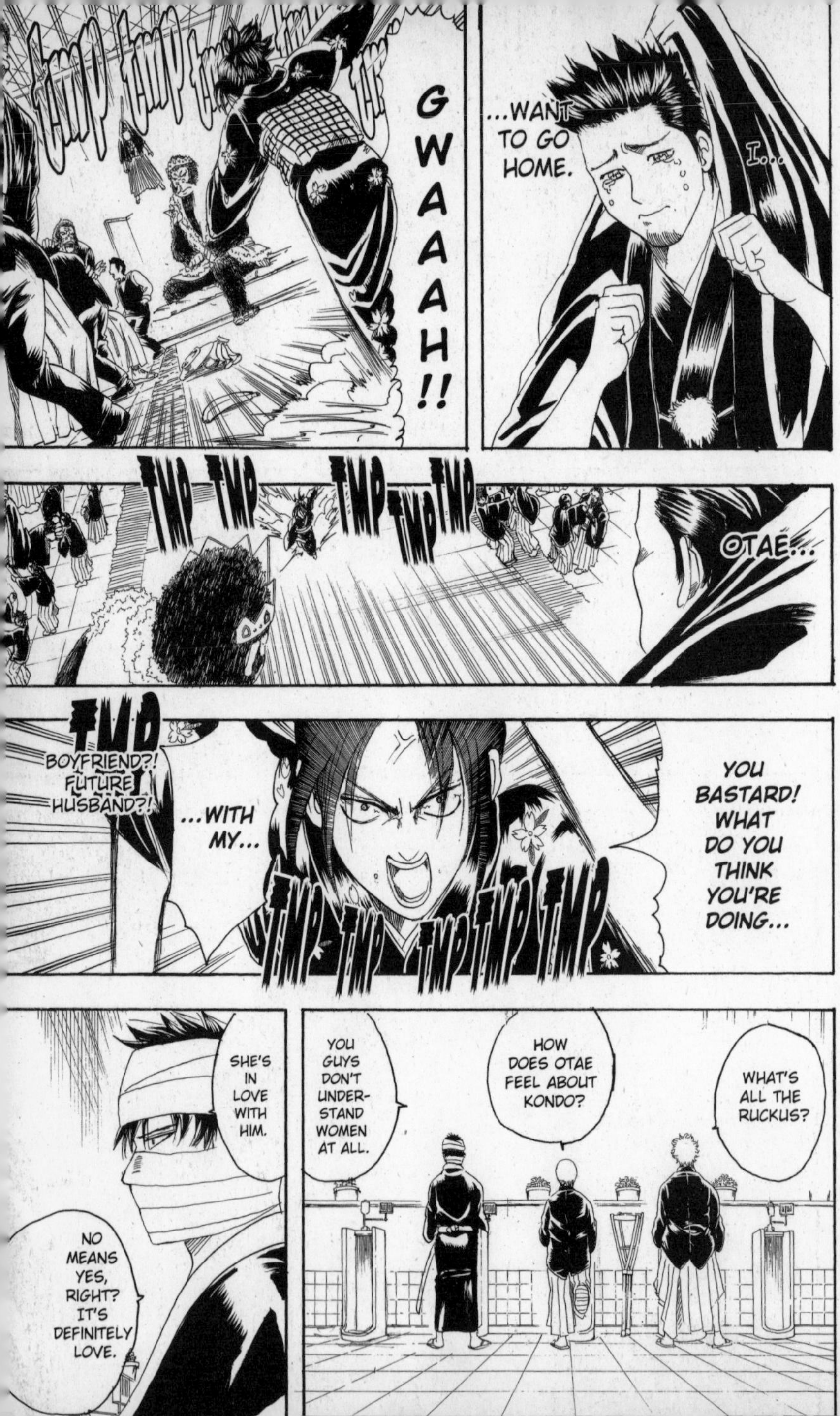
I...
...WANT TO GO HOME.
GWAAAAH!!
OTAE...
TMP TMP TMP TMP TMP
YOU BASTARD! WHAT DO YOU THINK YOU'RE DOING...
TMP TMP TMP TMP TMP TMP
...WITH MY...
BOYFRIEND?! FUTURE HUSBAND?!
TMP
WHAT'S ALL THE RUCKUS?
HOW DOES OTAE FEEL ABOUT KONDO?
YOU GUYS DON'T UNDER-STAND WOMEN AT ALL.
SHE'S IN LOVE WITH HIM.
NO MEANS YES, RIGHT? IT'S DEFINITELY LOVE.

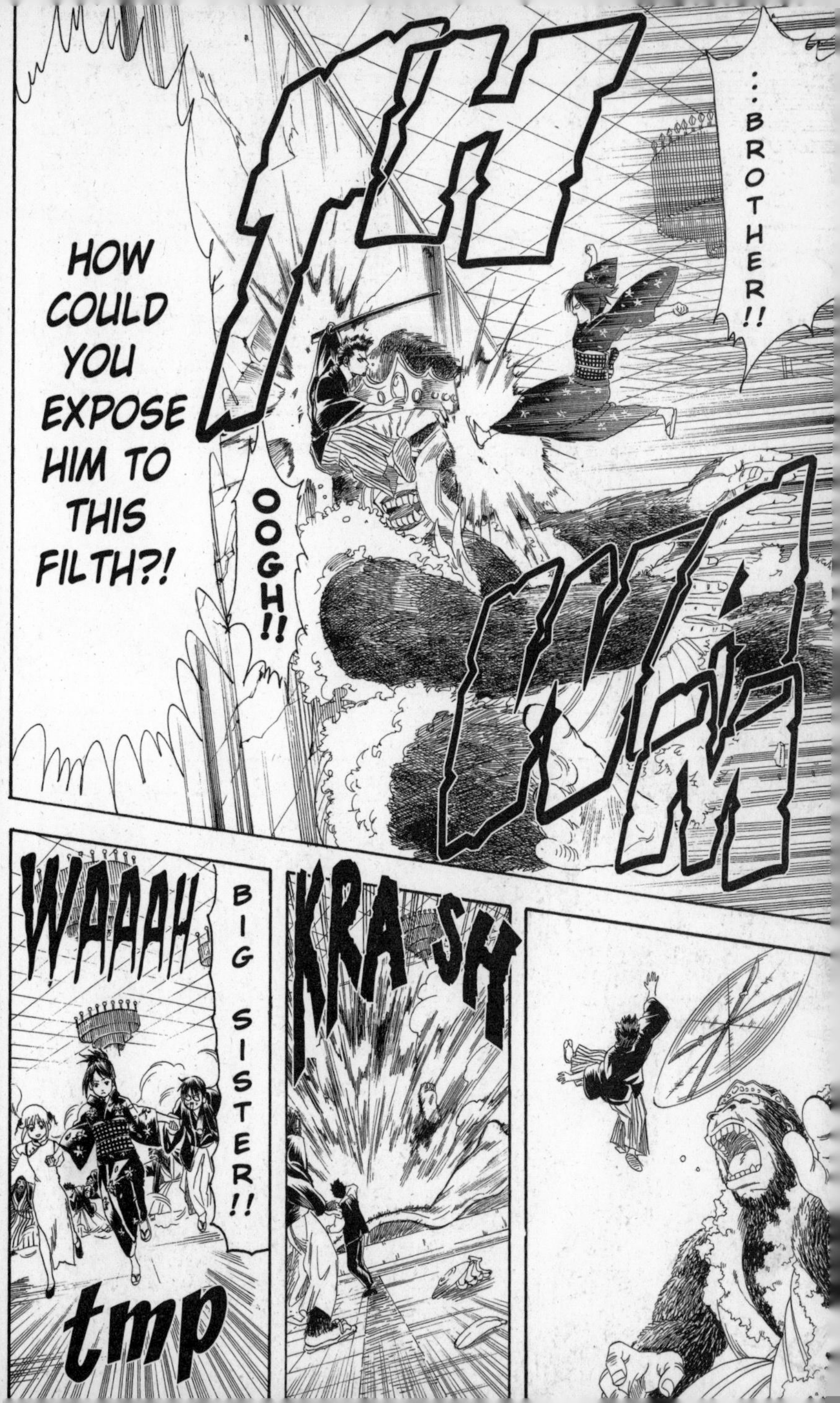
...BROTHER!!
OOGH!!
HOW COULD YOU EXPOSE HIM TO THIS FILTH?!
KRASH
BIG SISTER!!
WAAAH
tmp

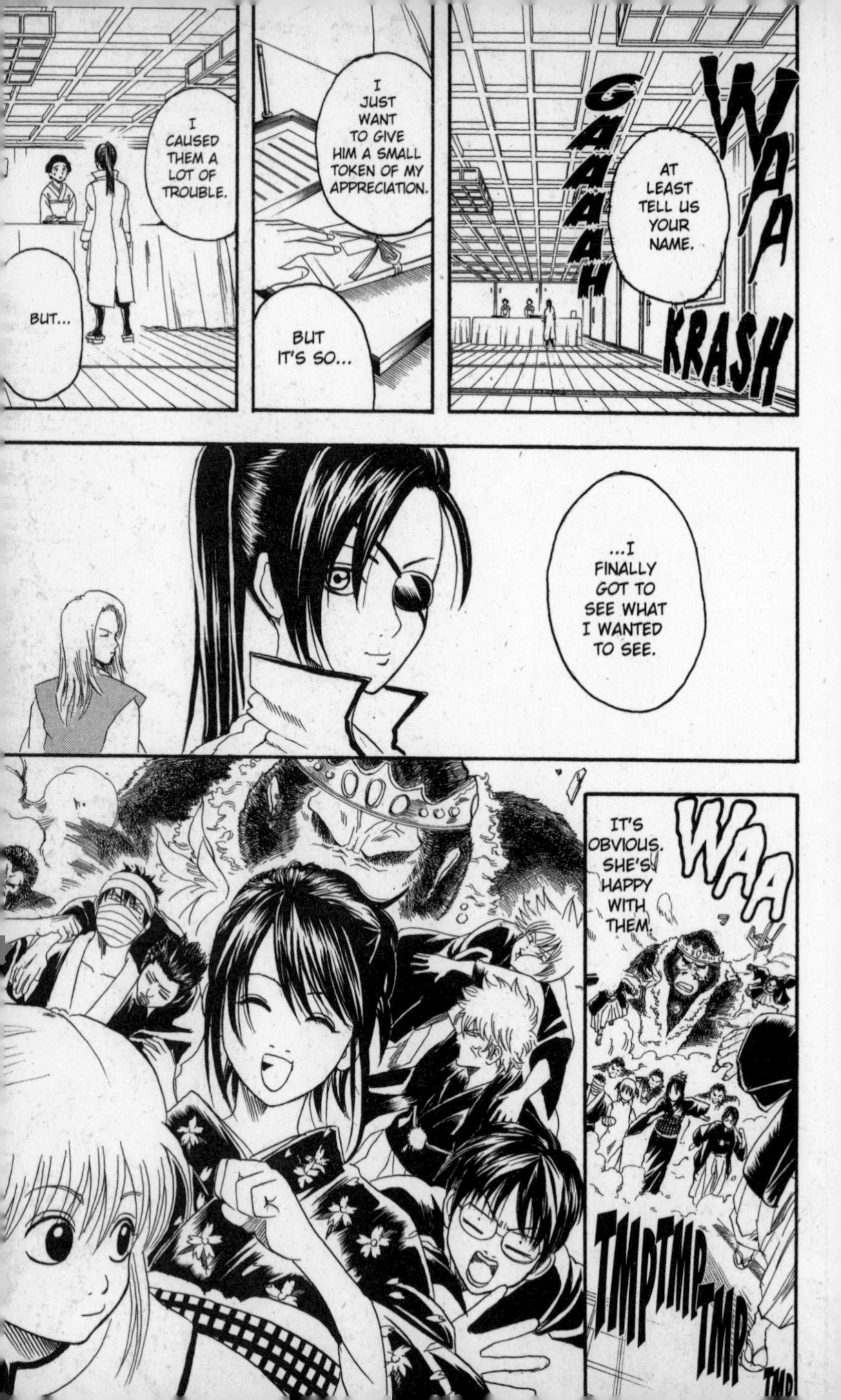
WAAA
GAAAAH
AT LEAST TELL US YOUR NAME.
KRASH
I JUST WANT TO GIVE HIM A SMALL TOKEN OF MY APPRECIATION.
BUT IT'S SO...
I CAUSED THEM A LOT OF TROUBLE.
BUT...
...I FINALLY GOT TO SEE WHAT I WANTED TO SEE.
WAA
IT'S OBVIOUS. SHE'S HAPPY WITH THEM.
TMPTMPTMP
TMP
TMP

● Published in *Weekly Shonen JUMP*, 2006 as the
cover illustration of Volume 36 & 37 joint issue

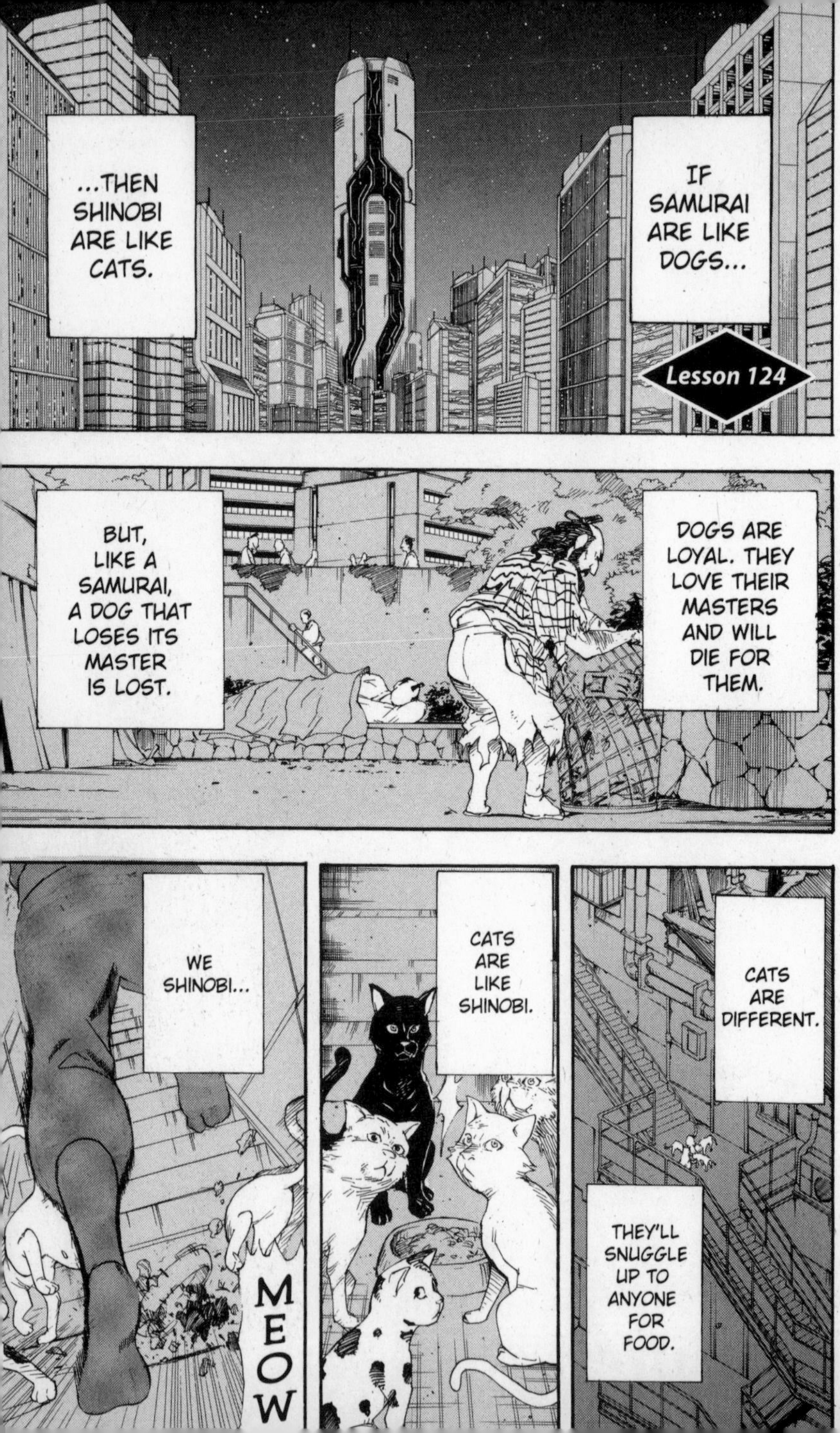
IF SAMURAI ARE LIKE DOGS...
Lesson 124
...THEN SHINOBI ARE LIKE CATS.
DOGS ARE LOYAL. THEY LOVE THEIR MASTERS AND WILL DIE FOR THEM.
BUT, LIKE A SAMURAI, A DOG THAT LOSES ITS MASTER IS LOST.
CATS ARE DIFFERENT.
THEY'LL SNUGGLE UP TO ANYONE FOR FOOD.
CATS ARE LIKE SHINOBI.
WE SHINOBI...
MEOW

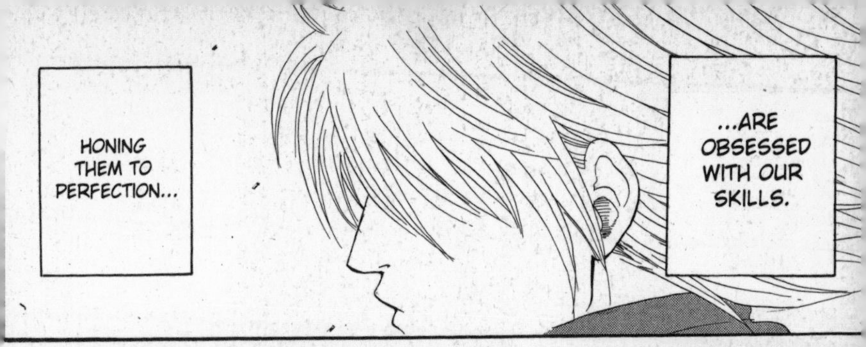
...ARE OBSESSED WITH OUR SKILLS.
HONING THEM TO PERFECTION...

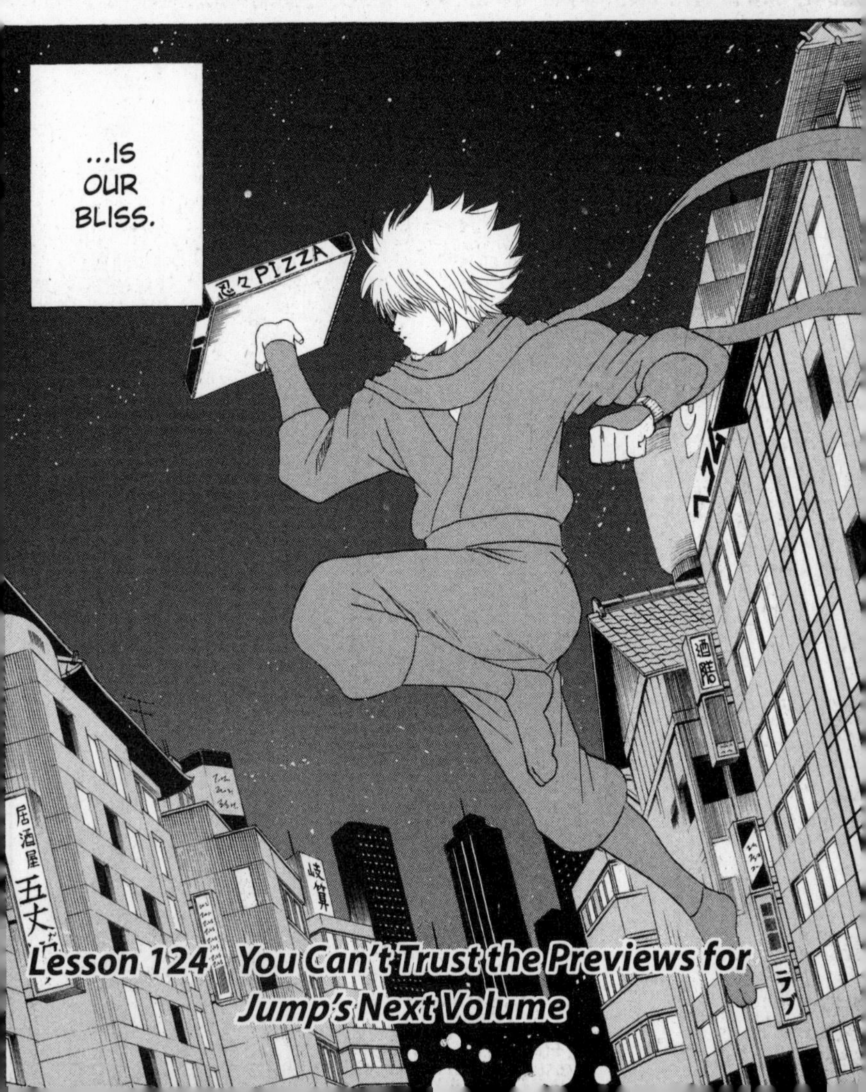
...IS OUR BLISS.
忍々PIZZA
居酒屋
ラブ

Lesson 124 You Can't Trust the Previews for Jump's Next Volume

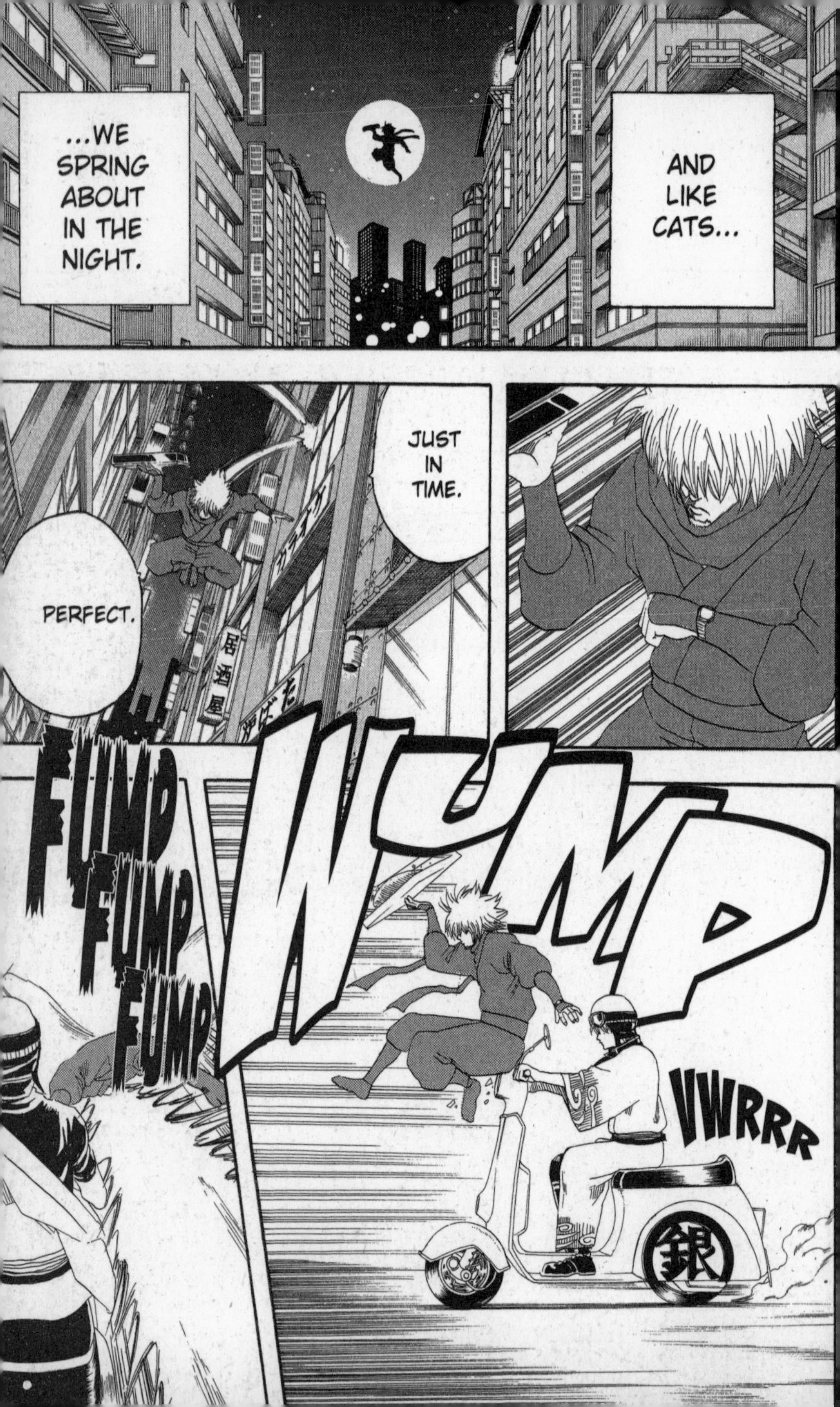
AND LIKE CATS...
...WE SPRING ABOUT IN THE NIGHT.
JUST IN TIME.
PERFECT.
居酒屋
WUMP
VWRRR
FUMP FUMP FUMP

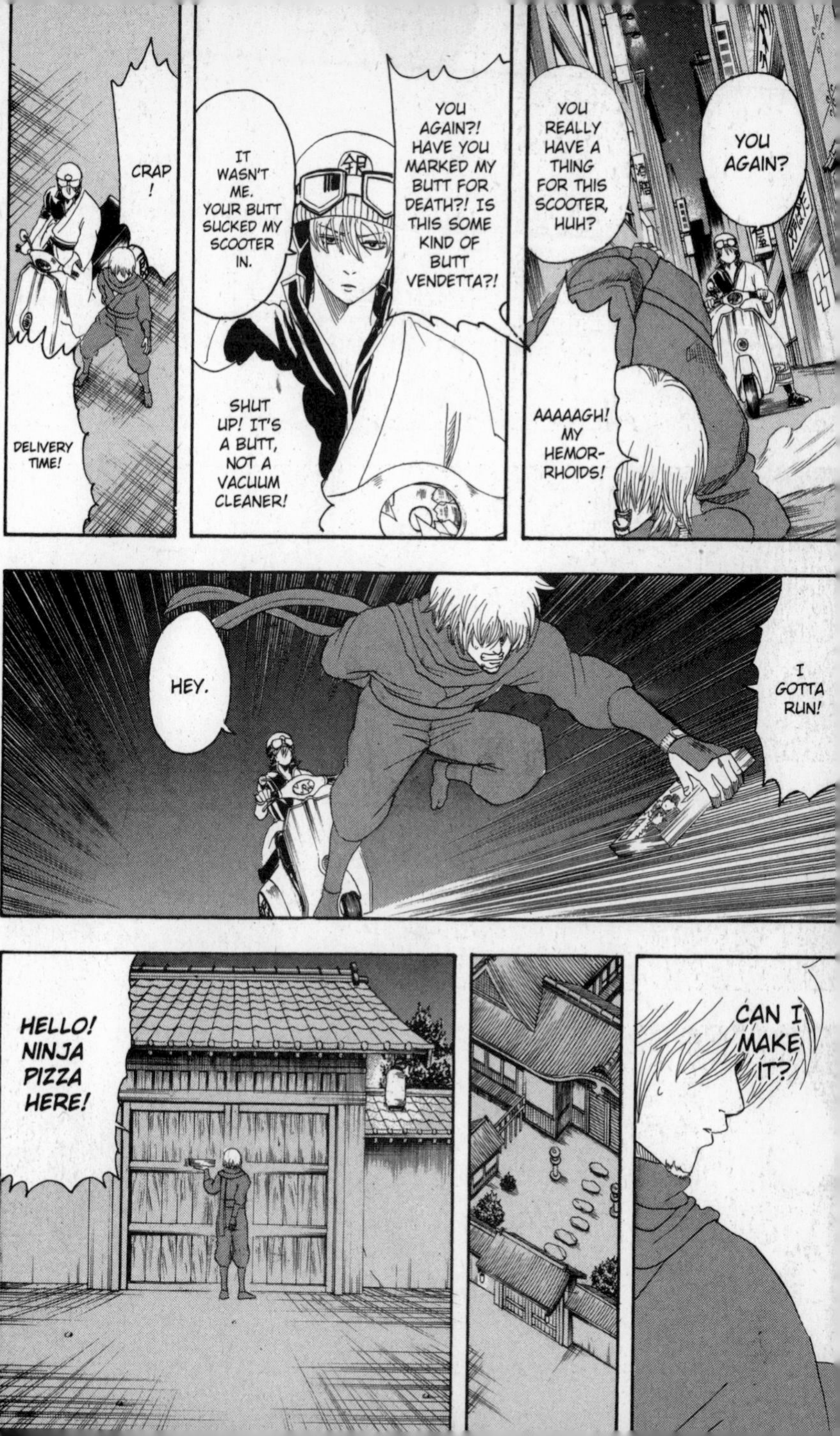
YOU AGAIN?
YOU REALLY HAVE A THING FOR THIS SCOOTER, HUH?
AAAAAGH! MY HEMOR-RHOIDS!
YOU AGAIN?! HAVE YOU MARKED MY BUTT FOR DEATH?! IS THIS SOME KIND OF BUTT VENDETTA?!
IT WASN'T ME. YOUR BUTT SUCKED MY SCOOTER IN.
SHUT UP! IT'S A BUTT, NOT A VACUUM CLEANER!
CRAP!
DELIVERY TIME!
I GOTTA RUN!
HEY.
CAN I MAKE IT?
HELLO! NINJA PIZZA HERE!

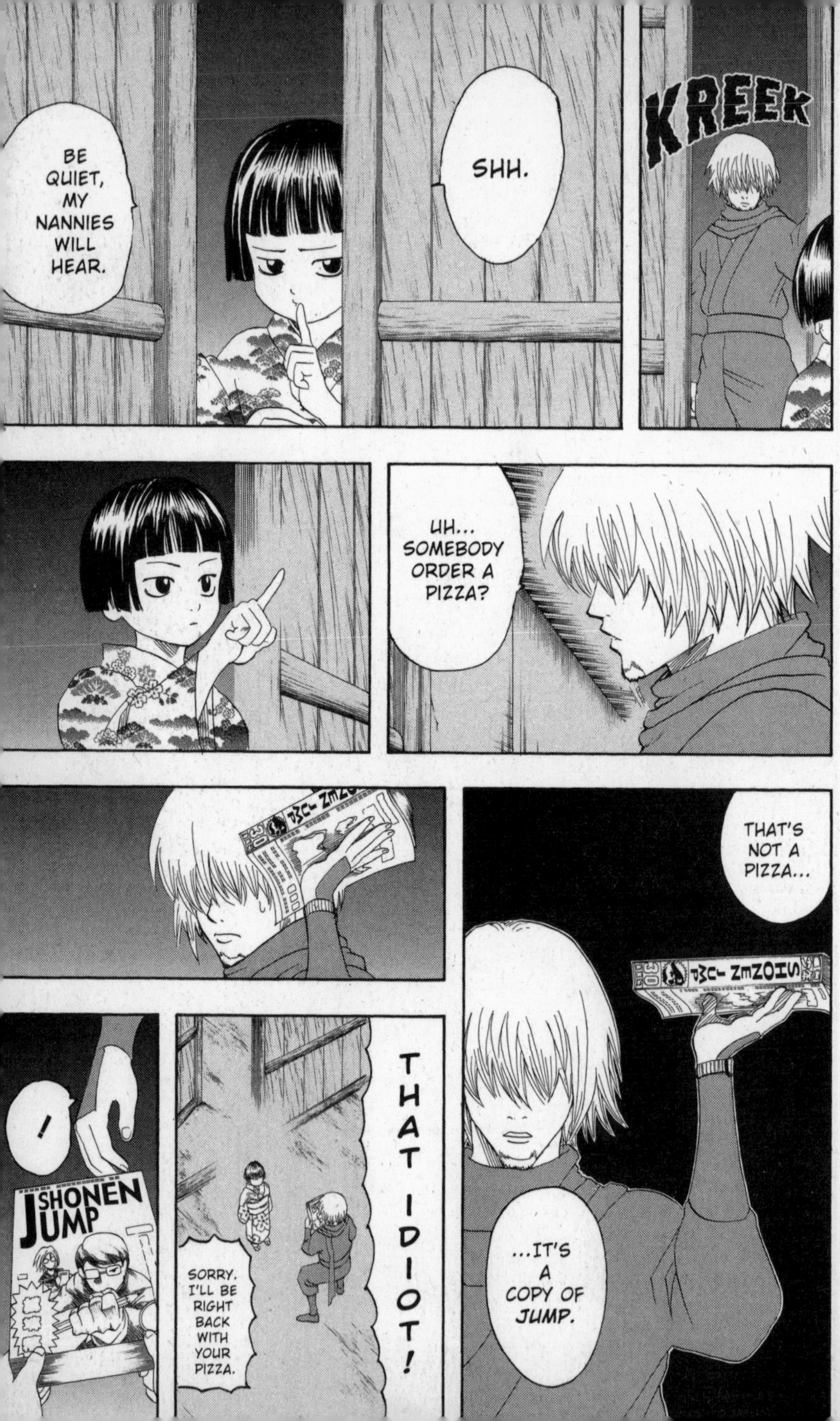
KREEK
SHH.
BE QUIET, MY NANNIES WILL HEAR.
UH... SOMEBODY ORDER A PIZZA?
THAT'S NOT A PIZZA...
...IT'S A COPY OF JUMP.
THAT IDIOT!
SORRY. I'LL BE RIGHT BACK WITH YOUR PIZZA.
!
SHONEN JUMP

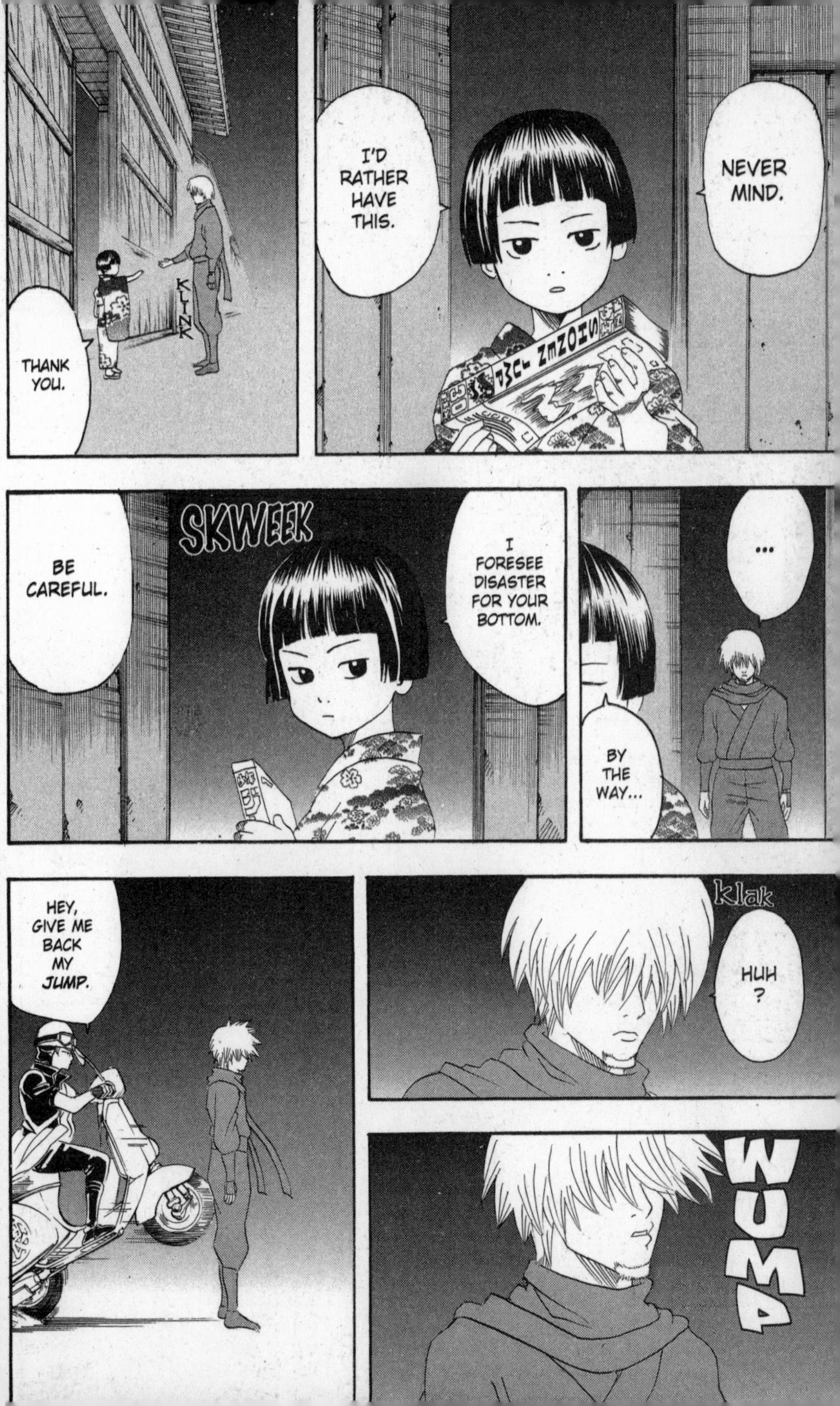
NEVER MIND.
I'D RATHER HAVE THIS.
KLINK
THANK YOU.
...
BY THE WAY...
I FORESEE DISASTER FOR YOUR BOTTOM.
SKWEEK
BE CAREFUL.
klak
HUH?
WUMP
HEY, GIVE ME BACK MY JUMP.

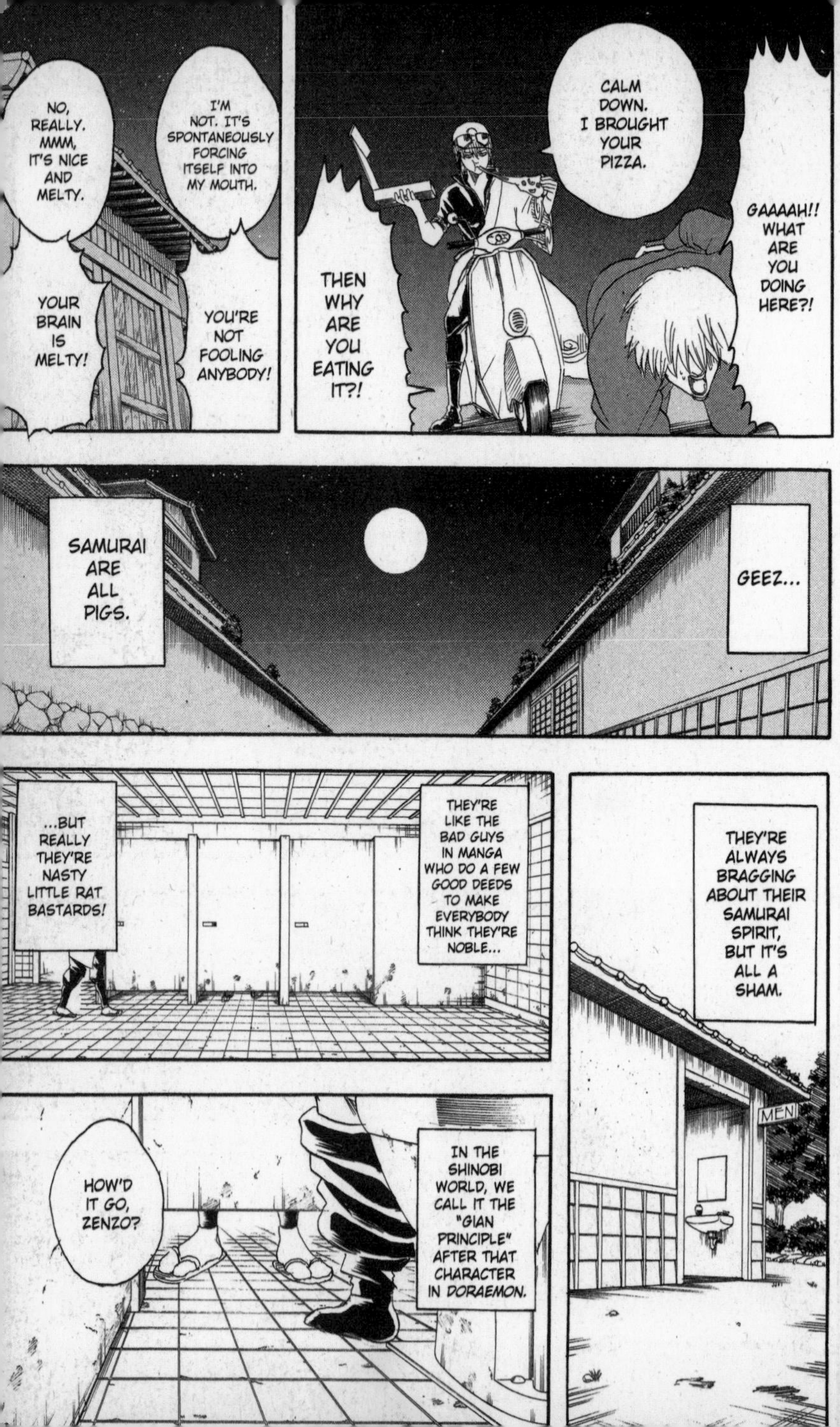
GAAAAH!! WHAT ARE YOU DOING HERE?!
CALM DOWN. I BROUGHT YOUR PIZZA.
THEN WHY ARE YOU EATING IT?!
I'M NOT. IT'S SPONTANEOUSLY FORCING ITSELF INTO MY MOUTH.
YOU'RE NOT FOOLING ANYBODY!
NO, REALLY. MMM, IT'S NICE AND MELTY.
YOUR BRAIN IS MELTY!
GEEZ...
SAMURAI ARE ALL PIGS.
THEY'RE ALWAYS BRAGGING ABOUT THEIR SAMURAI SPIRIT, BUT IT'S ALL A SHAM.
MEN
THEY'RE LIKE THE BAD GUYS IN MANGA WHO DO A FEW GOOD DEEDS TO MAKE EVERYBODY THINK THEY'RE NOBLE...
...BUT REALLY THEY'RE NASTY LITTLE RAT BASTARDS!
IN THE SHINOBI WORLD, WE CALL IT THE "GIAN PRINCIPLE" AFTER THAT CHARACTER IN *DORAEMON.*
HOW'D IT GO, ZENZO?

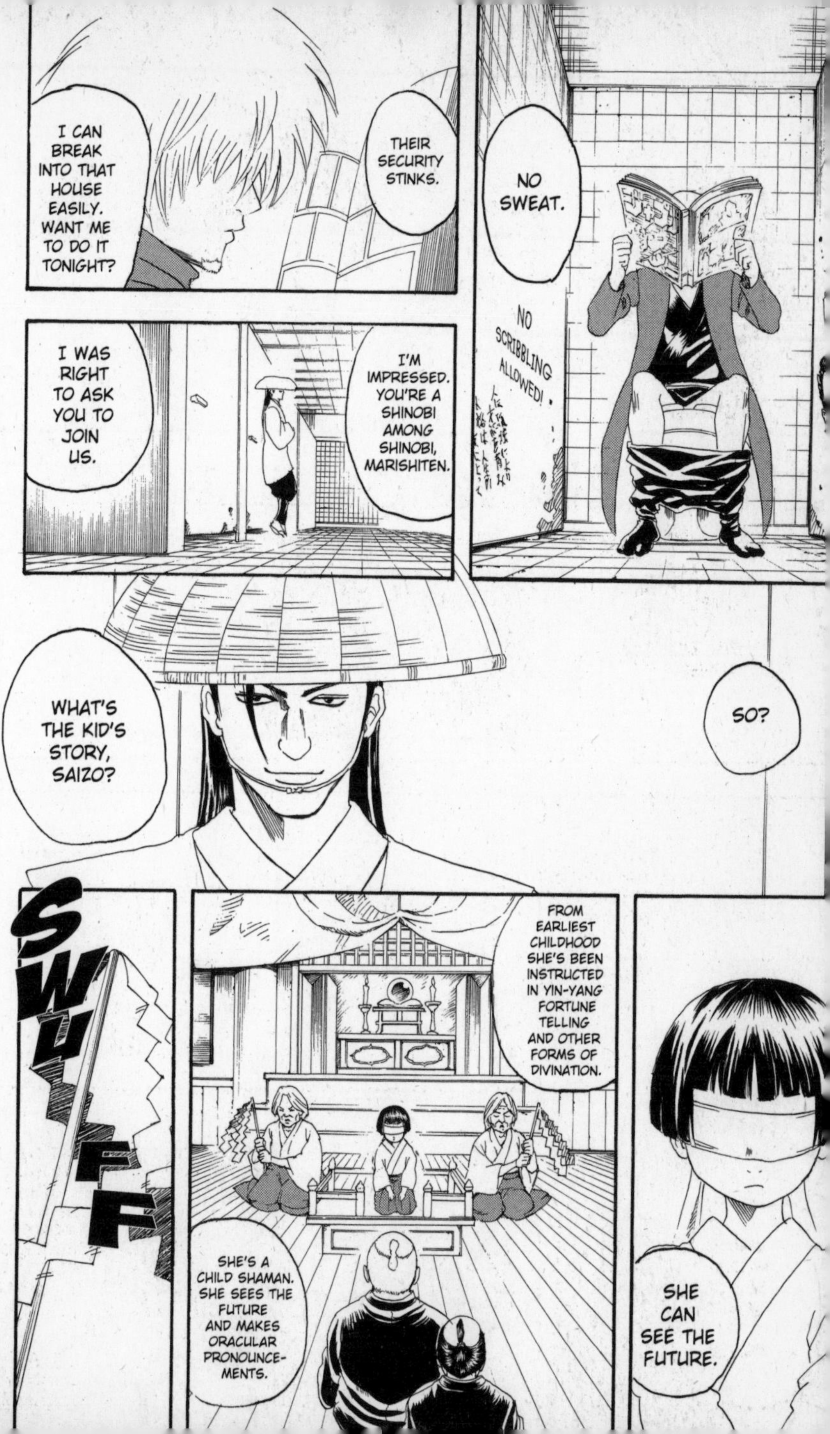
NO SWEAT.
NO SCRIBBLING ALLOWED!
THEIR SECURITY STINKS.
I CAN BREAK INTO THAT HOUSE EASILY. WANT ME TO DO IT TONIGHT?
I'M IMPRESSED. YOU'RE A SHINOBI AMONG SHINOBI, MARISHITEN.
I WAS RIGHT TO ASK YOU TO JOIN US.
SO?
WHAT'S THE KID'S STORY, SAIZO?
SHE CAN SEE THE FUTURE.
FROM EARLIEST CHILDHOOD SHE'S BEEN INSTRUCTED IN YIN-YANG FORTUNE TELLING AND OTHER FORMS OF DIVINATION.
SHE'S A CHILD SHAMAN. SHE SEES THE FUTURE AND MAKES ORACULAR PRONOUNCE-MENTS.
SWUFF

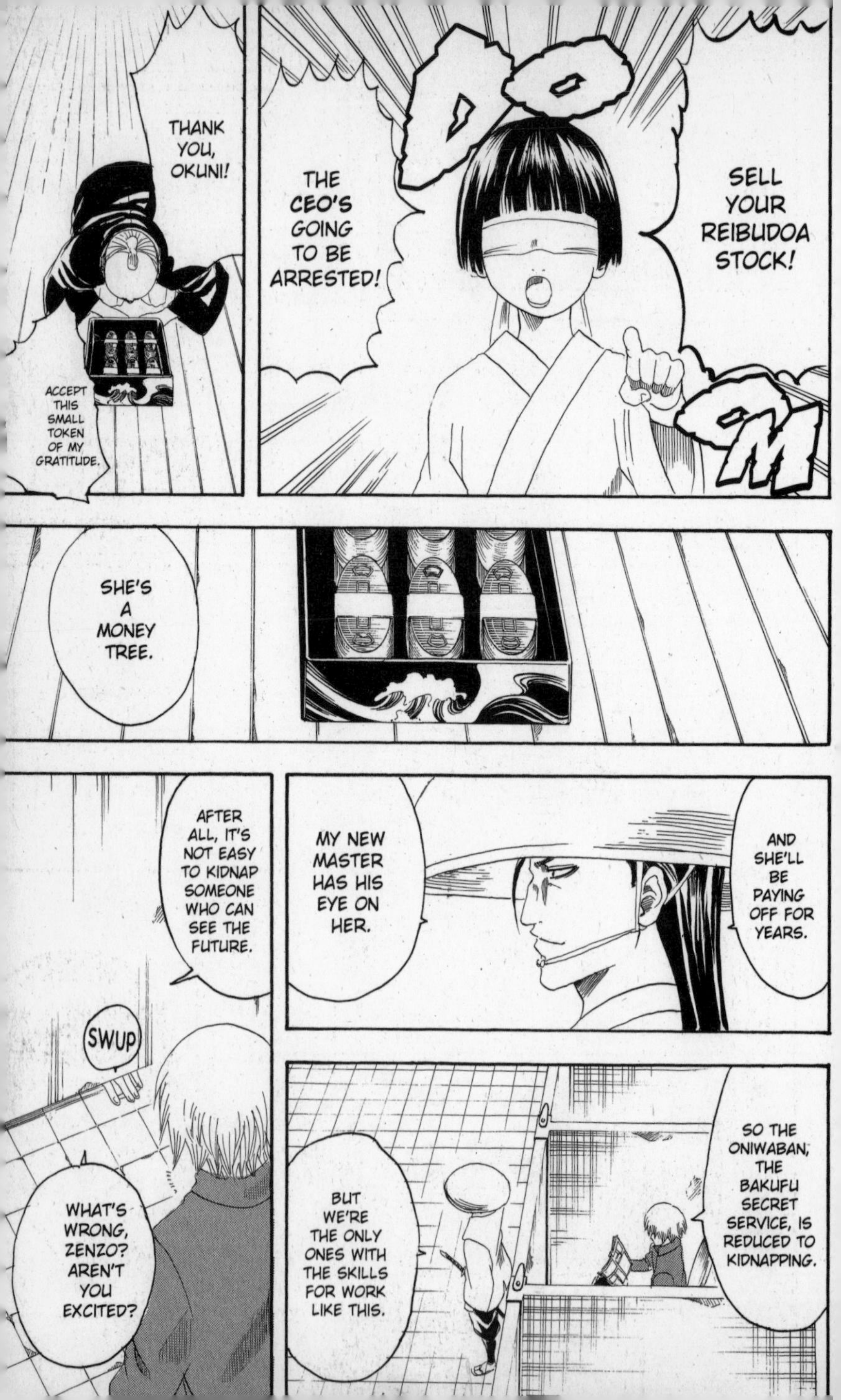
DO
SELL YOUR REIBUDOA STOCK!
THE CEO'S GOING TO BE ARRESTED!
OM
THANK YOU, OKUNI!
ACCEPT THIS SMALL TOKEN OF MY GRATITUDE.
SHE'S A MONEY TREE.
AND SHE'LL BE PAYING OFF FOR YEARS.
MY NEW MASTER HAS HIS EYE ON HER.
AFTER ALL, IT'S NOT EASY TO KIDNAP SOMEONE WHO CAN SEE THE FUTURE.
SO THE ONIWABAN, THE BAKUFU SECRET SERVICE, IS REDUCED TO KIDNAPPING.
BUT WE'RE THE ONLY ONES WITH THE SKILLS FOR WORK LIKE THIS.
SWUP
WHAT'S WRONG, ZENZO? AREN'T YOU EXCITED?

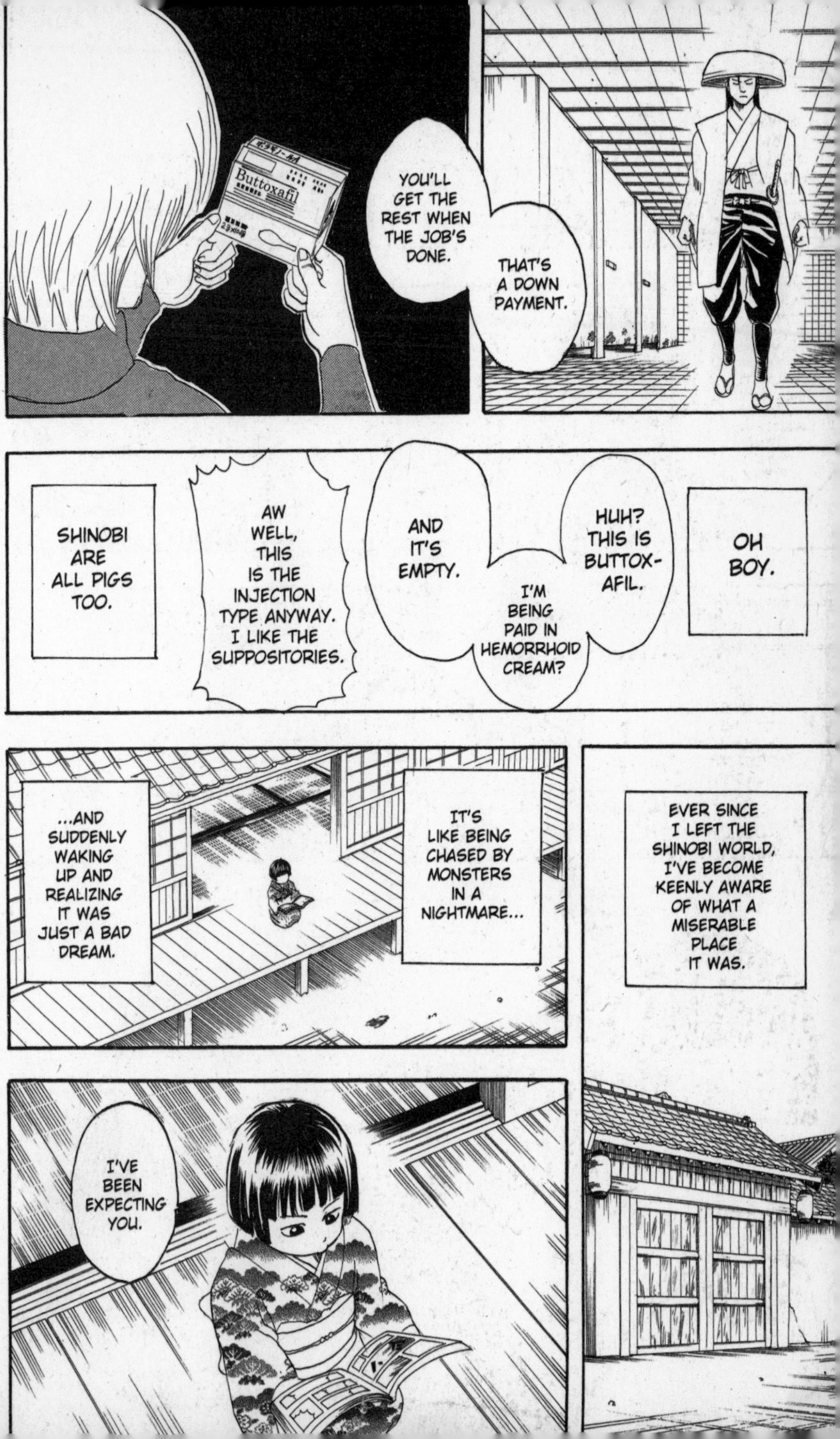
THAT'S A DOWN PAYMENT.
YOU'LL GET THE REST WHEN THE JOB'S DONE.
Buttoxafil
OH BOY.
HUH? THIS IS BUTTOX-AFIL.
I'M BEING PAID IN HEMORRHOID CREAM?
AND IT'S EMPTY.
AW WELL, THIS IS THE INJECTION TYPE ANYWAY. I LIKE THE SUPPOSITORIES.
SHINOBI ARE ALL PIGS TOO.
EVER SINCE I LEFT THE SHINOBI WORLD, I'VE BECOME KEENLY AWARE OF WHAT A MISERABLE PLACE IT WAS.
IT'S LIKE BEING CHASED BY MONSTERS IN A NIGHTMARE...
...AND SUDDENLY WAKING UP AND REALIZING IT WAS JUST A BAD DREAM.
I'VE BEEN EXPECTING YOU.

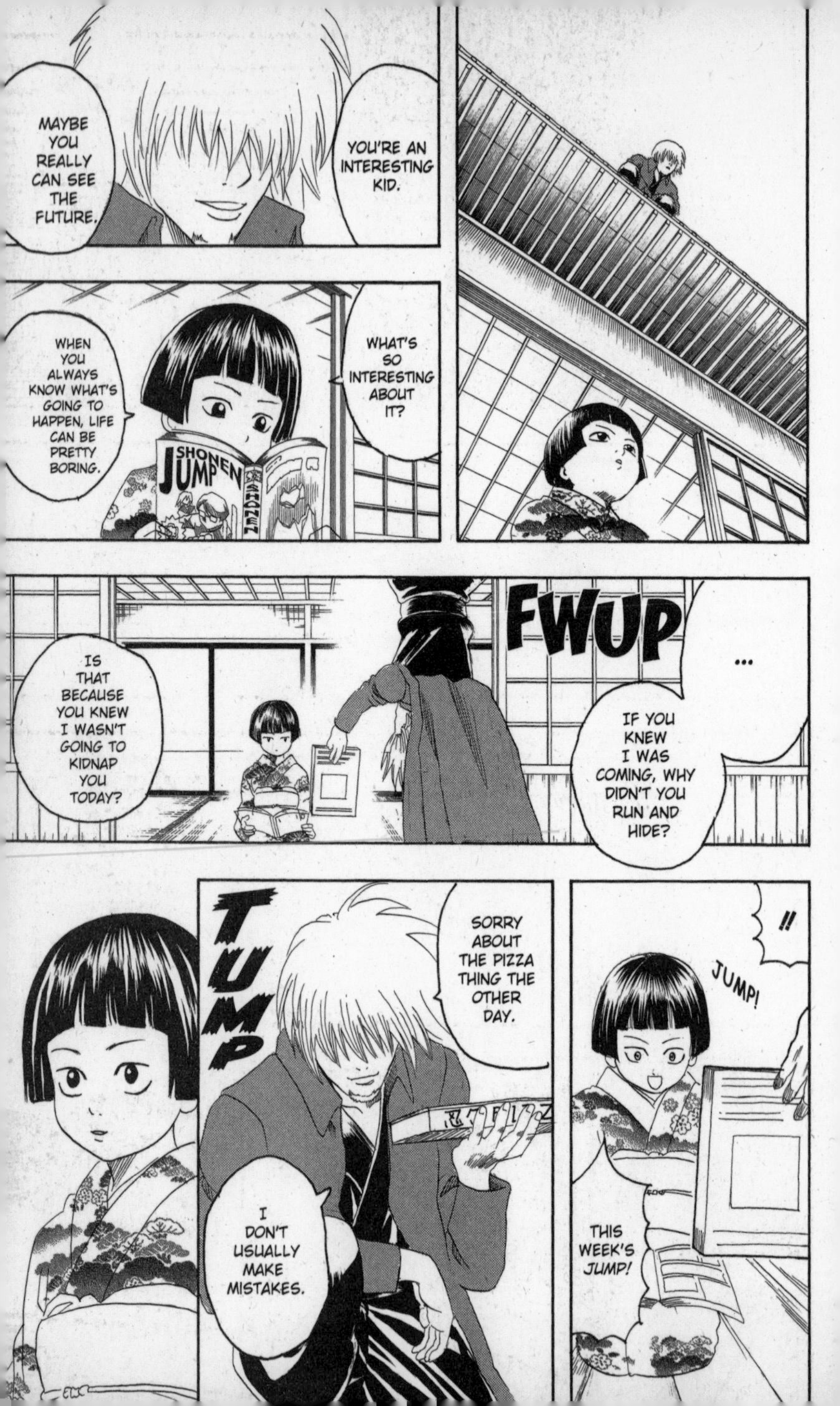
YOU'RE AN INTERESTING KID.
MAYBE YOU REALLY CAN SEE THE FUTURE.
WHAT'S SO INTERESTING ABOUT IT?
WHEN YOU ALWAYS KNOW WHAT'S GOING TO HAPPEN, LIFE CAN BE PRETTY BORING.
SHONEN JUMP
FWUP
...
IF YOU KNEW I WAS COMING, WHY DIDN'T YOU RUN AND HIDE?
IS THAT BECAUSE YOU KNEW I WASN'T GOING TO KIDNAP YOU TODAY?
!!
JUMP!
THIS WEEK'S JUMP!
TUMP
SORRY ABOUT THE PIZZA THING THE OTHER DAY.
I DON'T USUALLY MAKE MISTAKES.

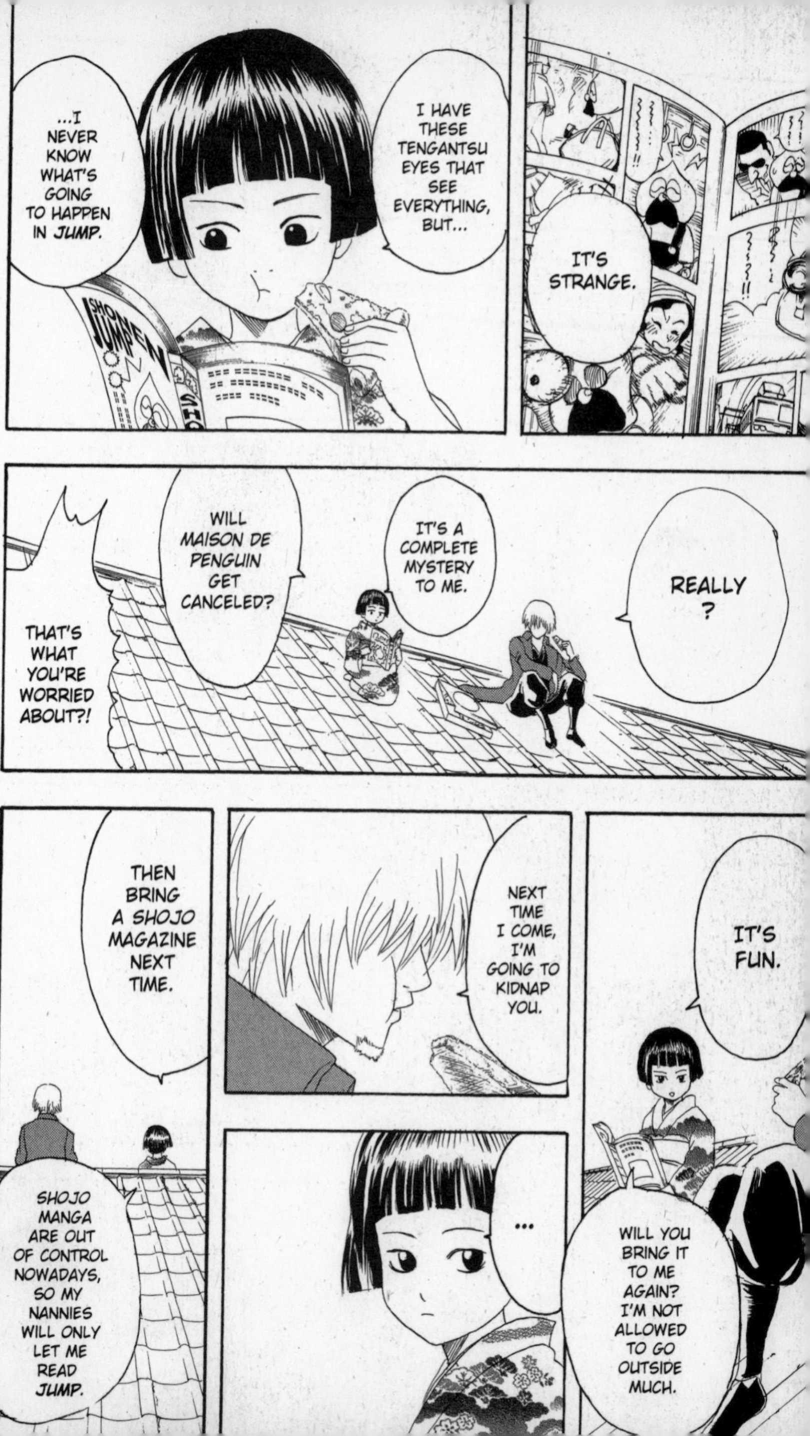
IT'S STRANGE.
I HAVE THESE TENGANTSU EYES THAT SEE EVERYTHING, BUT...
...I NEVER KNOW WHAT'S GOING TO HAPPEN IN *JUMP*.
SHONEN JUMP
REALLY?
IT'S A COMPLETE MYSTERY TO ME.
WILL MAISON DE PENGUIN GET CANCELED?
THAT'S WHAT YOU'RE WORRIED ABOUT?!
IT'S FUN.
WILL YOU BRING IT TO ME AGAIN? I'M NOT ALLOWED TO GO OUTSIDE MUCH.
NEXT TIME I COME, I'M GOING TO KIDNAP YOU.
...
THEN BRING A SHOJO MAGAZINE NEXT TIME.
SHOJO MANGA ARE OUT OF CONTROL NOWADAYS, SO MY NANNIES WILL ONLY LET ME READ *JUMP*.

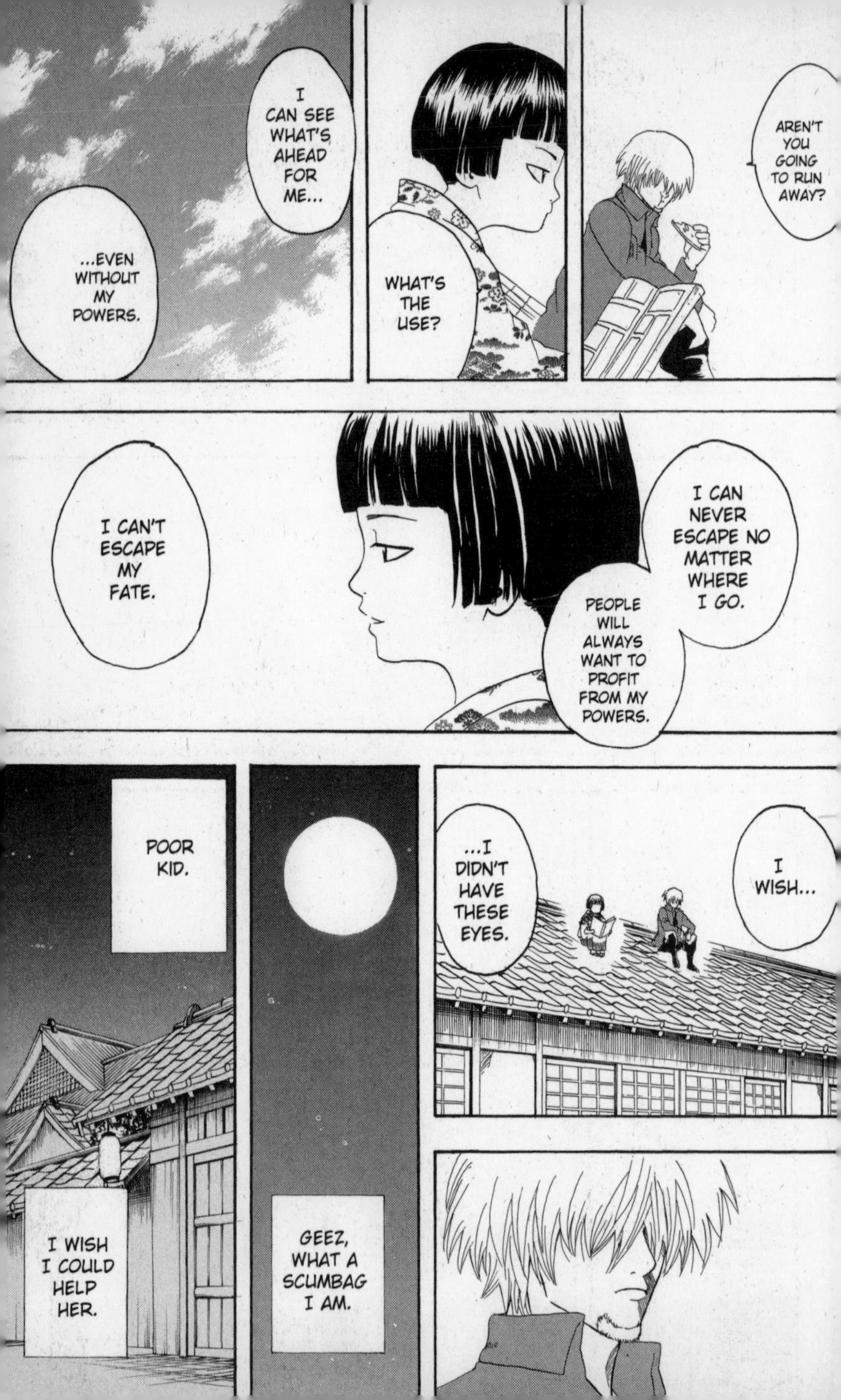
AREN'T YOU GOING TO RUN AWAY?
WHAT'S THE USE?
I CAN SEE WHAT'S AHEAD FOR ME...
...EVEN WITHOUT MY POWERS.
I CAN NEVER ESCAPE NO MATTER WHERE I GO.
PEOPLE WILL ALWAYS WANT TO PROFIT FROM MY POWERS.
I CAN'T ESCAPE MY FATE.
I WISH...
...I DIDN'T HAVE THESE EYES.
GEEZ, WHAT A SCUMBAG I AM.
POOR KID.
I WISH I COULD HELP HER.

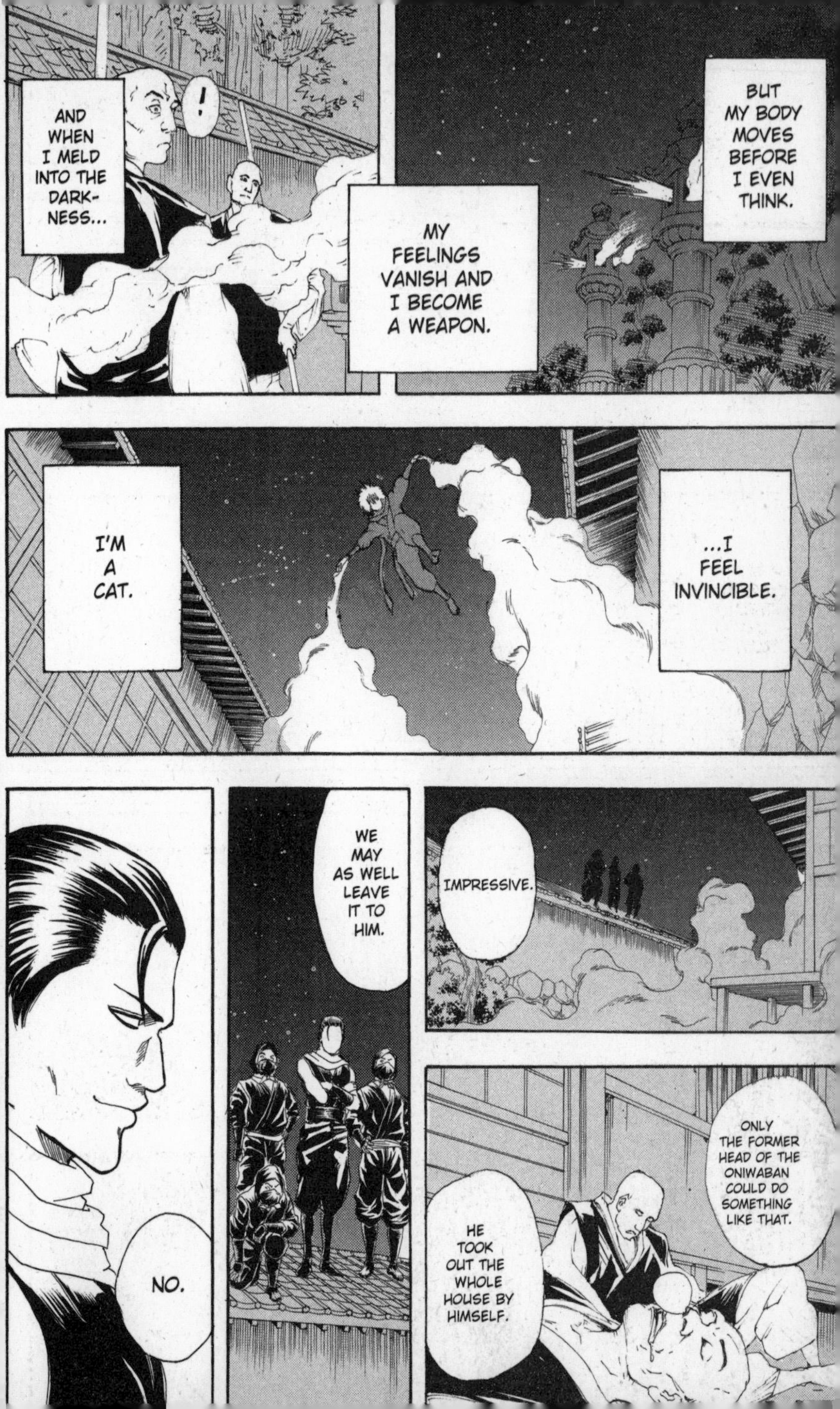
BUT MY BODY MOVES BEFORE I EVEN THINK.
MY FEELINGS VANISH AND I BECOME A WEAPON.
!
AND WHEN I MELD INTO THE DARK-NESS...
...I FEEL INVINCIBLE.
I'M A CAT.
IMPRESSIVE.
ONLY THE FORMER HEAD OF THE ONIWABAN COULD DO SOMETHING LIKE THAT.
HE TOOK OUT THE WHOLE HOUSE BY HIMSELF.
WE MAY AS WELL LEAVE IT TO HIM.
NO.

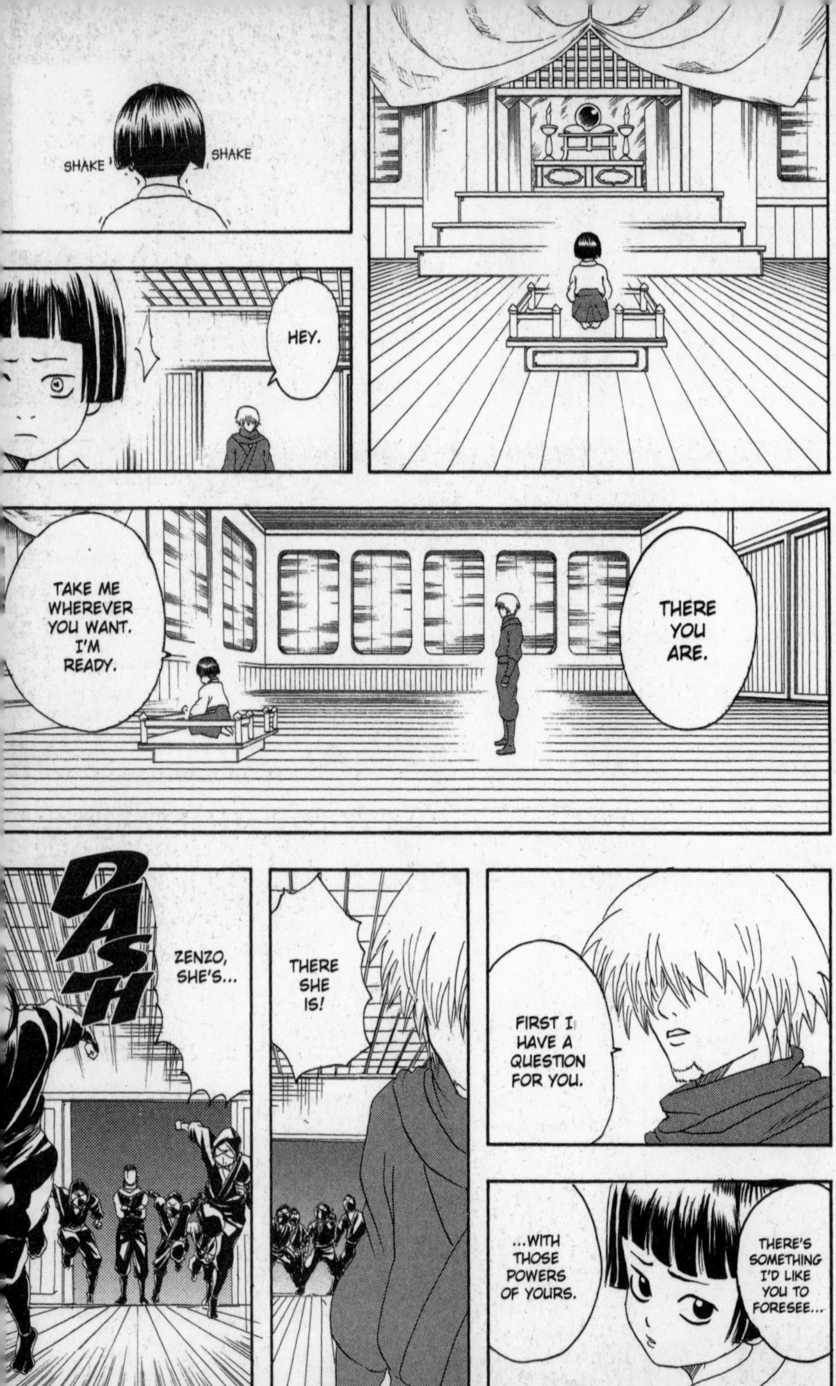
SHAKE
SHAKE
HEY.
THERE YOU ARE.
TAKE ME WHEREVER YOU WANT. I'M READY.
FIRST I HAVE A QUESTION FOR YOU.
THERE'S SOMETHING I'D LIKE YOU TO FORESEE...
...WITH THOSE POWERS OF YOURS.
THERE SHE IS!
DASH
ZENZO, SHE'S...

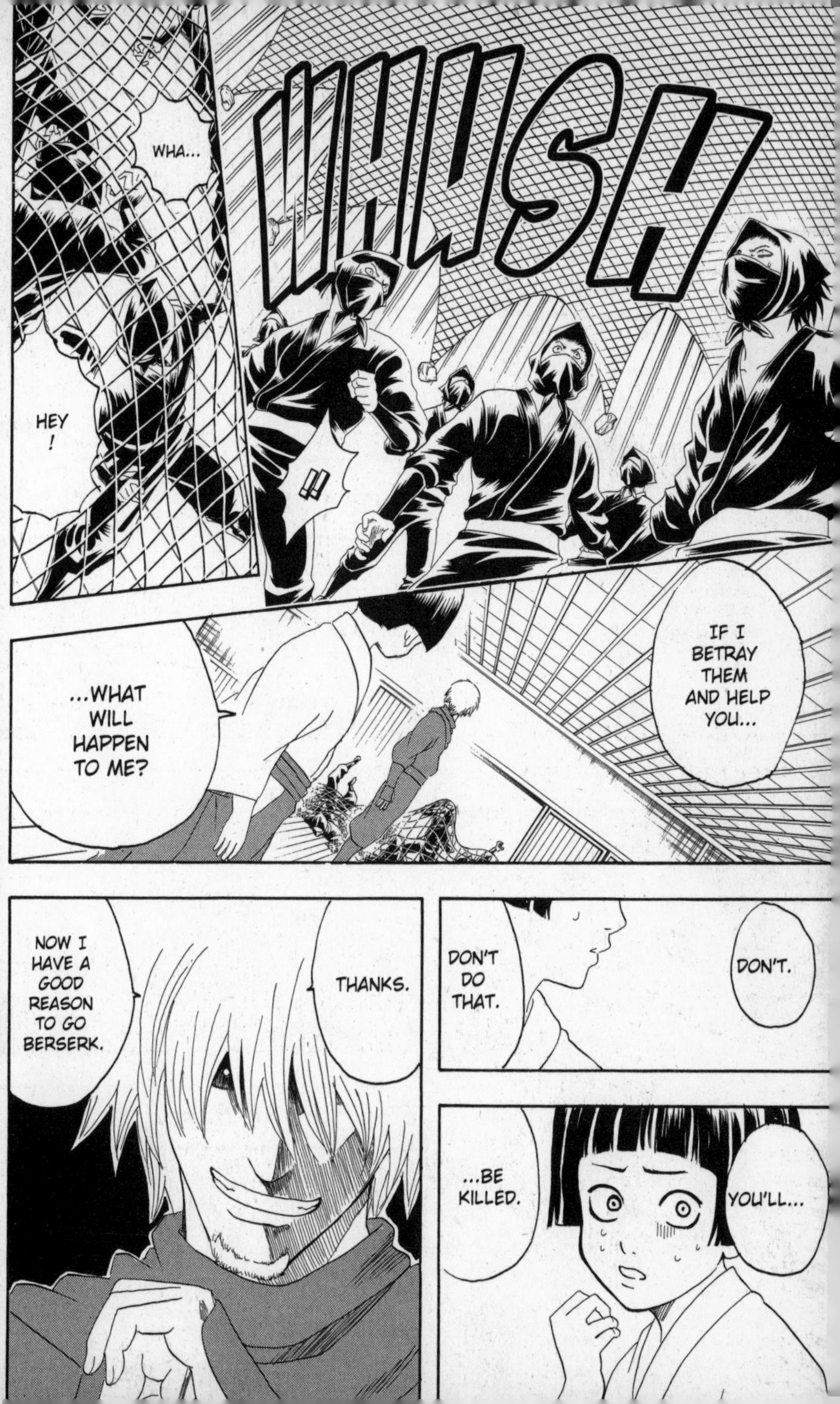
WHUSH
!!
WHA...
HEY!
IF I BETRAY THEM AND HELP YOU...
...WHAT WILL HAPPEN TO ME?
DON'T.
DON'T DO THAT.
YOU'LL...
...BE KILLED.
THANKS.
NOW I HAVE A GOOD REASON TO GO BERSERK.

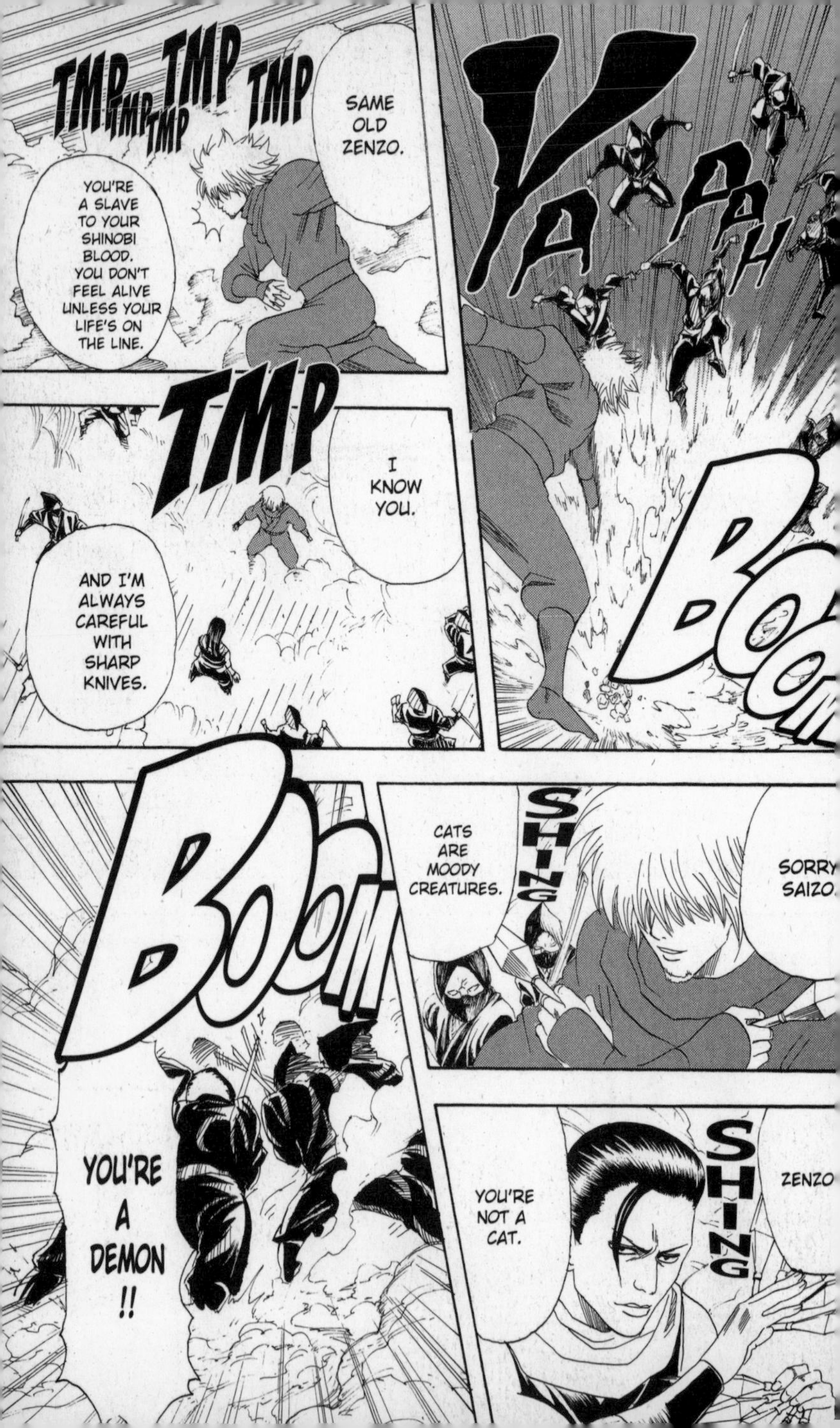

YAAAH
BOOM
TMP TMP TMP TMP TMP
SAME OLD ZENZO.
YOU'RE A SLAVE TO YOUR SHINOBI BLOOD. YOU DON'T FEEL ALIVE UNLESS YOUR LIFE'S ON THE LINE.
TMP
I KNOW YOU.
AND I'M ALWAYS CAREFUL WITH SHARP KNIVES.
SORRY SAIZO.
SHING
CATS ARE MOODY CREATURES.
ZENZO
SHING
YOU'RE NOT A CAT.
BOOM
YOU'RE A DEMON!!

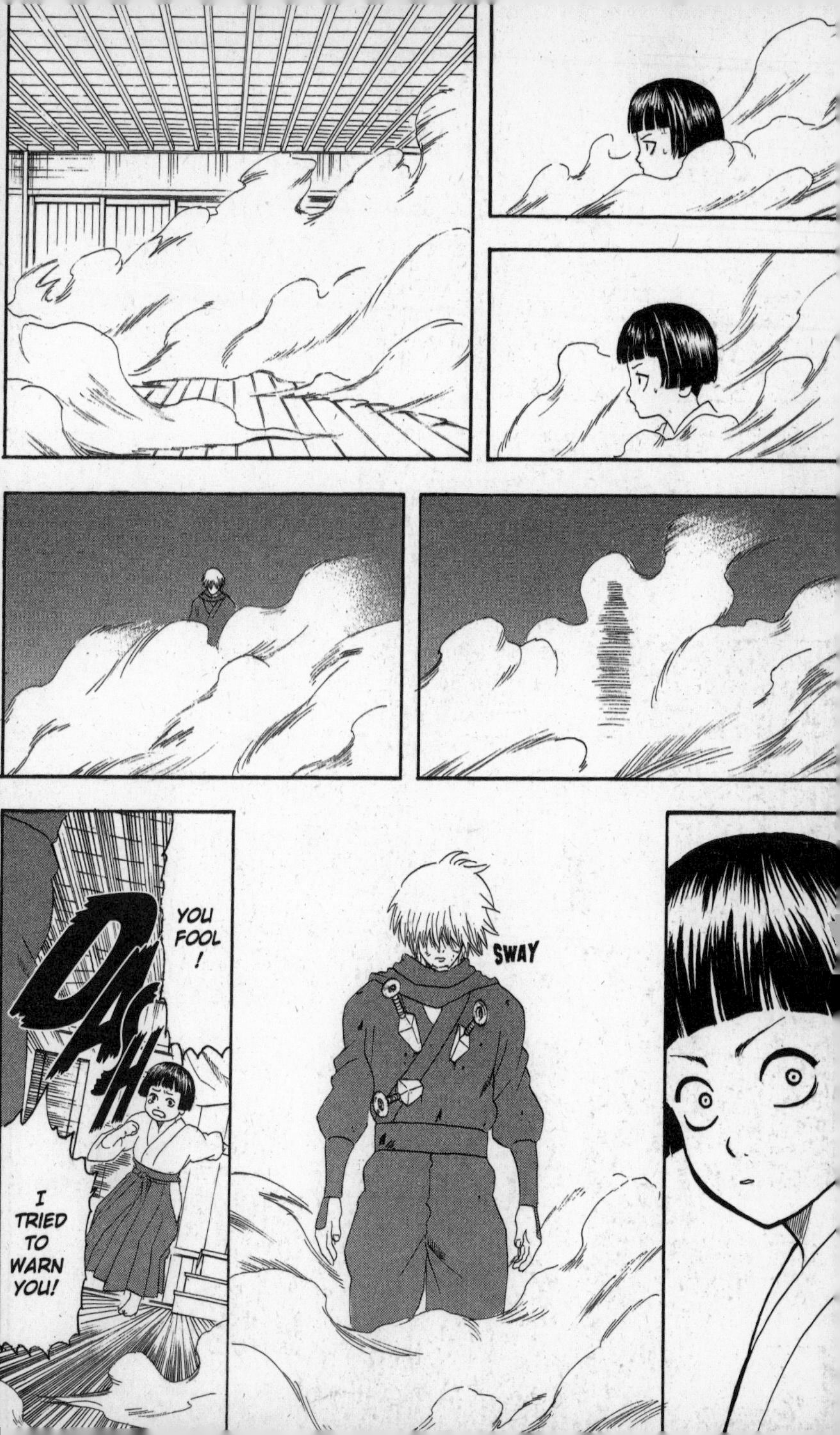
SWAY
DASH
YOU FOOL!
I TRIED TO WARN YOU!

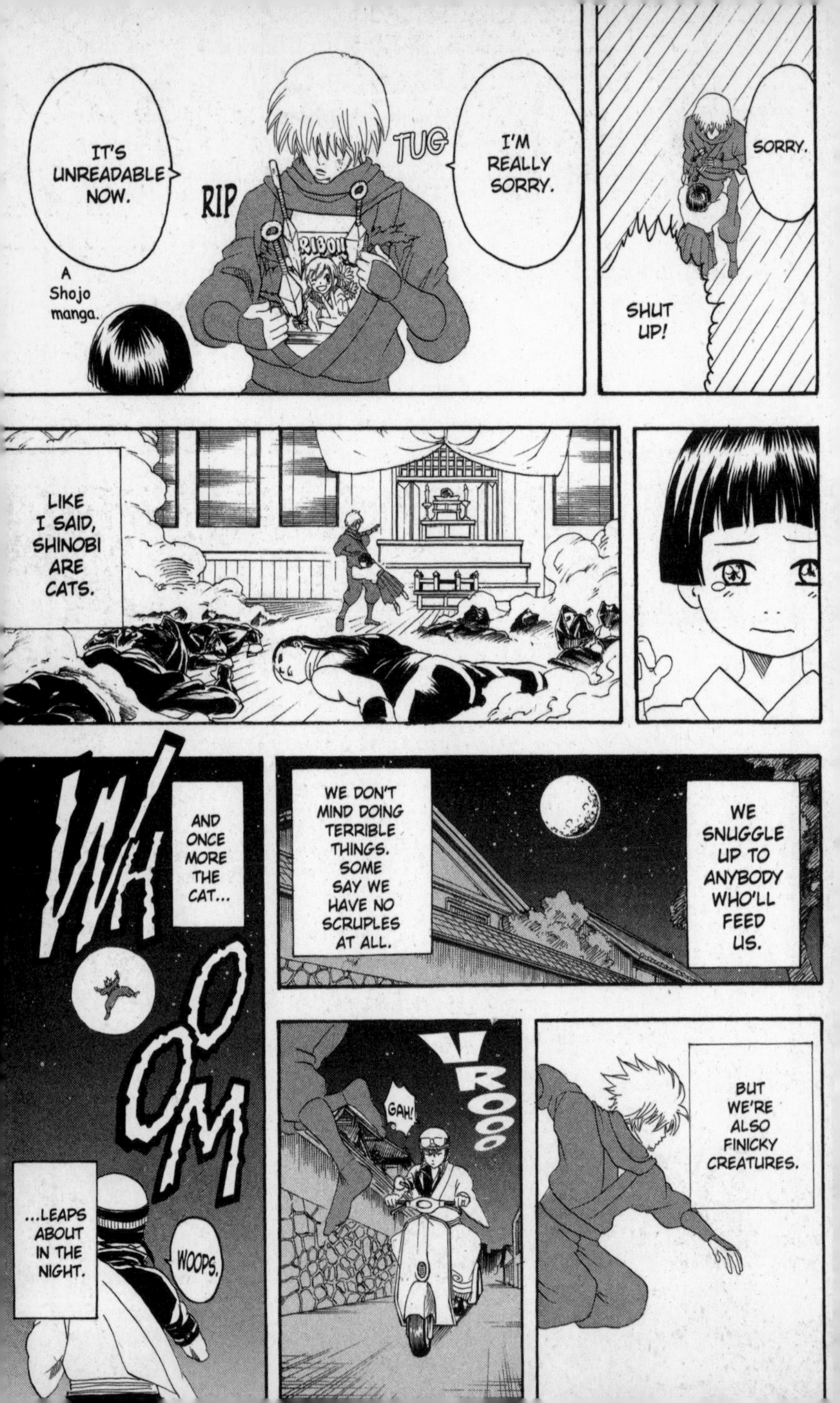
SORRY.
SHUT UP!
I'M REALLY SORRY.
TUG
IT'S UNREADABLE NOW.
RIP
RIBON
A Shojo manga.
LIKE I SAID, SHINOBI ARE CATS.
WE SNUGGLE UP TO ANYBODY WHO'LL FEED US.
WE DON'T MIND DOING TERRIBLE THINGS. SOME SAY WE HAVE NO SCRUPLES AT ALL.
BUT WE'RE ALSO FINICKY CREATURES.
VROOO
GAH!
AND ONCE MORE THE CAT...
WHOOOM
...LEAPS ABOUT IN THE NIGHT.
WOOPS.

Sorachi's Q&A
Hanging with the Readers #41

<Question from "Catharine's cat ears are the most terrible weapons in history" from Kagawa prefecture>

What's the point of *Gin Tama*? I don't understand what you're trying to do here. It seems like meaningless tripe to me.

<Answer>

Me too.
 Thank you for purchasing *Gin Tama*. Even though we're up to volume 15, I still get postcards like this. It's sad. I should've had my characters say catchy things like "I'm gonna be king of the samurai!" or something.
 I guess the point of this manga will become clear around volume 20, if it makes it that far. When the series ends, I hope readers will think: "So that's what it was all about." Please continue reading *Gin Tama* until then.

(Q&A #42 is on page 86)

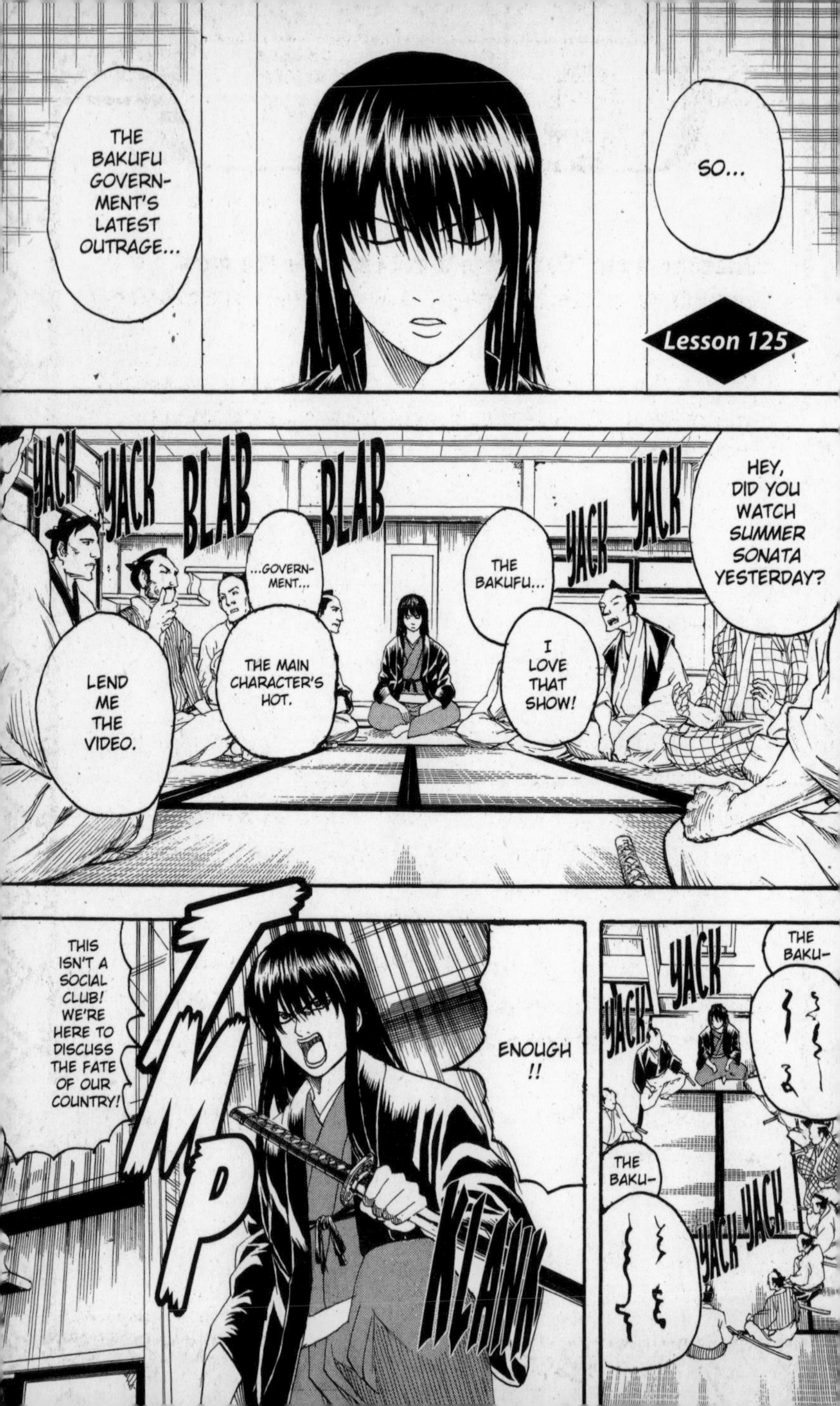
SO...
Lesson 125
THE BAKUFU GOVERNMENT'S LATEST OUTRAGE...
HEY, DID YOU WATCH SUMMER SONATA YESTERDAY?
YACK YACK
THE BAKUFU...
I LOVE THAT SHOW!
BLAB
...GOVERNMENT...
THE MAIN CHARACTER'S HOT.
BLAB
YACK YACK
LEND ME THE VIDEO.
THE BAKU-
YACK YACK
THE BAKU-
YACK YACK
ENOUGH!!
KLANK
THIS ISN'T A SOCIAL CLUB! WE'RE HERE TO DISCUSS THE FATE OF OUR COUNTRY!

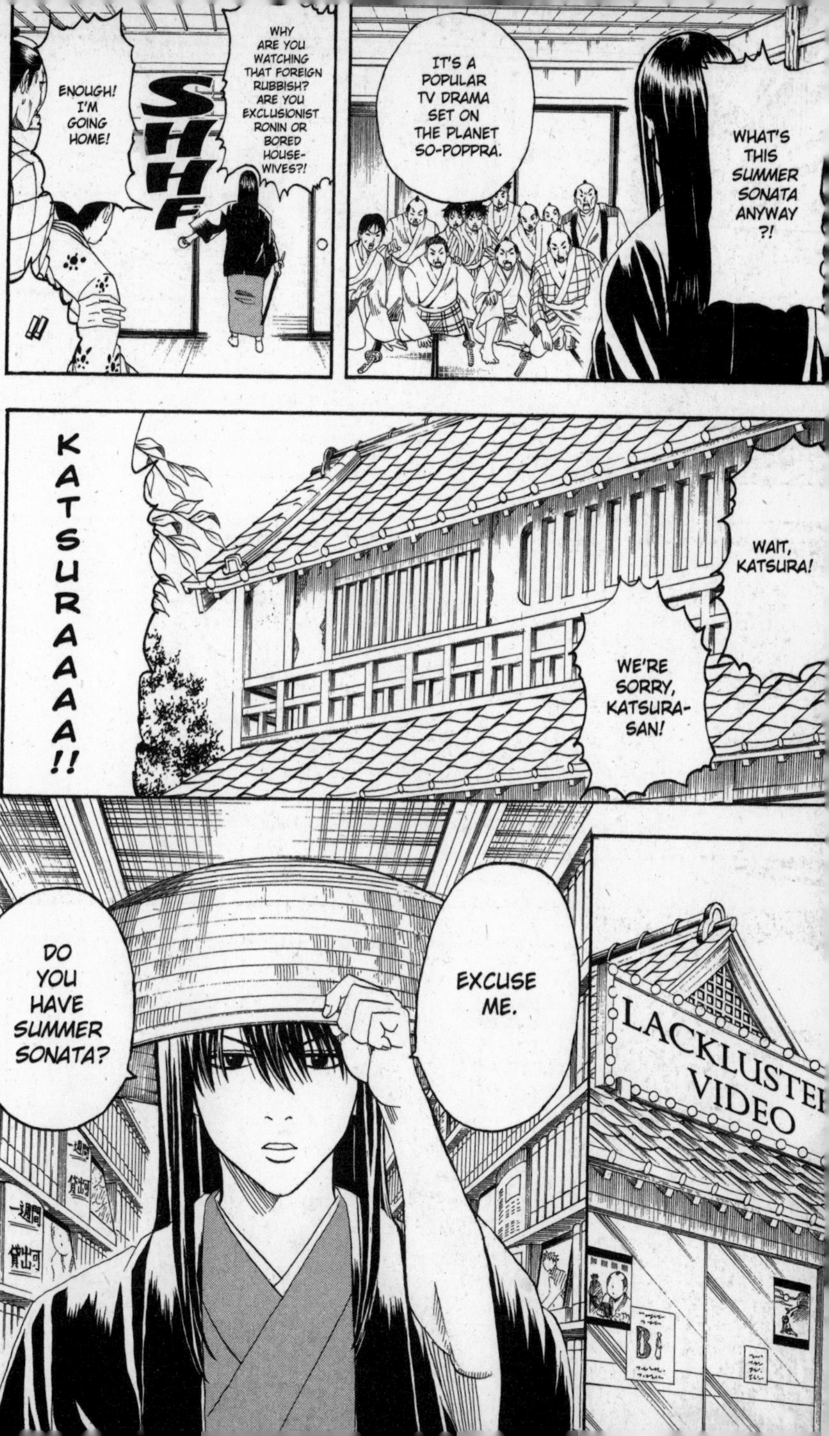
WHAT'S THIS SUMMER SONATA ANYWAY?!
IT'S A POPULAR TV DRAMA SET ON THE PLANET SO-POPPRA.
WHY ARE YOU WATCHING THAT FOREIGN RUBBISH? ARE YOU EXCLUSIONIST RONIN OR BORED HOUSE-WIVES?!
SHHF
ENOUGH! I'M GOING HOME!
!!
WAIT, KATSURA!
WE'RE SORRY, KATSURA-SAN!
KATSURAAAAAA!!
LACKLUSTER VIDEO
EXCUSE ME.
DO YOU HAVE SUMMER SONATA?

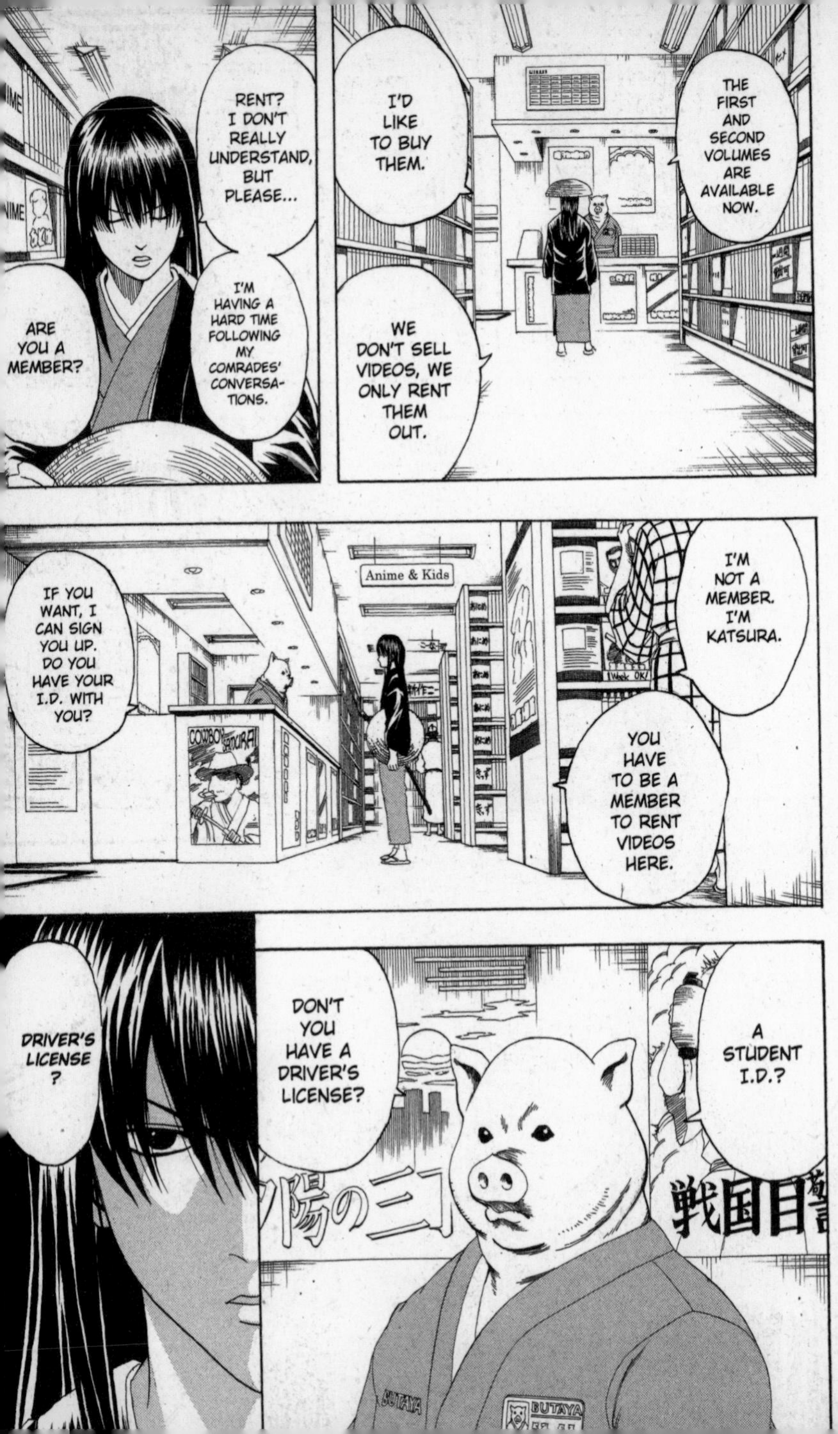
THE FIRST AND SECOND VOLUMES ARE AVAILABLE NOW.
I'D LIKE TO BUY THEM.
WE DON'T SELL VIDEOS, WE ONLY RENT THEM OUT.
RENT? I DON'T REALLY UNDERSTAND, BUT PLEASE...
I'M HAVING A HARD TIME FOLLOWING MY COMRADES' CONVERSATIONS.
ARE YOU A MEMBER?
I'M NOT A MEMBER. I'M KATSURA.
YOU HAVE TO BE A MEMBER TO RENT VIDEOS HERE.
1Week OK!
Anime & Kids
IF YOU WANT, I CAN SIGN YOU UP. DO YOU HAVE YOUR I.D. WITH YOU?
COWBOY SAMURAI
A STUDENT I.D.?
DON'T YOU HAVE A DRIVER'S LICENSE?
BUTAYA
BUTAYA
DRIVER'S LICENSE ?

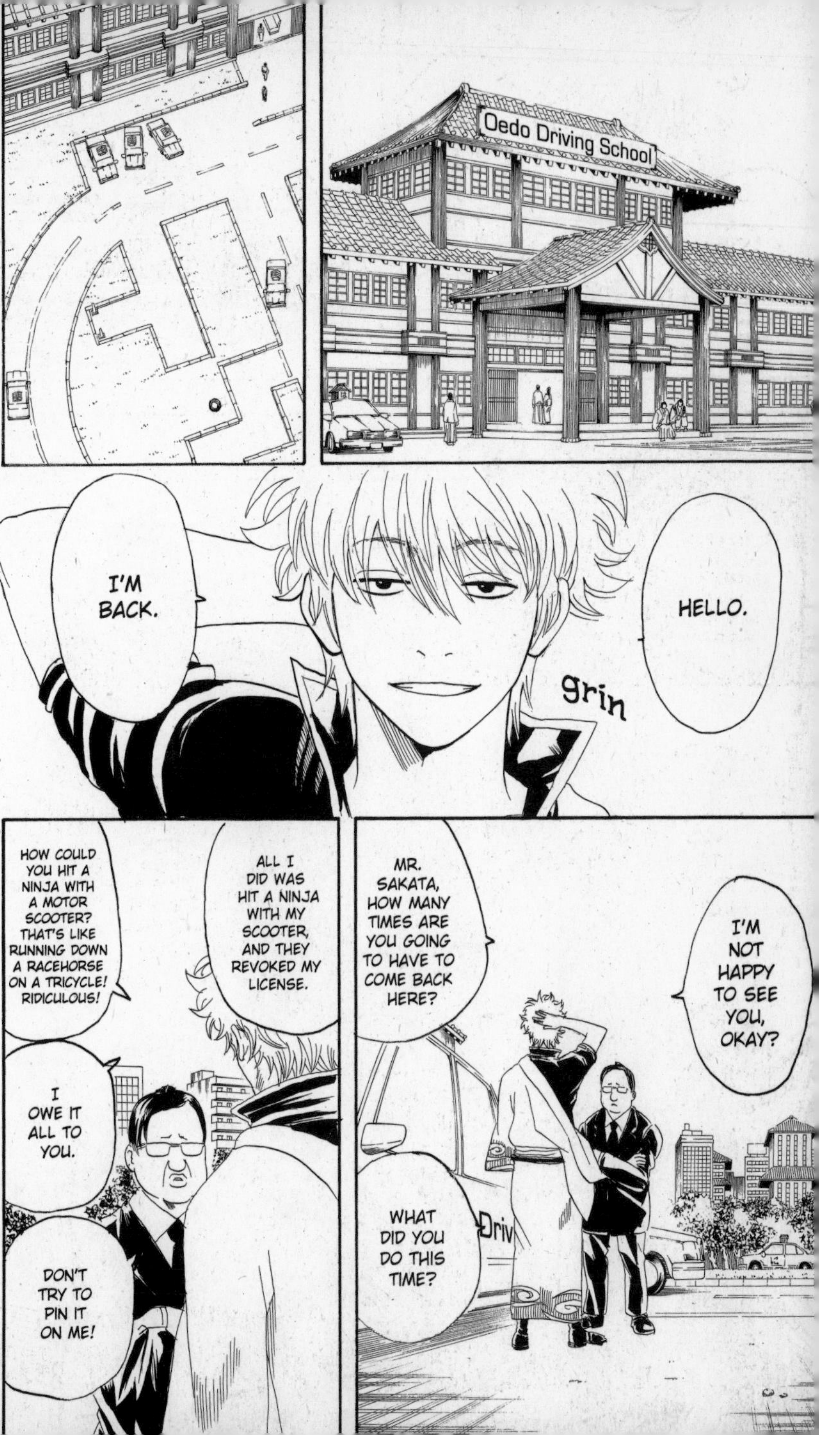
Oedo Driving School
HELLO.
grin
I'M BACK.
I'M NOT HAPPY TO SEE YOU, OKAY?
MR. SAKATA, HOW MANY TIMES ARE YOU GOING TO HAVE TO COME BACK HERE?
WHAT DID YOU DO THIS TIME?
ALL I DID WAS HIT A NINJA WITH MY SCOOTER, AND THEY REVOKED MY LICENSE.
HOW COULD YOU HIT A NINJA WITH A MOTOR SCOOTER? THAT'S LIKE RUNNING DOWN A RACEHORSE ON A TRICYCLE! RIDICULOUS!
I OWE IT ALL TO YOU.
DON'T TRY TO PIN IT ON ME!

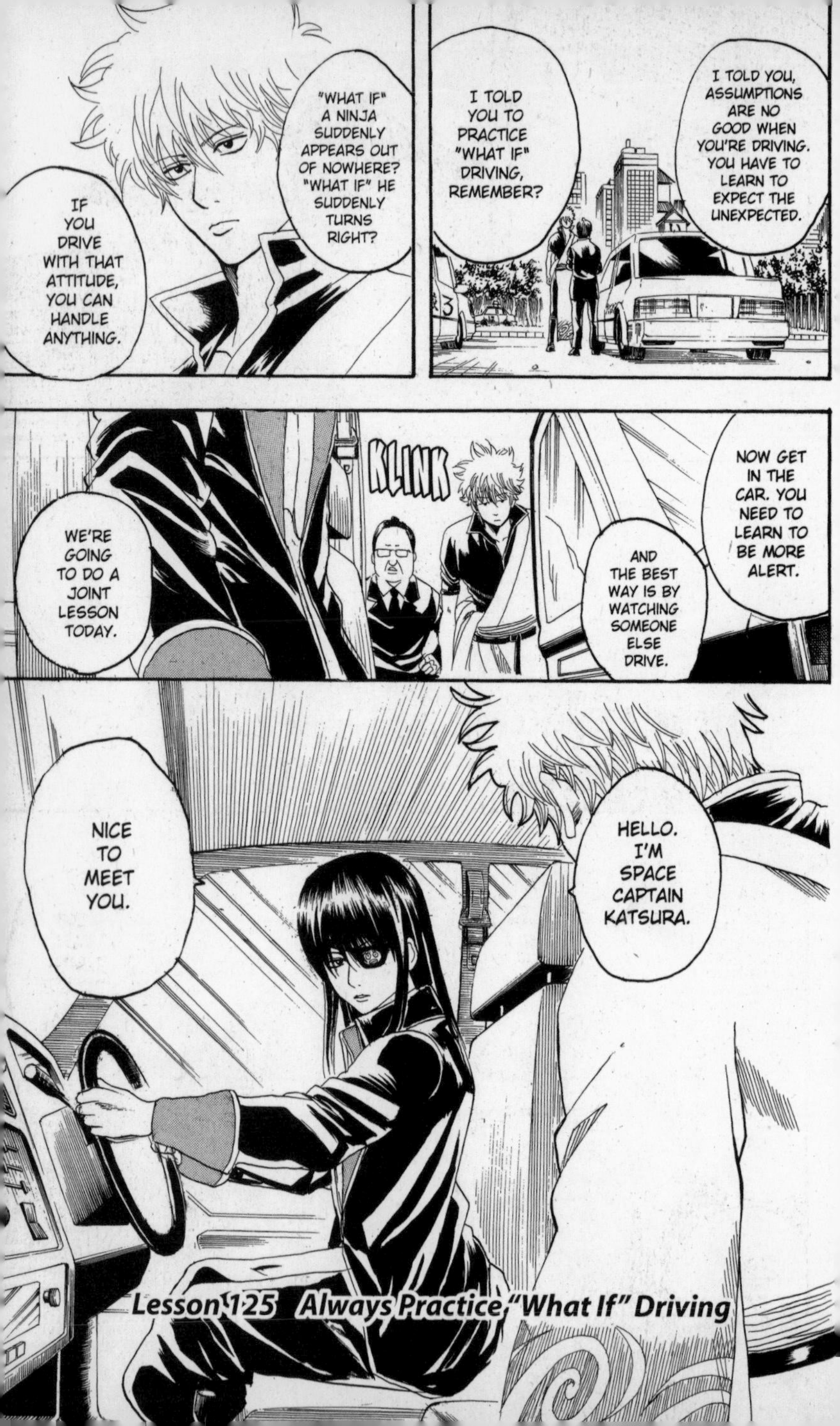
I TOLD YOU, ASSUMPTIONS ARE NO GOOD WHEN YOU'RE DRIVING. YOU HAVE TO LEARN TO EXPECT THE UNEXPECTED.
I TOLD YOU TO PRACTICE "WHAT IF" DRIVING, REMEMBER?
"WHAT IF" A NINJA SUDDENLY APPEARS OUT OF NOWHERE? "WHAT IF" HE SUDDENLY TURNS RIGHT?
IF YOU DRIVE WITH THAT ATTITUDE, YOU CAN HANDLE ANYTHING.
NOW GET IN THE CAR. YOU NEED TO LEARN TO BE MORE ALERT.
AND THE BEST WAY IS BY WATCHING SOMEONE ELSE DRIVE.
KLINK
WE'RE GOING TO DO A JOINT LESSON TODAY.
HELLO. I'M SPACE CAPTAIN KATSURA.
NICE TO MEET YOU.

Lesson 125 Always Practice "What If" Driving

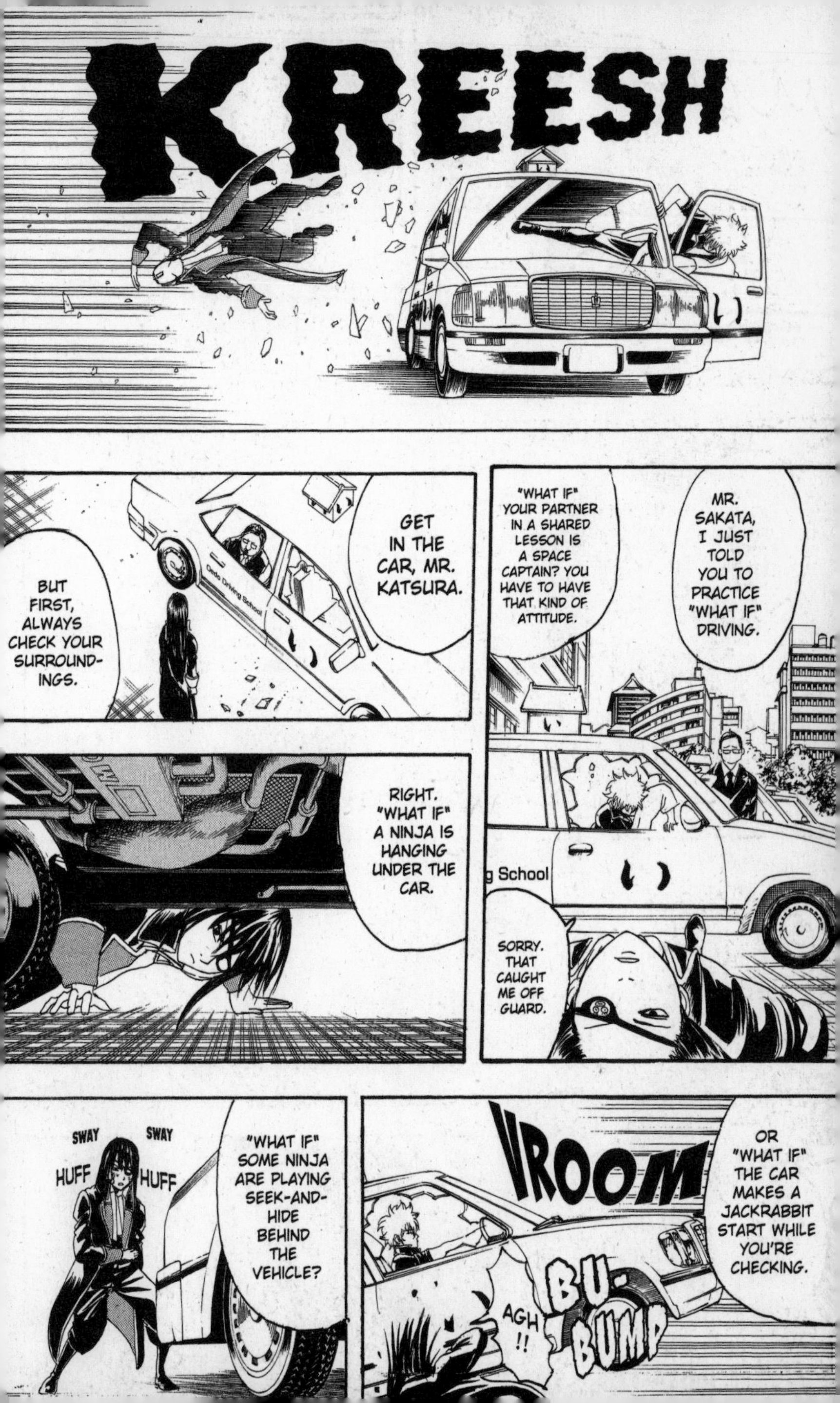
KREESH
MR. SAKATA, I JUST TOLD YOU TO PRACTICE "WHAT IF" DRIVING.
"WHAT IF" YOUR PARTNER IN A SHARED LESSON IS A SPACE CAPTAIN? YOU HAVE TO HAVE THAT KIND OF ATTITUDE.
SORRY. THAT CAUGHT ME OFF GUARD.
GET IN THE CAR, MR. KATSURA.
Oedo Driving School
BUT FIRST, ALWAYS CHECK YOUR SURROUND-INGS.
RIGHT. "WHAT IF" A NINJA IS HANGING UNDER THE CAR.
OR "WHAT IF" THE CAR MAKES A JACKRABBIT START WHILE YOU'RE CHECKING.
VROOM
BU-BUMP
AGH !!
"WHAT IF" SOME NINJA ARE PLAYING SEEK-AND-HIDE BEHIND THE VEHICLE?
SWAY SWAY
HUFF HUFF

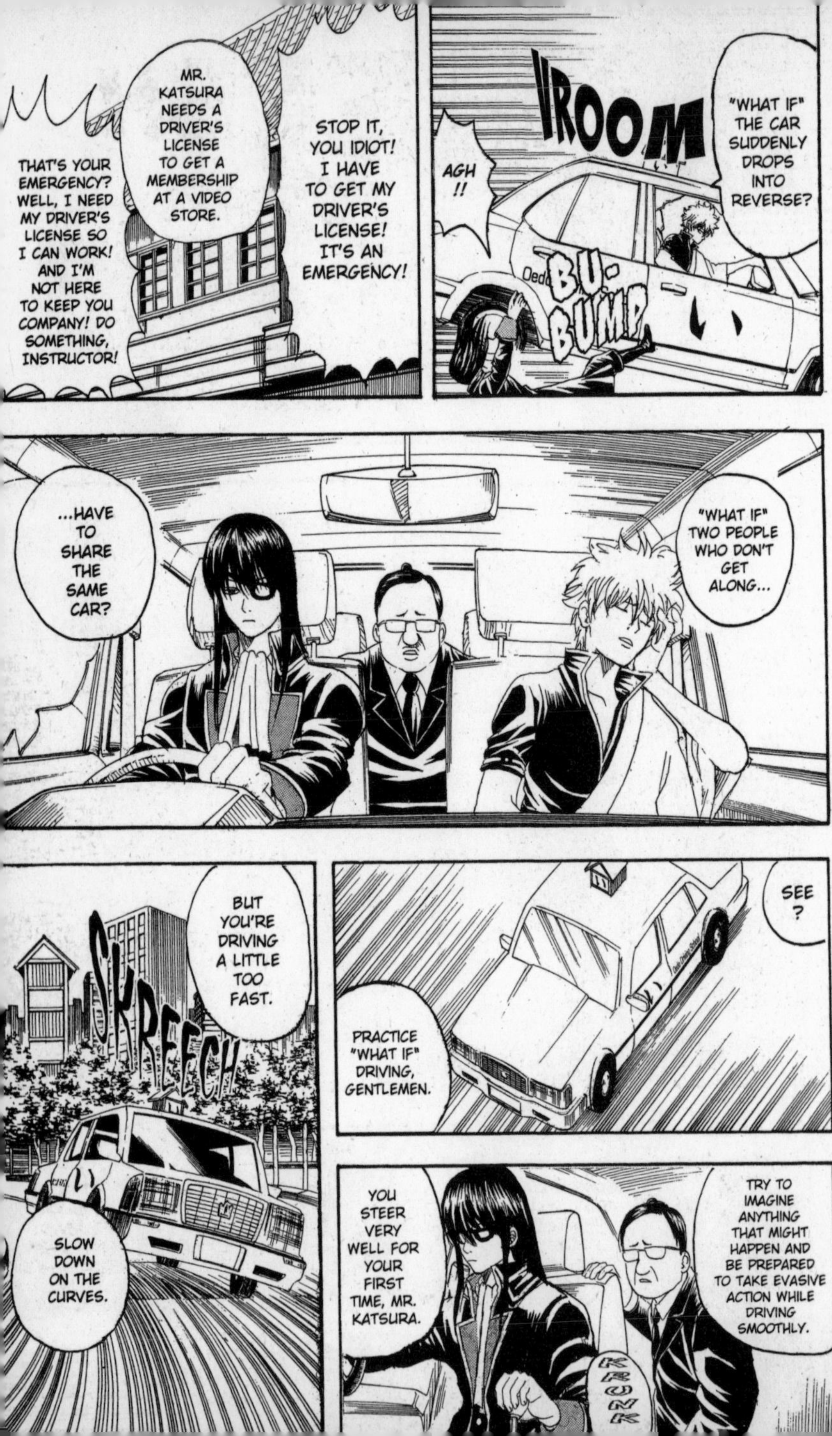
"WHAT IF" THE CAR SUDDENLY DROPS INTO REVERSE?
VROOM
AGH !!
BU-BUMP
STOP IT, YOU IDIOT! I HAVE TO GET MY DRIVER'S LICENSE! IT'S AN EMERGENCY!
MR. KATSURA NEEDS A DRIVER'S LICENSE TO GET A MEMBERSHIP AT A VIDEO STORE.
THAT'S YOUR EMERGENCY? WELL, I NEED MY DRIVER'S LICENSE SO I CAN WORK! AND I'M NOT HERE TO KEEP YOU COMPANY! DO SOMETHING, INSTRUCTOR!
"WHAT IF" TWO PEOPLE WHO DON'T GET ALONG...
...HAVE TO SHARE THE SAME CAR?
SEE ?
PRACTICE "WHAT IF" DRIVING, GENTLEMEN.
TRY TO IMAGINE ANYTHING THAT MIGHT HAPPEN AND BE PREPARED TO TAKE EVASIVE ACTION WHILE DRIVING SMOOTHLY.
YOU STEER VERY WELL FOR YOUR FIRST TIME, MR. KATSURA.
KRUNK
BUT YOU'RE DRIVING A LITTLE TOO FAST.
SKREECH
SLOW DOWN ON THE CURVES.

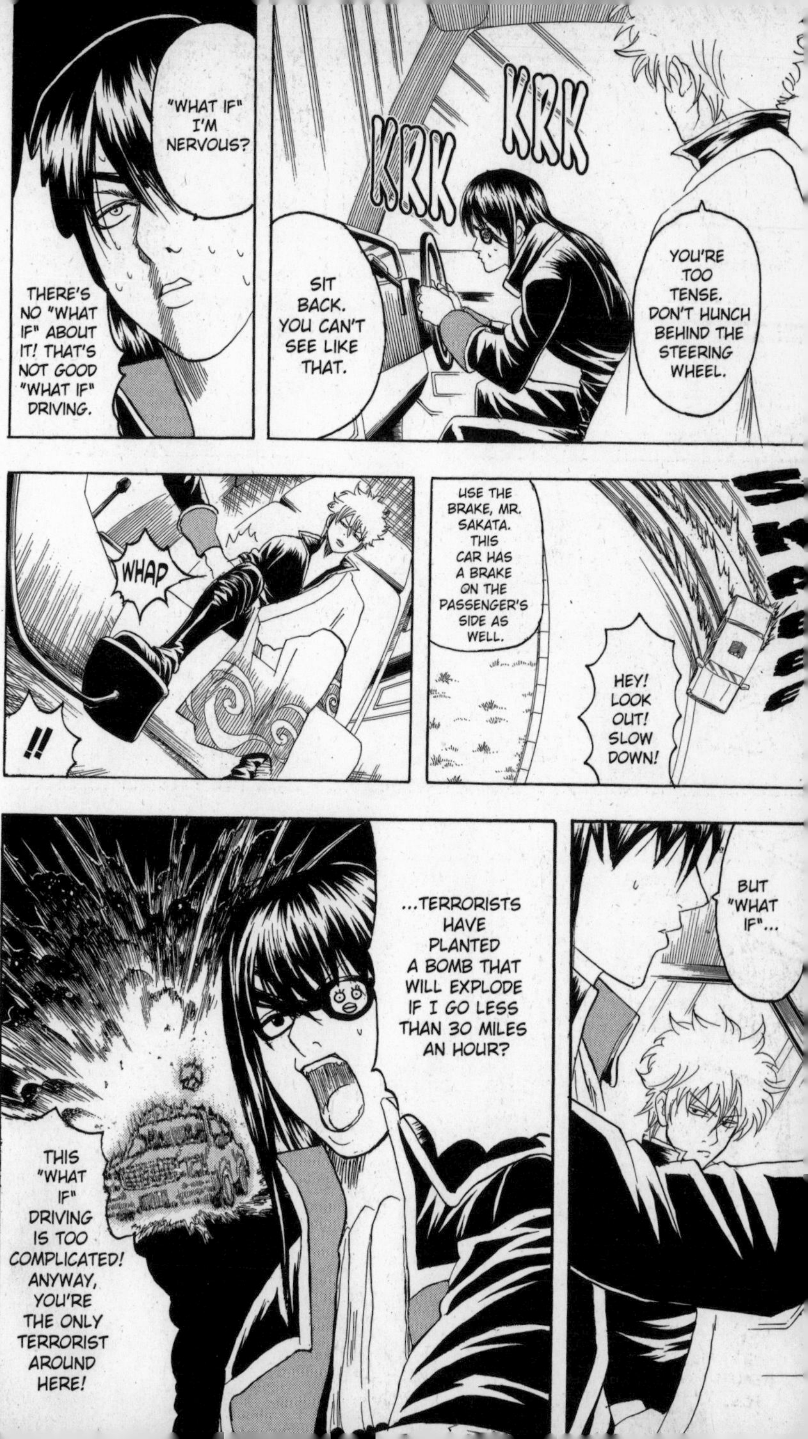
YOU'RE TOO TENSE. DON'T HUNCH BEHIND THE STEERING WHEEL.
KRK
KRK
SIT BACK. YOU CAN'T SEE LIKE THAT.
"WHAT IF" I'M NERVOUS?
THERE'S NO "WHAT IF" ABOUT IT! THAT'S NOT GOOD "WHAT IF" DRIVING.
HEY! LOOK OUT! SLOW DOWN!
USE THE BRAKE, MR. SAKATA. THIS CAR HAS A BRAKE ON THE PASSENGER'S SIDE AS WELL.
WHAP
!!
BUT "WHAT IF"...
...TERRORISTS HAVE PLANTED A BOMB THAT WILL EXPLODE IF I GO LESS THAN 30 MILES AN HOUR?
THIS "WHAT IF" DRIVING IS TOO COMPLICATED! ANYWAY, YOU'RE THE ONLY TERRORIST AROUND HERE!

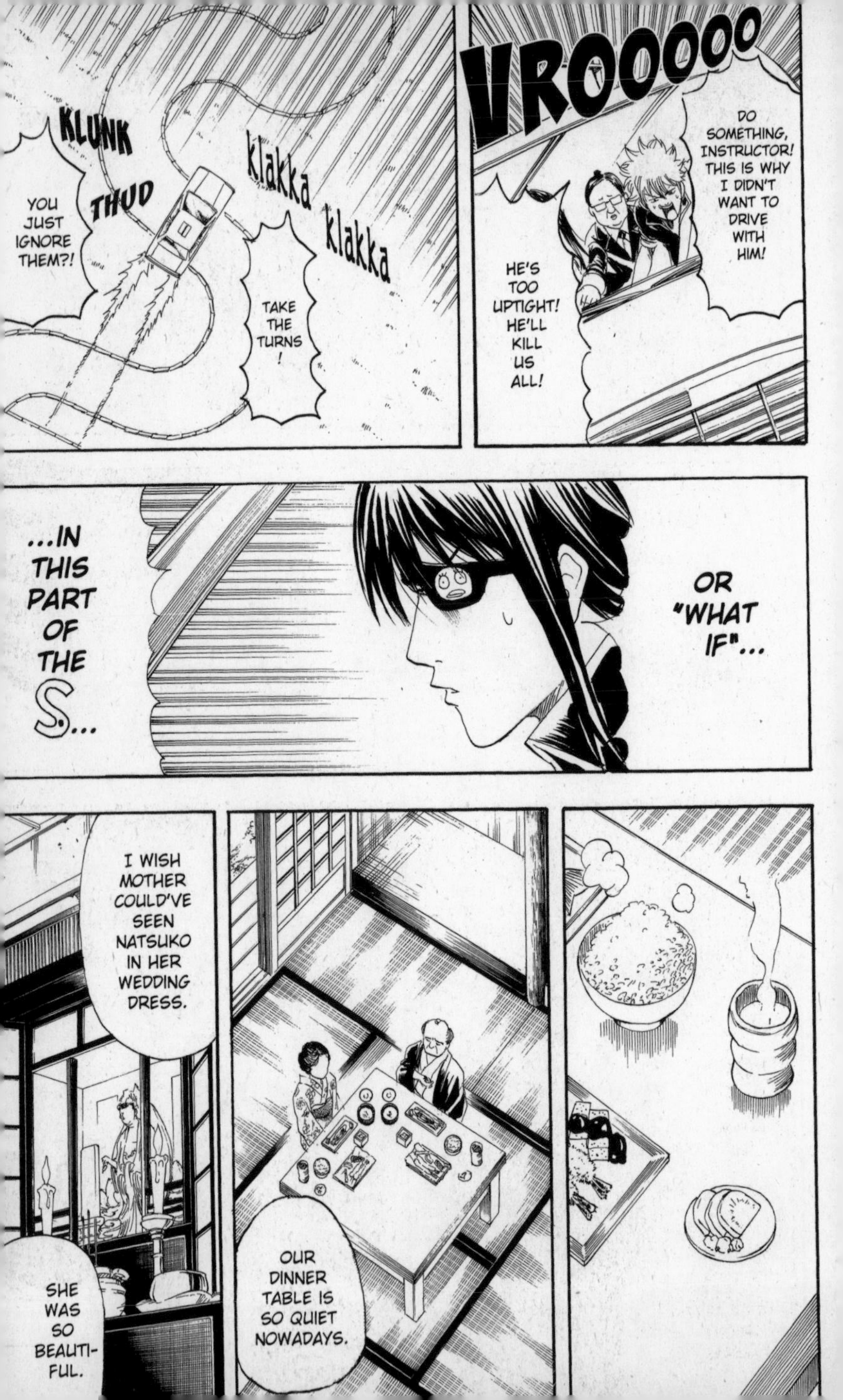
VROOOOO
DO SOMETHING, INSTRUCTOR! THIS IS WHY I DIDN'T WANT TO DRIVE WITH HIM!
HE'S TOO UPTIGHT! HE'LL KILL US ALL!
klakka klakka
KLUNK
THUD
TAKE THE TURNS!
YOU JUST IGNORE THEM?!
OR "WHAT IF"...
...IN THIS PART OF THE S...
OUR DINNER TABLE IS SO QUIET NOWADAYS.
I WISH MOTHER COULD'VE SEEN NATSUKO IN HER WEDDING DRESS.
SHE WAS SO BEAUTI-FUL.

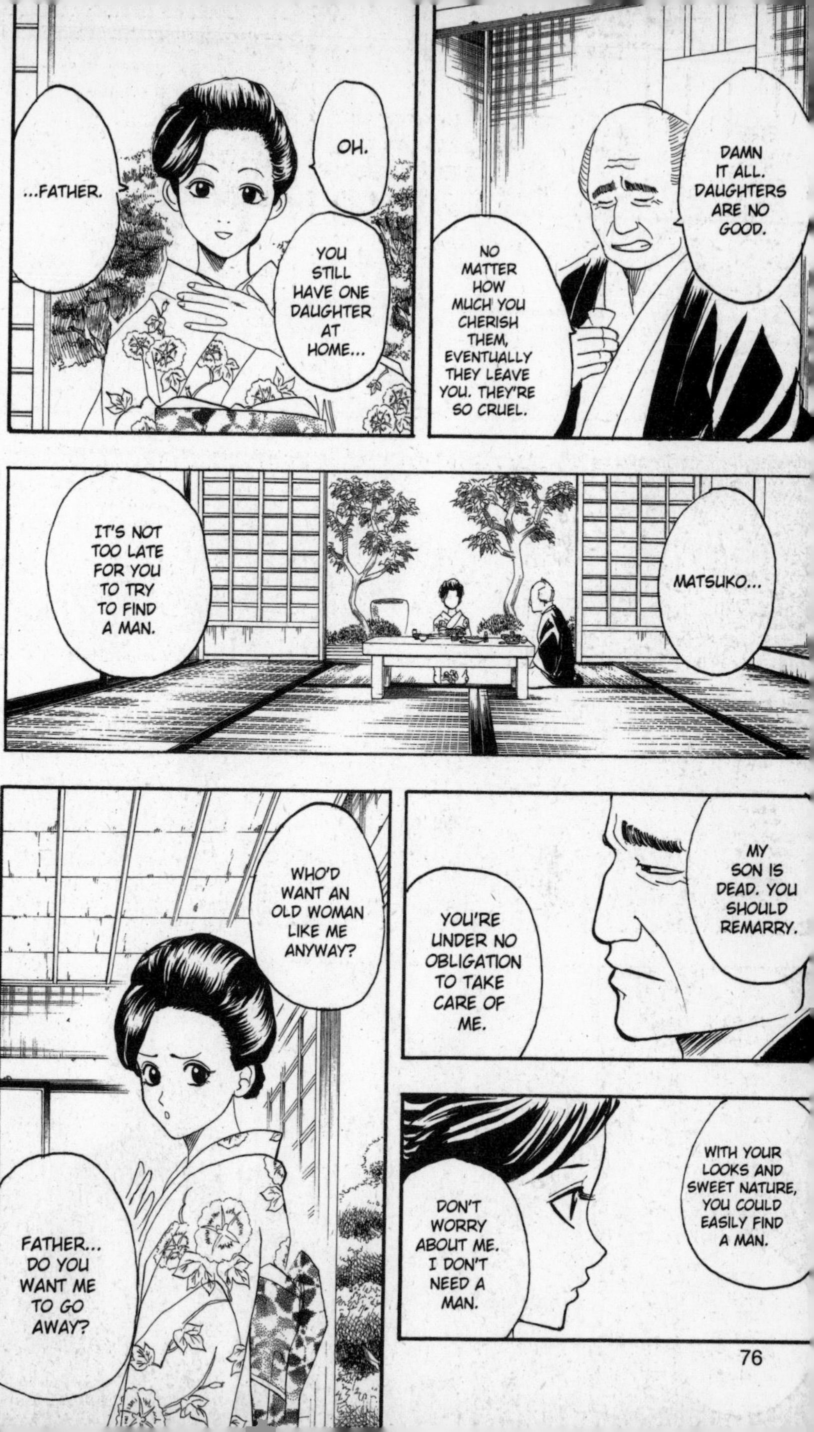
DAMN IT ALL. DAUGHTERS ARE NO GOOD.
NO MATTER HOW MUCH YOU CHERISH THEM, EVENTUALLY THEY LEAVE YOU. THEY'RE SO CRUEL.
OH.
YOU STILL HAVE ONE DAUGHTER AT HOME...
...FATHER.
MATSUKO...
IT'S NOT TOO LATE FOR YOU TO TRY TO FIND A MAN.
MY SON IS DEAD. YOU SHOULD REMARRY.
YOU'RE UNDER NO OBLIGATION TO TAKE CARE OF ME.
WITH YOUR LOOKS AND SWEET NATURE, YOU COULD EASILY FIND A MAN.
DON'T WORRY ABOUT ME. I DON'T NEED A MAN.
WHO'D WANT AN OLD WOMAN LIKE ME ANYWAY?
FATHER... DO YOU WANT ME TO GO AWAY?

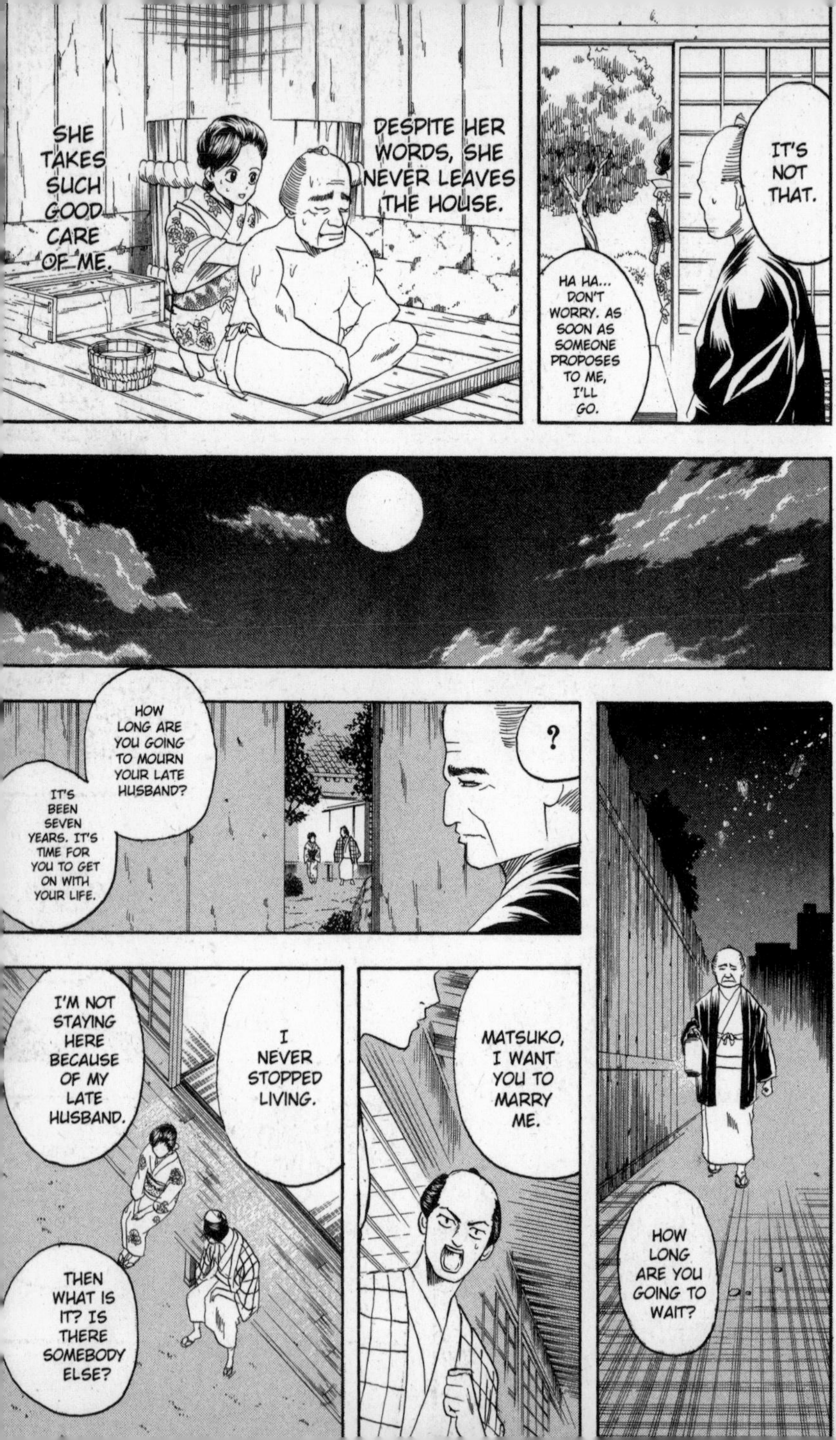

IT'S NOT THAT.
HA HA... DON'T WORRY. AS SOON AS SOMEONE PROPOSES TO ME, I'LL GO.
DESPITE HER WORDS, SHE NEVER LEAVES THE HOUSE.
SHE TAKES SUCH GOOD CARE OF ME.
HOW LONG ARE YOU GOING TO WAIT?
?
HOW LONG ARE YOU GOING TO MOURN YOUR LATE HUSBAND?
IT'S BEEN SEVEN YEARS. IT'S TIME FOR YOU TO GET ON WITH YOUR LIFE.
MATSUKO, I WANT YOU TO MARRY ME.
I NEVER STOPPED LIVING.
I'M NOT STAYING HERE BECAUSE OF MY LATE HUSBAND.
THEN WHAT IS IT? IS THERE SOMEBODY ELSE?

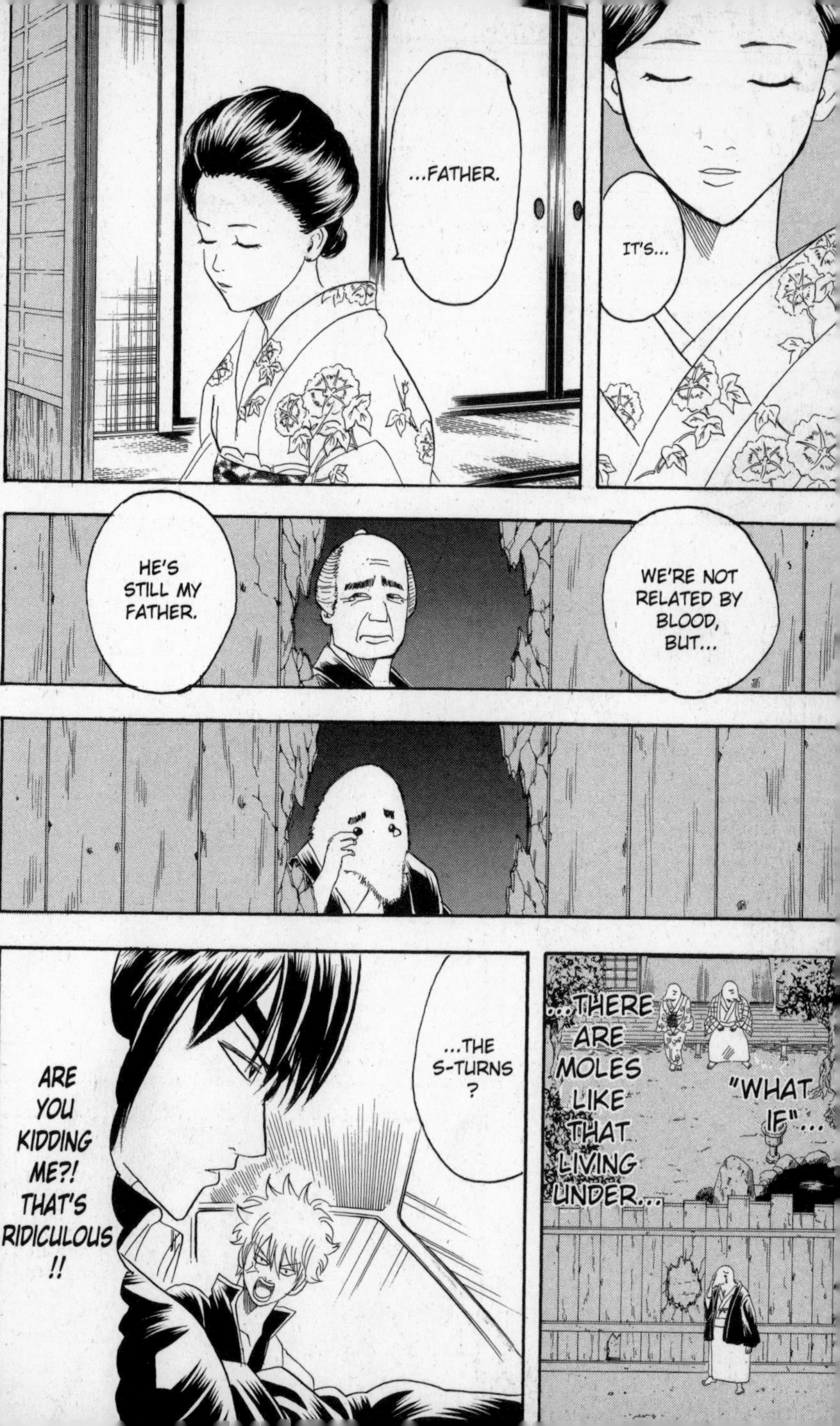
IT'S...
...FATHER.
WE'RE NOT RELATED BY BLOOD, BUT...
HE'S STILL MY FATHER.
"WHAT IF"...
...THERE ARE MOLES LIKE THAT LIVING UNDER...
...THE S-TURNS?
ARE YOU KIDDING ME?! THAT'S RIDICULOUS!!

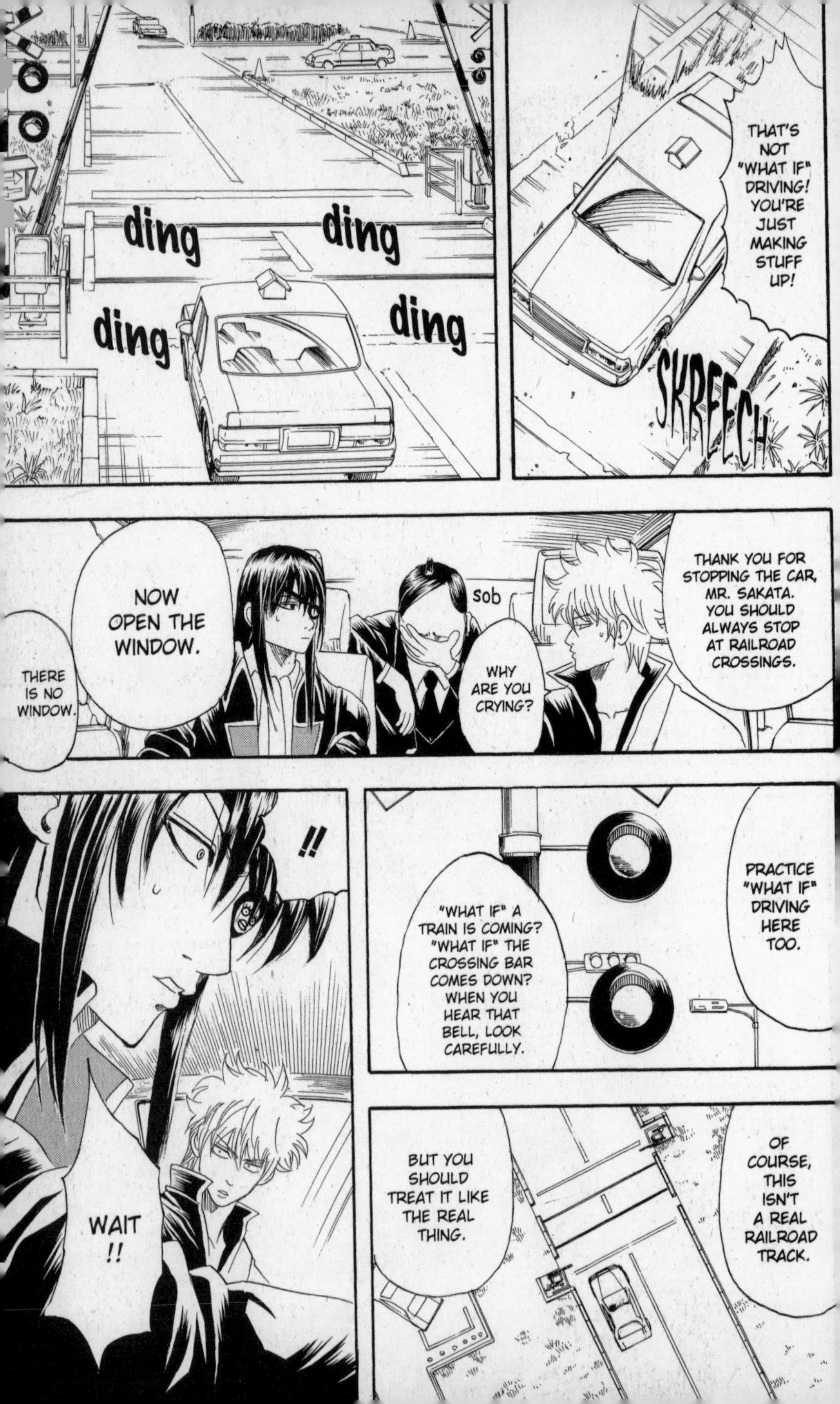
THAT'S NOT "WHAT IF" DRIVING! YOU'RE JUST MAKING STUFF UP!
SKREECH
ding ding
ding ding
THANK YOU FOR STOPPING THE CAR, MR. SAKATA. YOU SHOULD ALWAYS STOP AT RAILROAD CROSSINGS.
WHY ARE YOU CRYING?
sob
NOW OPEN THE WINDOW.
THERE IS NO WINDOW.
PRACTICE "WHAT IF" DRIVING HERE TOO.
"WHAT IF" A TRAIN IS COMING? "WHAT IF" THE CROSSING BAR COMES DOWN? WHEN YOU HEAR THAT BELL, LOOK CAREFULLY.
OF COURSE, THIS ISN'T A REAL RAILROAD TRACK.
BUT YOU SHOULD TREAT IT LIKE THE REAL THING.
!!
WAIT !!

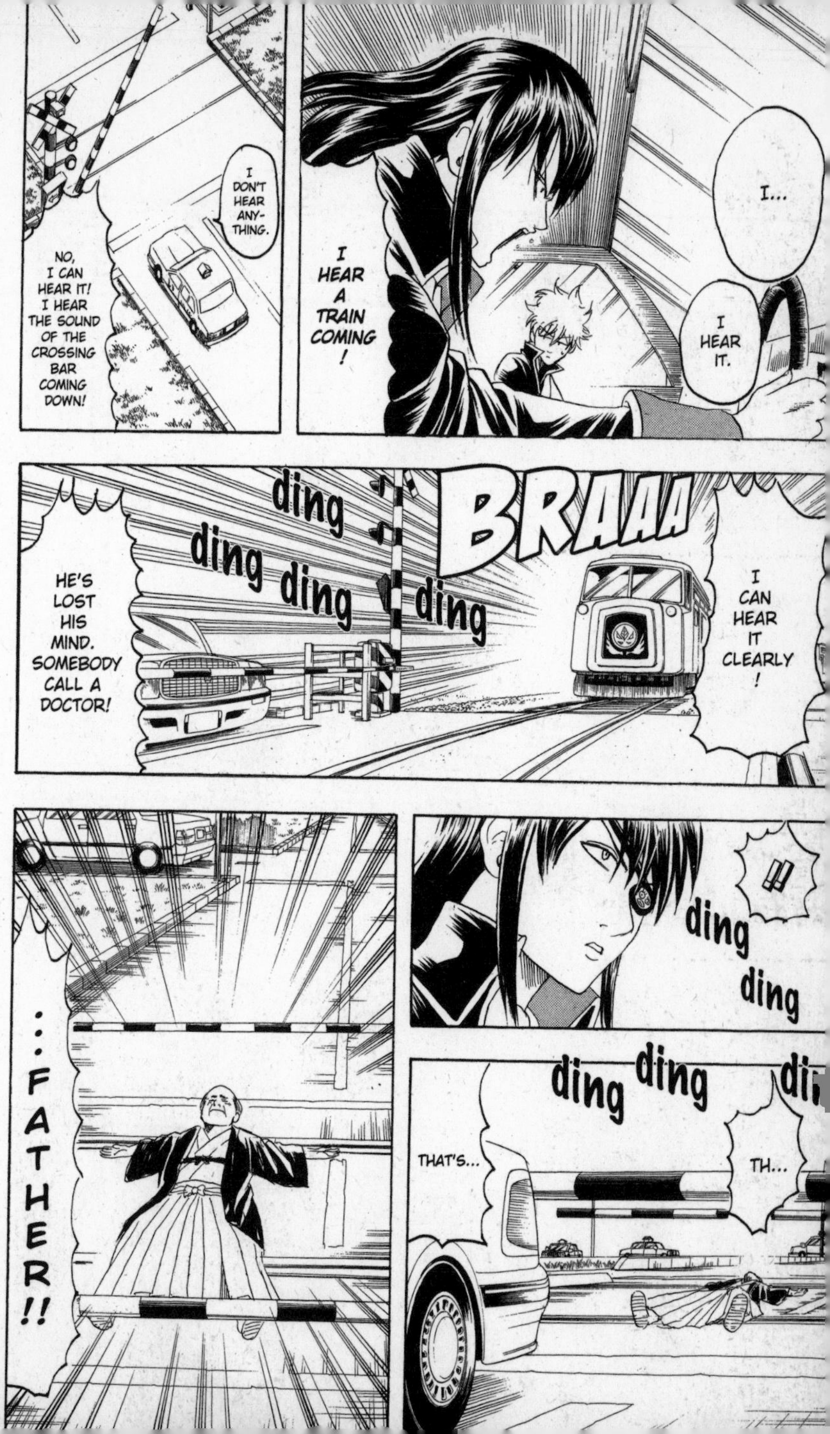
I...
I HEAR IT.
I HEAR A TRAIN COMING!
I DON'T HEAR ANY-THING.
NO, I CAN HEAR IT! I HEAR THE SOUND OF THE CROSSING BAR COMING DOWN!
I CAN HEAR IT CLEARLY!
BRAAA
ding
ding
ding
ding
HE'S LOST HIS MIND. SOMEBODY CALL A DOCTOR!
!!
ding
ding
ding
ding
TH...
THAT'S...
...FATHER!!

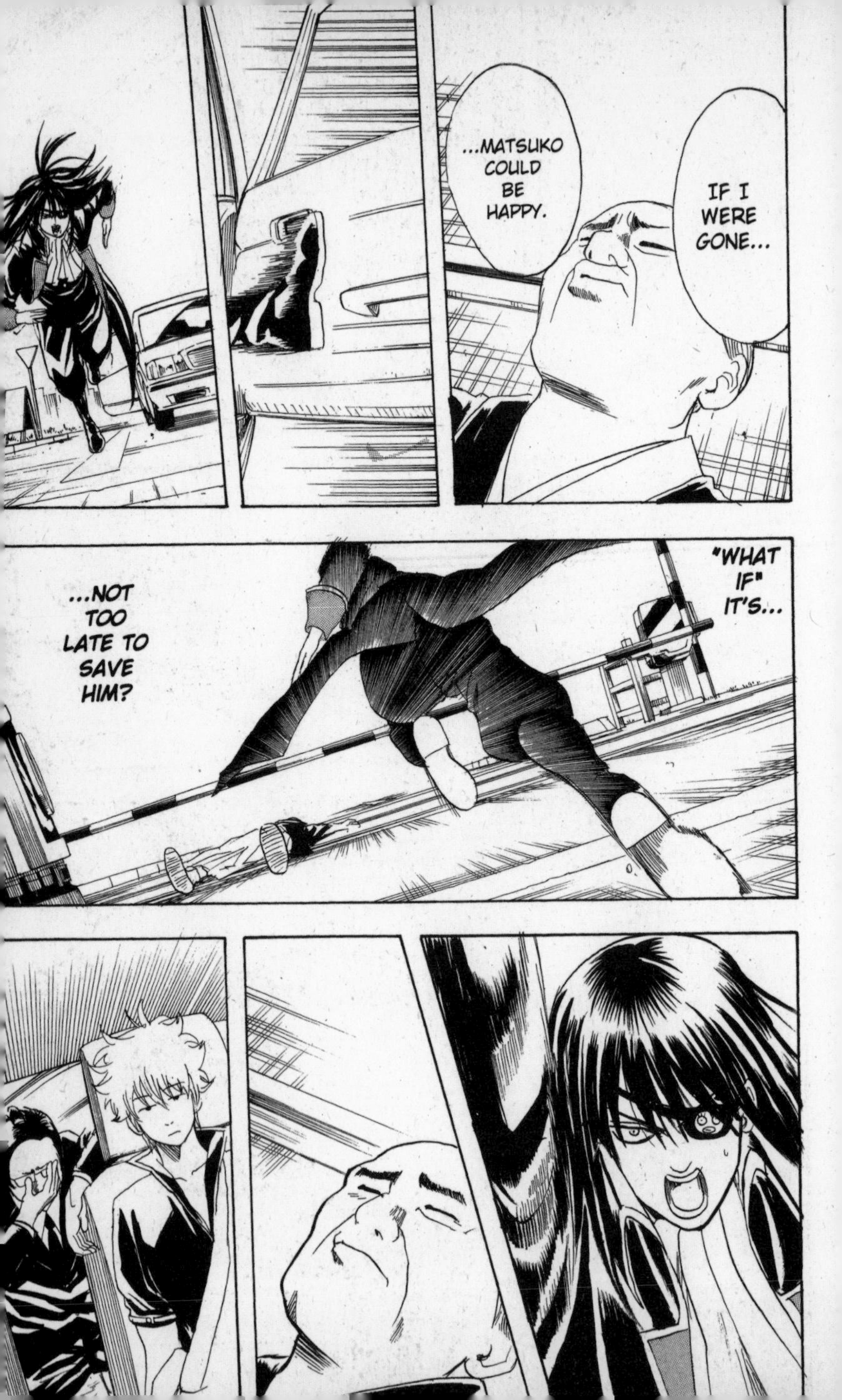
IF I WERE GONE...
...MATSUKO COULD BE HAPPY.
"WHAT IF" IT'S...
...NOT TOO LATE TO SAVE HIM?

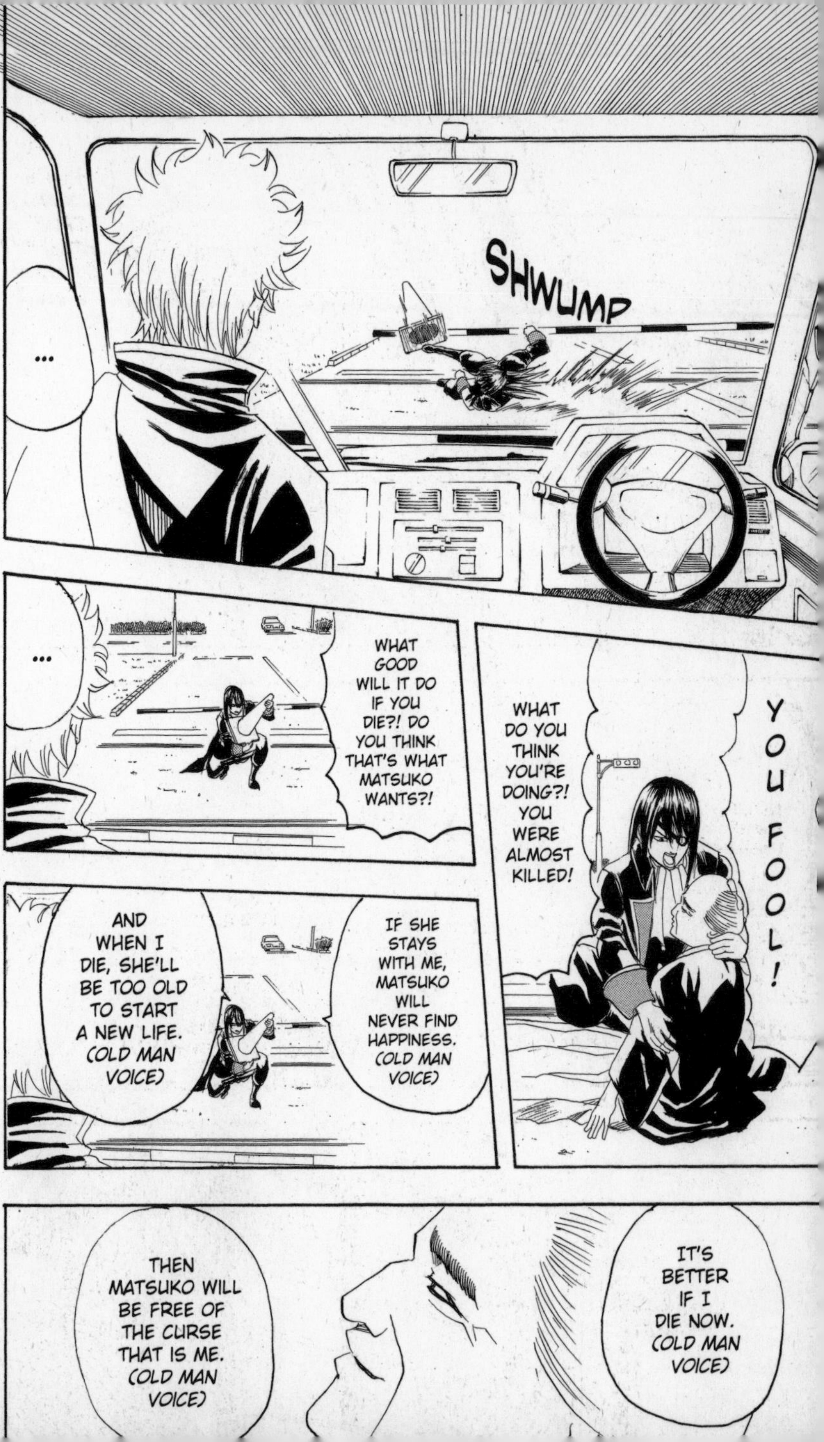
SHWUMP
...
YOU FOOL!
WHAT DO YOU THINK YOU'RE DOING?! YOU WERE ALMOST KILLED!
WHAT GOOD WILL IT DO IF YOU DIE?! DO YOU THINK THAT'S WHAT MATSUKO WANTS?!
...
IF SHE STAYS WITH ME, MATSUKO WILL NEVER FIND HAPPINESS. (OLD MAN VOICE)
AND WHEN I DIE, SHE'LL BE TOO OLD TO START A NEW LIFE. (OLD MAN VOICE)
IT'S BETTER IF I DIE NOW. (OLD MAN VOICE)
THEN MATSUKO WILL BE FREE OF THE CURSE THAT IS ME. (OLD MAN VOICE)

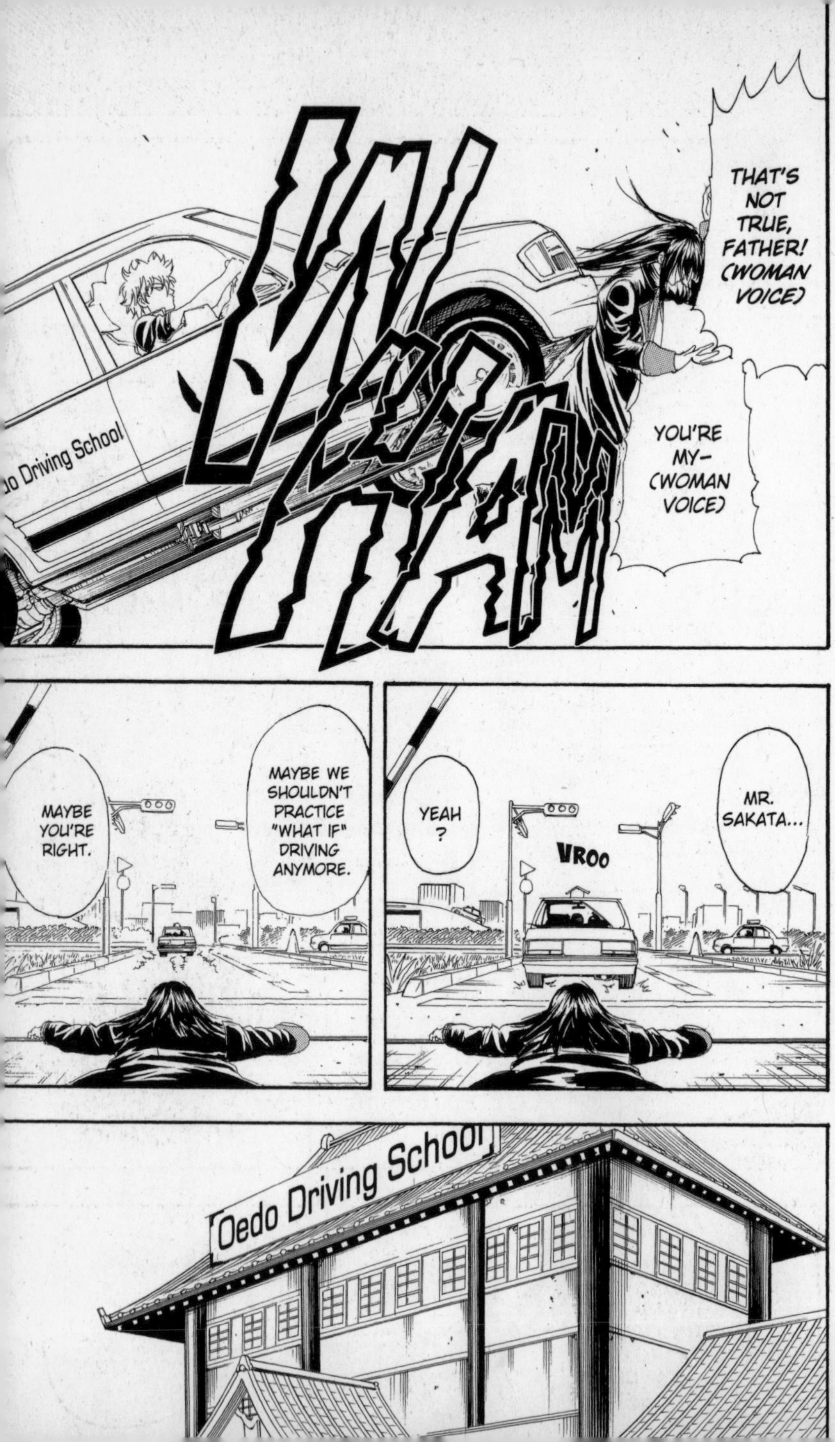
THAT'S NOT TRUE, FATHER! (WOMAN VOICE)
YOU'RE MY— (WOMAN VOICE)
VROOM
do Driving School
MR. SAKATA...
VROO
YEAH ?
MAYBE WE SHOULDN'T PRACTICE "WHAT IF" DRIVING ANYMORE.
MAYBE YOU'RE RIGHT.
Oedo Driving School

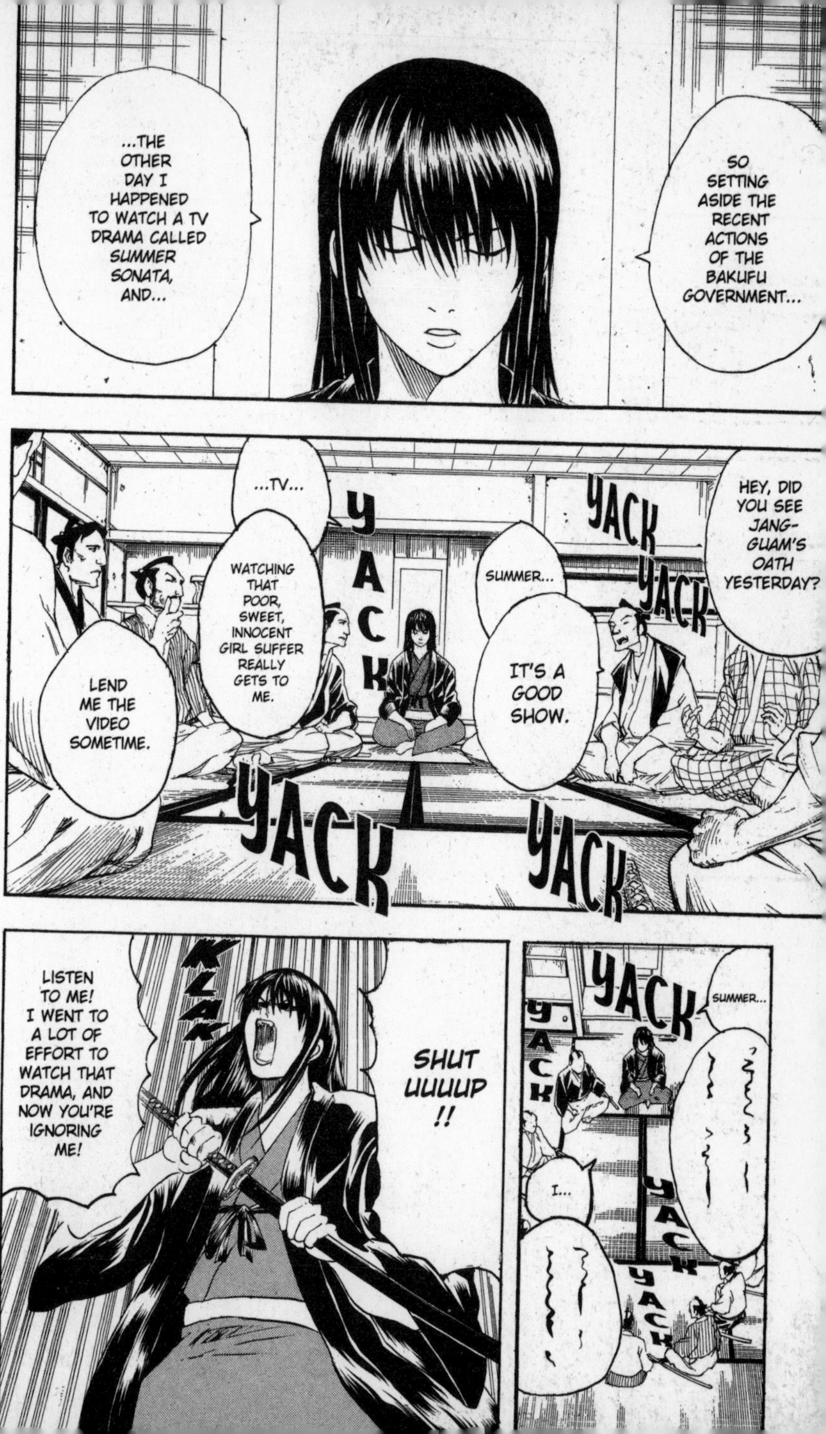
SO SETTING ASIDE THE RECENT ACTIONS OF THE BAKUFU GOVERNMENT...
...THE OTHER DAY I HAPPENED TO WATCH A TV DRAMA CALLED SUMMER SONATA, AND...
HEY, DID YOU SEE JANG-GUAM'S OATH YESTERDAY?
YACK
YACK
SUMMER...
IT'S A GOOD SHOW.
...TV...
WATCHING THAT POOR, SWEET, INNOCENT GIRL SUFFER REALLY GETS TO ME.
YACK
LEND ME THE VIDEO SOMETIME.
YACK
YACK
YACK
SUMMER...
YACK
I...
YACK
YACK
KLAK
SHUT UUUUP!!
LISTEN TO ME! I WENT TO A LOT OF EFFORT TO WATCH THAT DRAMA, AND NOW YOU'RE IGNORING ME!

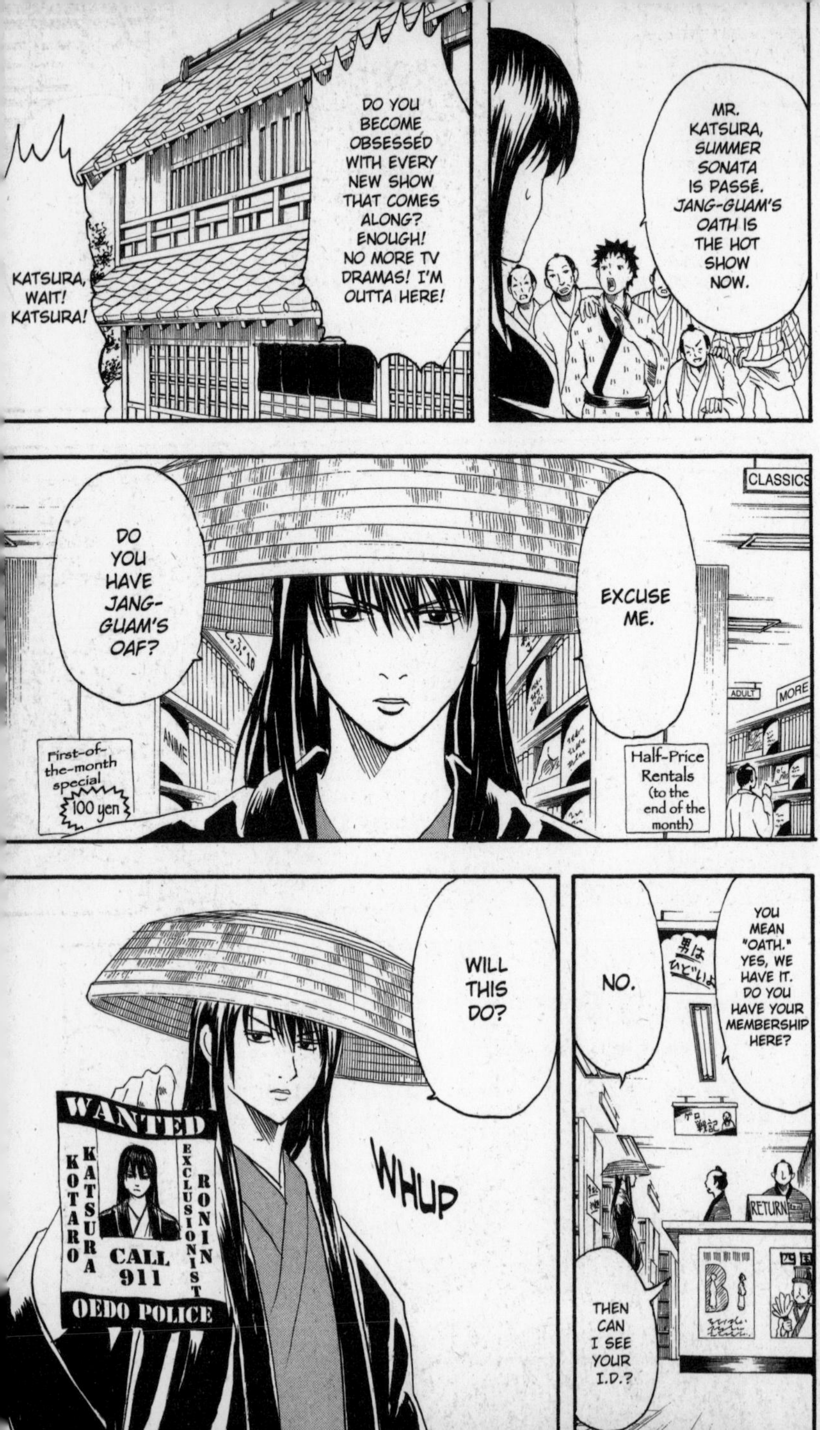
MR. KATSURA, SUMMER SONATA IS PASSÉ. JANG-GUAM'S OATH IS THE HOT SHOW NOW.
DO YOU BECOME OBSESSED WITH EVERY NEW SHOW THAT COMES ALONG? ENOUGH! NO MORE TV DRAMAS! I'M OUTTA HERE!
KATSURA, WAIT! KATSURA!
CLASSICS
EXCUSE ME.
ADULT
MORE
Half-Price Rentals (to the end of the month)
DO YOU HAVE JANG-GUAM'S OAF?
ANIME
First-of-the-month special 100 yen
YOU MEAN "OATH." YES, WE HAVE IT. DO YOU HAVE YOUR MEMBERSHIP HERE?
NO.
RETURN
THEN CAN I SEE YOUR I.D.?
WILL THIS DO?
WHUP
WANTED
KOTARO KATSURA
EXCLUSIONIST RONIN
CALL 911
OEDO POLICE

Sorachi's Q&A
Hanging with the Readers #42

<Question from "DORK (I really like Okita)"
 from Osaka>

I have a question, Mr. Sorachi. In *Lesson 87*, the
doorplate of Hatsu's house reads "Hasegawa,"
but Hatsu has left the house, hasn't she? Or has
Hasegawa married into Hatsu's family?
I'm confused.

<Answer>

Hasegawa moved in with his wife's
family when he married. Though he
comes from an undistinguished
family, he won the heart of a
daughter of the Hasegawa family
who is a Jikisan (shogun's retainer).
Like a male Cinderella, he became the
head of the Immigration Bureau, but
because he lived with his wife's
family, his domestic position was
very weak. It seems like his DORK
side developed during that time.

(Q&A #43 is on page 106)

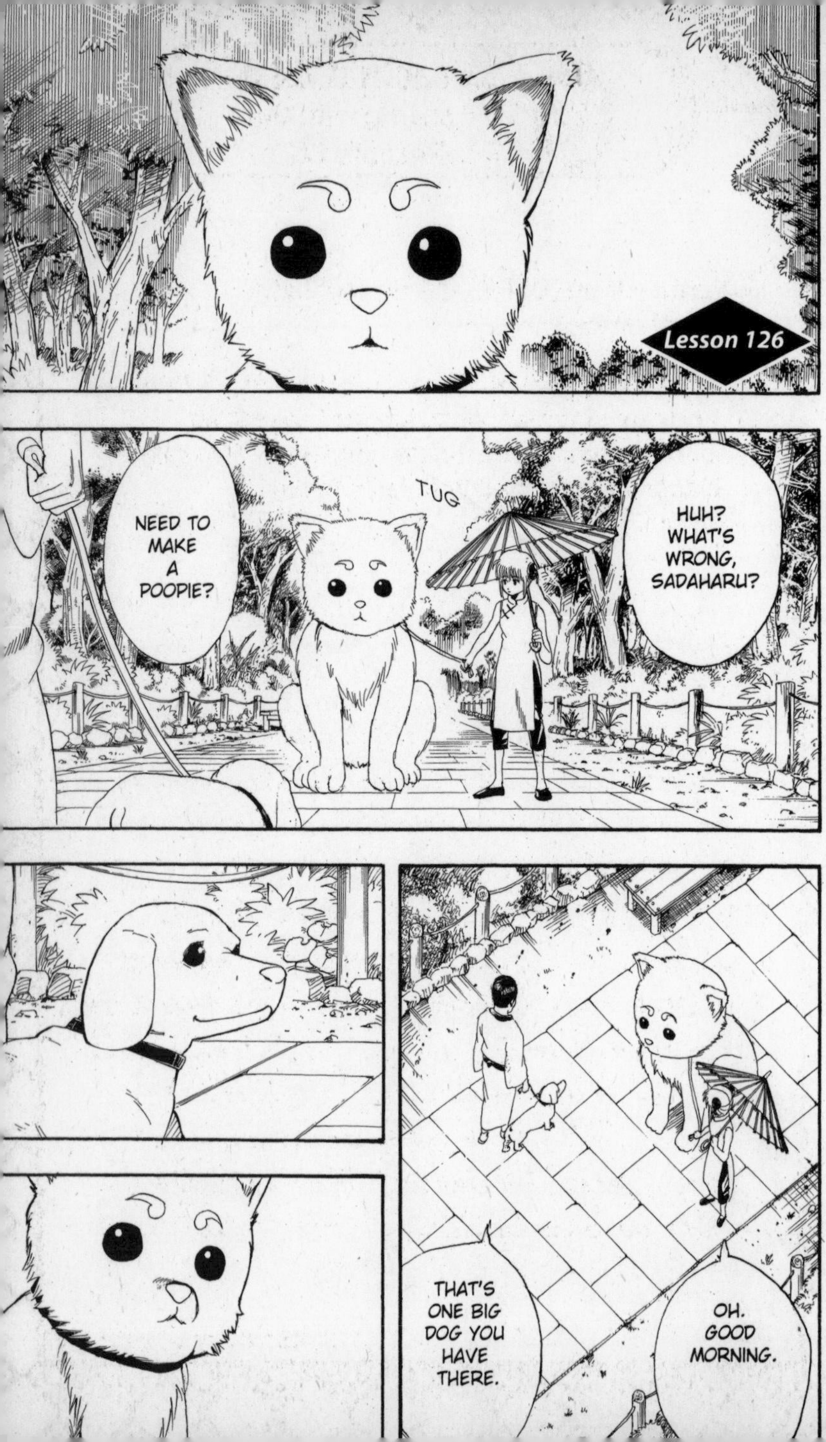
Lesson 126
HUH? WHAT'S WRONG, SADAHARU?
TUG
NEED TO MAKE A POOPIE?
OH. GOOD MORNING.
THAT'S ONE BIG DOG YOU HAVE THERE.

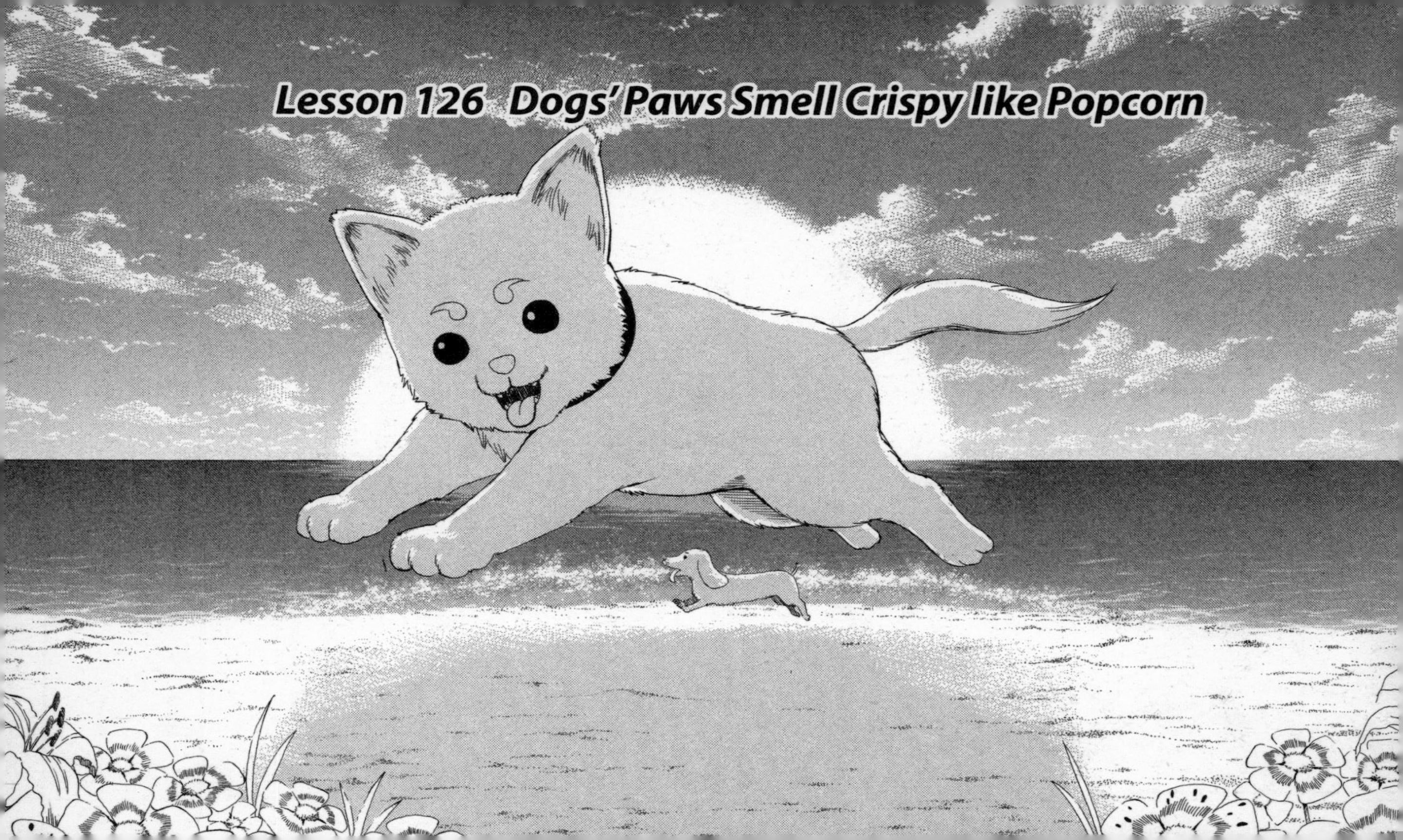
Lesson 126 Dogs' Paws Smell Crispy like Popcorn

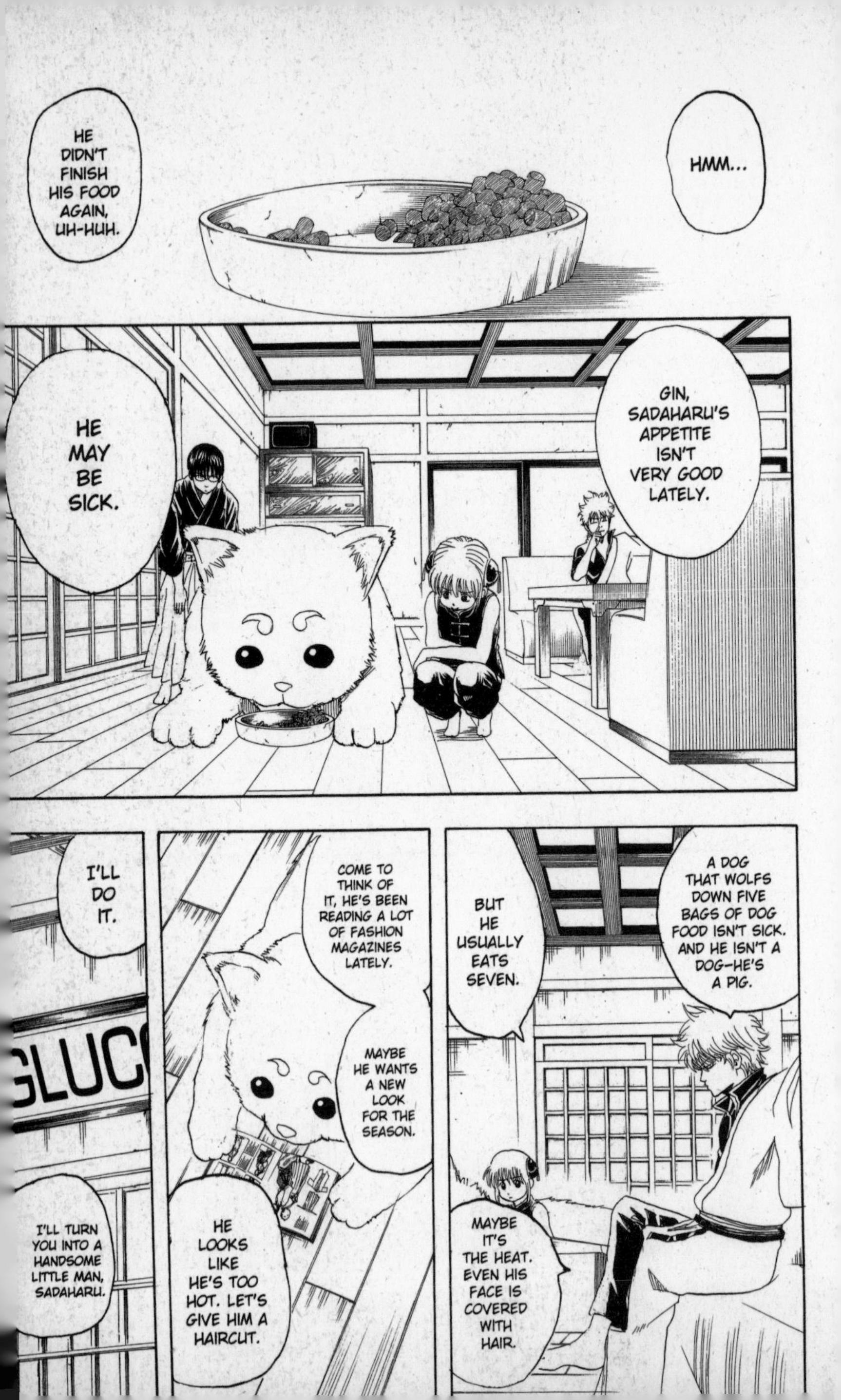
HMM...
HE DIDN'T FINISH HIS FOOD AGAIN, UH-HUH.
GIN, SADAHARU'S APPETITE ISN'T VERY GOOD LATELY.
HE MAY BE SICK.
A DOG THAT WOLFS DOWN FIVE BAGS OF DOG FOOD ISN'T SICK. AND HE ISN'T A DOG—HE'S A PIG.
BUT HE USUALLY EATS SEVEN.
MAYBE IT'S THE HEAT. EVEN HIS FACE IS COVERED WITH HAIR.
COME TO THINK OF IT, HE'S BEEN READING A LOT OF FASHION MAGAZINES LATELY.
MAYBE HE WANTS A NEW LOOK FOR THE SEASON.
HE LOOKS LIKE HE'S TOO HOT. LET'S GIVE HIM A HAIRCUT.
I'LL DO IT.
GLUC
I'LL TURN YOU INTO A HANDSOME LITTLE MAN, SADAHARU.

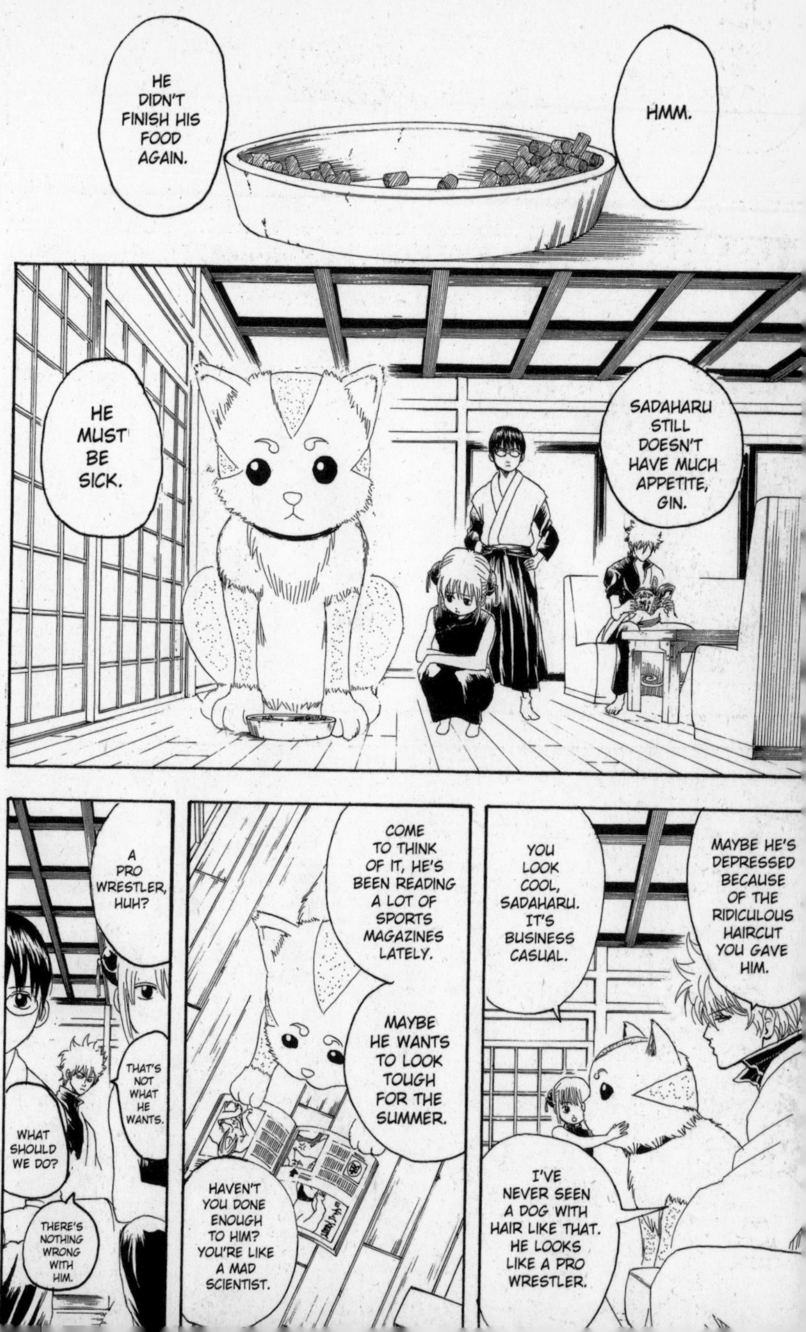
HMM.
HE DIDN'T FINISH HIS FOOD AGAIN.
SADAHARU STILL DOESN'T HAVE MUCH APPETITE, GIN.
HE MUST BE SICK.
MAYBE HE'S DEPRESSED BECAUSE OF THE RIDICULOUS HAIRCUT YOU GAVE HIM.
YOU LOOK COOL, SADAHARU. IT'S BUSINESS CASUAL.
I'VE NEVER SEEN A DOG WITH HAIR LIKE THAT. HE LOOKS LIKE A PRO WRESTLER.
COME TO THINK OF IT, HE'S BEEN READING A LOT OF SPORTS MAGAZINES LATELY.
MAYBE HE WANTS TO LOOK TOUGH FOR THE SUMMER.
HAVEN'T YOU DONE ENOUGH TO HIM? YOU'RE LIKE A MAD SCIENTIST.
A PRO WRESTLER, HUH?
THAT'S NOT WHAT HE WANTS.
WHAT SHOULD WE DO?
THERE'S NOTHING WRONG WITH HIM.

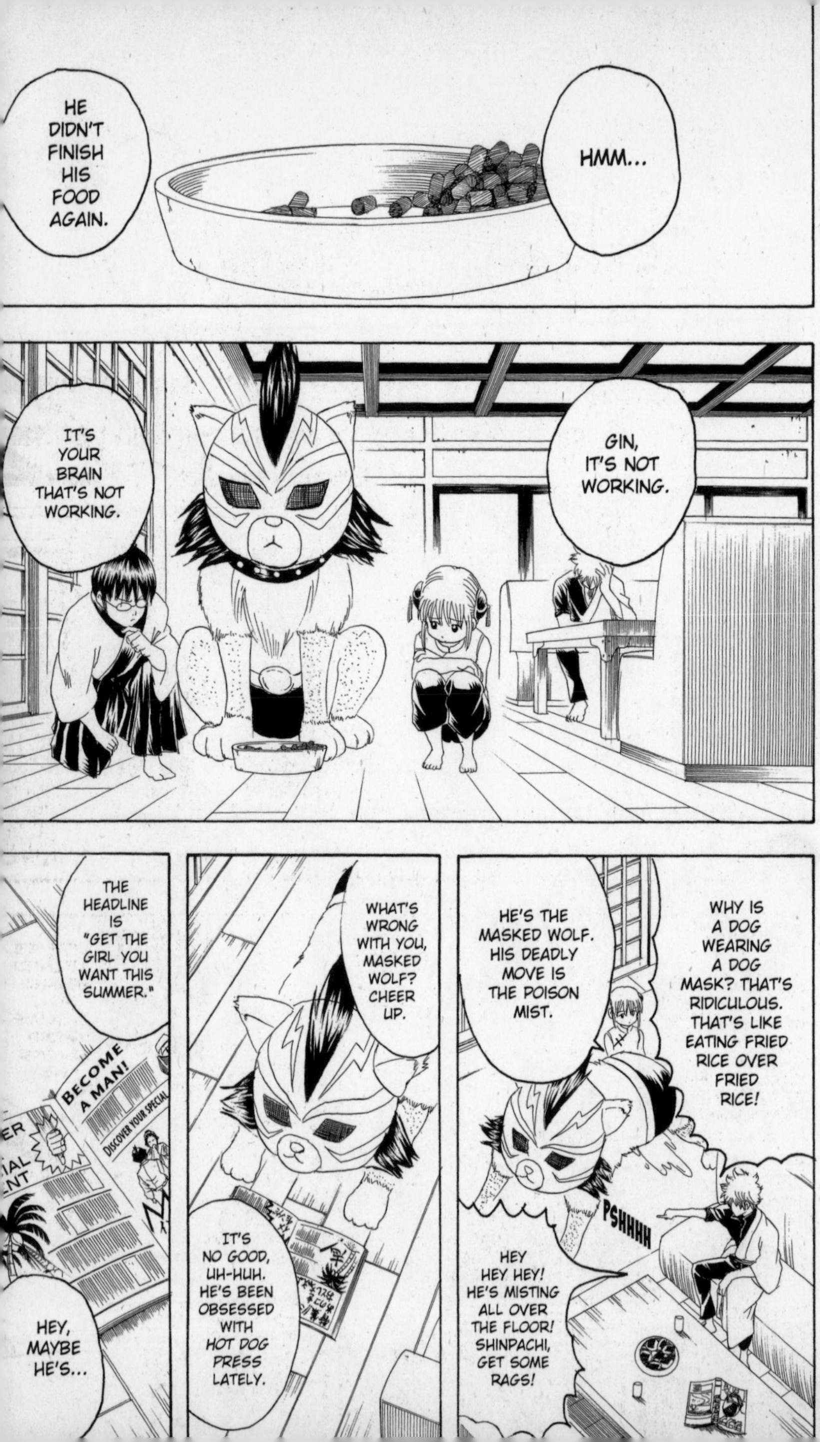
HMM...
HE DIDN'T FINISH HIS FOOD AGAIN.
GIN, IT'S NOT WORKING.
IT'S YOUR BRAIN THAT'S NOT WORKING.
WHY IS A DOG WEARING A DOG MASK? THAT'S RIDICULOUS. THAT'S LIKE EATING FRIED RICE OVER FRIED RICE!
HE'S THE MASKED WOLF. HIS DEADLY MOVE IS THE POISON MIST.
PSHHHH
HEY HEY HEY! HE'S MISTING ALL OVER THE FLOOR! SHINPACHI, GET SOME RAGS!
WHAT'S WRONG WITH YOU, MASKED WOLF? CHEER UP.
IT'S NO GOOD, UH-HUH. HE'S BEEN OBSESSED WITH HOT DOG PRESS LATELY.
THE HEADLINE IS "GET THE GIRL YOU WANT THIS SUMMER."
BECOME A MAN!
DISCOVER YOUR SPECIAL
HEY, MAYBE HE'S...

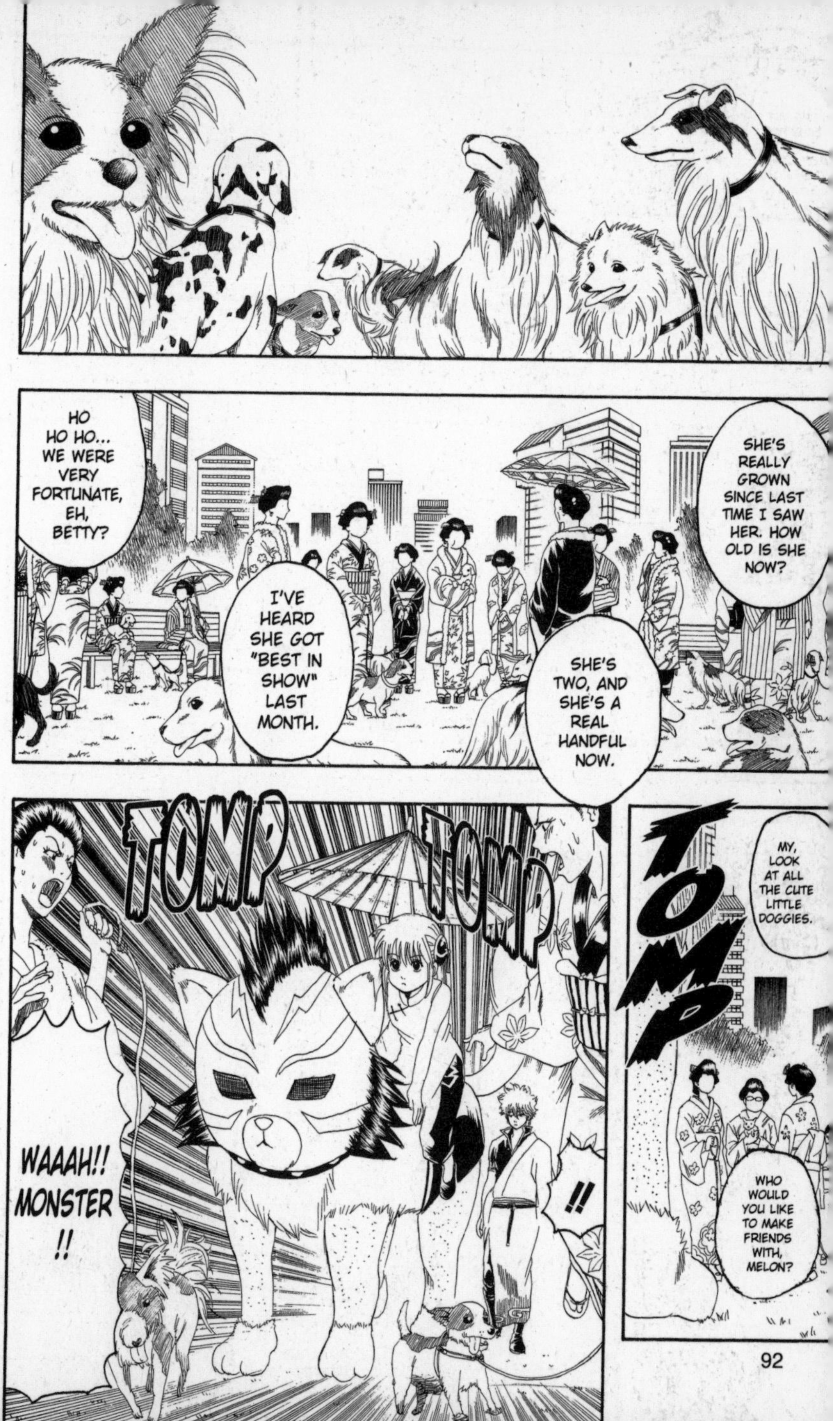
SHE'S REALLY GROWN SINCE LAST TIME I SAW HER. HOW OLD IS SHE NOW?
SHE'S TWO, AND SHE'S A REAL HANDFUL NOW.
I'VE HEARD SHE GOT "BEST IN SHOW" LAST MONTH.
HO HO HO... WE WERE VERY FORTUNATE, EH, BETTY?
TOMP
MY, LOOK AT ALL THE CUTE LITTLE DOGGIES.
WHO WOULD YOU LIKE TO MAKE FRIENDS WITH, MELON?
TOMP
TOMP
!!
WAAAH!! MONSTER !!

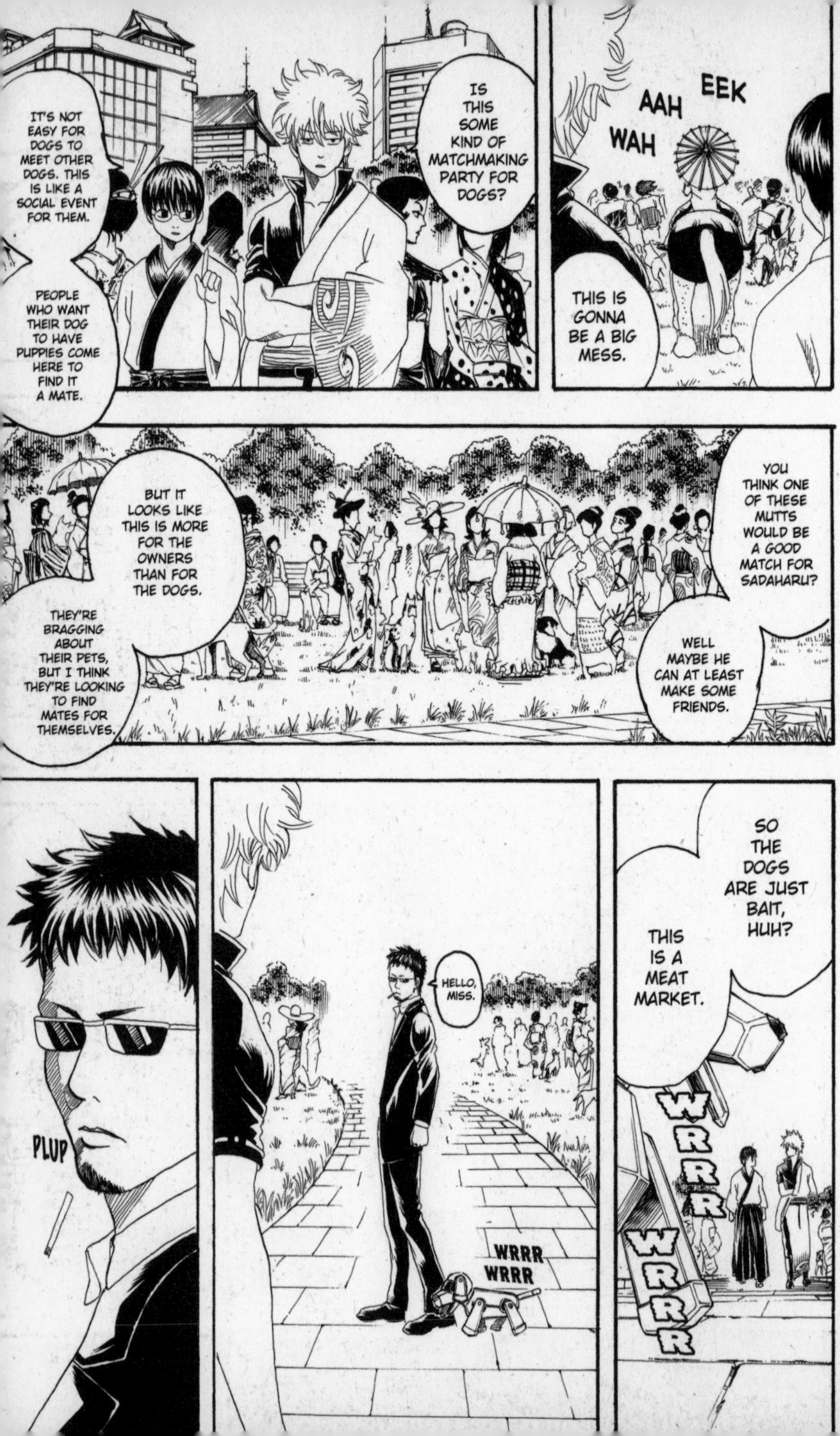
EEK
AAH
WAH
THIS IS GONNA BE A BIG MESS.
IS THIS SOME KIND OF MATCHMAKING PARTY FOR DOGS?
IT'S NOT EASY FOR DOGS TO MEET OTHER DOGS. THIS IS LIKE A SOCIAL EVENT FOR THEM.
PEOPLE WHO WANT THEIR DOG TO HAVE PUPPIES COME HERE TO FIND IT A MATE.
YOU THINK ONE OF THESE MUTTS WOULD BE A GOOD MATCH FOR SADAHARU?
WELL MAYBE HE CAN AT LEAST MAKE SOME FRIENDS.
BUT IT LOOKS LIKE THIS IS MORE FOR THE OWNERS THAN FOR THE DOGS.
THEY'RE BRAGGING ABOUT THEIR PETS, BUT I THINK THEY'RE LOOKING TO FIND MATES FOR THEMSELVES.
SO THE DOGS ARE JUST BAIT, HUH?
THIS IS A MEAT MARKET.
WRRR
WRRR
HELLO, MISS.
WRRR
WRRR
PLUP

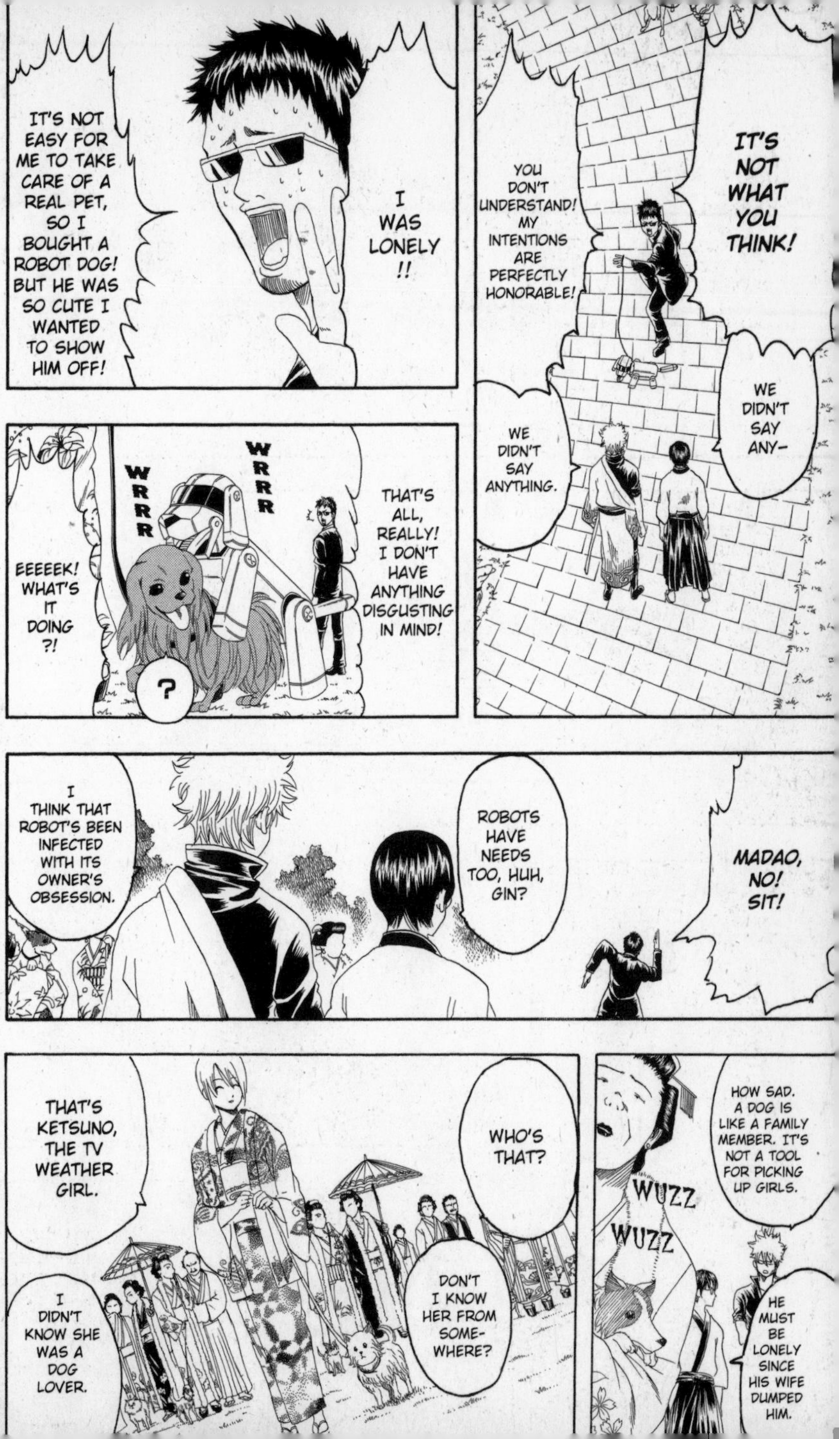
IT'S NOT WHAT YOU THINK!
YOU DON'T UNDERSTAND! MY INTENTIONS ARE PERFECTLY HONORABLE!
WE DIDN'T SAY ANY-
WE DIDN'T SAY ANYTHING.
I WAS LONELY!!
IT'S NOT EASY FOR ME TO TAKE CARE OF A REAL PET, SO I BOUGHT A ROBOT DOG! BUT HE WAS SO CUTE I WANTED TO SHOW HIM OFF!
WRRR
WRRR
THAT'S ALL, REALLY! I DON'T HAVE ANYTHING DISGUSTING IN MIND!
EEEEEK! WHAT'S IT DOING?!
?
MADAO, NO! SIT!
ROBOTS HAVE NEEDS TOO, HUH, GIN?
I THINK THAT ROBOT'S BEEN INFECTED WITH ITS OWNER'S OBSESSION.
HOW SAD. A DOG IS LIKE A FAMILY MEMBER. IT'S NOT A TOOL FOR PICKING UP GIRLS.
WUZZ
WUZZ
HE MUST BE LONELY SINCE HIS WIFE DUMPED HIM.
WHO'S THAT?
THAT'S KETSUNO, THE TV WEATHER GIRL.
DON'T I KNOW HER FROM SOMEWHERE?
I DIDN'T KNOW SHE WAS A DOG LOVER.

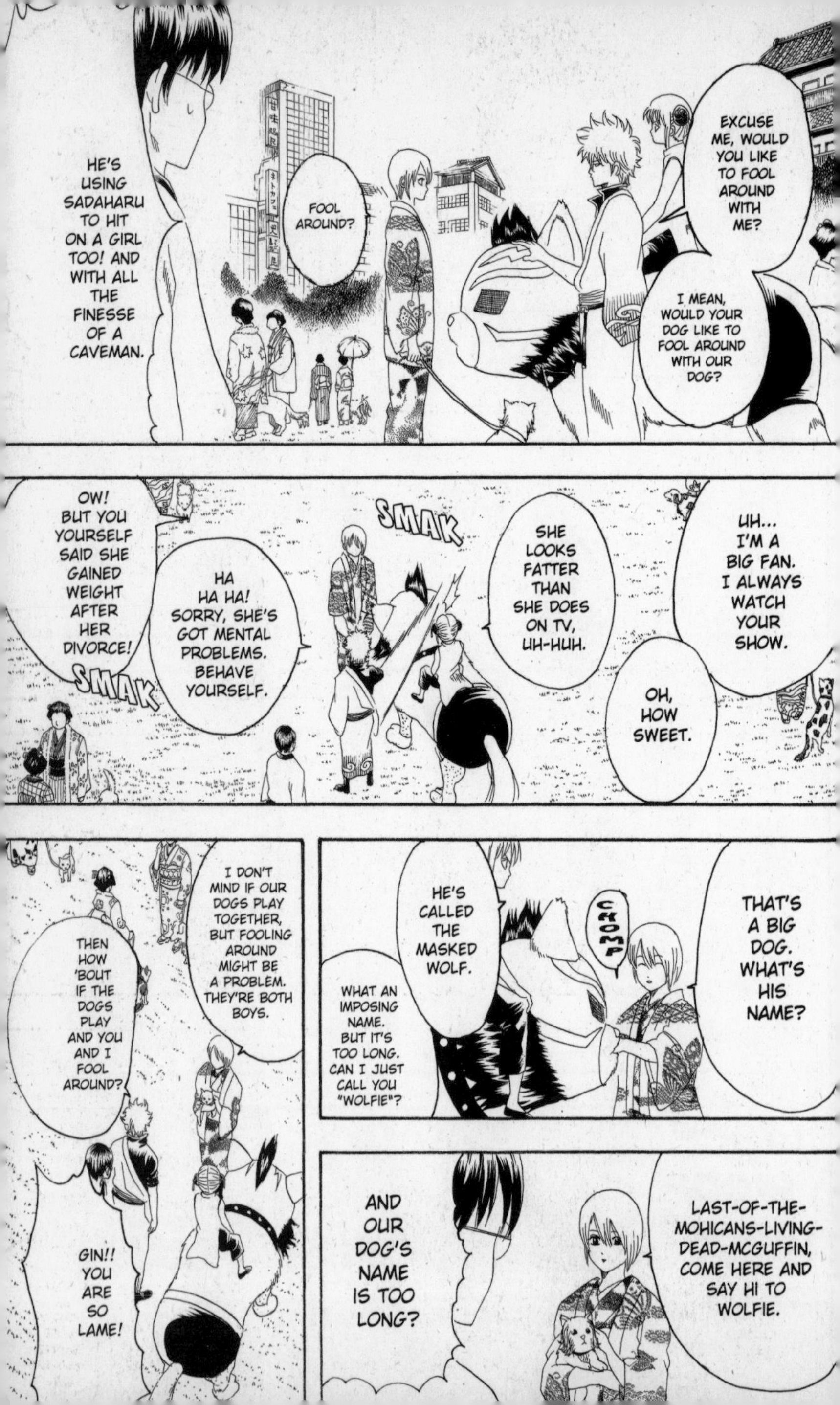
EXCUSE ME, WOULD YOU LIKE TO FOOL AROUND WITH ME?
FOOL AROUND?
I MEAN, WOULD YOUR DOG LIKE TO FOOL AROUND WITH OUR DOG?
HE'S USING SADAHARU TO HIT ON A GIRL TOO! AND WITH ALL THE FINESSE OF A CAVEMAN.
UH... I'M A BIG FAN. I ALWAYS WATCH YOUR SHOW.
OH, HOW SWEET.
SHE LOOKS FATTER THAN SHE DOES ON TV, UH-HUH.
SMAK
HA HA HA! SORRY, SHE'S GOT MENTAL PROBLEMS. BEHAVE YOURSELF.
OW! BUT YOU YOURSELF SAID SHE GAINED WEIGHT AFTER HER DIVORCE!
SMAK
THAT'S A BIG DOG. WHAT'S HIS NAME?
HE'S CALLED THE MASKED WOLF.
CHOMP
WHAT AN IMPOSING NAME. BUT IT'S TOO LONG. CAN I JUST CALL YOU "WOLFIE"?
LAST-OF-THE-MOHICANS-LIVING-DEAD-MCGUFFIN, COME HERE AND SAY HI TO WOLFIE.
AND OUR DOG'S NAME IS TOO LONG?
I DON'T MIND IF OUR DOGS PLAY TOGETHER, BUT FOOLING AROUND MIGHT BE A PROBLEM. THEY'RE BOTH BOYS.
THEN HOW 'BOUT IF THE DOGS PLAY AND YOU AND I FOOL AROUND?
GIN!! YOU ARE SO LAME!

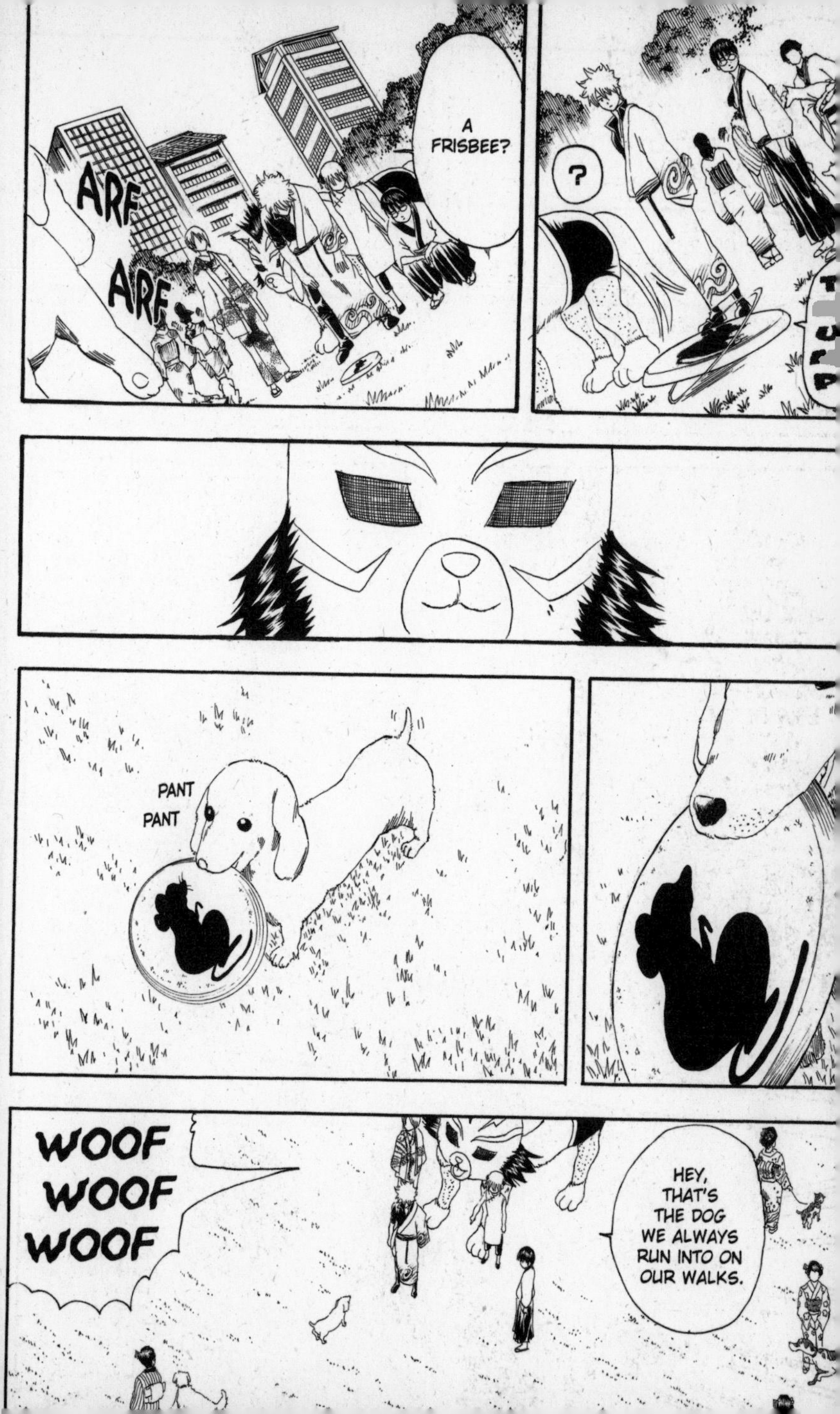
?
A FRISBEE?
ARF ARF
PANT PANT
HEY, THAT'S THE DOG WE ALWAYS RUN INTO ON OUR WALKS.
WOOF WOOF WOOF

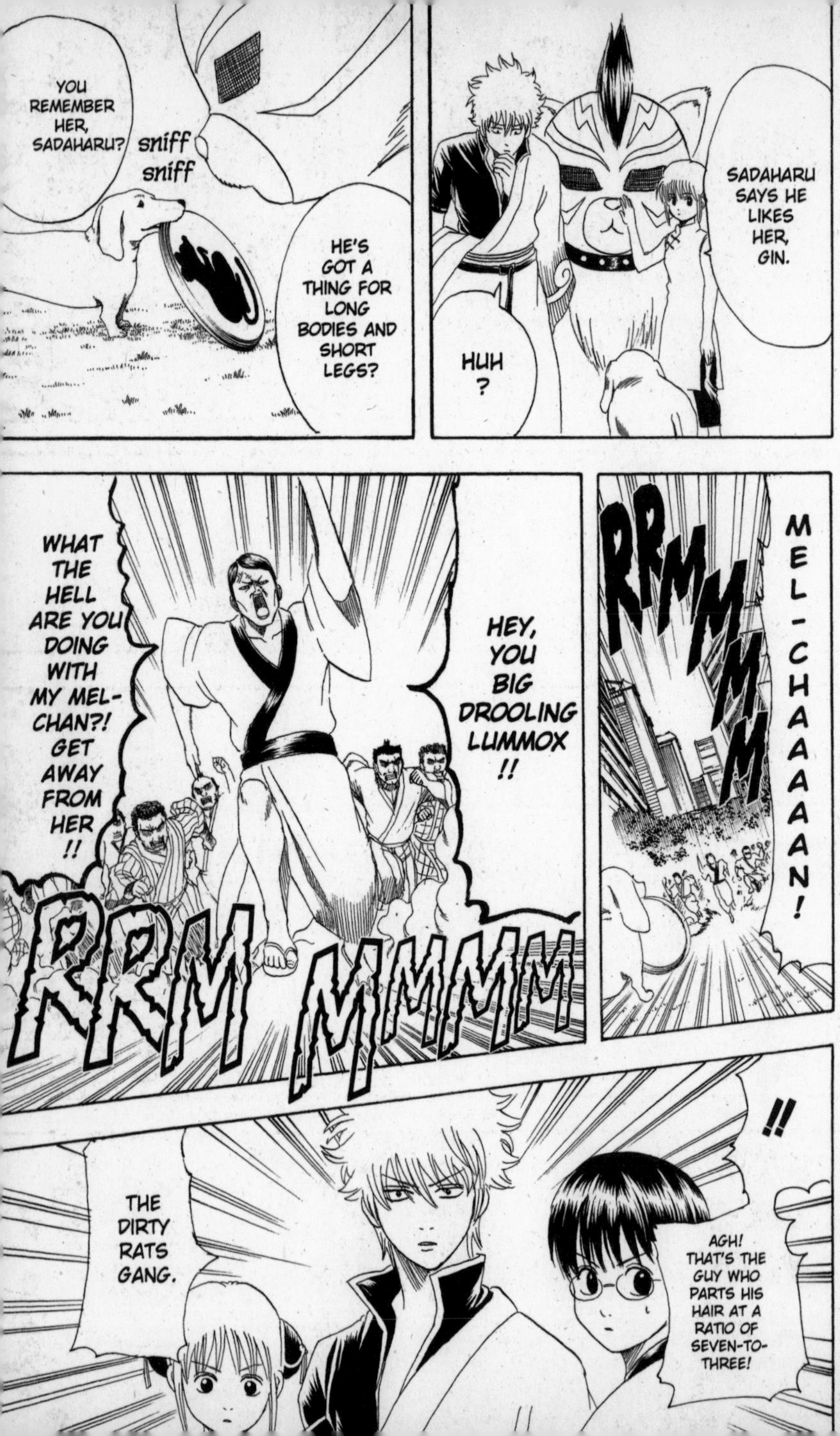
SADAHARU SAYS HE LIKES HER, GIN.
HUH?
YOU REMEMBER HER, SADAHARU?
sniff sniff
HE'S GOT A THING FOR LONG BODIES AND SHORT LEGS?
MEL-CHAAAAAAN!
RRMMMMM
HEY, YOU BIG DROOLING LUMMOX!!
WHAT THE HELL ARE YOU DOING WITH MY MEL-CHAN?! GET AWAY FROM HER!!
RRM MMMMM
!!
AGH! THAT'S THE GUY WHO PARTS HIS HAIR AT A RATIO OF SEVEN-TO-THREE!
THE DIRTY RATS GANG.

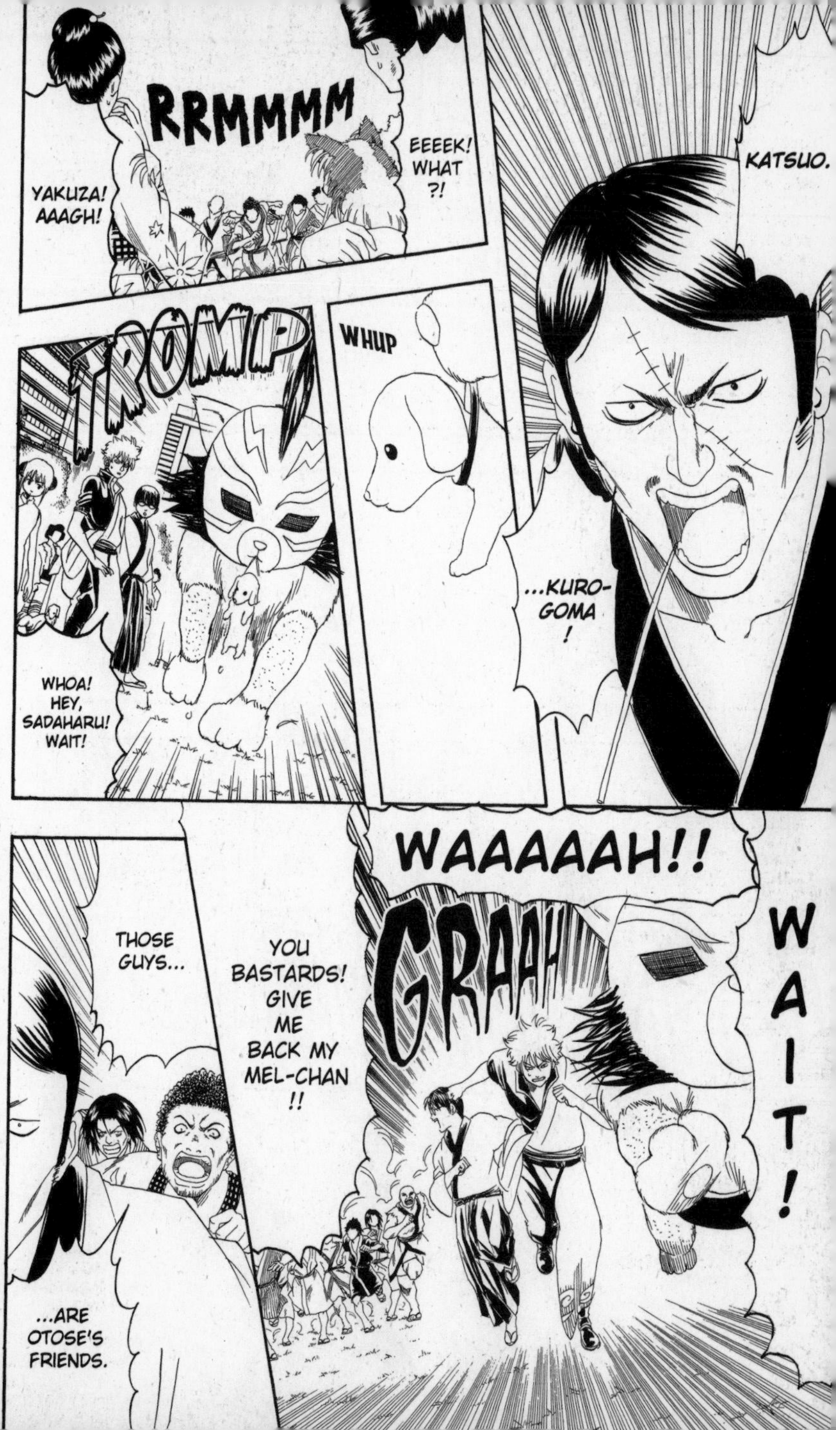
KATSUO.
...KURO-GOMA!
EEEEK! WHAT?!
RRMMMM
YAKUZA! AAAGH!
WHUP
TROMP
WHOA! HEY, SADAHARU! WAIT!
WAIT!
WAAAAAH!!
GRAAH
YOU BASTARDS! GIVE ME BACK MY MEL-CHAN!!
THOSE GUYS...
...ARE OTOSE'S FRIENDS.

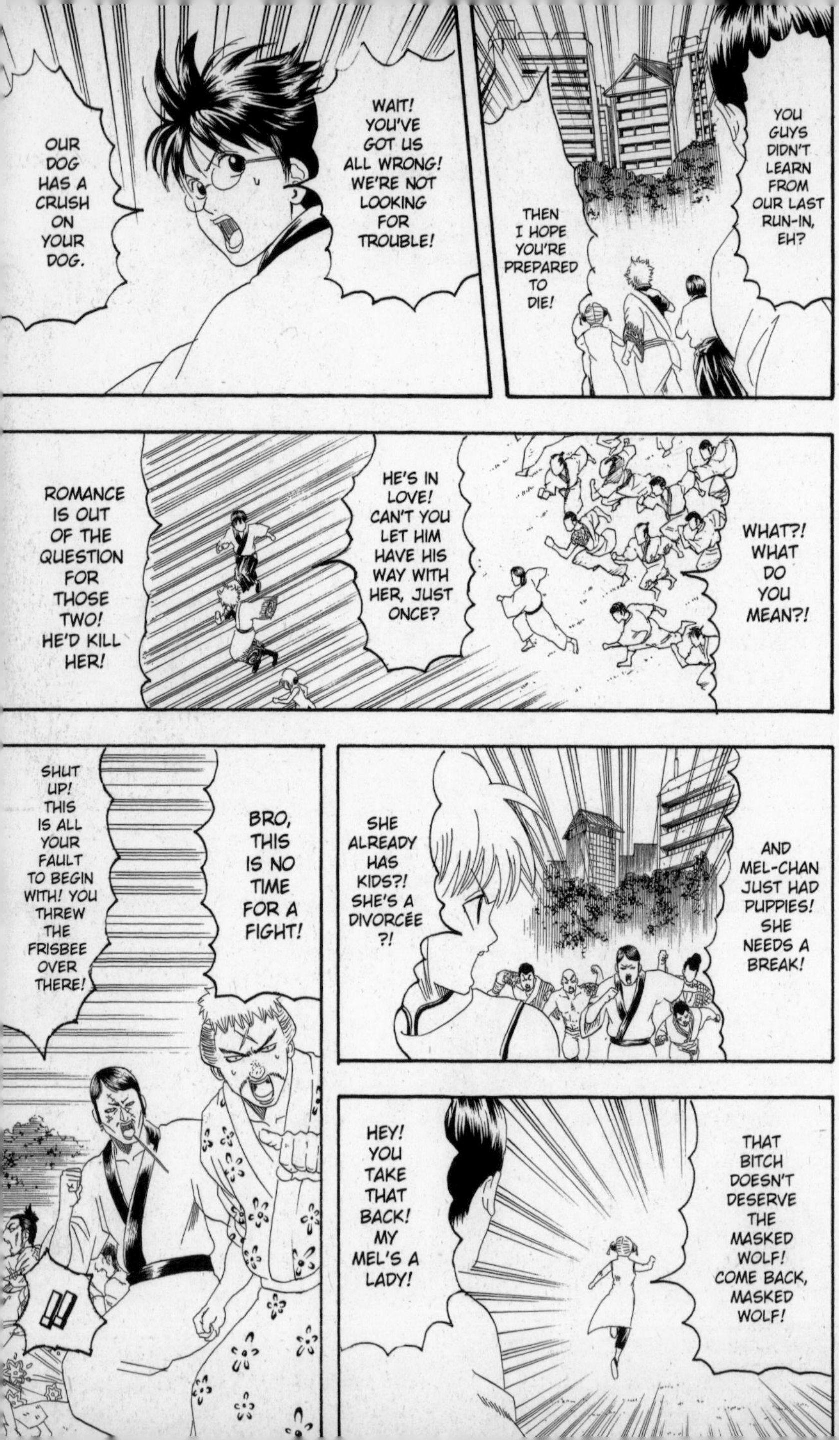
YOU GUYS DIDN'T LEARN FROM OUR LAST RUN-IN, EH?
THEN I HOPE YOU'RE PREPARED TO DIE!
WAIT! YOU'VE GOT US ALL WRONG! WE'RE NOT LOOKING FOR TROUBLE!
OUR DOG HAS A CRUSH ON YOUR DOG.
WHAT?! WHAT DO YOU MEAN?!
HE'S IN LOVE! CAN'T YOU LET HIM HAVE HIS WAY WITH HER, JUST ONCE?
ROMANCE IS OUT OF THE QUESTION FOR THOSE TWO! HE'D KILL HER!
AND MEL-CHAN JUST HAD PUPPIES! SHE NEEDS A BREAK!
SHE ALREADY HAS KIDS?! SHE'S A DIVORCÉE?!
THAT BITCH DOESN'T DESERVE THE MASKED WOLF! COME BACK, MASKED WOLF!
HEY! YOU TAKE THAT BACK! MY MEL'S A LADY!
BRO, THIS IS NO TIME FOR A FIGHT!
SHUT UP! THIS IS ALL YOUR FAULT TO BEGIN WITH! YOU THREW THE FRISBEE OVER THERE!
!!

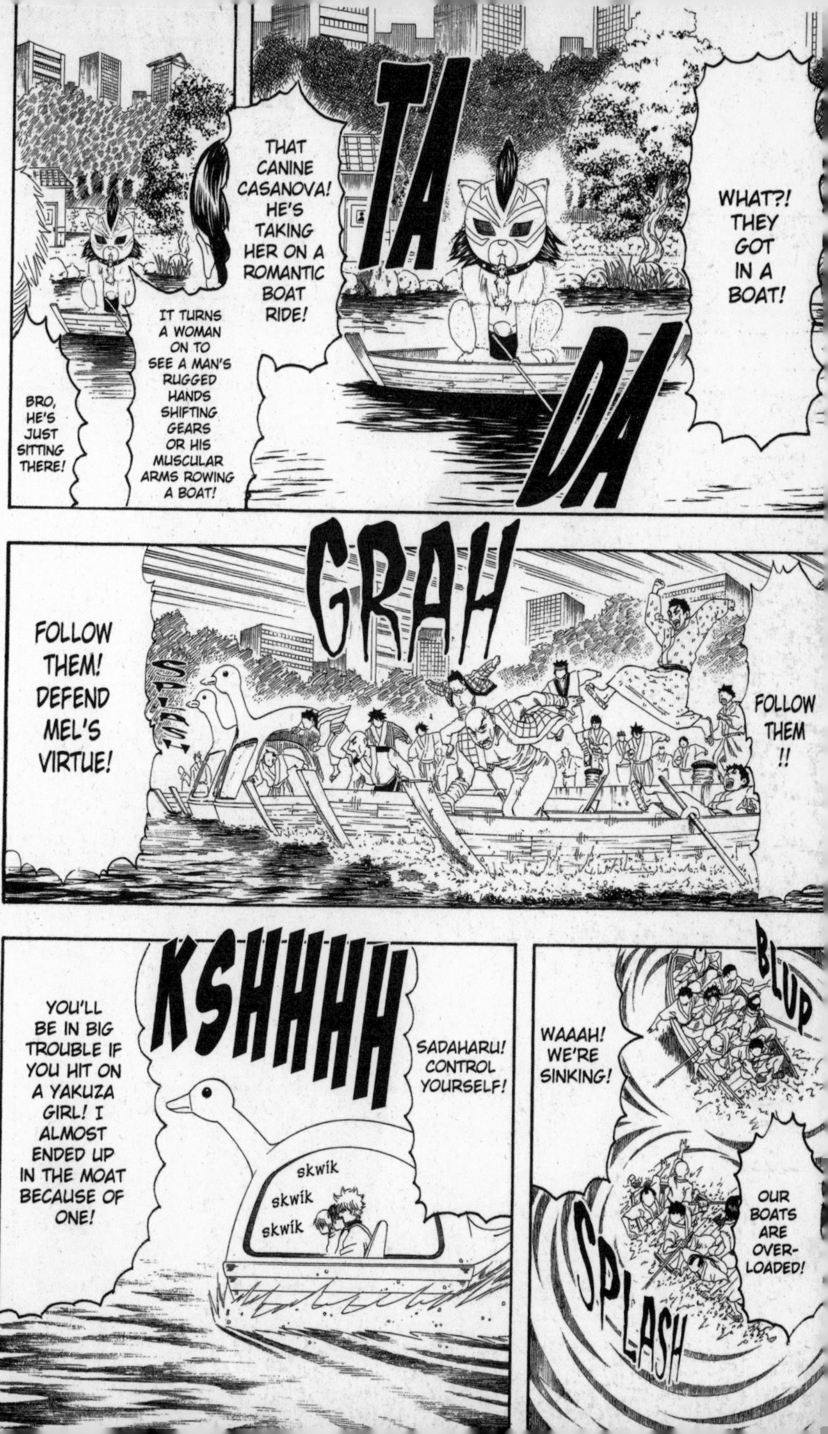
WHAT?! THEY GOT IN A BOAT!
TA
DA
THAT CANINE CASANOVA! HE'S TAKING HER ON A ROMANTIC BOAT RIDE!
IT TURNS A WOMAN ON TO SEE A MAN'S RUGGED HANDS SHIFTING GEARS OR HIS MUSCULAR ARMS ROWING A BOAT!
BRO, HE'S JUST SITTING THERE!
FOLLOW THEM !!
GRAH
FOLLOW THEM! DEFEND MEL'S VIRTUE!
BLUP
WAAAH! WE'RE SINKING!
OUR BOATS ARE OVER-LOADED!
SPLASH
SADAHARU! CONTROL YOURSELF!
KSHHHH
skwik
skwik
skwik
YOU'LL BE IN BIG TROUBLE IF YOU HIT ON A YAKUZA GIRL! I ALMOST ENDED UP IN THE MOAT BECAUSE OF ONE!

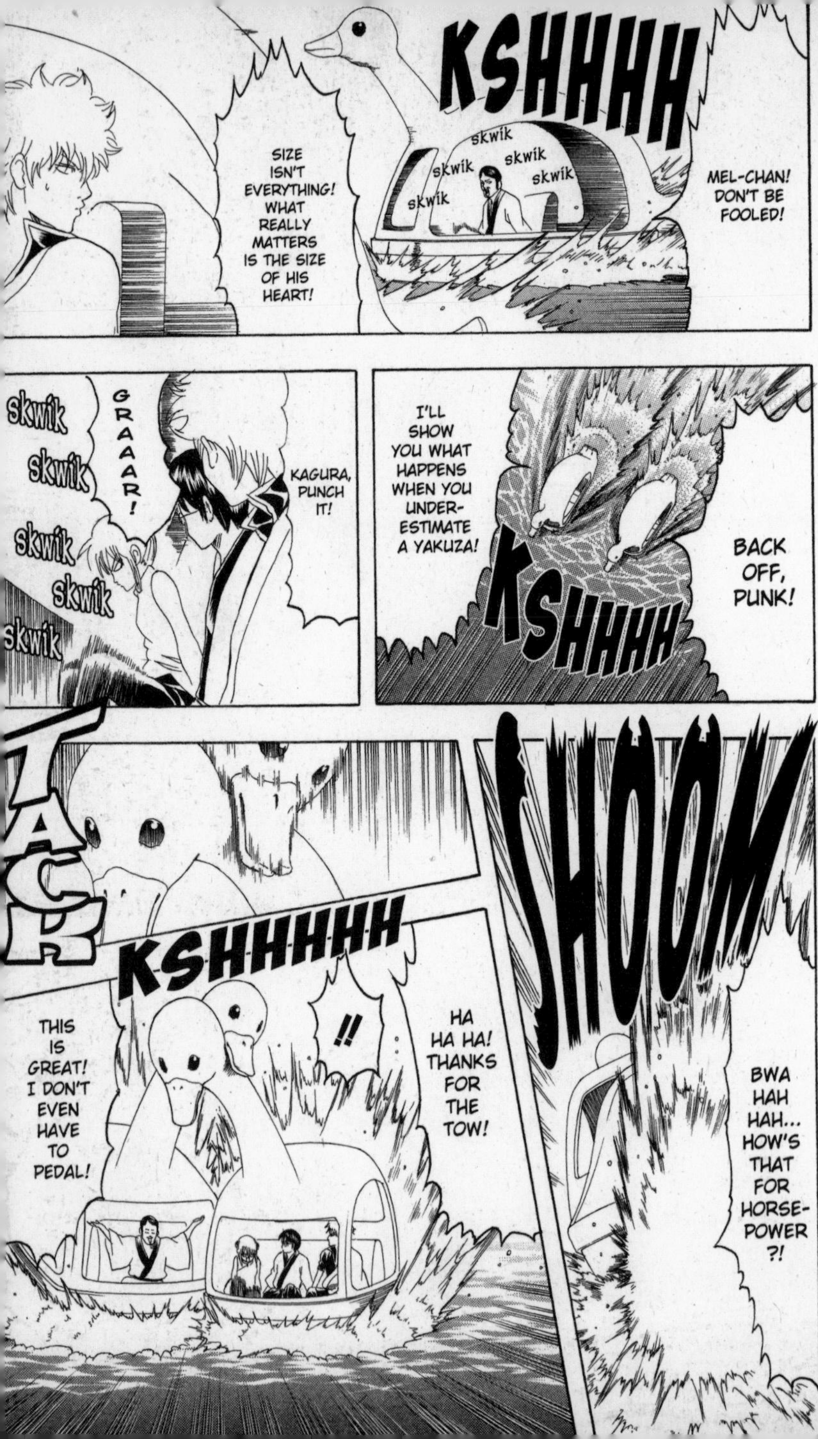
MEL-CHAN! DON'T BE FOOLED!
KSHHHH
skwik skwik skwik skwik skwik
SIZE ISN'T EVERYTHING! WHAT REALLY MATTERS IS THE SIZE OF HIS HEART!
BACK OFF, PUNK!
I'LL SHOW YOU WHAT HAPPENS WHEN YOU UNDER-ESTIMATE A YAKUZA!
KSHHHH
KAGURA, PUNCH IT!
GRAAAAR!
skwik skwik skwik skwik skwik
SHOOM
BWA HAH HAH... HOW'S THAT FOR HORSE-POWER?!
TACK
KSHHHHHH
HA HA HA! THANKS FOR THE TOW!
!!
THIS IS GREAT! I DON'T EVEN HAVE TO PEDAL!

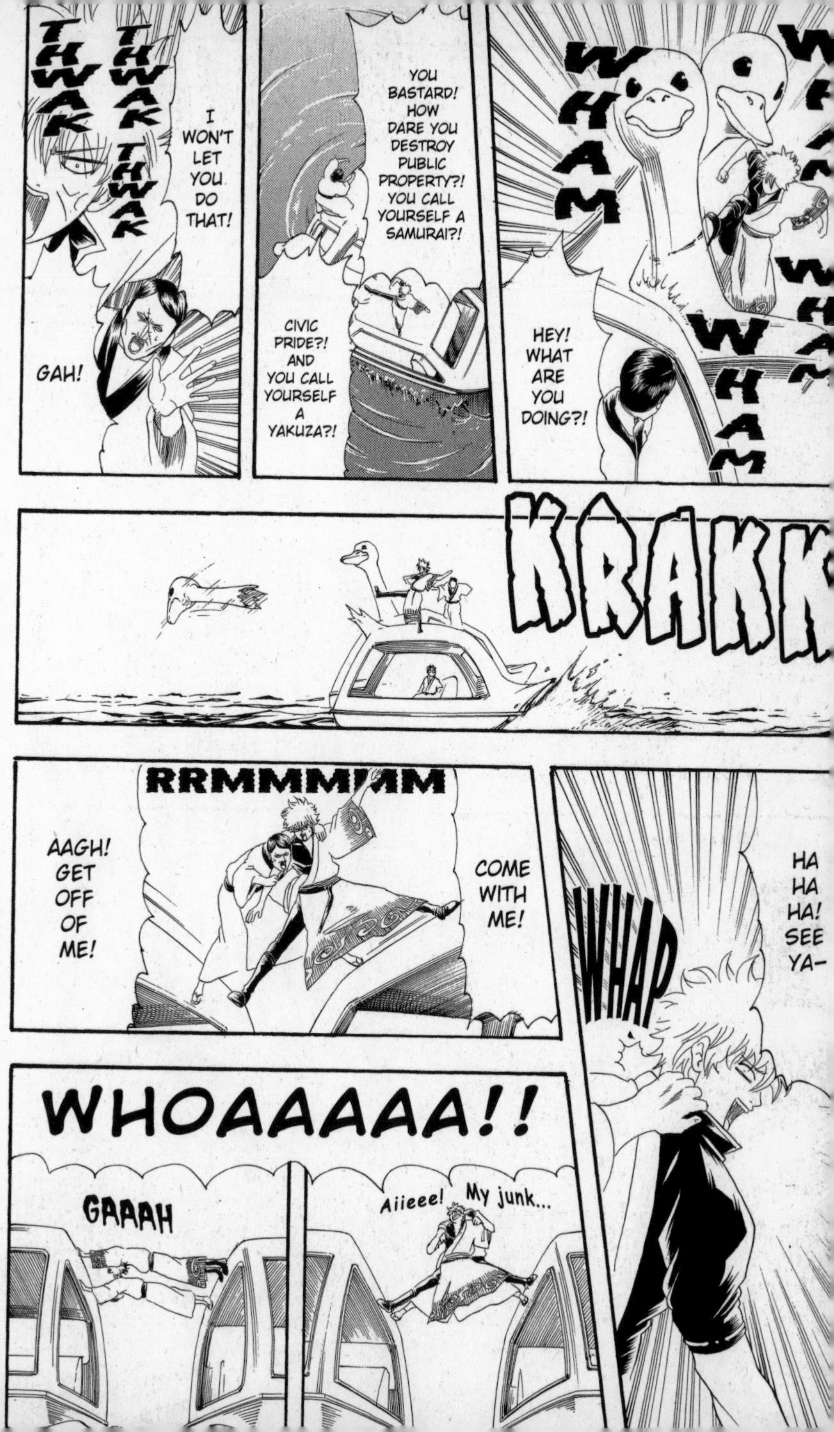
WHAM WHAM
WHAM
HEY! WHAT ARE YOU DOING?!
WHAM
YOU BASTARD! HOW DARE YOU DESTROY PUBLIC PROPERTY?! YOU CALL YOURSELF A SAMURAI?!
CIVIC PRIDE?! AND YOU CALL YOURSELF A YAKUZA?!
THWAK THWAK
I WON'T LET YOU DO THAT!
THWAK
GAH!
KRAKK
HA HA HA! SEE YA-
WHAP
RRMMMMMM
COME WITH ME!
AAGH! GET OFF OF ME!
WHOAAAAA!!
Aiieee! My junk...
GAAAH

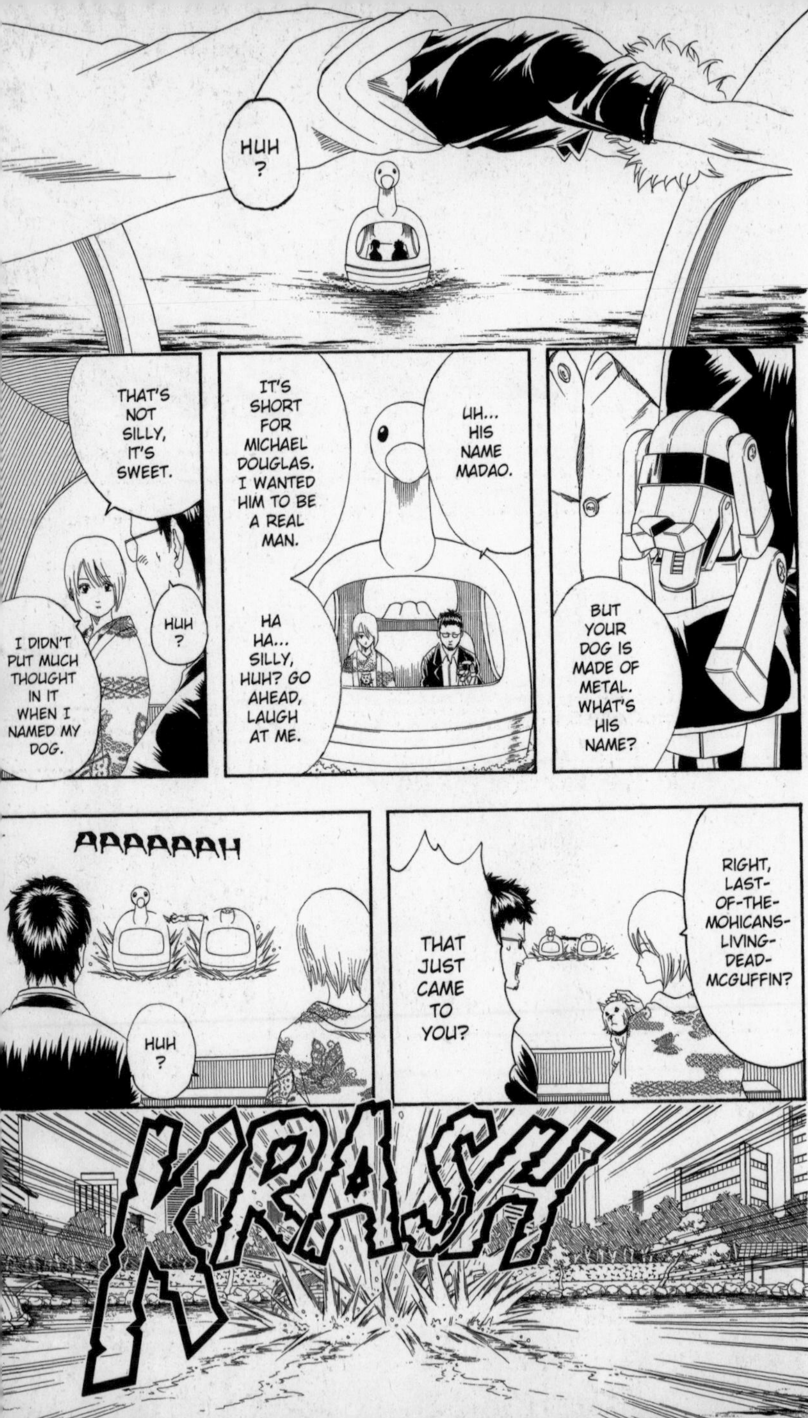
HUH ?
BUT YOUR DOG IS MADE OF METAL. WHAT'S HIS NAME?
UH... HIS NAME MADAO.
IT'S SHORT FOR MICHAEL DOUGLAS. I WANTED HIM TO BE A REAL MAN.
HA HA... SILLY, HUH? GO AHEAD, LAUGH AT ME.
THAT'S NOT SILLY, IT'S SWEET.
HUH ?
I DIDN'T PUT MUCH THOUGHT IN IT WHEN I NAMED MY DOG.
RIGHT, LAST-OF-THE-MOHICANS-LIVING-DEAD-MCGUFFIN?
THAT JUST CAME TO YOU?
AAAAAAH
HUH ?
KRASH

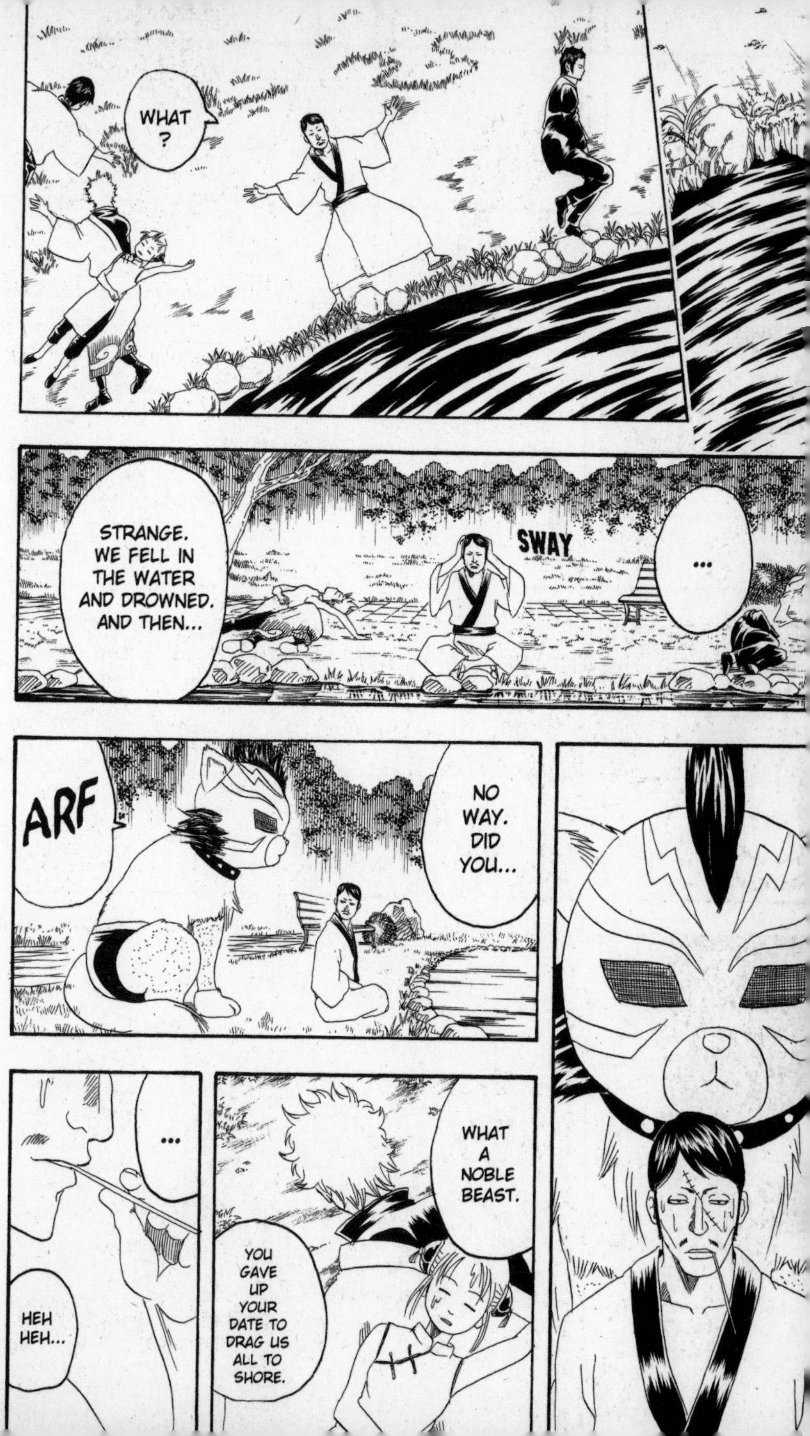
WHAT ?
...
SWAY
STRANGE. WE FELL IN THE WATER AND DROWNED. AND THEN...
NO WAY. DID YOU...
ARF
WHAT A NOBLE BEAST.
YOU GAVE UP YOUR DATE TO DRAG US ALL TO SHORE.
...
HEH HEH...

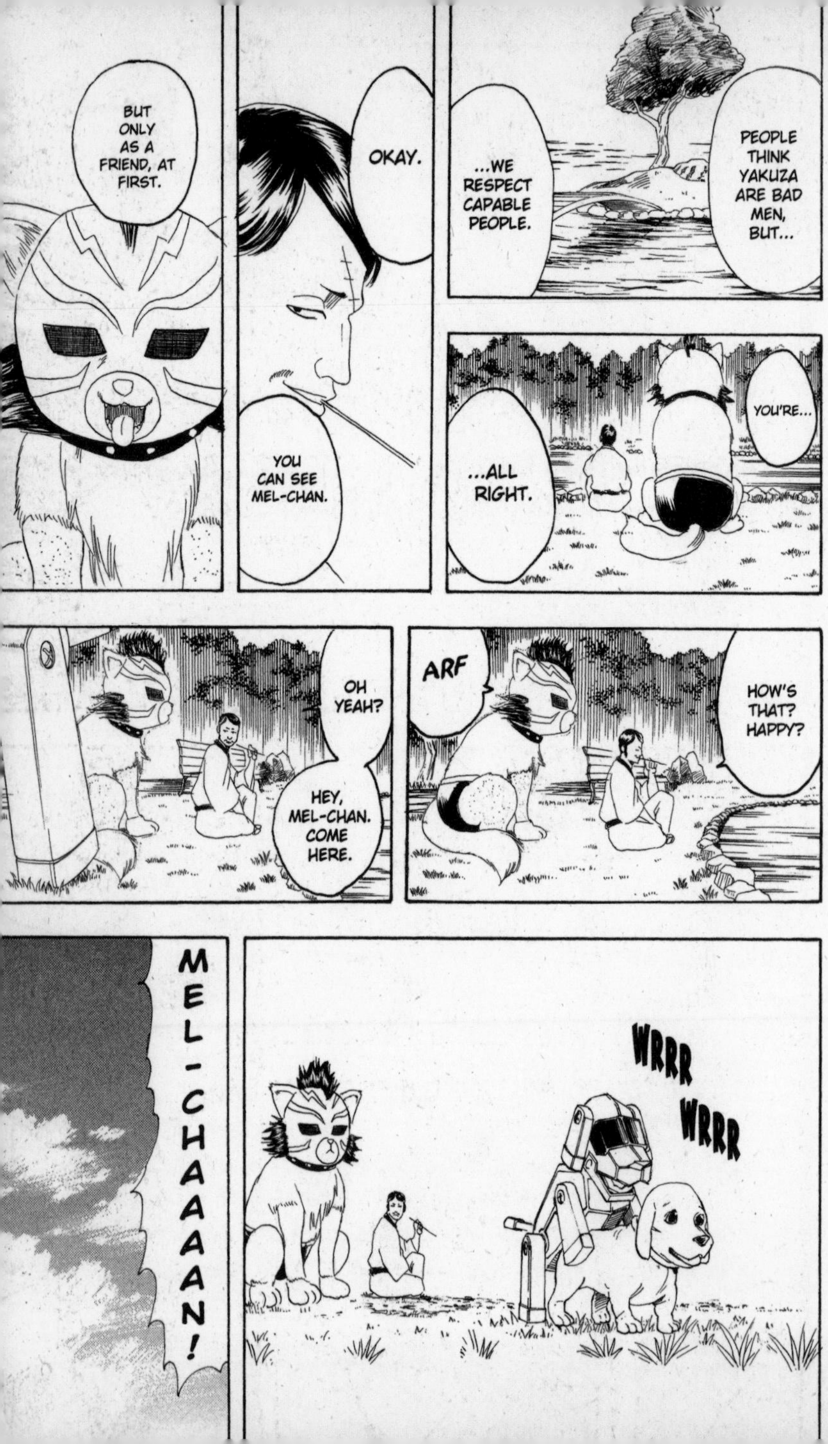
PEOPLE THINK YAKUZA ARE BAD MEN, BUT...
...WE RESPECT CAPABLE PEOPLE.
YOU'RE...
...ALL RIGHT.
OKAY.
YOU CAN SEE MEL-CHAN.
BUT ONLY AS A FRIEND, AT FIRST.
HOW'S THAT? HAPPY?
ARF
OH YEAH?
HEY, MEL-CHAN. COME HERE.
WRRR
WRRR
MEL-CHAAAAN!

Sorachi's Q&A
Hanging with the Readers #43

<Question from "Java 100%" from Tokyo>

What kind of careful consideration led you to put that stupid prince on the cover of volume 13? And Kyube is on the cover of volume 14. So when will Yamazaki make the cover?

<Answer>

Yamazaki will never be on the cover. What makes Yamazaki Yamazaki is his banality—he doesn't make the cover of manga. If he ever made the cover, he would cease to be Yamazaki. Yamazaki is someone who could be around you all day without you noticing him. When you're talking about the good old days, you say, "Those were good times, huh? But who else was with us?" "Well, there was Takahashi, Sato, you, me and... There was one more. Who was that?" That's Yamazaki. He's that green stuff in a bento box. He's the guy who looks better than usual at graduation. He's the guy who walks around all day with toilet paper stuck to his shoe. Yamazaki is always in your heart. Even if he doesn't make the cover, you can find Yamazaki all over the place. He's right beside you.

(Q&A #44 is on page 126)

SORRY, BUT I CAN TAKE THE DAY OFF TOMORROW?

Lesson 127

I'M SORRY.

KOFF

KOFF

KOFF

WHAT? HAVE YOU CAUGHT A COLD TOO, HANAKO?

ALL RIGHT.

BUNDLE UP, DRINK LOTS OF POCARI AND SWEAT AND SWEAT A LOT.

NEVER UNDER-ESTIMATE A LOW-GRADE FEVER! TAKE CARE OF YOURSELF!

OKAY.

ALL RIGHT, ALL RIGHT. GO HOME AND GET SOME REST.

MY FEVER'S NOT TOO BAD, BUT I CAN'T STOP COUGHING. I WOULDN'T WANT TO INFECT THE CUSTOMERS.

I'M SORRY.

BOW

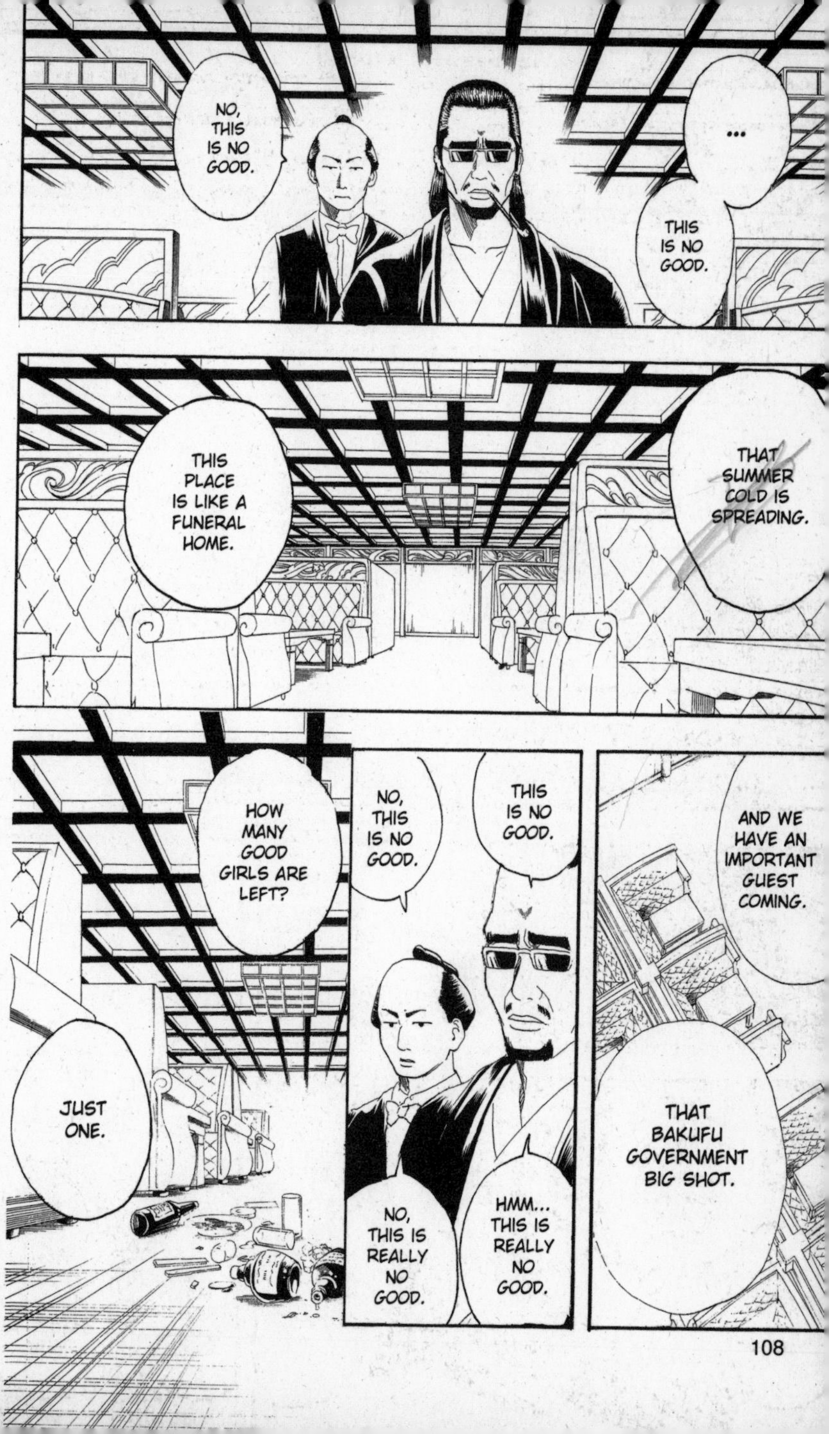
...
THIS IS NO GOOD.
NO, THIS IS NO GOOD.
THAT SUMMER COLD IS SPREADING.
THIS PLACE IS LIKE A FUNERAL HOME.
AND WE HAVE AN IMPORTANT GUEST COMING.
THAT BAKUFU GOVERNMENT BIG SHOT.
THIS IS NO GOOD.
NO, THIS IS NO GOOD.
HMM... THIS IS REALLY NO GOOD.
NO, THIS IS REALLY NO GOOD.
HOW MANY GOOD GIRLS ARE LEFT?
JUST ONE.

Lesson 127 If You Sleep with the Air Conditioner On, You'll Catch a Cold

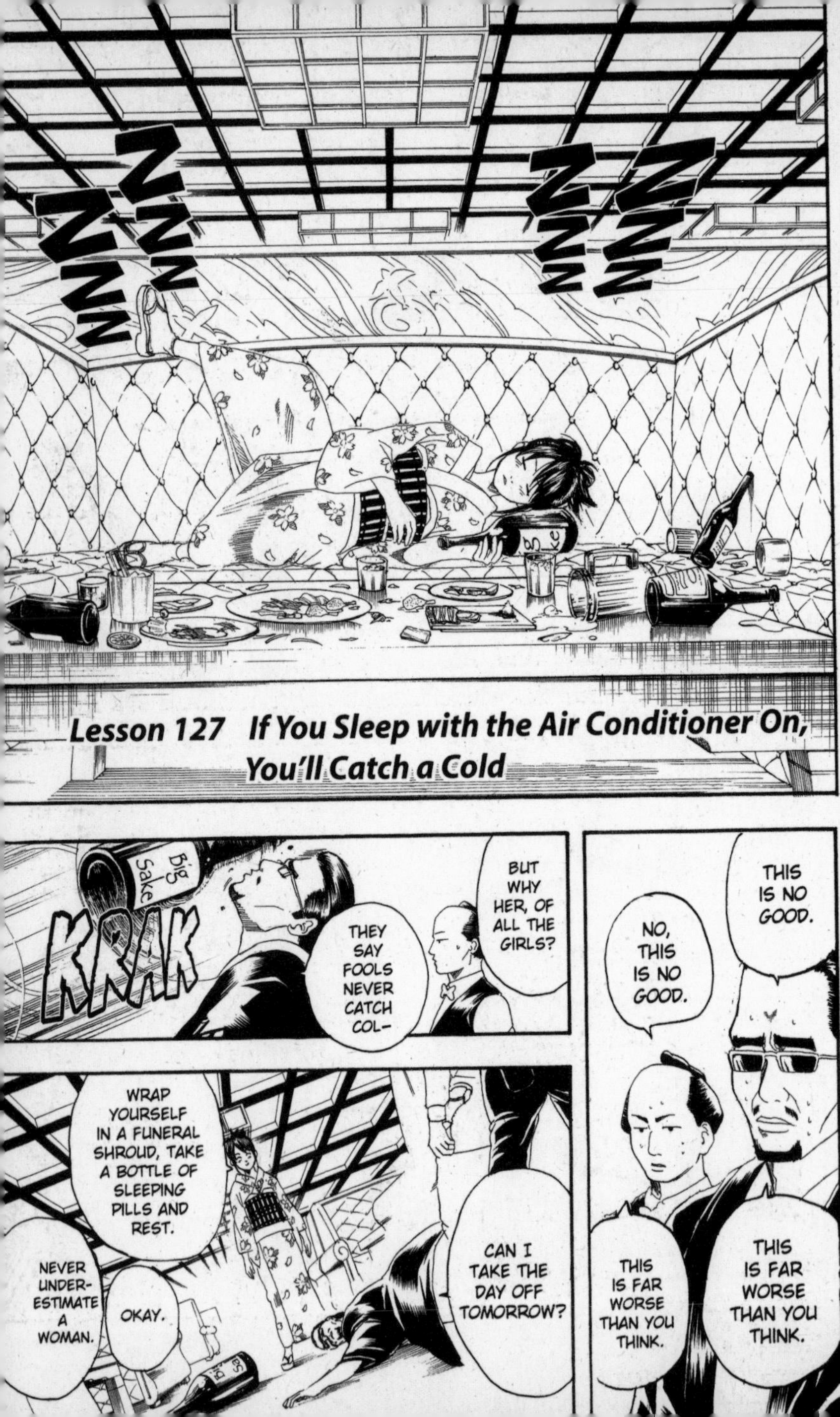
ZZZZ
ZZZZ
ZZZZ
ZZZZ
THIS IS NO GOOD.
NO, THIS IS NO GOOD.
THIS IS FAR WORSE THAN YOU THINK.
THIS IS FAR WORSE THAN YOU THINK.
BUT WHY HER, OF ALL THE GIRLS?
THEY SAY FOOLS NEVER CATCH COL-
Big Sake
KRAK
CAN I TAKE THE DAY OFF TOMORROW?
WRAP YOURSELF IN A FUNERAL SHROUD, TAKE A BOTTLE OF SLEEPING PILLS AND REST.
OKAY.
NEVER UNDER-ESTIMATE A WOMAN.

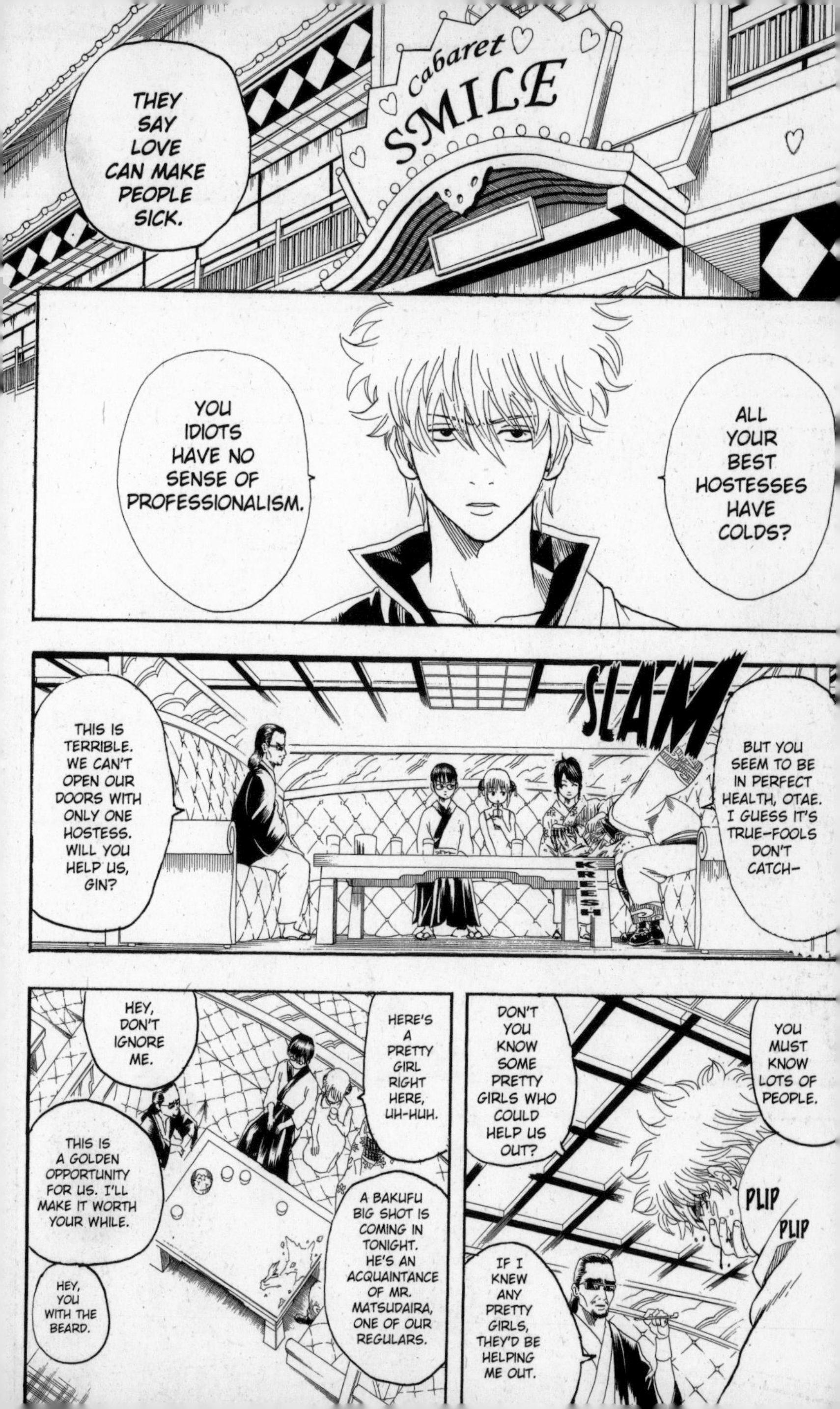
Cabaret SMILE
THEY SAY LOVE CAN MAKE PEOPLE SICK.
ALL YOUR BEST HOSTESSES HAVE COLDS?
YOU IDIOTS HAVE NO SENSE OF PROFESSIONALISM.
BUT YOU SEEM TO BE IN PERFECT HEALTH, OTAE. I GUESS IT'S TRUE—FOOLS DON'T CATCH—
SLAM
KREESH
THIS IS TERRIBLE. WE CAN'T OPEN OUR DOORS WITH ONLY ONE HOSTESS. WILL YOU HELP US, GIN?
YOU MUST KNOW LOTS OF PEOPLE.
DON'T YOU KNOW SOME PRETTY GIRLS WHO COULD HELP US OUT?
PLIP
PLIP
IF I KNEW ANY PRETTY GIRLS, THEY'D BE HELPING ME OUT.
HERE'S A PRETTY GIRL RIGHT HERE, UH-HUH.
HEY, DON'T IGNORE ME.
A BAKUFU BIG SHOT IS COMING IN TONIGHT. HE'S AN ACQUAINTANCE OF MR. MATSUDAIRA, ONE OF OUR REGULARS.
THIS IS A GOLDEN OPPORTUNITY FOR US. I'LL MAKE IT WORTH YOUR WHILE.
HEY, YOU WITH THE BEARD.

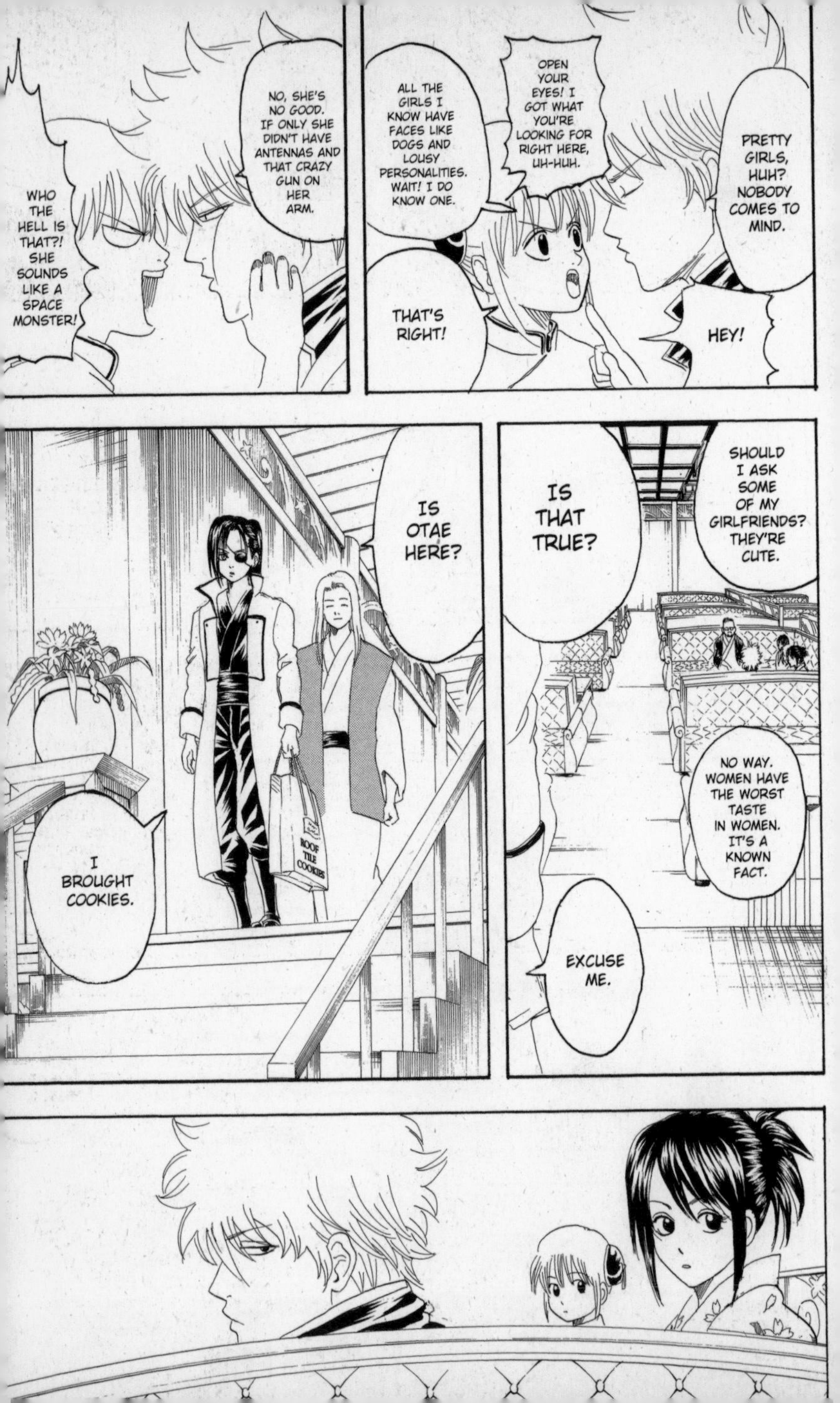
PRETTY GIRLS, HUH? NOBODY COMES TO MIND.
HEY!
OPEN YOUR EYES! I GOT WHAT YOU'RE LOOKING FOR RIGHT HERE, UH-HUH.
ALL THE GIRLS I KNOW HAVE FACES LIKE DOGS AND LOUSY PERSONALITIES. WAIT! I DO KNOW ONE.
THAT'S RIGHT!
NO, SHE'S NO GOOD. IF ONLY SHE DIDN'T HAVE ANTENNAS AND THAT CRAZY GUN ON HER ARM.
WHO THE HELL IS THAT?! SHE SOUNDS LIKE A SPACE MONSTER!
SHOULD I ASK SOME OF MY GIRLFRIENDS? THEY'RE CUTE.
IS THAT TRUE?
NO WAY. WOMEN HAVE THE WORST TASTE IN WOMEN. IT'S A KNOWN FACT.
EXCUSE ME.
IS OTAE HERE?
ROOF TILE COOKIES
I BROUGHT COOKIES.

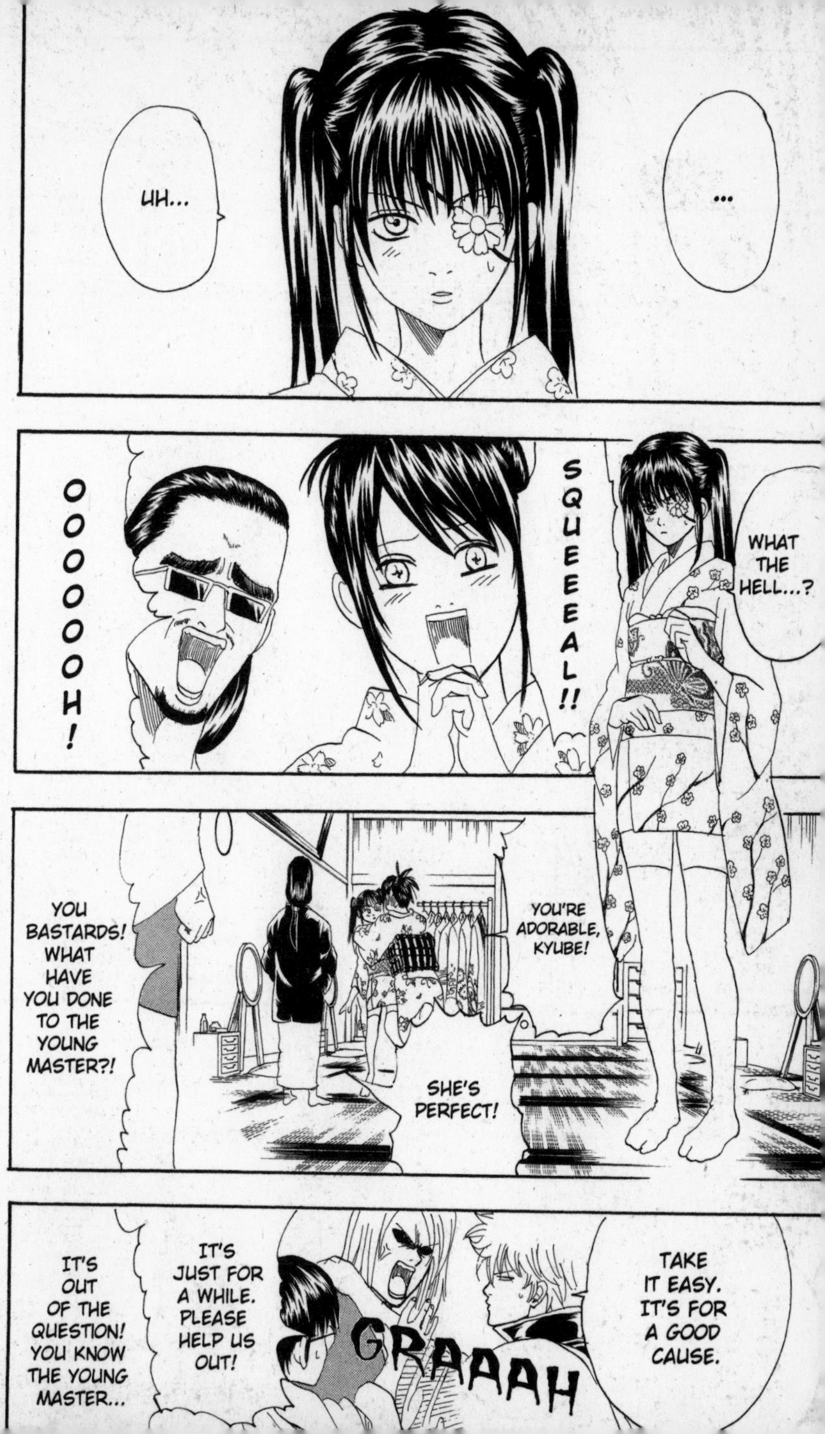
...
UH...
WHAT THE HELL...?
SQUEEEEAL!!
OOOOOOOH!
YOU'RE ADORABLE, KYUBE!
SHE'S PERFECT!
YOU BASTARDS! WHAT HAVE YOU DONE TO THE YOUNG MASTER?!
TAKE IT EASY. IT'S FOR A GOOD CAUSE.
GRAAAH
IT'S JUST FOR A WHILE. PLEASE HELP US OUT!
IT'S OUT OF THE QUESTION! YOU KNOW THE YOUNG MASTER...

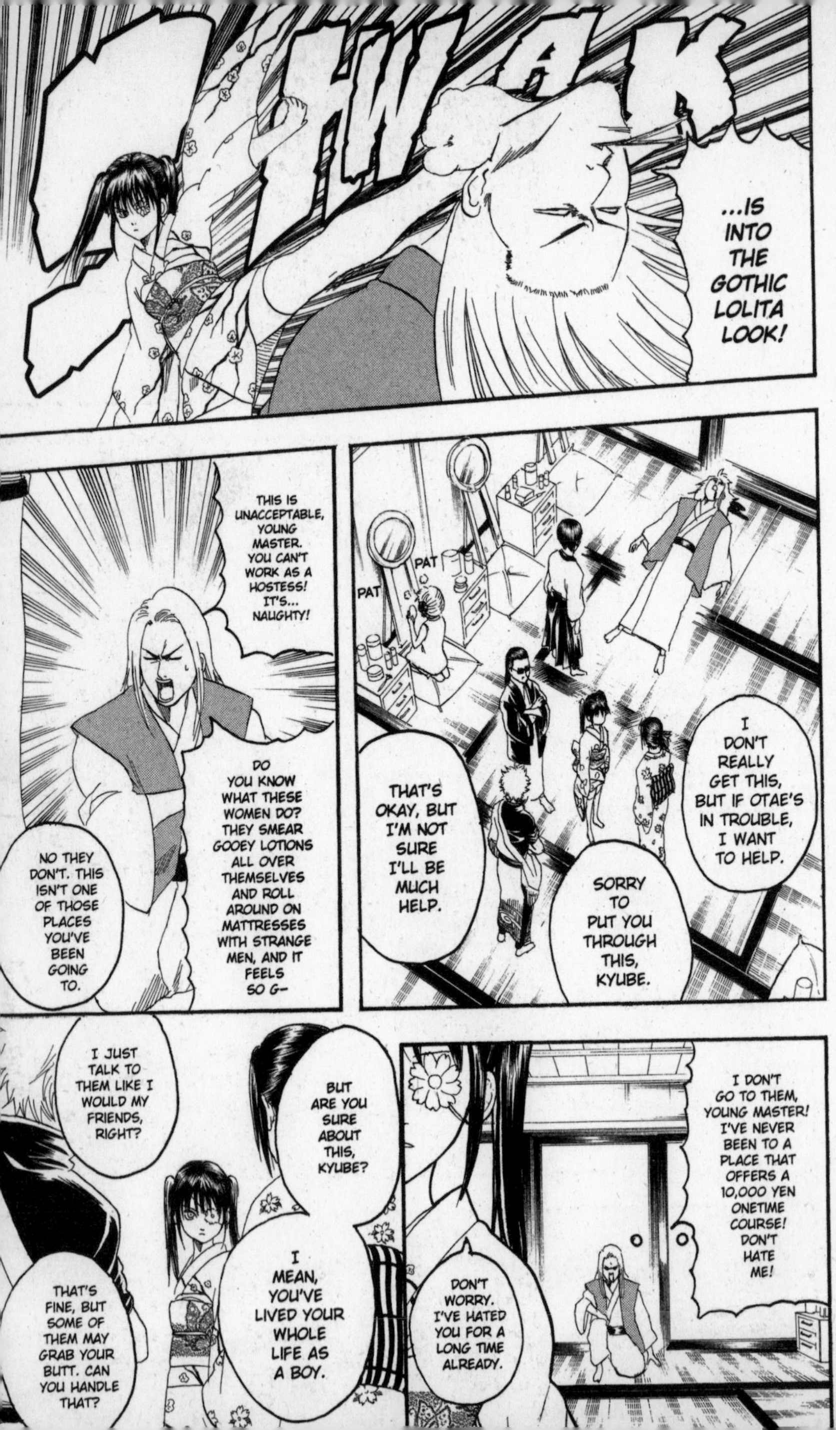

...IS INTO THE GOTHIC LOLITA LOOK!
I DON'T REALLY GET THIS, BUT IF OTAE'S IN TROUBLE, I WANT TO HELP.
THAT'S OKAY, BUT I'M NOT SURE I'LL BE MUCH HELP.
SORRY TO PUT YOU THROUGH THIS, KYUBE.
PAT
PAT
THIS IS UNACCEPTABLE, YOUNG MASTER. YOU CAN'T WORK AS A HOSTESS! IT'S... NAUGHTY!
DO YOU KNOW WHAT THESE WOMEN DO? THEY SMEAR GOOEY LOTIONS ALL OVER THEMSELVES AND ROLL AROUND ON MATTRESSES WITH STRANGE MEN, AND IT FEELS SO G—
NO THEY DON'T. THIS ISN'T ONE OF THOSE PLACES YOU'VE BEEN GOING TO.
I DON'T GO TO THEM, YOUNG MASTER! I'VE NEVER BEEN TO A PLACE THAT OFFERS A 10,000 YEN ONETIME COURSE! DON'T HATE ME!
DON'T WORRY. I'VE HATED YOU FOR A LONG TIME ALREADY.
BUT ARE YOU SURE ABOUT THIS, KYUBE?
I JUST TALK TO THEM LIKE I WOULD MY FRIENDS, RIGHT?
I MEAN, YOU'VE LIVED YOUR WHOLE LIFE AS A BOY.
THAT'S FINE, BUT SOME OF THEM MAY GRAB YOUR BUTT. CAN YOU HANDLE THAT?

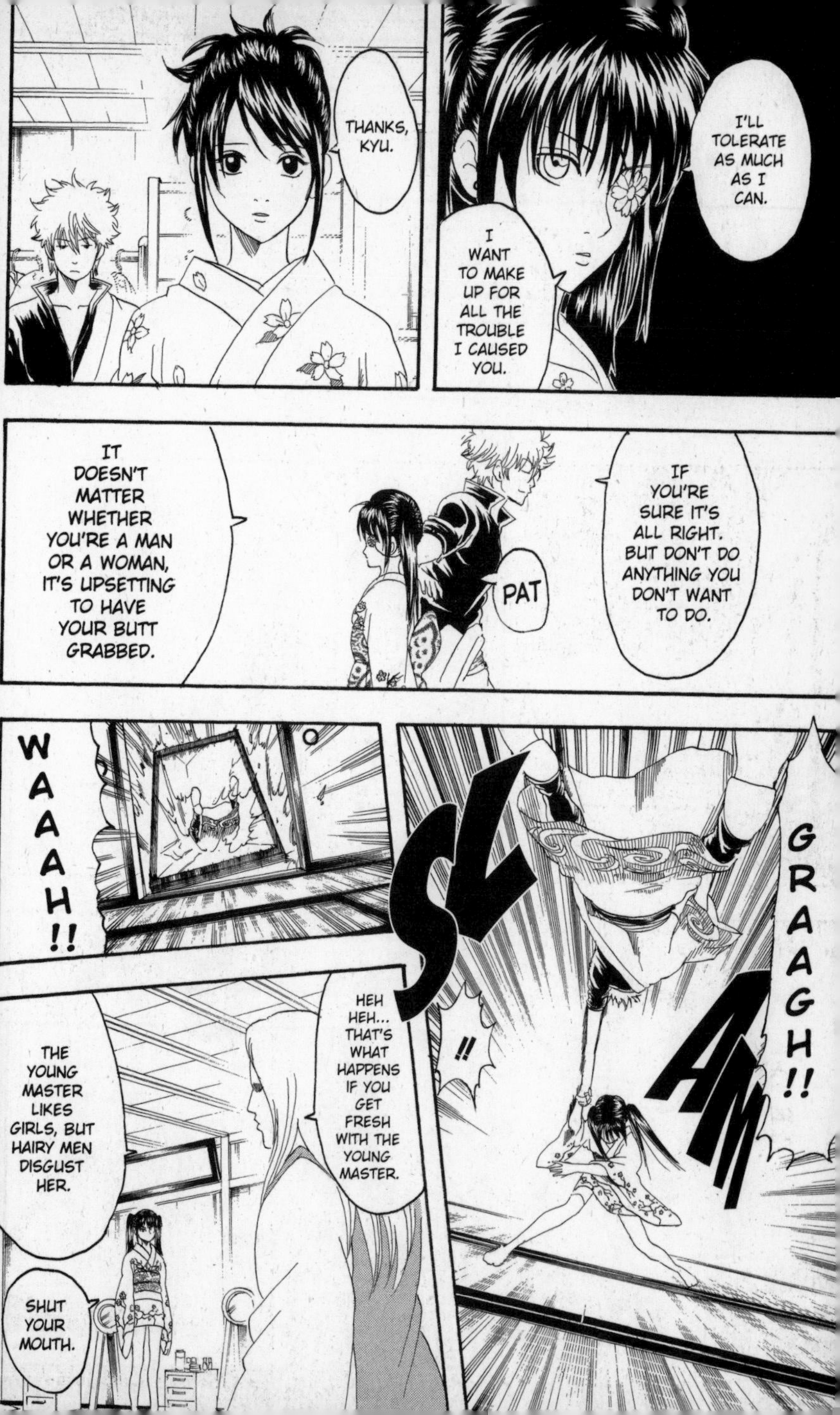
I'LL TOLERATE AS MUCH AS I CAN.
I WANT TO MAKE UP FOR ALL THE TROUBLE I CAUSED YOU.
THANKS, KYU.
IF YOU'RE SURE IT'S ALL RIGHT. BUT DON'T DO ANYTHING YOU DON'T WANT TO DO.
PAT
IT DOESN'T MATTER WHETHER YOU'RE A MAN OR A WOMAN, IT'S UPSETTING TO HAVE YOUR BUTT GRABBED.
GRAAGH!!
SLAM
!!
WAAAAH!!
HEH HEH... THAT'S WHAT HAPPENS IF YOU GET FRESH WITH THE YOUNG MASTER.
THE YOUNG MASTER LIKES GIRLS, BUT HAIRY MEN DISGUST HER.
SHUT YOUR MOUTH.

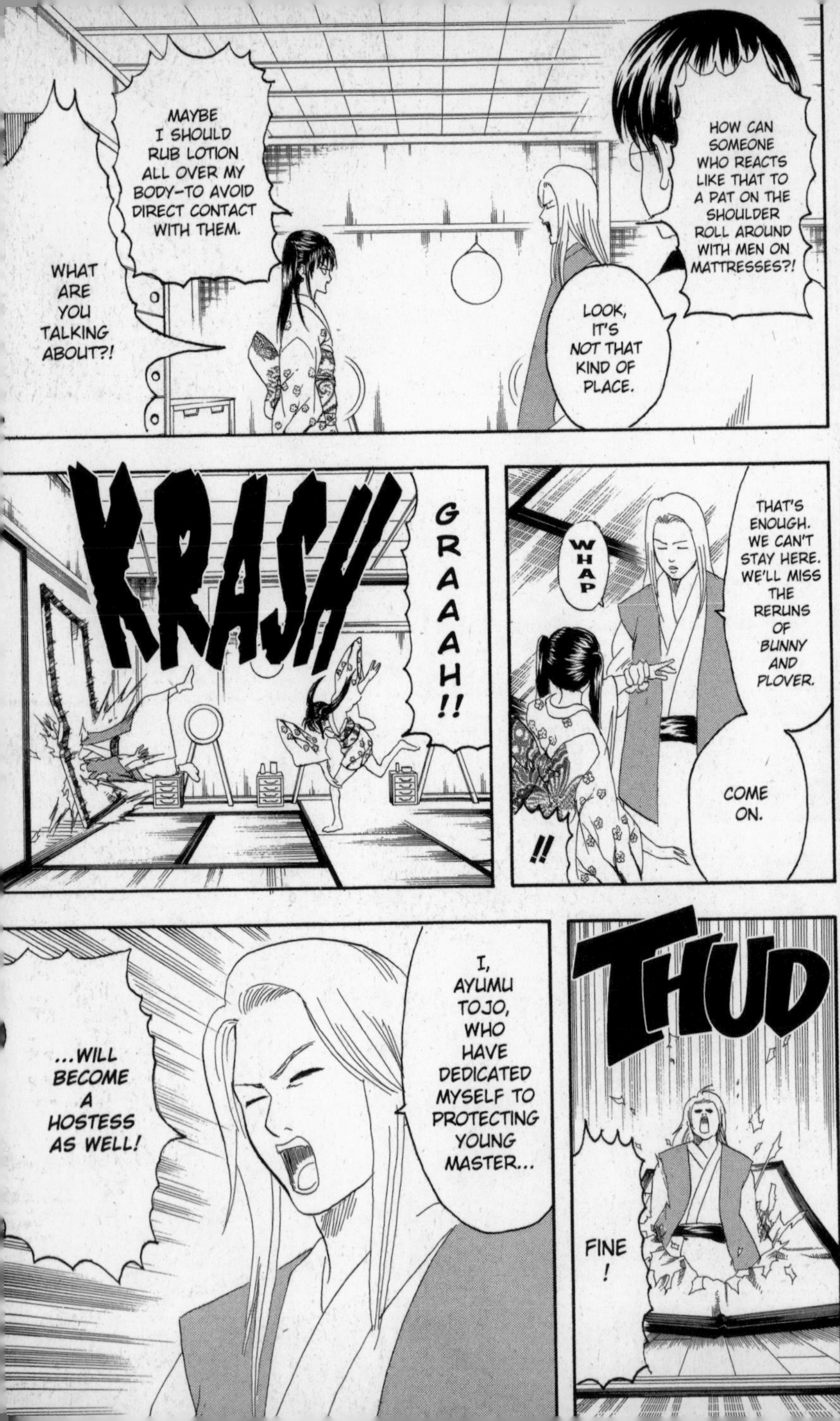
HOW CAN SOMEONE WHO REACTS LIKE THAT TO A PAT ON THE SHOULDER ROLL AROUND WITH MEN ON MATTRESSES?!
MAYBE I SHOULD RUB LOTION ALL OVER MY BODY—TO AVOID DIRECT CONTACT WITH THEM.
LOOK, IT'S NOT THAT KIND OF PLACE.
WHAT ARE YOU TALKING ABOUT?!
WHAP
THAT'S ENOUGH. WE CAN'T STAY HERE. WE'LL MISS THE RERUNS OF BUNNY AND PLOVER.
COME ON.
!!
KRASH
GRAAAAH!!
THUD
FINE!
I, AYUMU TOJO, WHO HAVE DEDICATED MYSELF TO PROTECTING YOUNG MASTER...
...WILL BECOME A HOSTESS AS WELL!

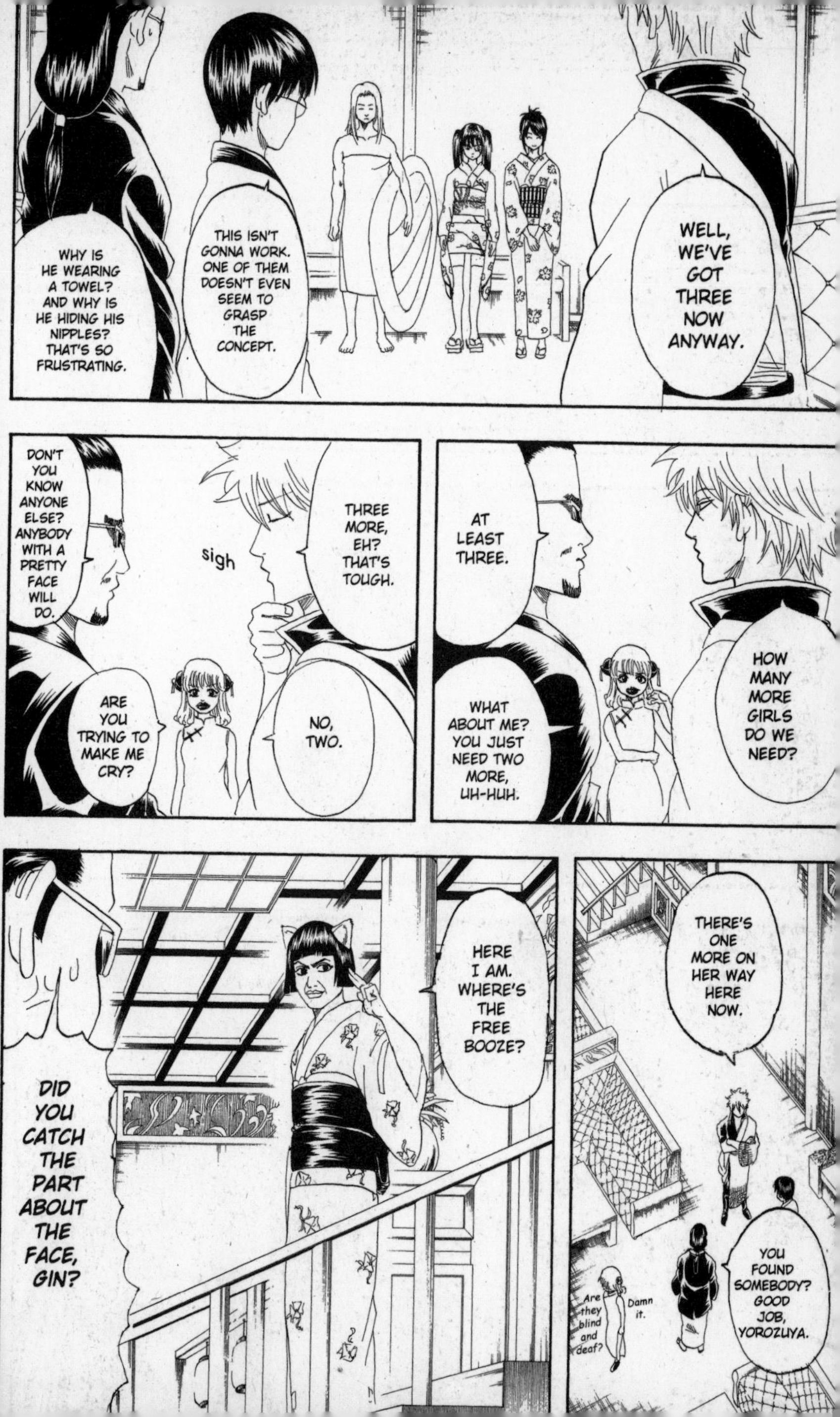
WELL, WE'VE GOT THREE NOW ANYWAY.
THIS ISN'T GONNA WORK. ONE OF THEM DOESN'T EVEN SEEM TO GRASP THE CONCEPT.
WHY IS HE WEARING A TOWEL? AND WHY IS HE HIDING HIS NIPPLES? THAT'S SO FRUSTRATING.
HOW MANY MORE GIRLS DO WE NEED?
AT LEAST THREE.
WHAT ABOUT ME? YOU JUST NEED TWO MORE, UH-HUH.
THREE MORE, EH? THAT'S TOUGH.
sigh
NO, TWO.
DON'T YOU KNOW ANYONE ELSE? ANYBODY WITH A PRETTY FACE WILL DO.
ARE YOU TRYING TO MAKE ME CRY?
THERE'S ONE MORE ON HER WAY HERE NOW.
YOU FOUND SOMEBODY? GOOD JOB, YOROZUYA.
Damn it.
Are they blind and deaf?
HERE I AM. WHERE'S THE FREE BOOZE?
DID YOU CATCH THE PART ABOUT THE FACE, GIN?

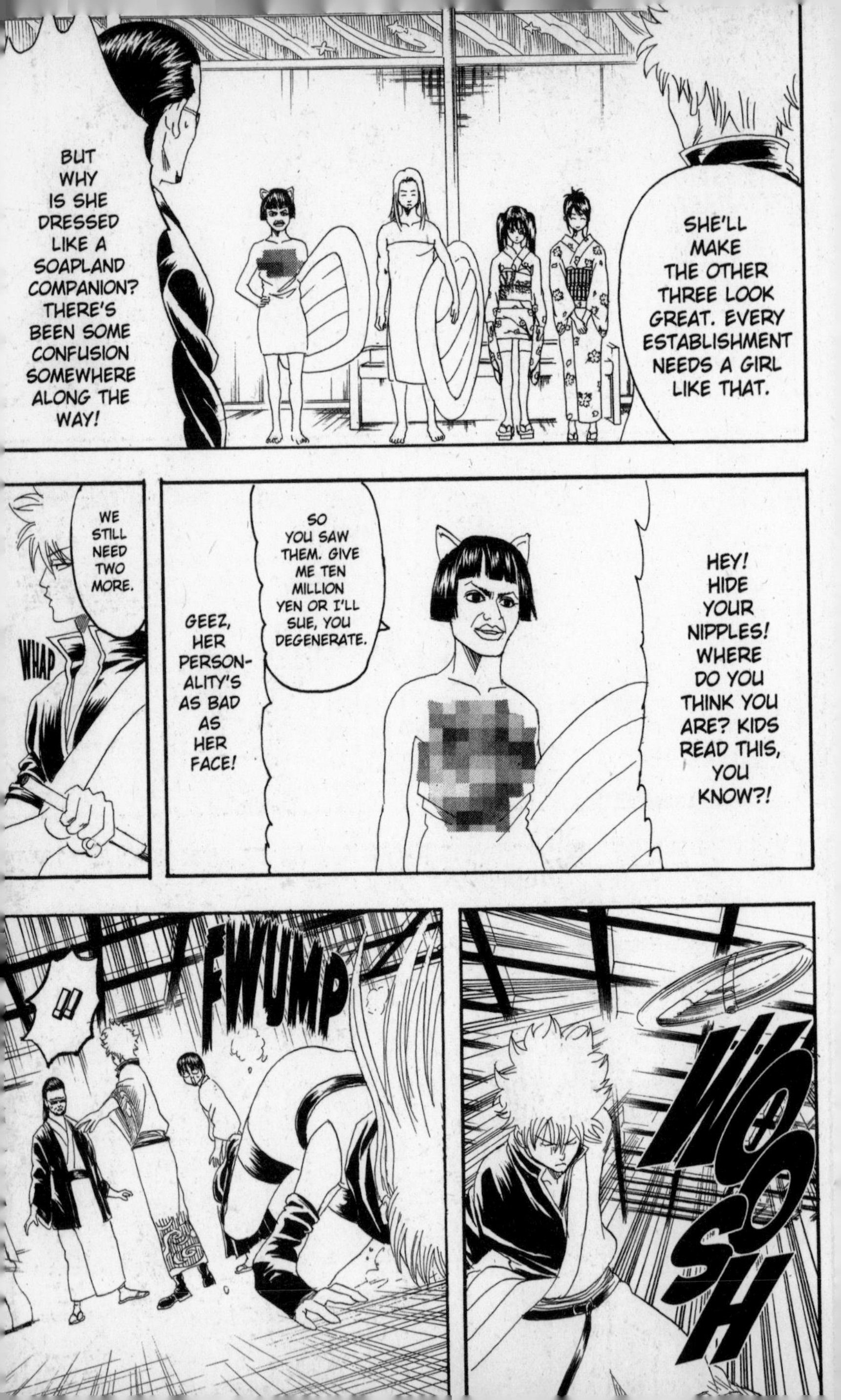
SHE'LL MAKE THE OTHER THREE LOOK GREAT. EVERY ESTABLISHMENT NEEDS A GIRL LIKE THAT.
BUT WHY IS SHE DRESSED LIKE A SOAPLAND COMPANION? THERE'S BEEN SOME CONFUSION SOMEWHERE ALONG THE WAY!
HEY! HIDE YOUR NIPPLES! WHERE DO YOU THINK YOU ARE? KIDS READ THIS, YOU KNOW?!
SO YOU SAW THEM. GIVE ME TEN MILLION YEN OR I'LL SUE, YOU DEGENERATE.
GEEZ, HER PERSON-ALITY'S AS BAD AS HER FACE!
WE STILL NEED TWO MORE.
WHAP
WHOOSH
FWUMP
!!

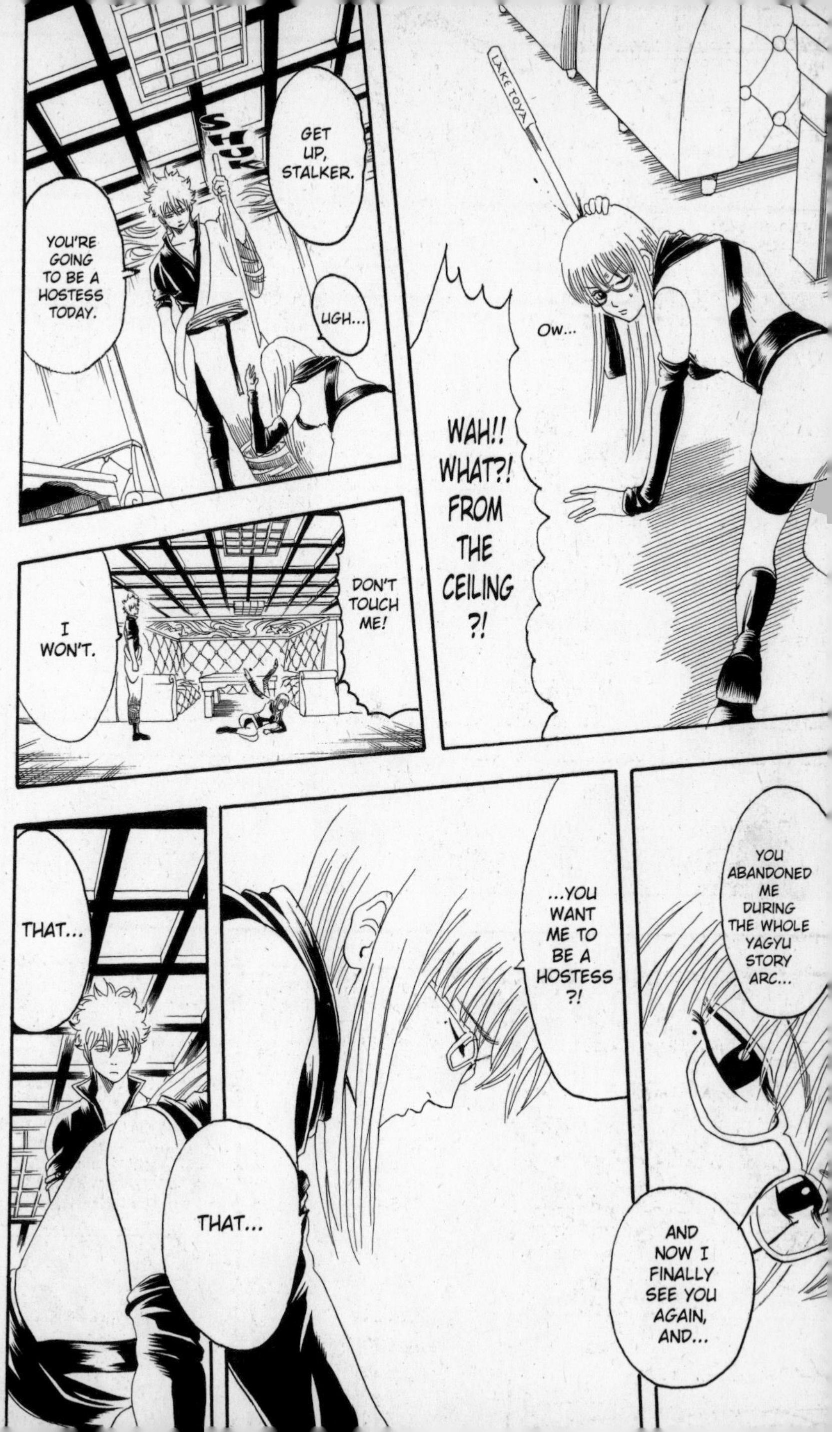
LAKE TOYA
Ow...
WAH!! WHAT?! FROM THE CEILING?!
GET UP, STALKER.
SHUK
UGH...
YOU'RE GOING TO BE A HOSTESS TODAY.
DON'T TOUCH ME!
I WON'T.
YOU ABANDONED ME DURING THE WHOLE YAGYU STORY ARC...
AND NOW I FINALLY SEE YOU AGAIN, AND...
...YOU WANT ME TO BE A HOSTESS?!
THAT...
THAT...

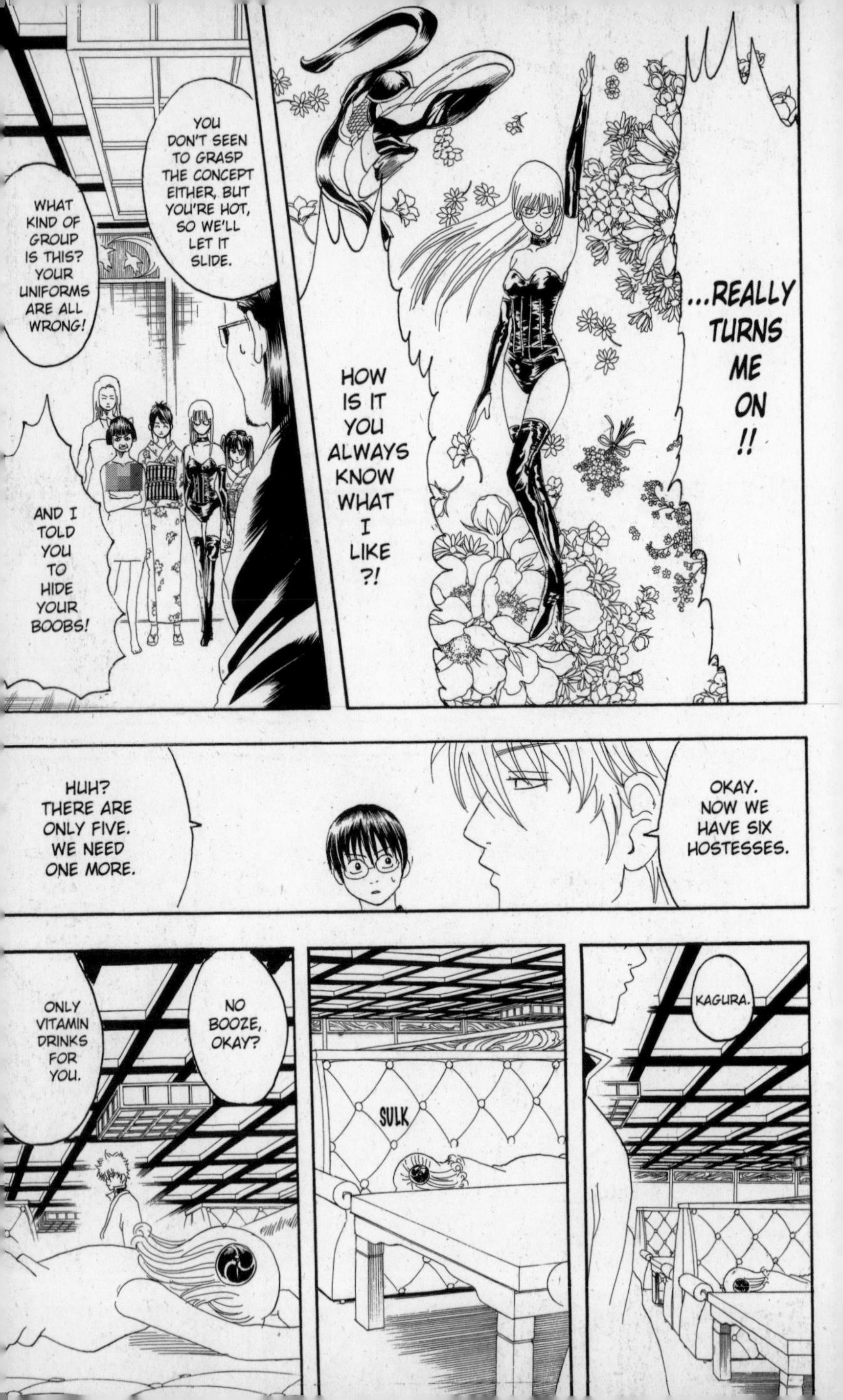
...REALLY TURNS ME ON!!
HOW IS IT YOU ALWAYS KNOW WHAT I LIKE?!
YOU DON'T SEEN TO GRASP THE CONCEPT EITHER, BUT YOU'RE HOT, SO WE'LL LET IT SLIDE.
WHAT KIND OF GROUP IS THIS? YOUR UNIFORMS ARE ALL WRONG!
AND I TOLD YOU TO HIDE YOUR BOOBS!
OKAY. NOW WE HAVE SIX HOSTESSES.
HUH? THERE ARE ONLY FIVE. WE NEED ONE MORE.
KAGURA.
SULK
NO BOOZE, OKAY?
ONLY VITAMIN DRINKS FOR YOU.

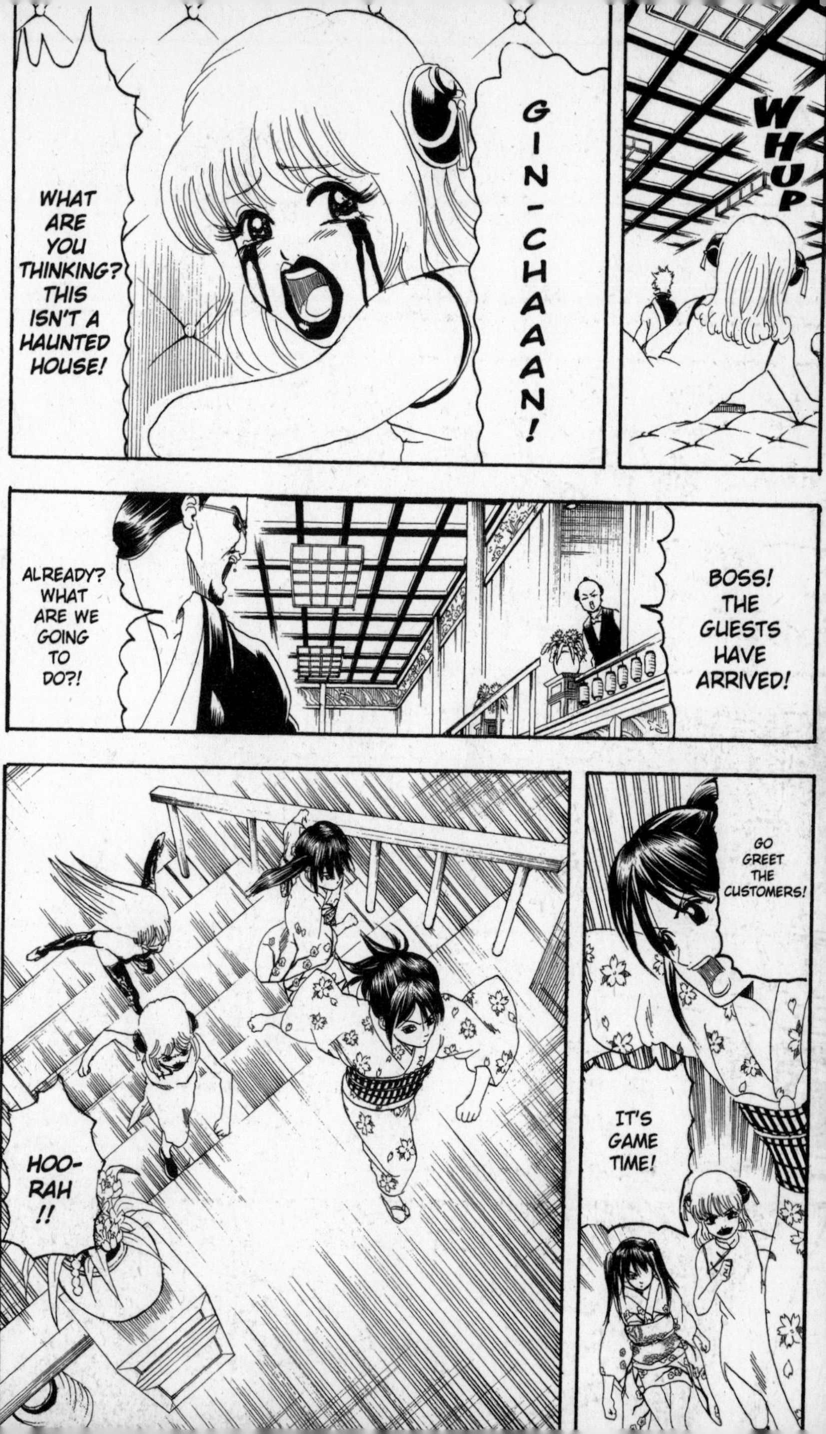
WHUP
GIN-CHAAAN!
WHAT ARE YOU THINKING? THIS ISN'T A HAUNTED HOUSE!
BOSS! THE GUESTS HAVE ARRIVED!
ALREADY? WHAT ARE WE GOING TO DO?!
GO GREET THE CUSTOMERS!
IT'S GAME TIME!
HOO-RAH!!

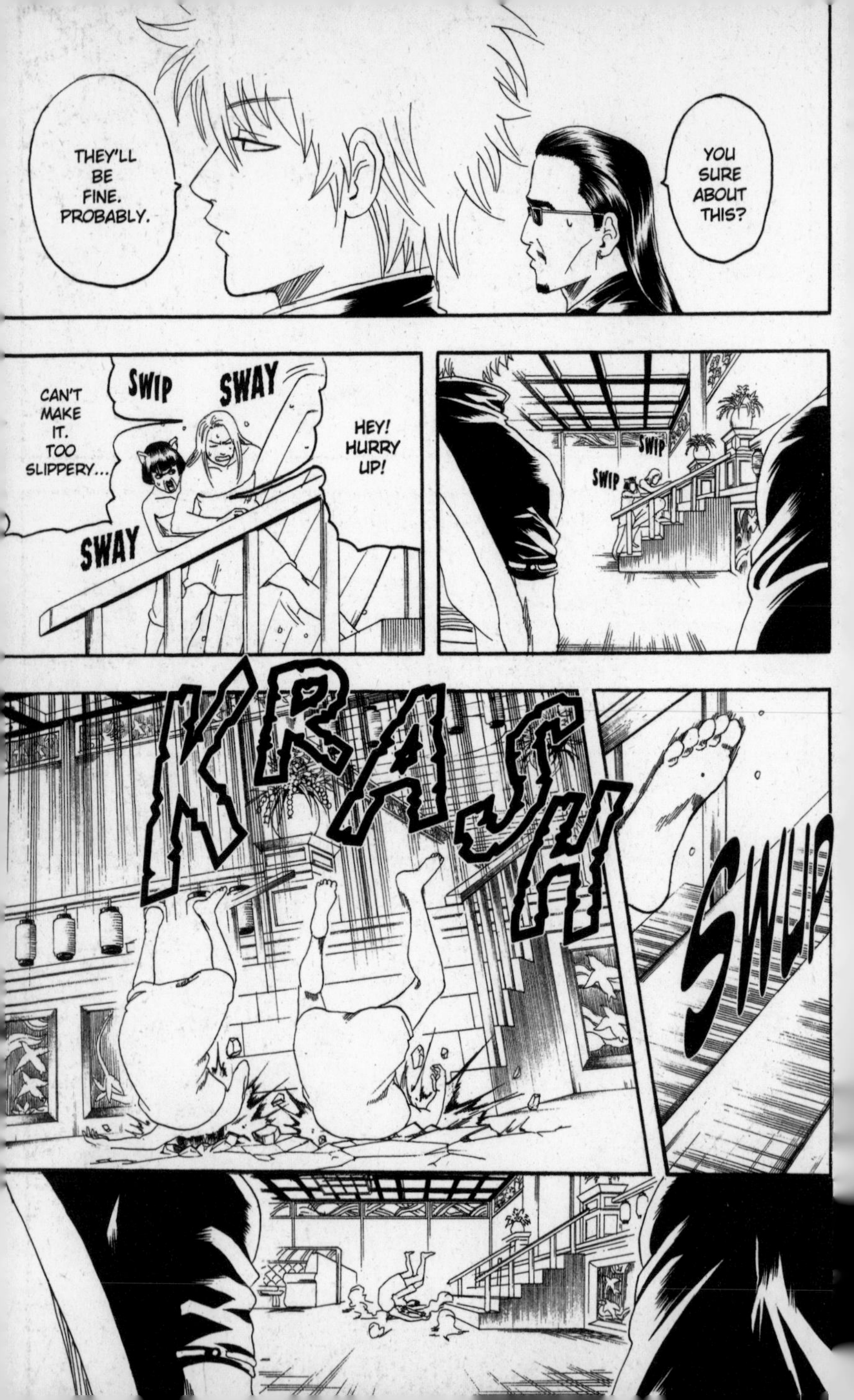
YOU SURE ABOUT THIS?
THEY'LL BE FINE. PROBABLY.
SWIP
SWIP
HEY! HURRY UP!
SWAY
SWIP
CAN'T MAKE IT. TOO SLIPPERY...
SWAY
SWUP
KRASH

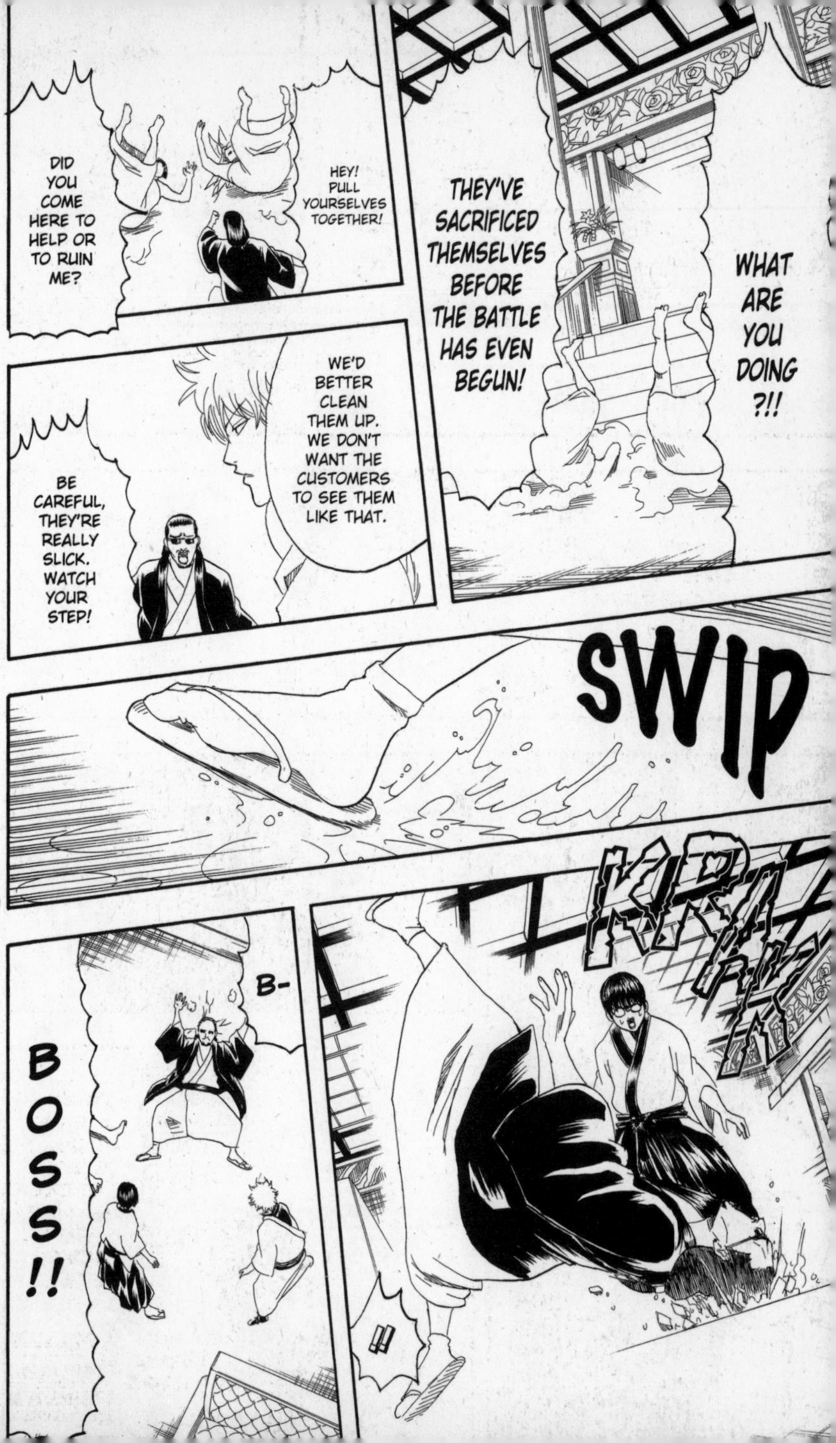
WHAT ARE YOU DOING ?!!
THEY'VE SACRIFICED THEMSELVES BEFORE THE BATTLE HAS EVEN BEGUN!
HEY! PULL YOURSELVES TOGETHER!
DID YOU COME HERE TO HELP OR TO RUIN ME?
WE'D BETTER CLEAN THEM UP. WE DON'T WANT THE CUSTOMERS TO SEE THEM LIKE THAT.
BE CAREFUL, THEY'RE REALLY SLICK. WATCH YOUR STEP!
SWIP
KRAK
!!
B-
BOSS!!

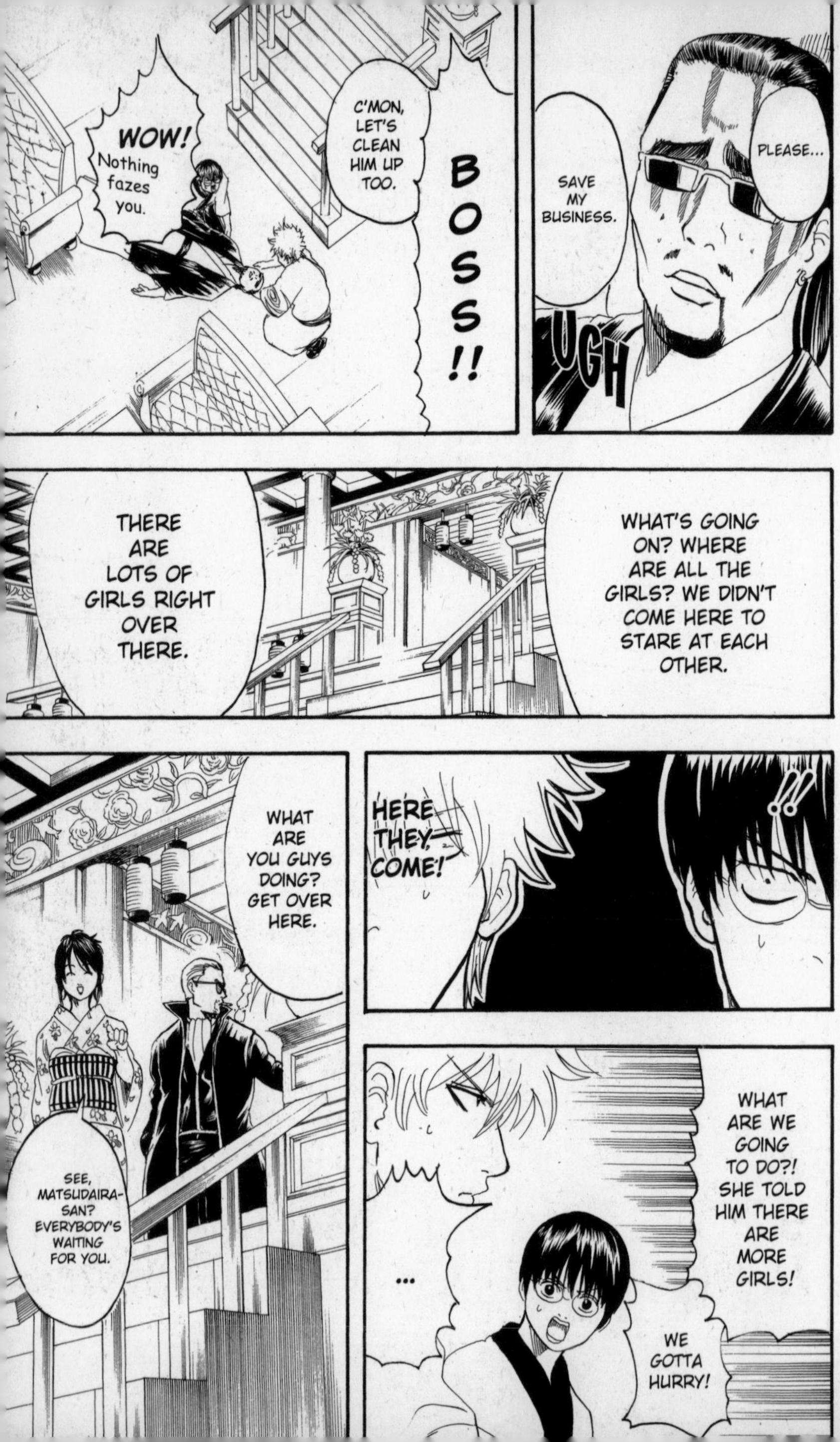
PLEASE...
SAVE MY BUSINESS.
UGH
BOSS!!
C'MON, LET'S CLEAN HIM UP TOO.
WOW! Nothing fazes you.
WHAT'S GOING ON? WHERE ARE ALL THE GIRLS? WE DIDN'T COME HERE TO STARE AT EACH OTHER.
THERE ARE LOTS OF GIRLS RIGHT OVER THERE.
!!
HERE THEY COME!
WHAT ARE WE GOING TO DO?! SHE TOLD HIM THERE ARE MORE GIRLS!
...
WE GOTTA HURRY!
WHAT ARE YOU GUYS DOING? GET OVER HERE.
SEE, MATSUDAIRA-SAN? EVERYBODY'S WAITING FOR YOU.

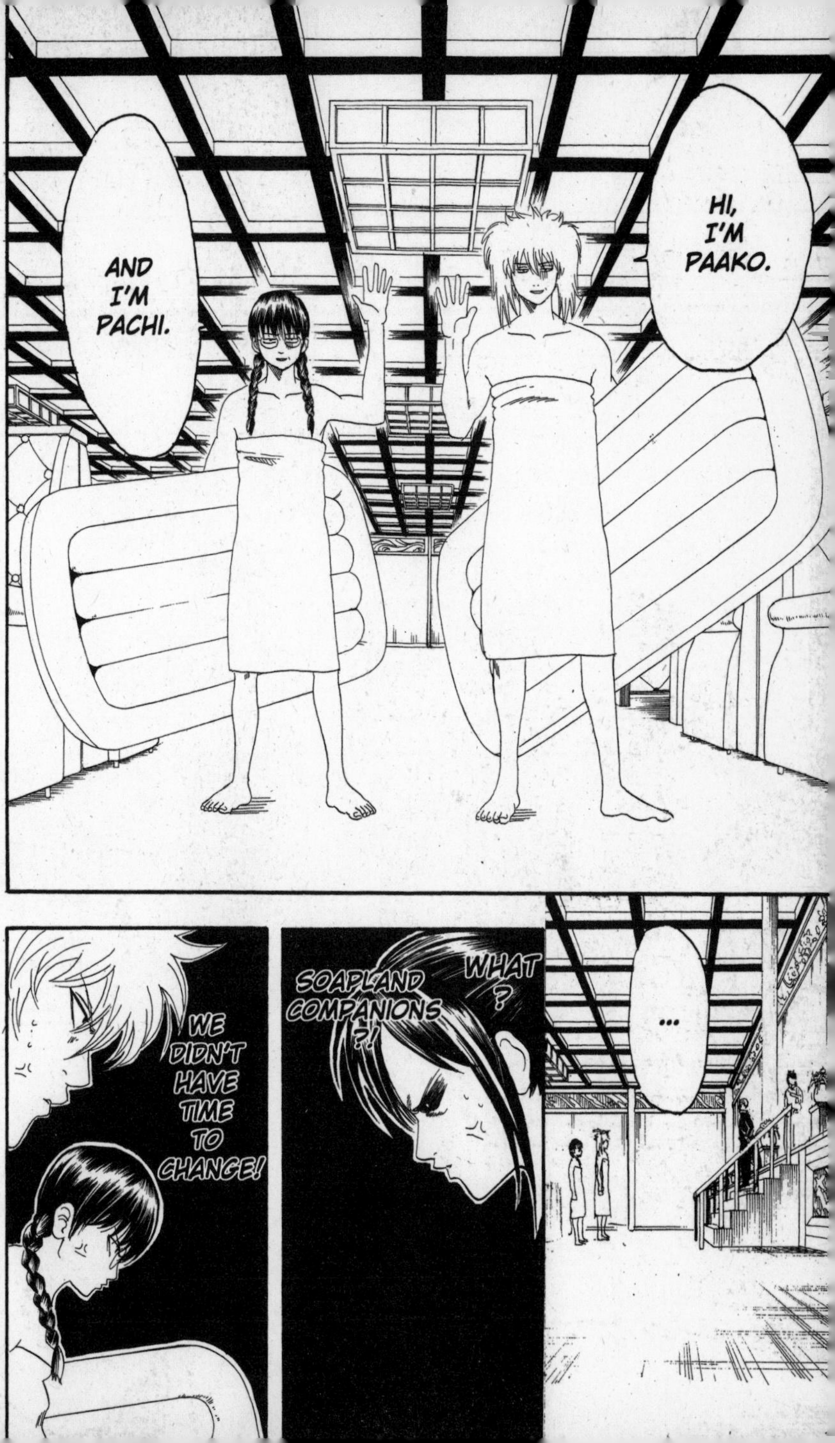
HI, I'M PAAKO.
AND I'M PACHI.
...
WHAT?
SOAPLAND COMPANIONS?!
WE DIDN'T HAVE TIME TO CHANGE!

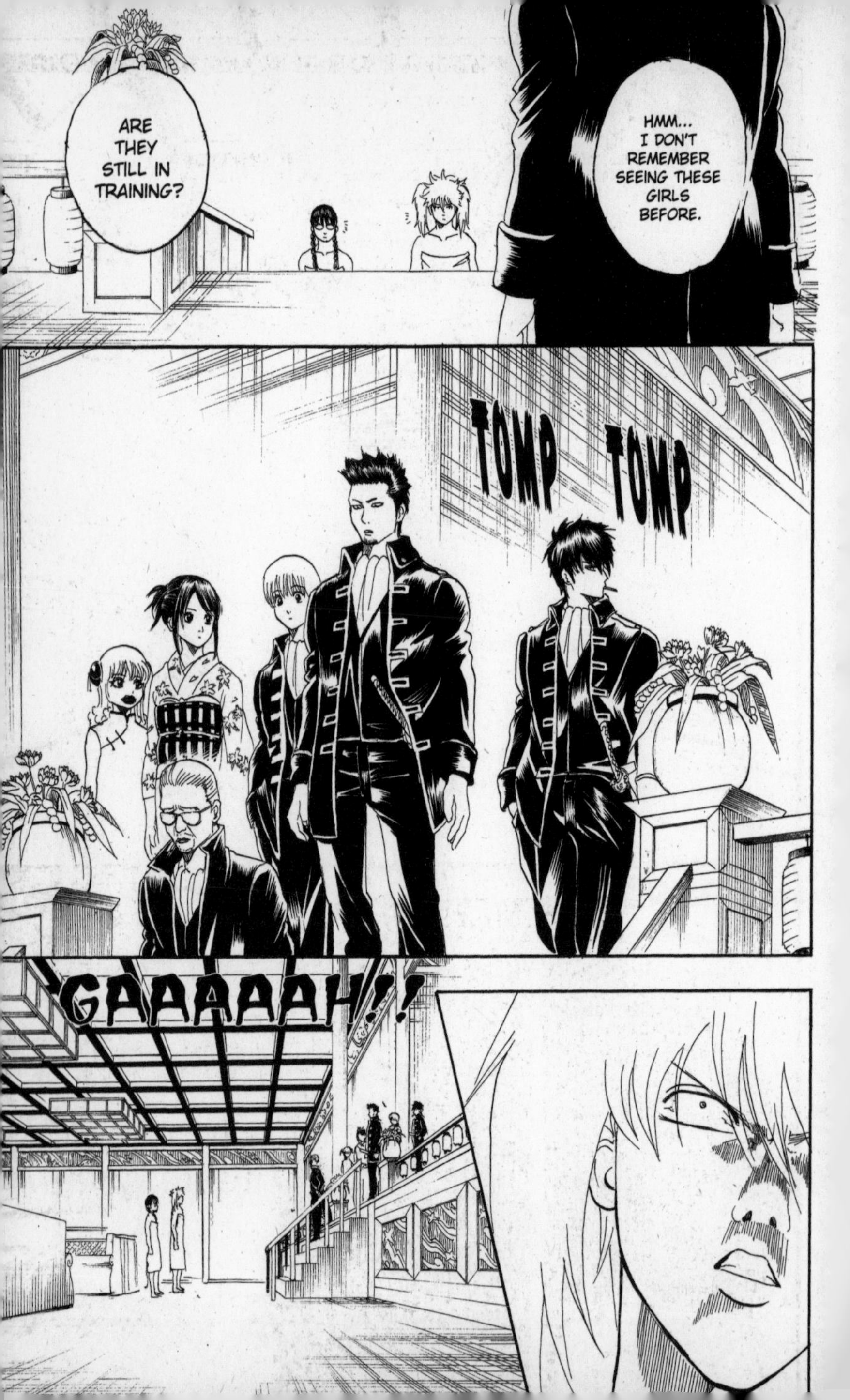
HMM... I DON'T REMEMBER SEEING THESE GIRLS BEFORE.
ARE THEY STILL IN TRAINING?
TOMP TOMP
GAAAAAH!!

Sorachi's Q&A
Hanging with the Readers #44

<Question from "STTα" from Aichi Prefecture>

I have a question. To me Shinpachi seems like a wisecracking loser with glasses, but he's a pretty good fighter too. And he runs the family dojo. So just how strong is Shinpachi?

<Answer>

Shinpachi may seem like a wimp compared to the monsters around him, but he's actually very strong. When I was in junior high, there was a school gang leader named Kosuke who was a year older than me, and Shinpachi is about three times stronger than he was. Kosuke was one tough guy, so Shinpachi is very strong. But despite being a gangster, Kosuke had excellent posture when he rode his bicycle. He was really something.

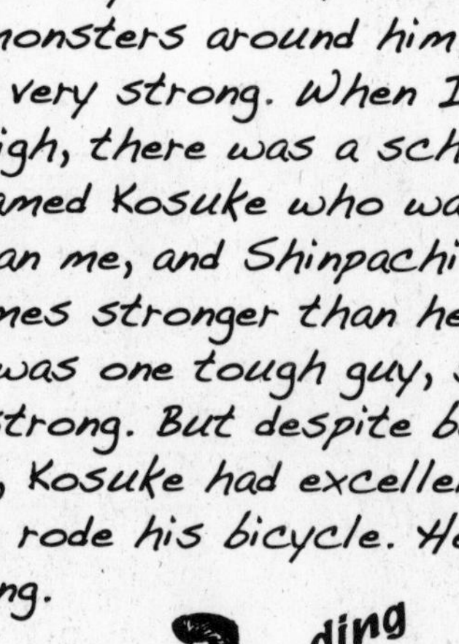

ding
ding

(Q&A #45 is on page 146)

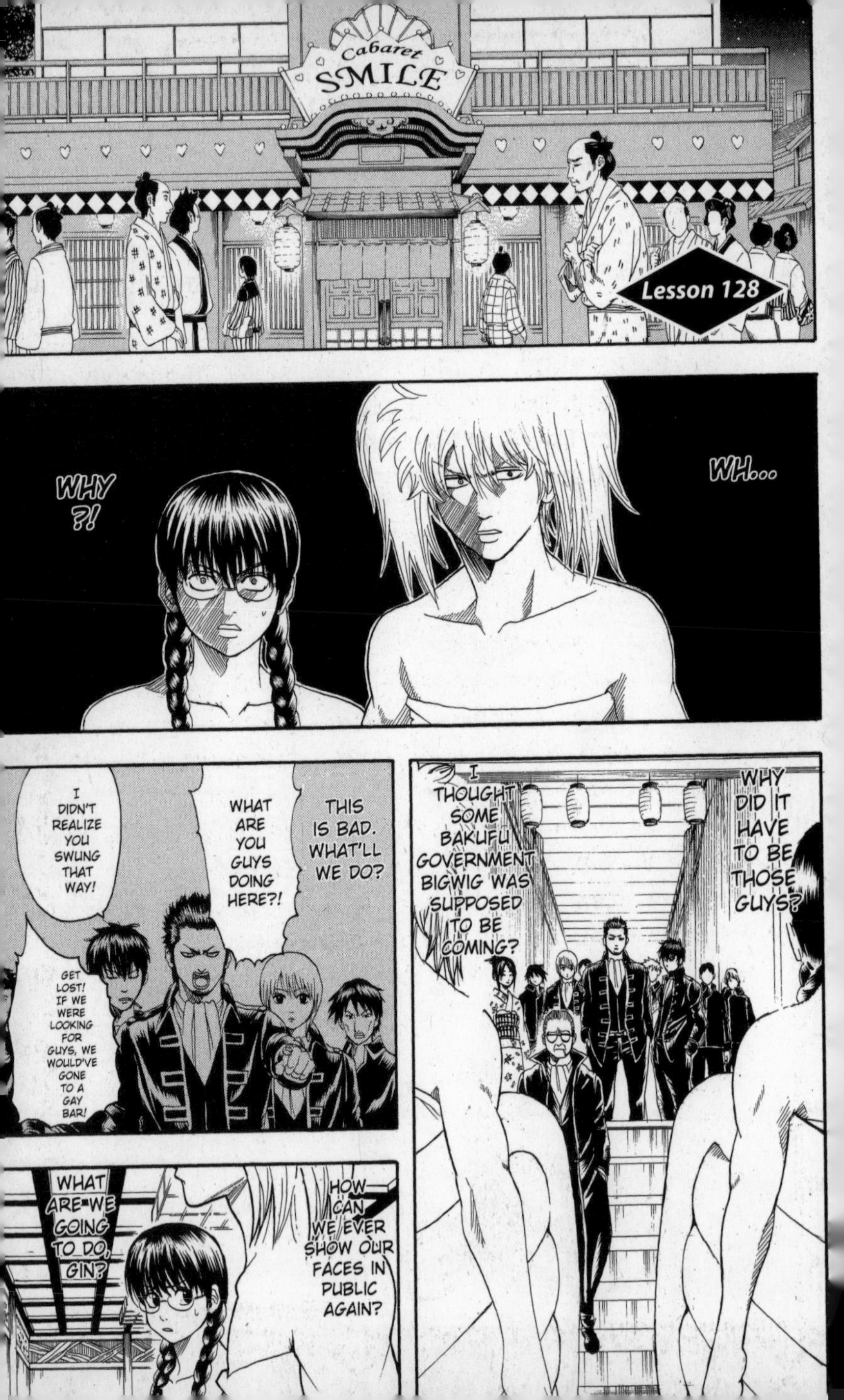
Cabaret SMILE
Lesson 128
WH...
WHY ?!
WHY DID IT HAVE TO BE THOSE GUYS?
I THOUGHT SOME BAKUFU GOVERNMENT BIGWIG WAS SUPPOSED TO BE COMING?
THIS IS BAD. WHAT'LL WE DO?
WHAT ARE YOU GUYS DOING HERE?!
I DIDN'T REALIZE YOU SWUNG THAT WAY!
GET LOST! IF WE WERE LOOKING FOR GUYS, WE WOULD'VE GONE TO A GAY BAR!
HOW CAN WE EVER SHOW OUR FACES IN PUBLIC AGAIN?
WHAT ARE WE GOING TO DO, GIN?

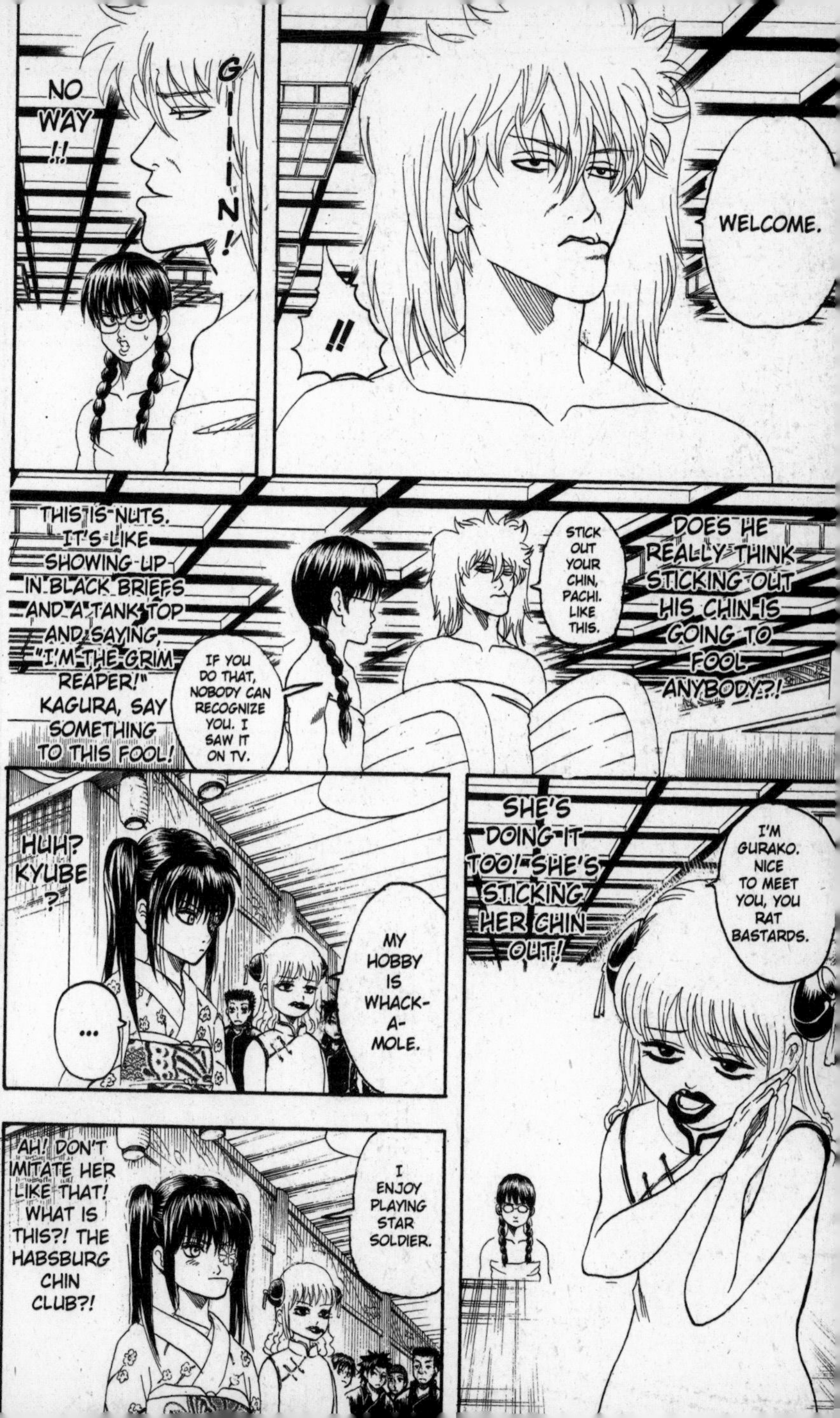
WELCOME.
!!
GIIIN!
NO WAY!!
DOES HE REALLY THINK STICKING OUT HIS CHIN IS GOING TO FOOL ANYBODY?!
STICK OUT YOUR CHIN, PACHI. LIKE THIS.
IF YOU DO THAT, NOBODY CAN RECOGNIZE YOU. I SAW IT ON TV.
THIS IS NUTS. IT'S LIKE SHOWING UP IN BLACK BRIEFS AND A TANK TOP AND SAYING, "I'M THE GRIM REAPER!" KAGURA, SAY SOMETHING TO THIS FOOL!
I'M GURAKO. NICE TO MEET YOU, YOU RAT BASTARDS.
SHE'S DOING IT TOO! SHE'S STICKING HER CHIN OUT!
MY HOBBY IS WHACK-A-MOLE.
...
HUH? KYUBE?
I ENJOY PLAYING STAR SOLDIER.
AH! DON'T IMITATE HER LIKE THAT! WHAT IS THIS?! THE HABSBURG CHIN CLUB?!

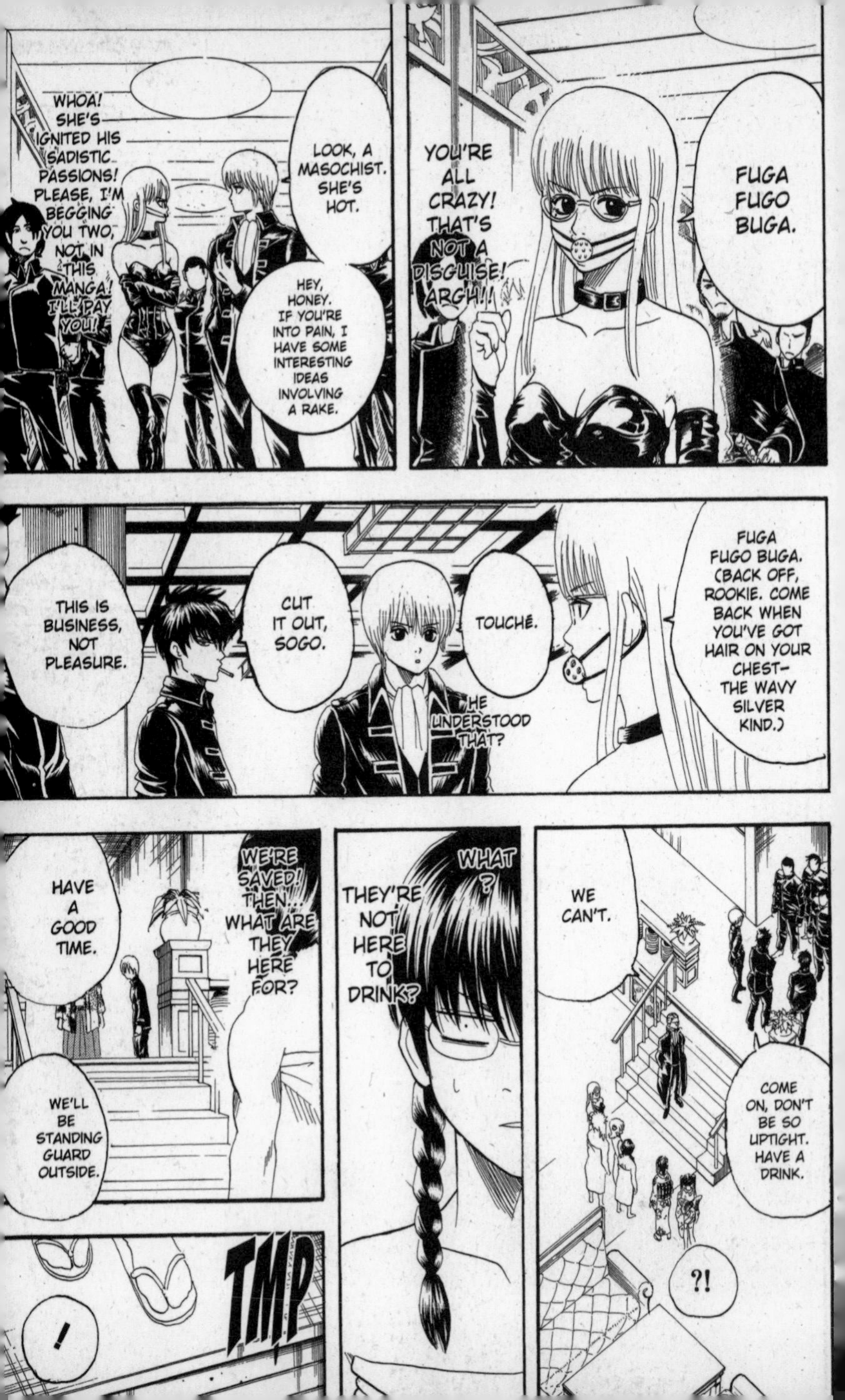
FUGA FUGO BUGA.
YOU'RE ALL CRAZY! THAT'S NOT A DISGUISE! ARGH!!
LOOK, A MASOCHIST. SHE'S HOT.
HEY, HONEY. IF YOU'RE INTO PAIN, I HAVE SOME INTERESTING IDEAS INVOLVING A RAKE.
WHOA! SHE'S IGNITED HIS SADISTIC PASSIONS! PLEASE, I'M BEGGING YOU TWO, NOT IN THIS MANGA! I'LL PAY YOU!
FUGA FUGO BUGA. (BACK OFF, ROOKIE. COME BACK WHEN YOU'VE GOT HAIR ON YOUR CHEST- THE WAVY SILVER KIND.)
TOUCHÉ.
HE UNDERSTOOD THAT?
CUT IT OUT, SOGO.
THIS IS BUSINESS, NOT PLEASURE.
WE CAN'T.
COME ON, DON'T BE SO UPTIGHT. HAVE A DRINK.
?!
WHAT ?
THEY'RE NOT HERE TO DRINK?
WE'RE SAVED! THEN... WHAT ARE THEY HERE FOR?
HAVE A GOOD TIME.
WE'LL BE STANDING GUARD OUTSIDE.
TMP
!

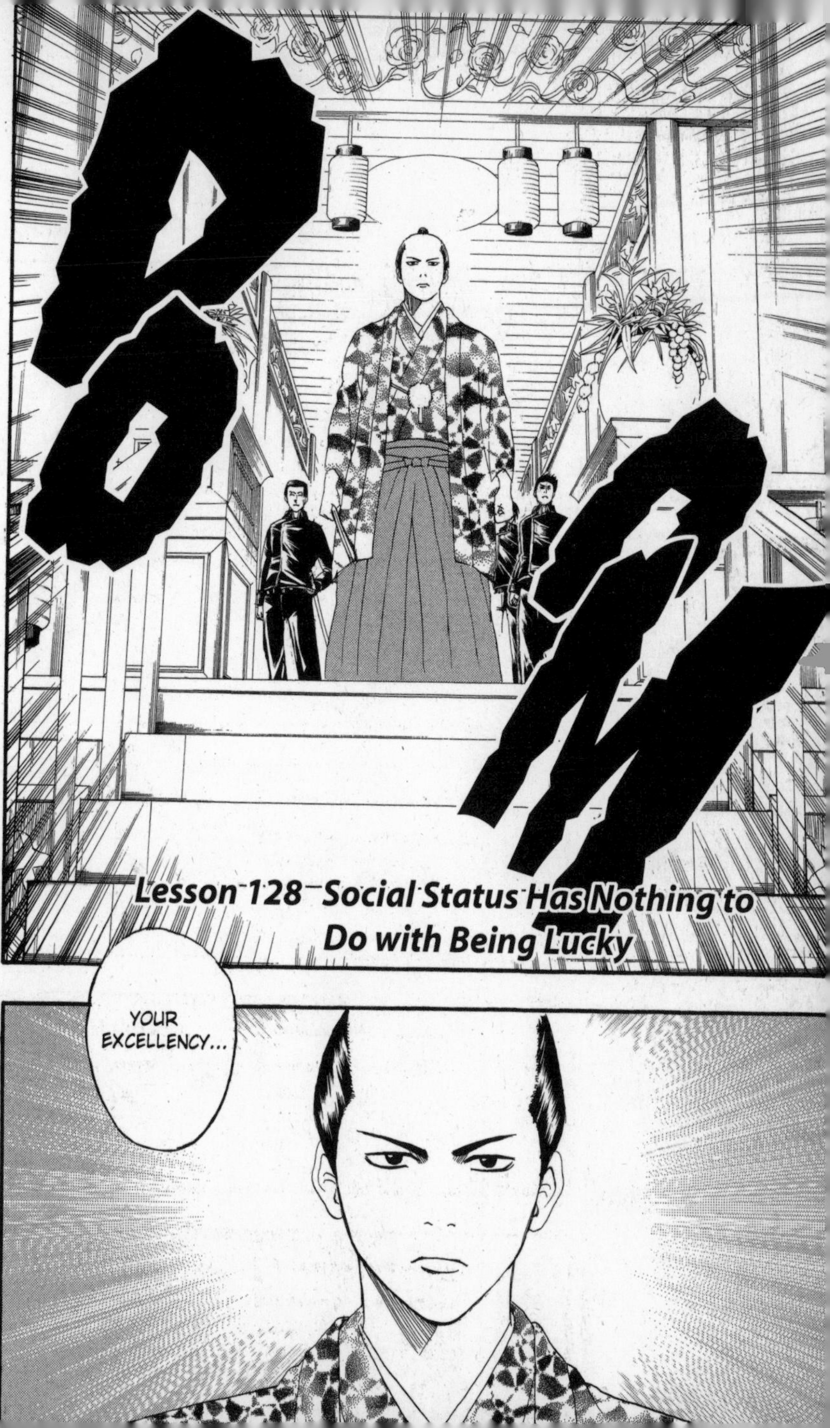
DOM
Lesson 128 Social Status Has Nothing to Do with Being Lucky
YOUR EXCELLENCY...

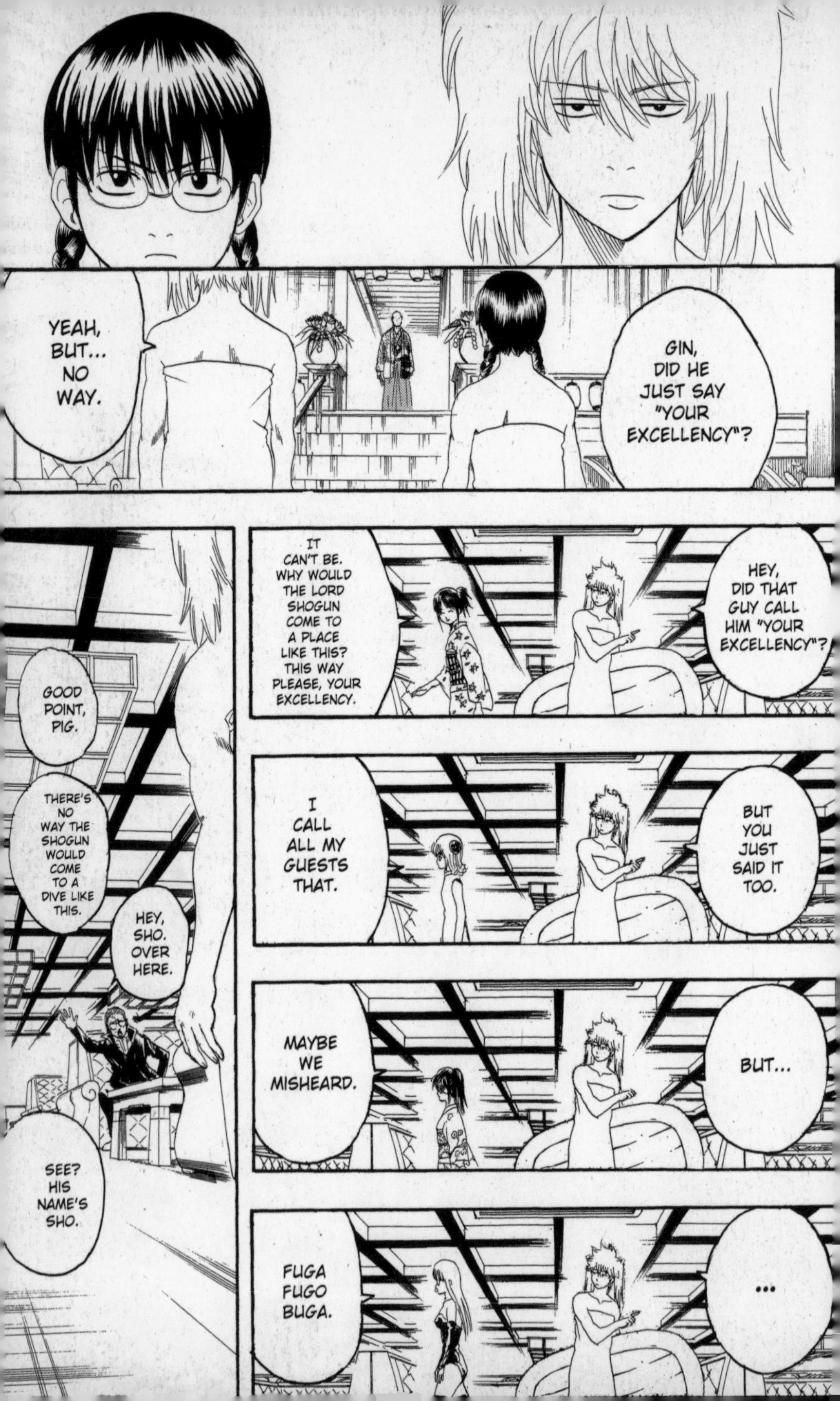
GIN, DID HE JUST SAY "YOUR EXCELLENCY"?
YEAH, BUT... NO WAY.
HEY, DID THAT GUY CALL HIM "YOUR EXCELLENCY"?
IT CAN'T BE. WHY WOULD THE LORD SHOGUN COME TO A PLACE LIKE THIS? THIS WAY PLEASE, YOUR EXCELLENCY.
BUT YOU JUST SAID IT TOO.
I CALL ALL MY GUESTS THAT.
BUT...
MAYBE WE MISHEARD.
...
FUGA FUGO BUGA.
GOOD POINT, PIG.
THERE'S NO WAY THE SHOGUN WOULD COME TO A DIVE LIKE THIS.
HEY, SHO. OVER HERE.
SEE? HIS NAME'S SHO.

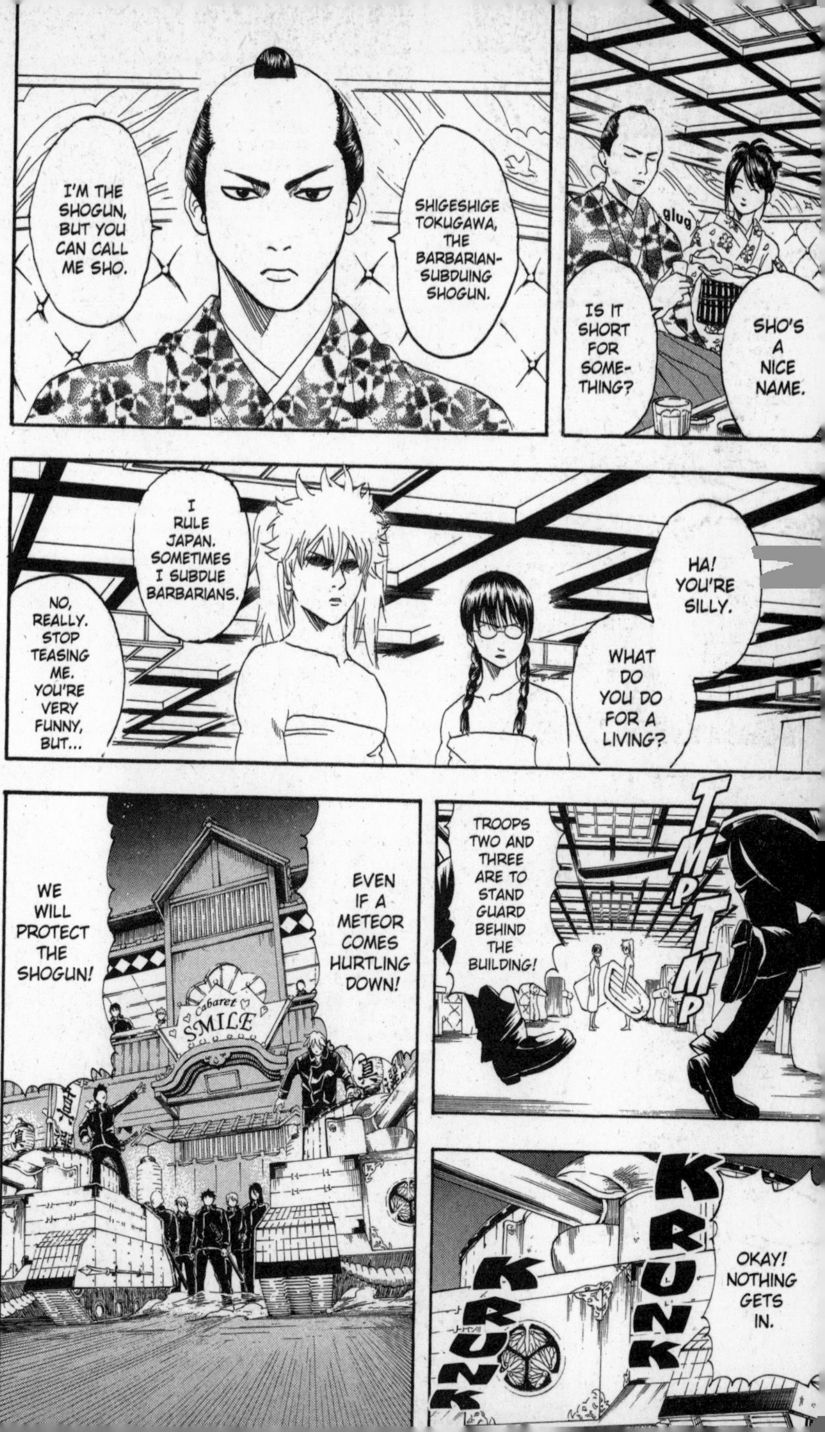
glug
SHO'S A NICE NAME.
IS IT SHORT FOR SOMETHING?
SHIGESHIGE TOKUGAWA, THE BARBARIAN-SUBDUING SHOGUN.
I'M THE SHOGUN, BUT YOU CAN CALL ME SHO.
HA! YOU'RE SILLY.
WHAT DO YOU DO FOR A LIVING?
I RULE JAPAN. SOMETIMES I SUBDUE BARBARIANS.
NO, REALLY. STOP TEASING ME. YOU'RE VERY FUNNY, BUT...
TMP TMP
TROOPS TWO AND THREE ARE TO STAND GUARD BEHIND THE BUILDING!
KRUNK KRUNK
OKAY! NOTHING GETS IN.
Cabaret SMILE
EVEN IF A METEOR COMES HURTLING DOWN!
WE WILL PROTECT THE SHOGUN!

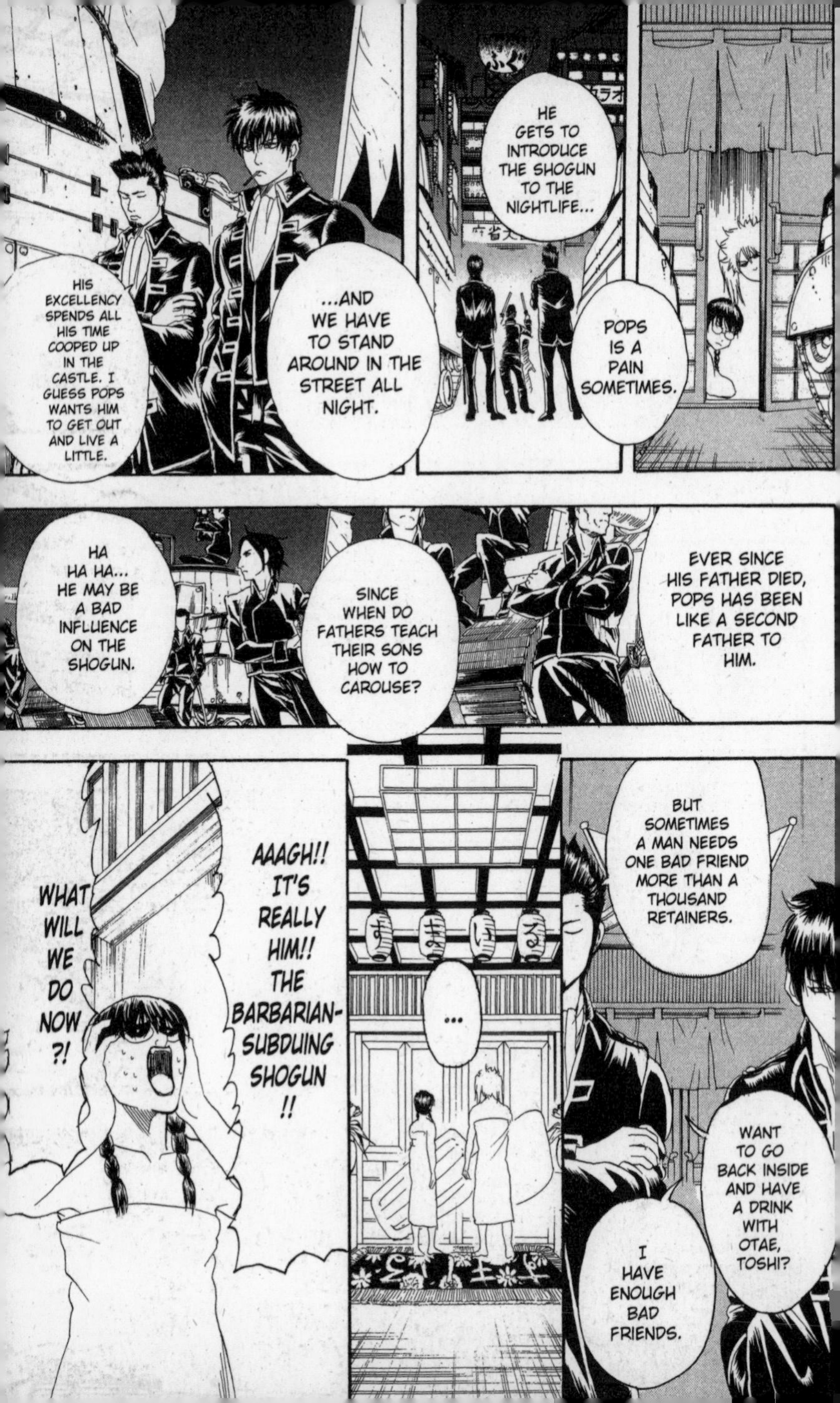
HE GETS TO INTRODUCE THE SHOGUN TO THE NIGHTLIFE...
POPS IS A PAIN SOMETIMES.
...AND WE HAVE TO STAND AROUND IN THE STREET ALL NIGHT.
HIS EXCELLENCY SPENDS ALL HIS TIME COOPED UP IN THE CASTLE. I GUESS POPS WANTS HIM TO GET OUT AND LIVE A LITTLE.
EVER SINCE HIS FATHER DIED, POPS HAS BEEN LIKE A SECOND FATHER TO HIM.
SINCE WHEN DO FATHERS TEACH THEIR SONS HOW TO CAROUSE?
HA HA HA... HE MAY BE A BAD INFLUENCE ON THE SHOGUN.
BUT SOMETIMES A MAN NEEDS ONE BAD FRIEND MORE THAN A THOUSAND RETAINERS.
WANT TO GO BACK INSIDE AND HAVE A DRINK WITH OTAE, TOSHI?
I HAVE ENOUGH BAD FRIENDS.
すまいる
...
AAAGH!! IT'S REALLY HIM!! THE BARBARIAN-SUBDUING SHOGUN!!
WHAT WILL WE DO NOW?!

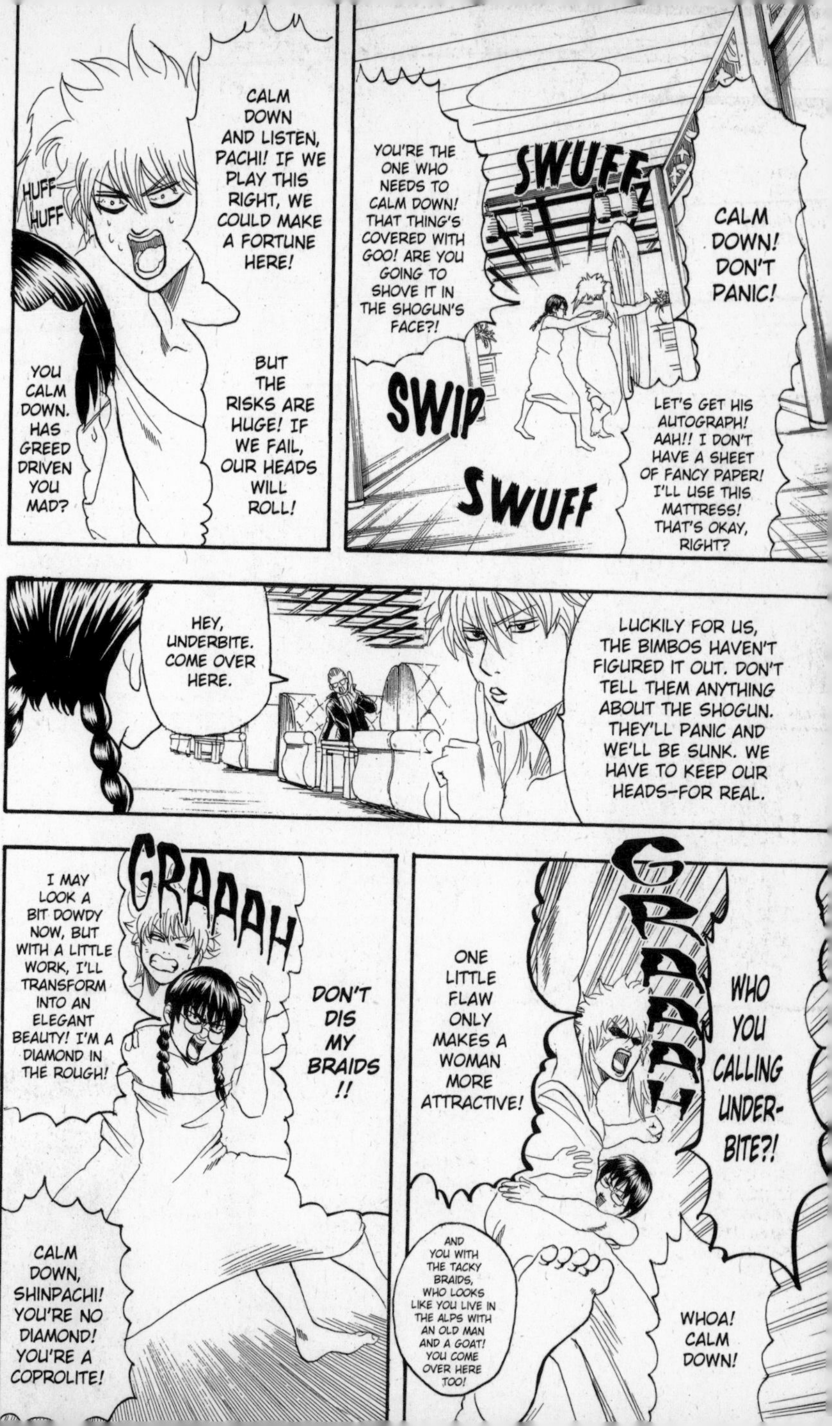
CALM DOWN! DON'T PANIC!
SWUFF
YOU'RE THE ONE WHO NEEDS TO CALM DOWN! THAT THING'S COVERED WITH GOO! ARE YOU GOING TO SHOVE IT IN THE SHOGUN'S FACE?!
LET'S GET HIS AUTOGRAPH! AAH!! I DON'T HAVE A SHEET OF FANCY PAPER! I'LL USE THIS MATTRESS! THAT'S OKAY, RIGHT?
SWIP
SWUFF
CALM DOWN AND LISTEN, PACHI! IF WE PLAY THIS RIGHT, WE COULD MAKE A FORTUNE HERE!
HUFF HUFF
BUT THE RISKS ARE HUGE! IF WE FAIL, OUR HEADS WILL ROLL!
YOU CALM DOWN. HAS GREED DRIVEN YOU MAD?
LUCKILY FOR US, THE BIMBOS HAVEN'T FIGURED IT OUT. DON'T TELL THEM ANYTHING ABOUT THE SHOGUN. THEY'LL PANIC AND WE'LL BE SUNK. WE HAVE TO KEEP OUR HEADS—FOR REAL.
HEY, UNDERBITE. COME OVER HERE.
GRAAAH
WHO YOU CALLING UNDER-BITE?!
ONE LITTLE FLAW ONLY MAKES A WOMAN MORE ATTRACTIVE!
WHOA! CALM DOWN!
AND YOU WITH THE TACKY BRAIDS, WHO LOOKS LIKE YOU LIVE IN THE ALPS WITH AN OLD MAN AND A GOAT! YOU COME OVER HERE TOO!
GRAAAH
DON'T DIS MY BRAIDS !!
I MAY LOOK A BIT DOWDY NOW, BUT WITH A LITTLE WORK, I'LL TRANSFORM INTO AN ELEGANT BEAUTY! I'M A DIAMOND IN THE ROUGH!
CALM DOWN, SHINPACHI! YOU'RE NO DIAMOND! YOU'RE A COPROLITE!

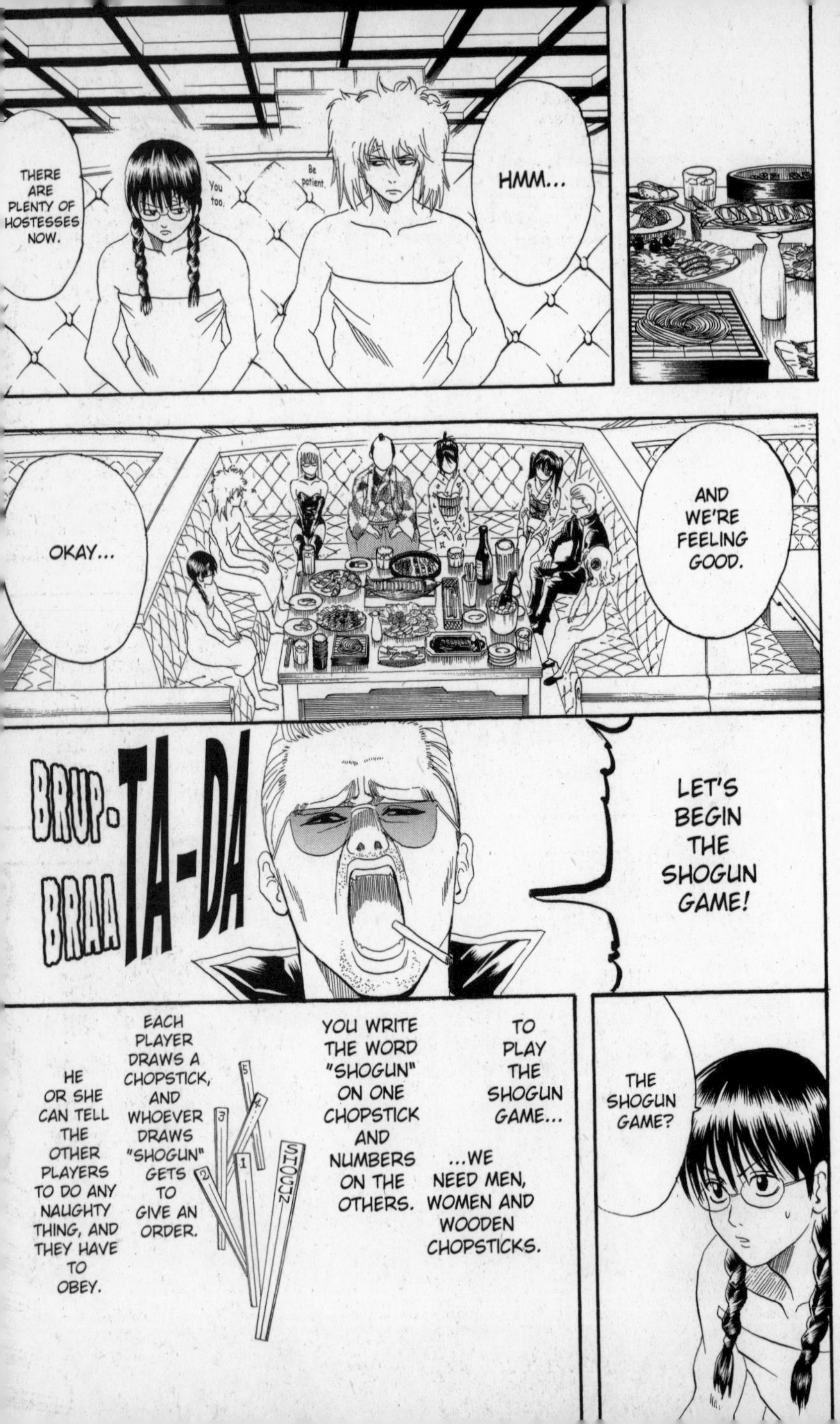
HMM...
Be patient.
You too.
THERE ARE PLENTY OF HOSTESSES NOW.
AND WE'RE FEELING GOOD.
OKAY...
LET'S BEGIN THE SHOGUN GAME!
BRUP-BRAA TA-DA
THE SHOGUN GAME?
TO PLAY THE SHOGUN GAME...
...WE NEED MEN, WOMEN AND WOODEN CHOPSTICKS.
YOU WRITE THE WORD "SHOGUN" ON ONE CHOPSTICK AND NUMBERS ON THE OTHERS.
EACH PLAYER DRAWS A CHOPSTICK, AND WHOEVER DRAWS "SHOGUN" GETS TO GIVE AN ORDER.
HE OR SHE CAN TELL THE OTHER PLAYERS TO DO ANY NAUGHTY THING, AND THEY HAVE TO OBEY.

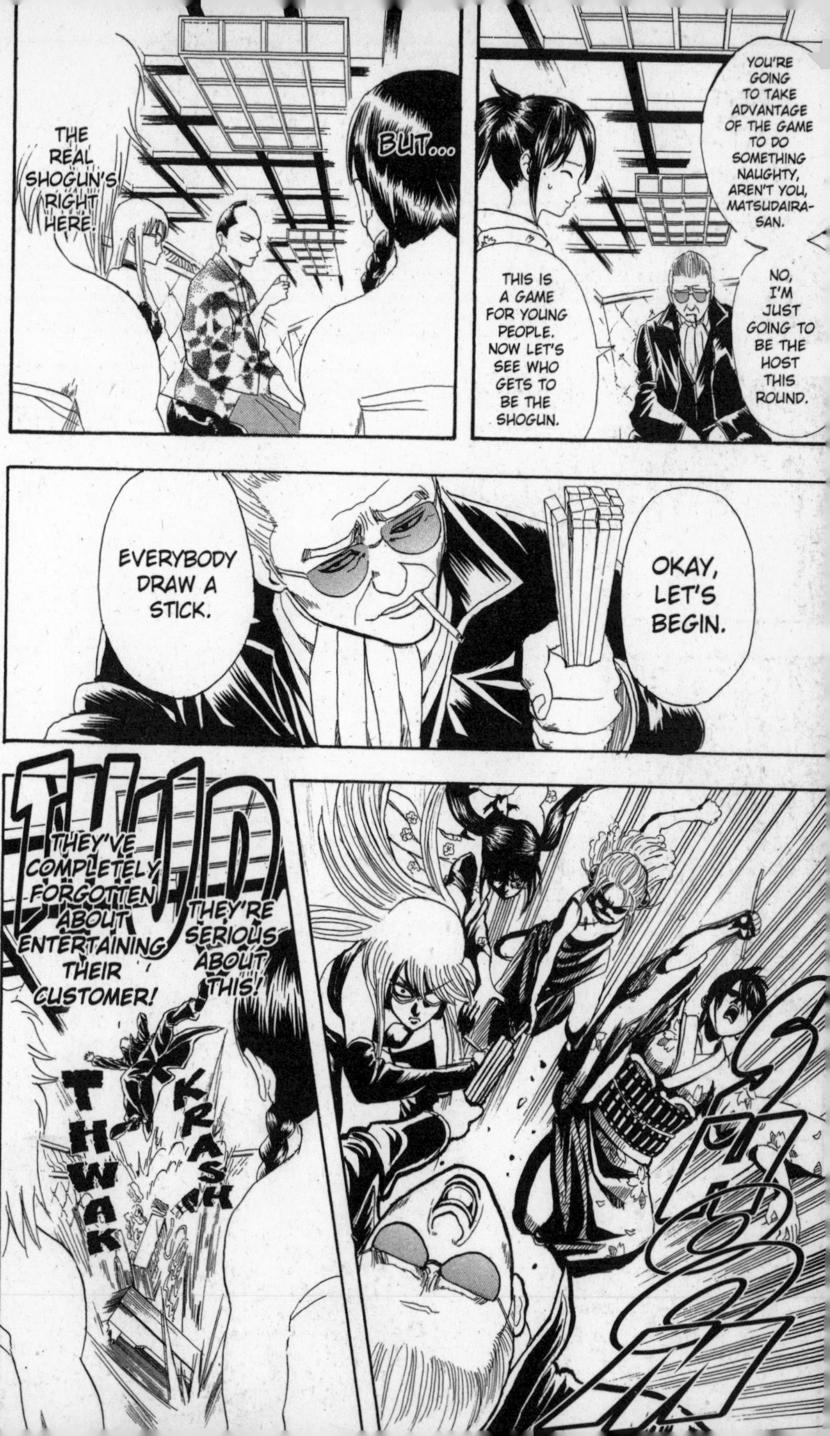
YOU'RE GOING TO TAKE ADVANTAGE OF THE GAME TO DO SOMETHING NAUGHTY, AREN'T YOU, MATSUDAIRA-SAN.
NO, I'M JUST GOING TO BE THE HOST THIS ROUND.
THIS IS A GAME FOR YOUNG PEOPLE. NOW LET'S SEE WHO GETS TO BE THE SHOGUN.
BUT...
THE REAL SHOGUN'S RIGHT HERE.
OKAY, LET'S BEGIN.
EVERYBODY DRAW A STICK.
THUD
THEY'RE SERIOUS ABOUT THIS!
THEY'VE COMPLETELY FORGOTTEN ABOUT ENTERTAINING THEIR CUSTOMER!
KRASH
THWAK

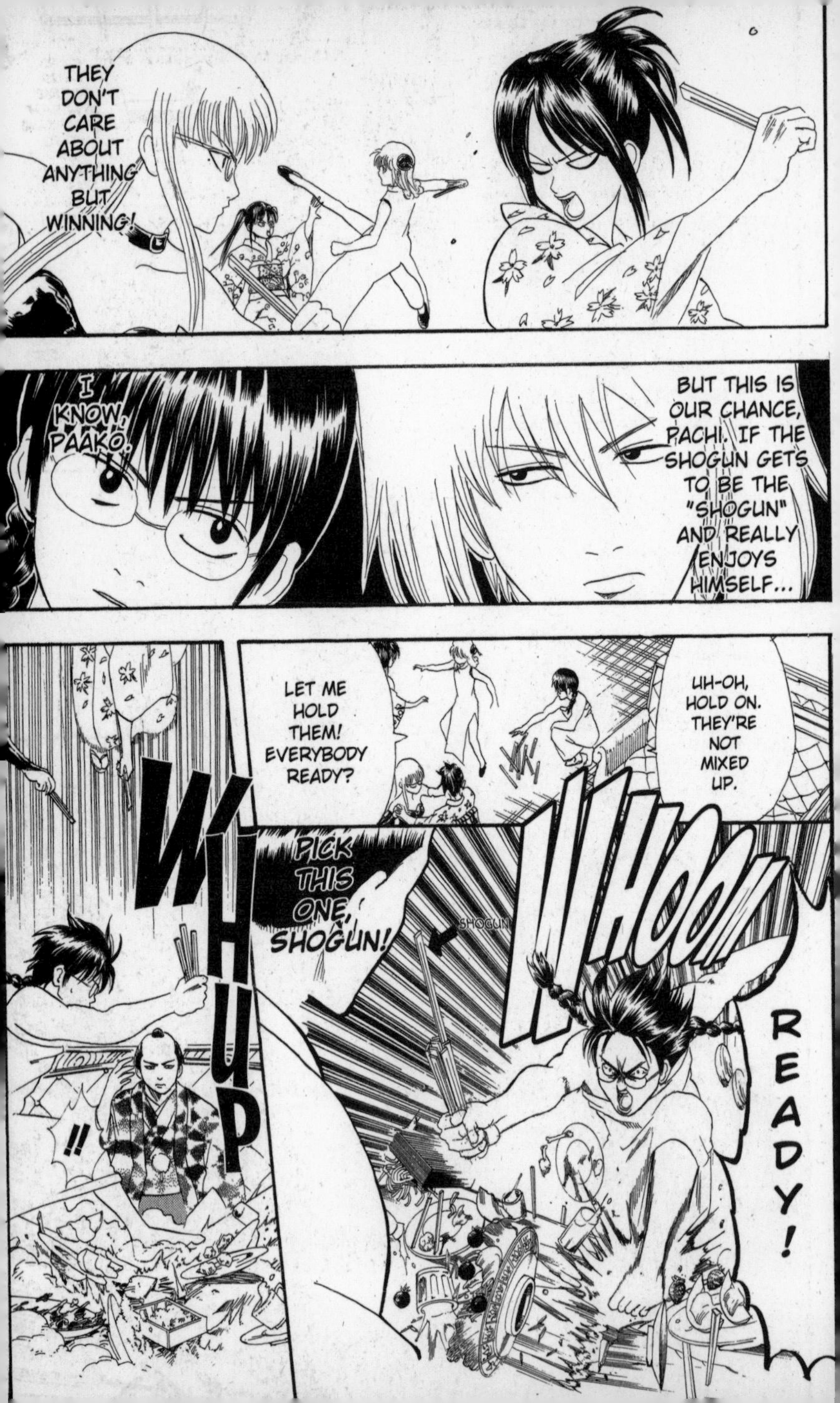
THEY DON'T CARE ABOUT ANYTHING BUT WINNING!
BUT THIS IS OUR CHANCE, PACHI. IF THE SHOGUN GETS TO BE THE "SHOGUN" AND REALLY ENJOYS HIMSELF...
I KNOW, PAAKO.
UH-OH, HOLD ON. THEY'RE NOT MIXED UP.
LET ME HOLD THEM! EVERYBODY READY?
READY!
WHOOM
SHOGUN
PICK THIS ONE, SHOGUN!
WHUP
!!

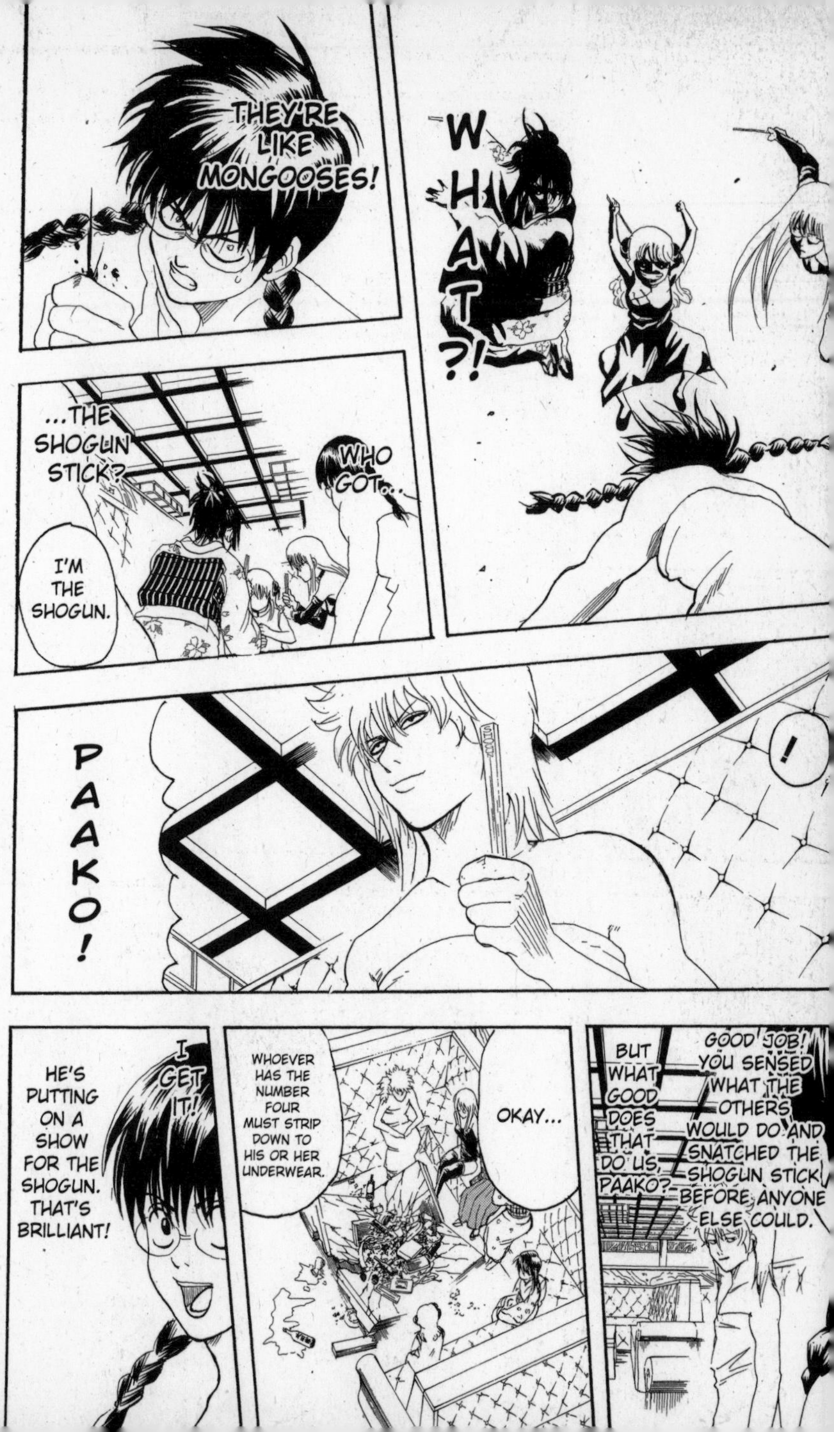
WHAT?!
THEY'RE LIKE MONGOOSES!
WHO GOT...
...THE SHOGUN STICK?
I'M THE SHOGUN.
!
PAAKO!
GOOD JOB! YOU SENSED WHAT THE OTHERS WOULD DO AND SNATCHED THE SHOGUN STICK BEFORE ANYONE ELSE COULD.
BUT WHAT GOOD DOES THAT DO US, PAAKO?
OKAY...
WHOEVER HAS THE NUMBER FOUR MUST STRIP DOWN TO HIS OR HER UNDERWEAR.
I GET IT!
HE'S PUTTING ON A SHOW FOR THE SHOGUN. THAT'S BRILLIANT!

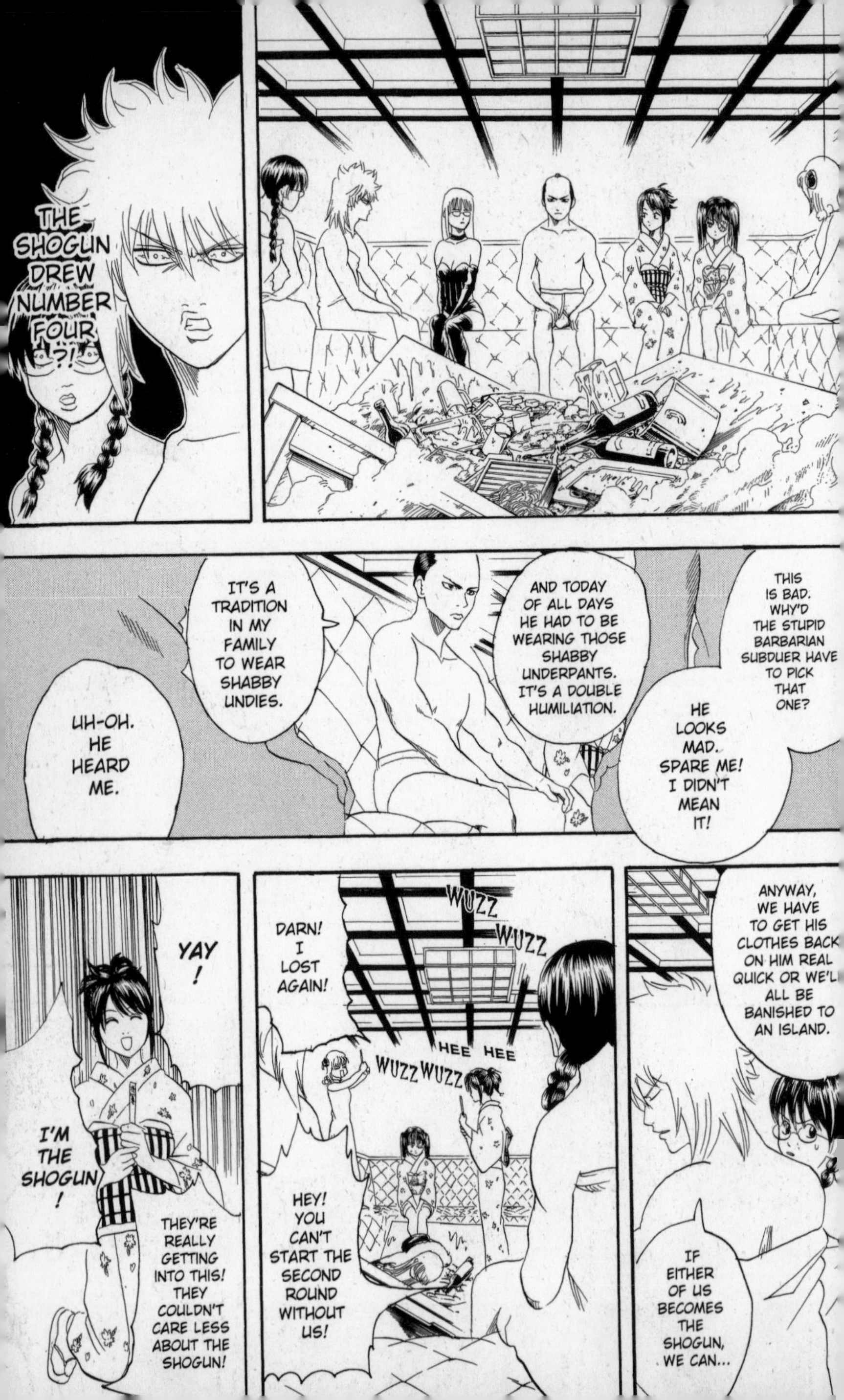
THE SHOGUN DREW NUMBER FOUR ?!
THIS IS BAD. WHY'D THE STUPID BARBARIAN SUBDUER HAVE TO PICK THAT ONE?
HE LOOKS MAD. SPARE ME! I DIDN'T MEAN IT!
AND TODAY OF ALL DAYS HE HAD TO BE WEARING THOSE SHABBY UNDERPANTS. IT'S A DOUBLE HUMILIATION.
IT'S A TRADITION IN MY FAMILY TO WEAR SHABBY UNDIES.
UH-OH. HE HEARD ME.
ANYWAY, WE HAVE TO GET HIS CLOTHES BACK ON HIM REAL QUICK OR WE'LL ALL BE BANISHED TO AN ISLAND.
IF EITHER OF US BECOMES THE SHOGUN, WE CAN...
WUZZ
WUZZ
DARN! I LOST AGAIN!
HEE HEE
WUZZ WUZZ
HEY! YOU CAN'T START THE SECOND ROUND WITHOUT US!
YAY!
I'M THE SHOGUN!
THEY'RE REALLY GETTING INTO THIS! THEY COULDN'T CARE LESS ABOUT THE SHOGUN!

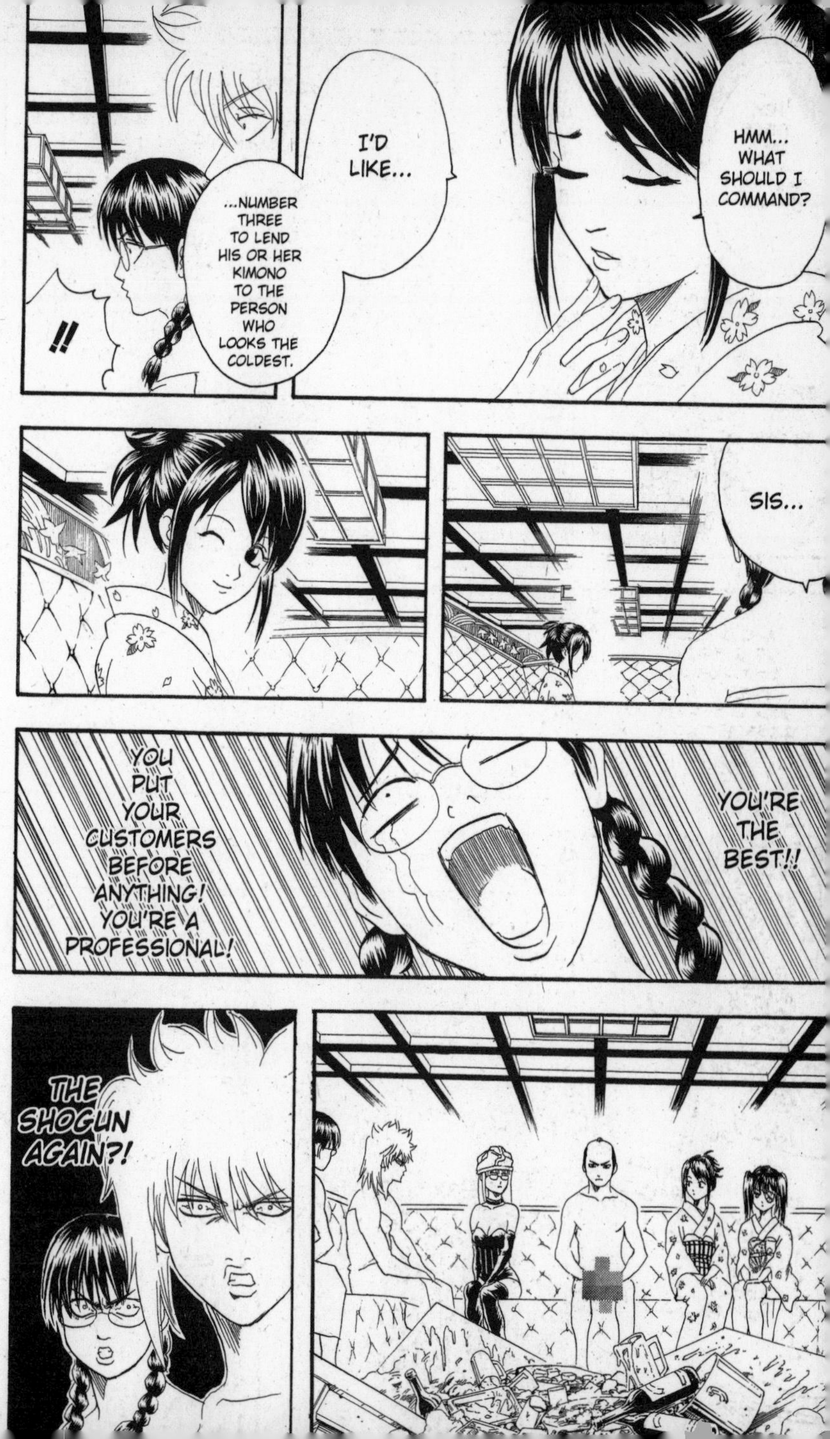
HMM... WHAT SHOULD I COMMAND?
I'D LIKE...
...NUMBER THREE TO LEND HIS OR HER KIMONO TO THE PERSON WHO LOOKS THE COLDEST.
!!
SIS...
YOU'RE THE BEST!!
YOU PUT YOUR CUSTOMERS BEFORE ANYTHING! YOU'RE A PROFESSIONAL!
THE SHOGUN AGAIN?!

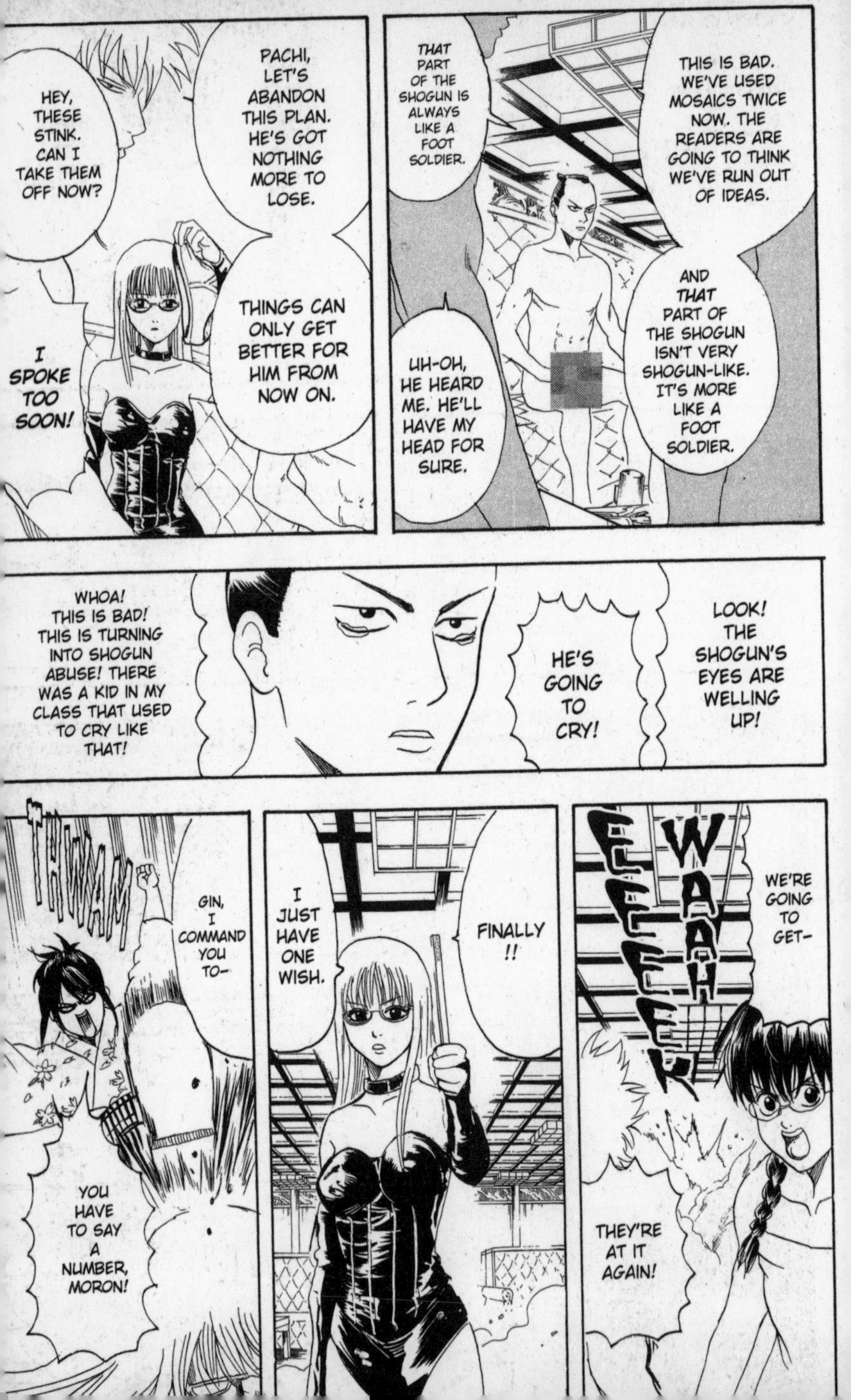
THIS IS BAD. WE'VE USED MOSAICS TWICE NOW. THE READERS ARE GOING TO THINK WE'VE RUN OUT OF IDEAS.
THAT PART OF THE SHOGUN IS ALWAYS LIKE A FOOT SOLDIER.
AND THAT PART OF THE SHOGUN ISN'T VERY SHOGUN-LIKE. IT'S MORE LIKE A FOOT SOLDIER.
UH-OH, HE HEARD ME. HE'LL HAVE MY HEAD FOR SURE.
PACHI, LET'S ABANDON THIS PLAN. HE'S GOT NOTHING MORE TO LOSE.
HEY, THESE STINK. CAN I TAKE THEM OFF NOW?
THINGS CAN ONLY GET BETTER FOR HIM FROM NOW ON.
I SPOKE TOO SOON!
LOOK! THE SHOGUN'S EYES ARE WELLING UP!
HE'S GOING TO CRY!
WHOA! THIS IS BAD! THIS IS TURNING INTO SHOGUN ABUSE! THERE WAS A KID IN MY CLASS THAT USED TO CRY LIKE THAT!
WE'RE GOING TO GET-
WAAH
EEEEEEK
THEY'RE AT IT AGAIN!
FINALLY!!
I JUST HAVE ONE WISH.
GIN, I COMMAND YOU TO-
THWAM
YOU HAVE TO SAY A NUMBER, MORON!

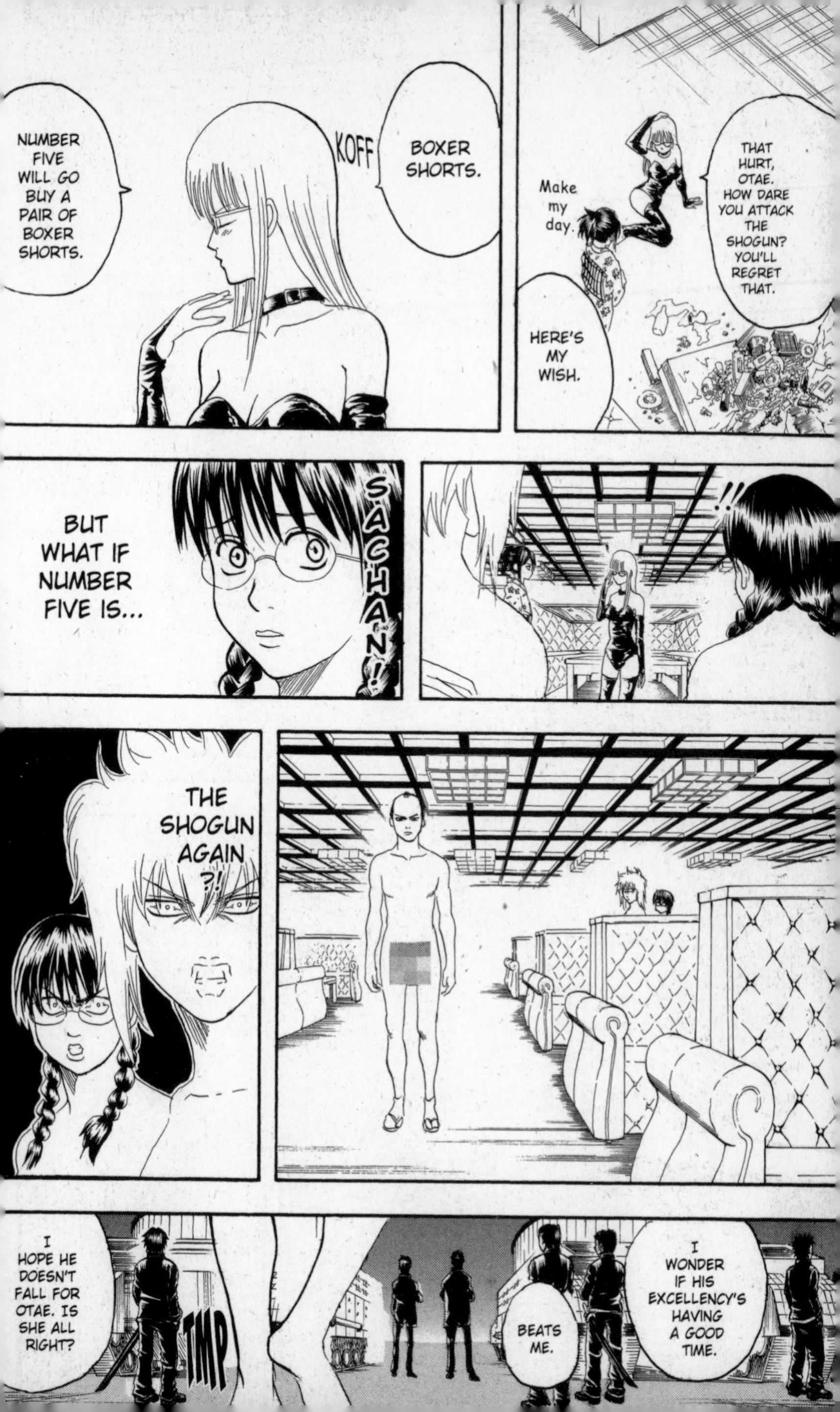
THAT HURT, OTAE. HOW DARE YOU ATTACK THE SHOGUN? YOU'LL REGRET THAT.
Make my day.
HERE'S MY WISH.
BOXER SHORTS.
KOFF
NUMBER FIVE WILL GO BUY A PAIR OF BOXER SHORTS.
!!
SACHAN!
BUT WHAT IF NUMBER FIVE IS...
THE SHOGUN AGAIN?!
I WONDER IF HIS EXCELLENCY'S HAVING A GOOD TIME.
BEATS ME.
TMP
I HOPE HE DOESN'T FALL FOR OTAE. IS SHE ALL RIGHT?

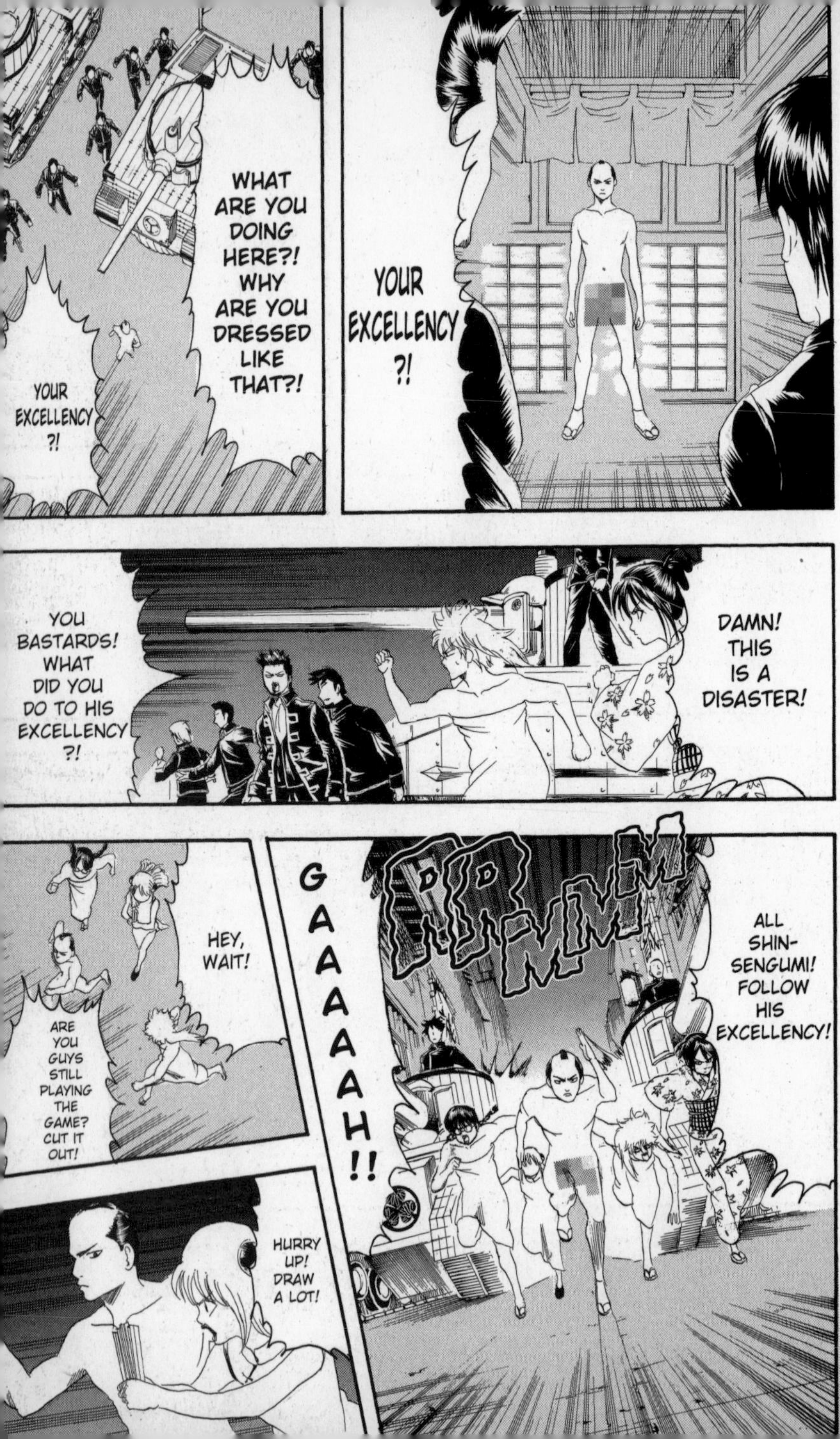
YOUR EXCELLENCY ?!
WHAT ARE YOU DOING HERE?! WHY ARE YOU DRESSED LIKE THAT?!
YOUR EXCELLENCY ?!
DAMN! THIS IS A DISASTER!
YOU BASTARDS! WHAT DID YOU DO TO HIS EXCELLENCY ?!
ALL SHIN-SENGUMI! FOLLOW HIS EXCELLENCY!
RRMMM
GAAAAAH!!
HEY, WAIT!
ARE YOU GUYS STILL PLAYING THE GAME? CUT IT OUT!
HURRY UP! DRAW A LOT!

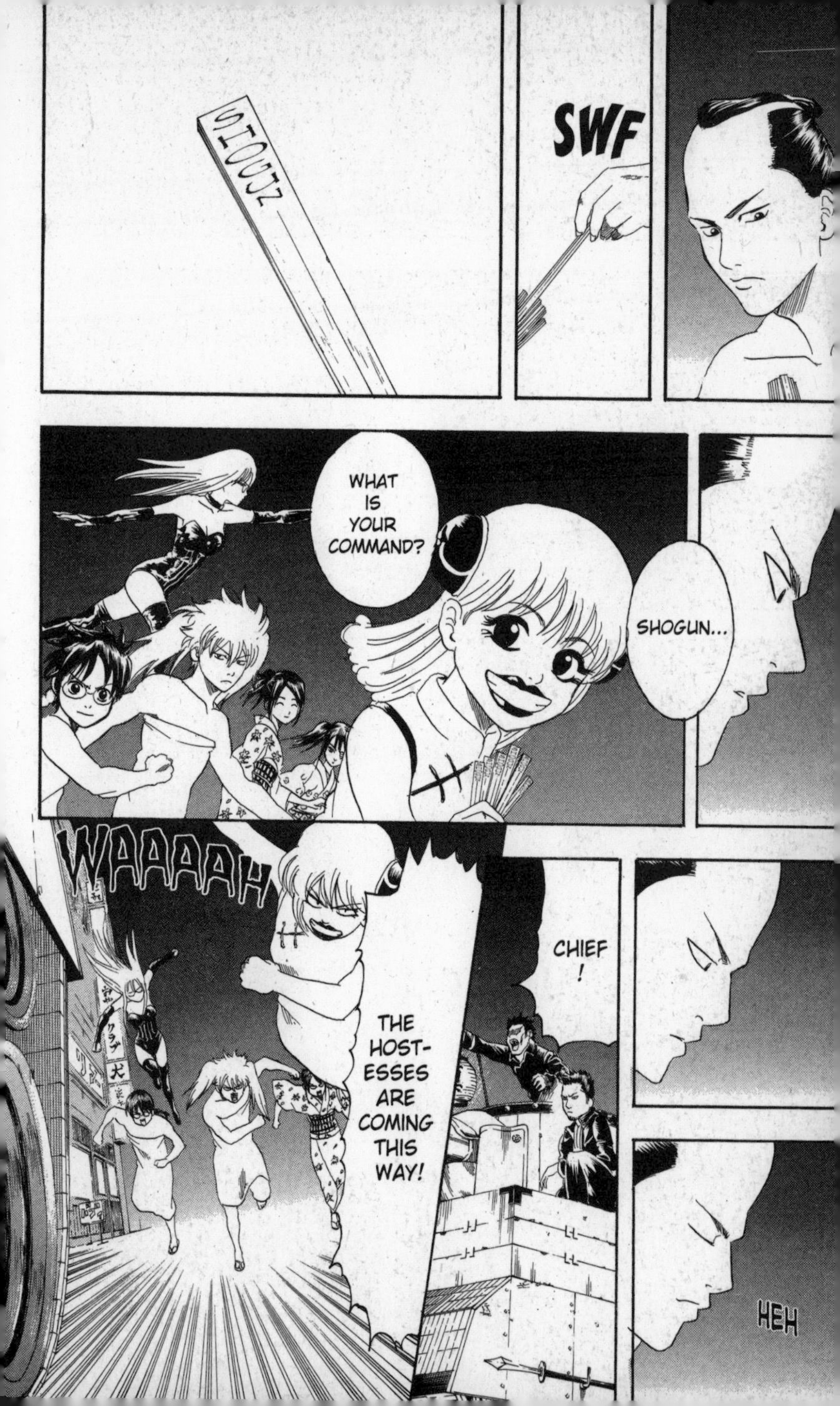
SWF
SHOGUN...
WHAT IS YOUR COMMAND?
HEH
CHIEF!
THE HOST-ESSES ARE COMING THIS WAY!
WAAAAH

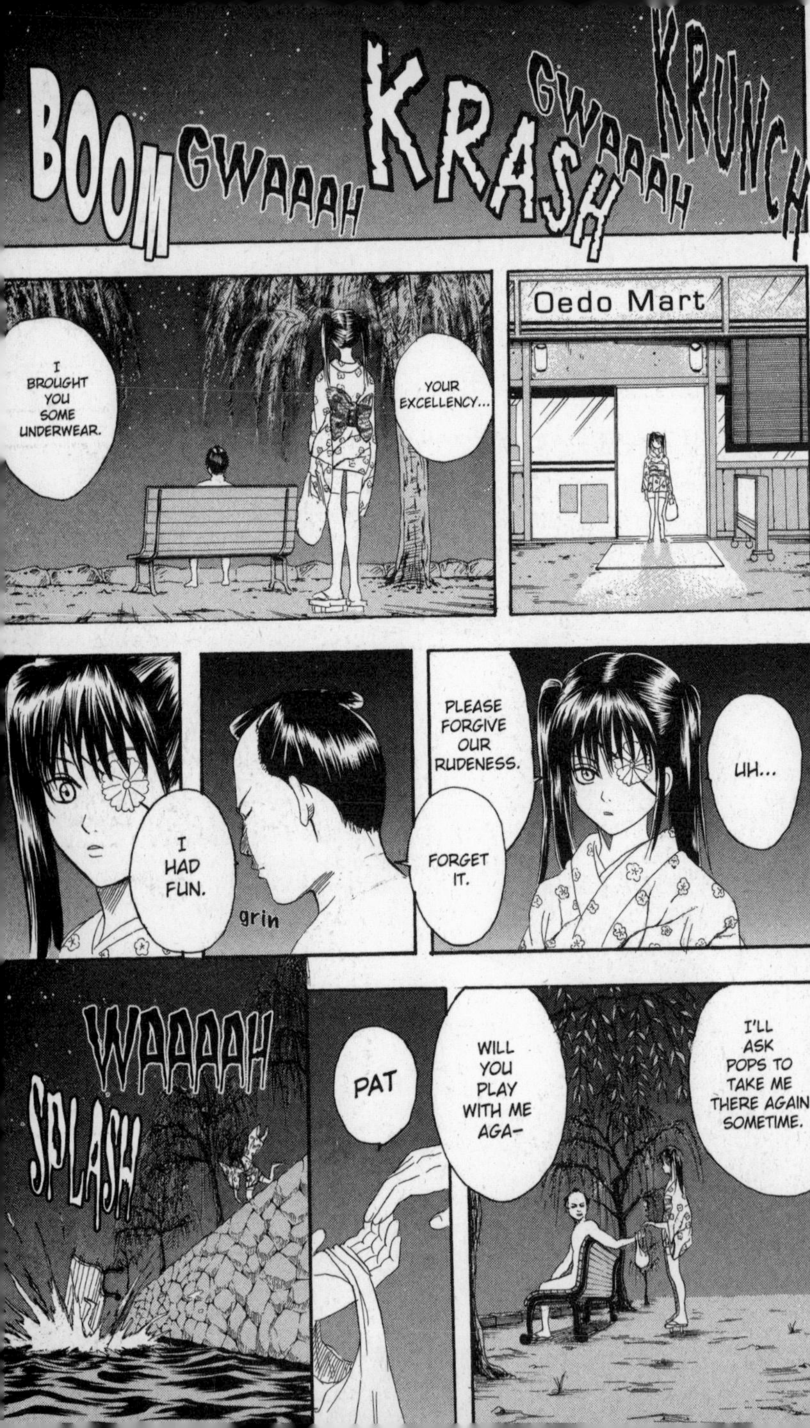
KRUNCH
GWAAAH
KRASH
GWAAAH
BOOM
Oedo Mart
YOUR EXCELLENCY...
I BROUGHT YOU SOME UNDERWEAR.
UH...
PLEASE FORGIVE OUR RUDENESS.
FORGET IT.
I HAD FUN.
grin
I'LL ASK POPS TO TAKE ME THERE AGAIN SOMETIME.
WILL YOU PLAY WITH ME AGA-
PAT
WAAAAH
SPLASH

\<Question from Anonymous\>

Teach me how to draw the faces of the yorozuya members!

\<Answer\>

I've already explained how to draw Gin, so this time I'll show you how to draw Shinpachi and Kagura.

Shinpachi

Draw an ordinary person's face however you like. Make it as boring as possible.

Give him a pair of glasses. There! That's it.

Kagura

Draw Shinpachi's face without glasses and with white hair.

Add dumplings. There! That's it.

Most of the characters are drawn using Shinpachi's face as a base. If you master Shinpachi's face, you can draw lots of characters! Now let's all Shinpachi!

(Q&A #46 is on page 166)

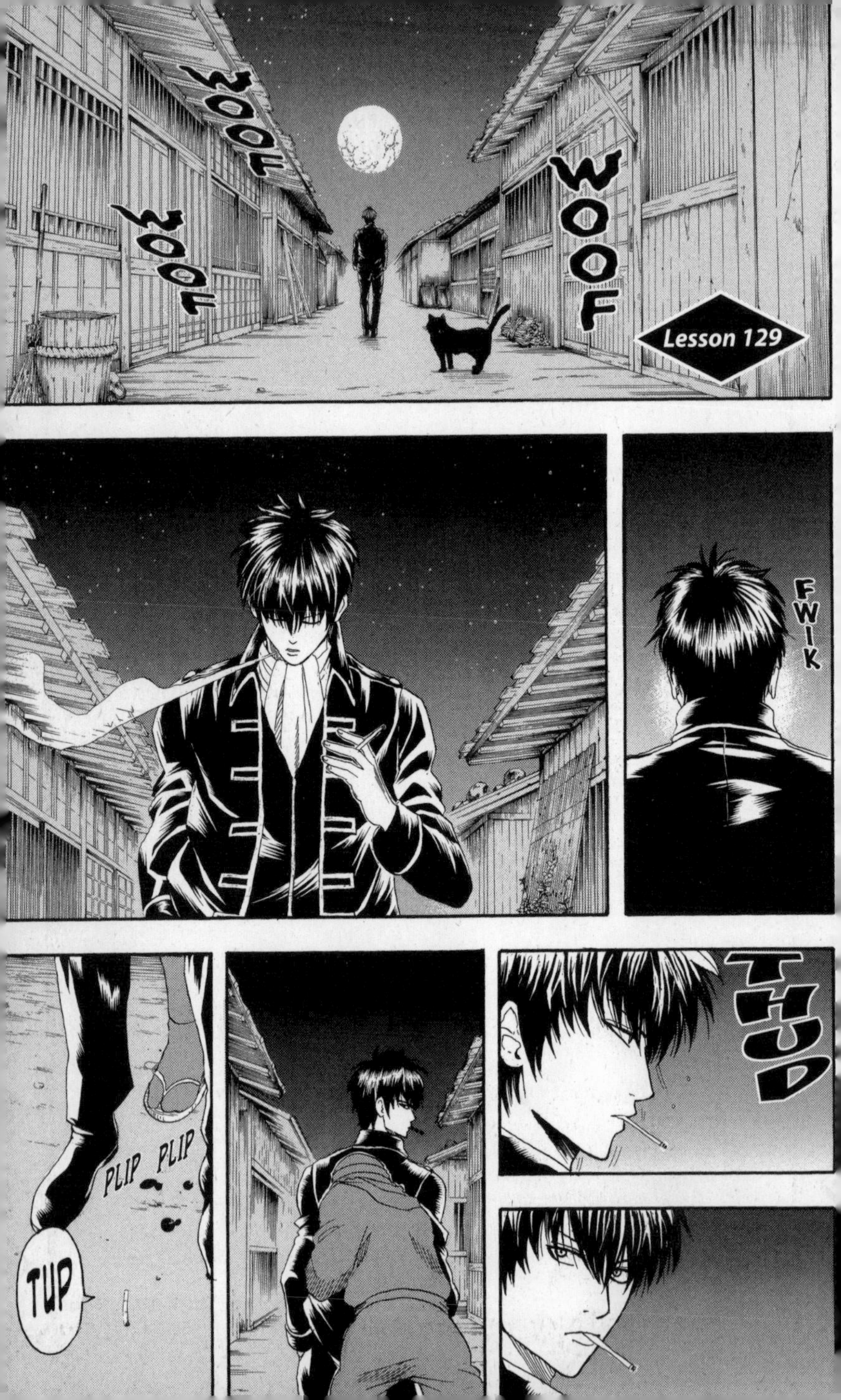
WOOF WOOF
WOOF WOOF
Lesson 129
FWIK
THUD
PLIP PLIP
TUP

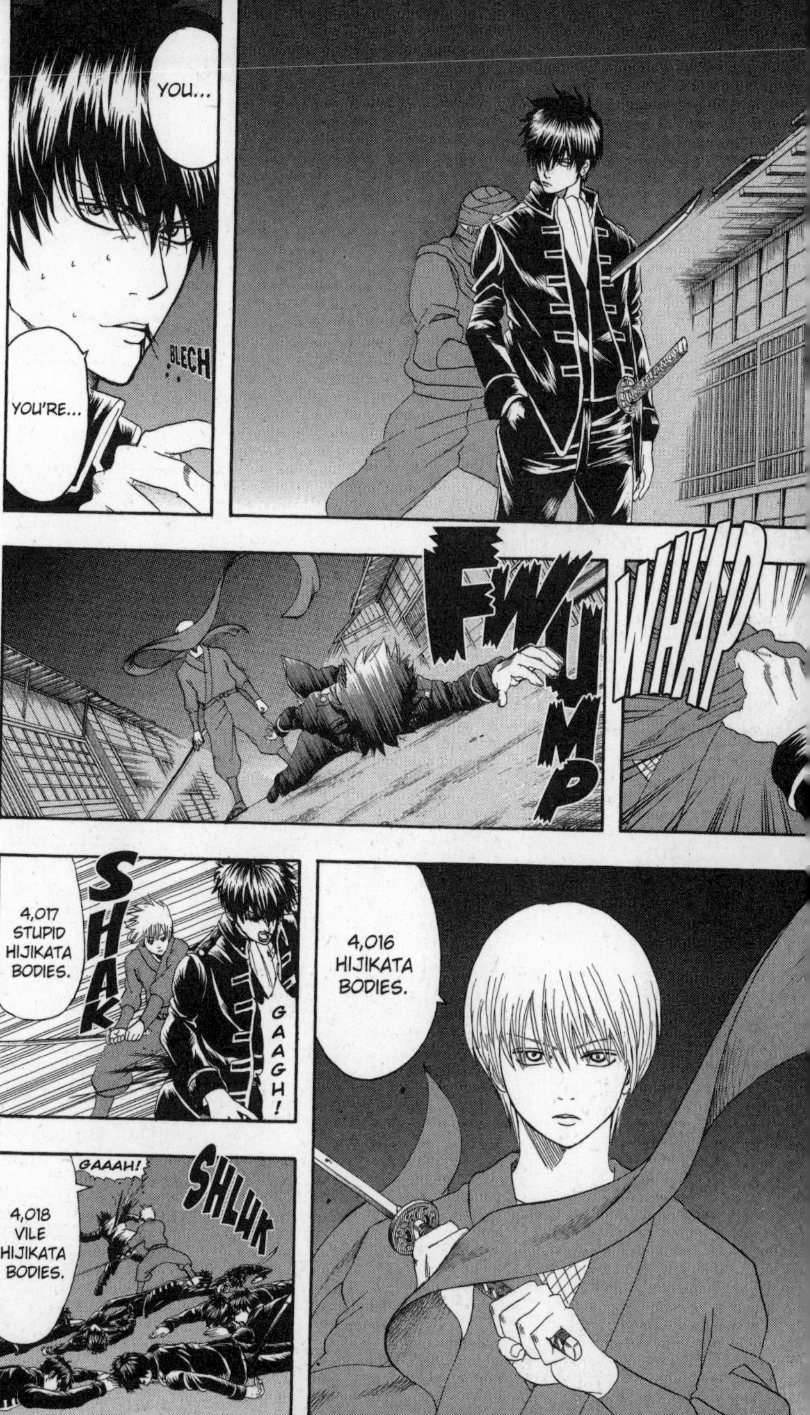
YOU...
BLECH
YOU'RE...
WHAP
FWUMP
4,016 HIJIKATA BODIES.
SHAK
4,017 STUPID HIJIKATA BODIES.
GAAGH!
SHLUK
GAAAH!
4,018 VILE HIJIKATA BODIES.

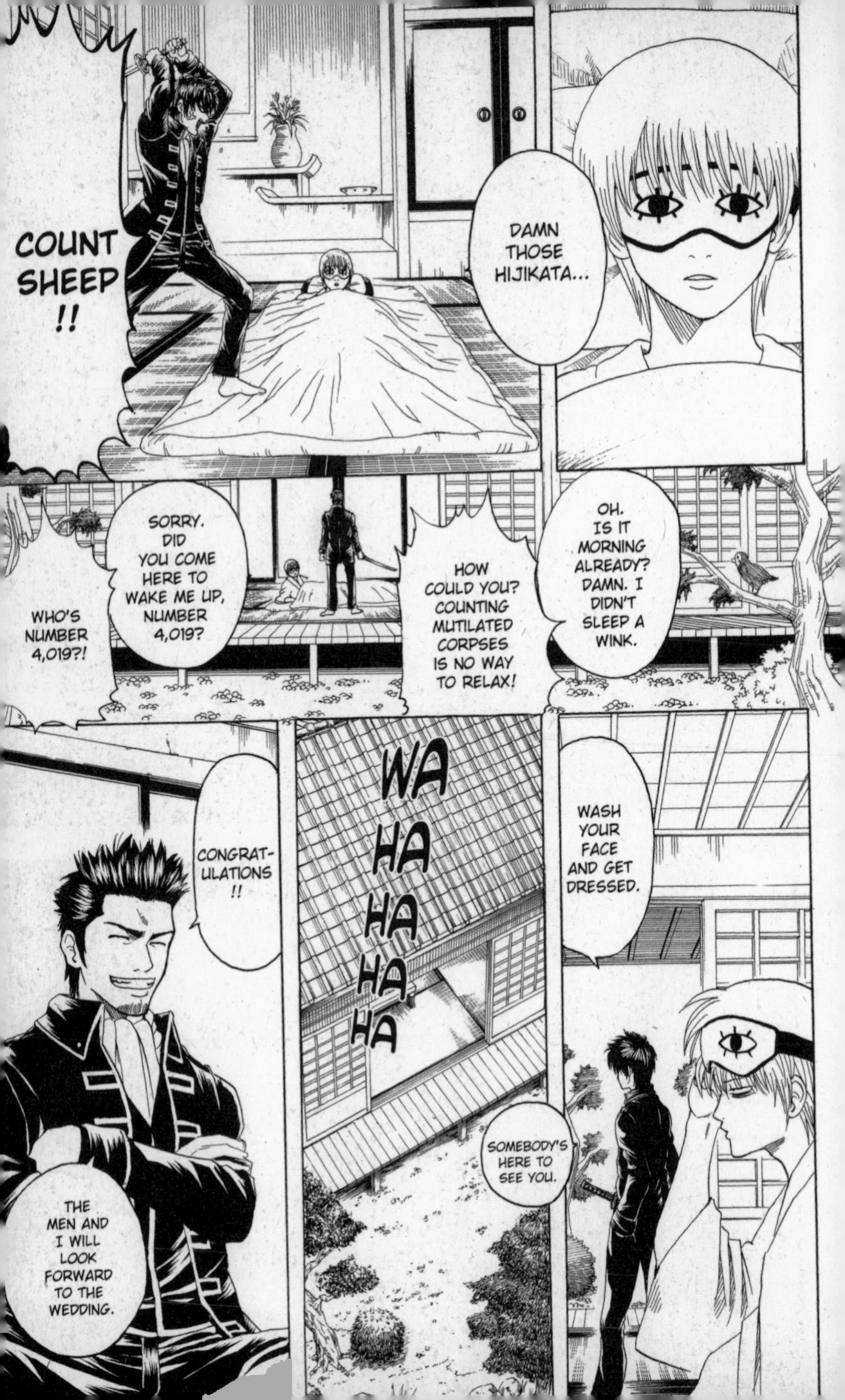
DAMN THOSE HIJIKATA...
COUNT SHEEP !!
OH. IS IT MORNING ALREADY? DAMN. I DIDN'T SLEEP A WINK.
HOW COULD YOU? COUNTING MUTILATED CORPSES IS NO WAY TO RELAX!
SORRY. DID YOU COME HERE TO WAKE ME UP, NUMBER 4,019?
WHO'S NUMBER 4,019?!
WASH YOUR FACE AND GET DRESSED.
SOMEBODY'S HERE TO SEE YOU.
WA HA HA HA HA HA
CONGRAT-ULATIONS !!
THE MEN AND I WILL LOOK FORWARD TO THE WEDDING.

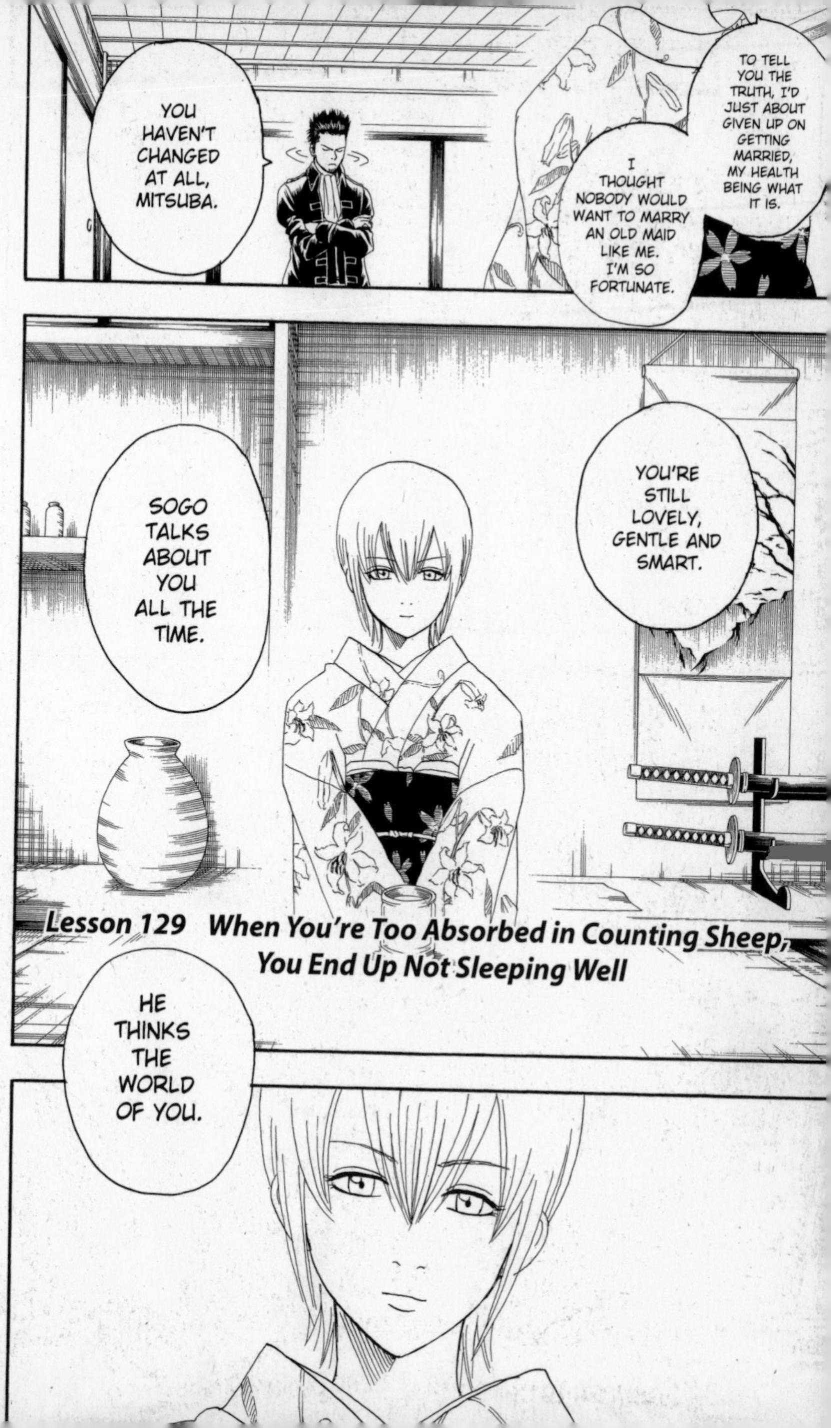
TO TELL YOU THE TRUTH, I'D JUST ABOUT GIVEN UP ON GETTING MARRIED, MY HEALTH BEING WHAT IT IS.
I THOUGHT NOBODY WOULD WANT TO MARRY AN OLD MAID LIKE ME. I'M SO FORTUNATE.
YOU HAVEN'T CHANGED AT ALL, MITSUBA.
YOU'RE STILL LOVELY, GENTLE AND SMART.
SOGO TALKS ABOUT YOU ALL THE TIME.
Lesson 129 When You're Too Absorbed in Counting Sheep, You End Up Not Sleeping Well
HE THINKS THE WORLD OF YOU.

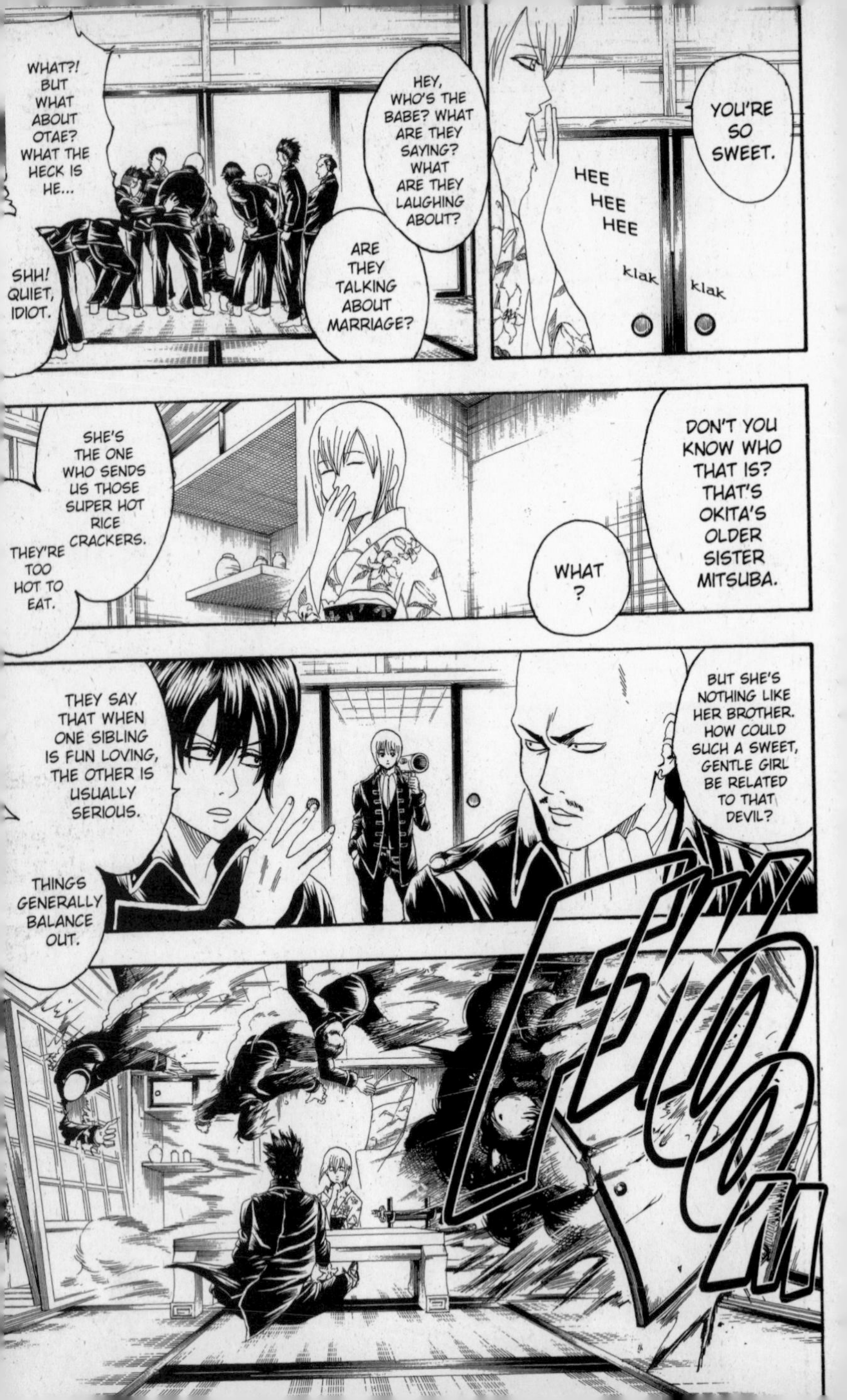
YOU'RE SO SWEET.
HEE HEE HEE
klak
klak
HEY, WHO'S THE BABE? WHAT ARE THEY SAYING? WHAT ARE THEY LAUGHING ABOUT?
ARE THEY TALKING ABOUT MARRIAGE?
WHAT?! BUT WHAT ABOUT OTAE? WHAT THE HECK IS HE...
SHH! QUIET, IDIOT.
DON'T YOU KNOW WHO THAT IS? THAT'S OKITA'S OLDER SISTER MITSUBA.
WHAT?
SHE'S THE ONE WHO SENDS US THOSE SUPER HOT RICE CRACKERS.
THEY'RE TOO HOT TO EAT.
BUT SHE'S NOTHING LIKE HER BROTHER. HOW COULD SUCH A SWEET, GENTLE GIRL BE RELATED TO THAT DEVIL?
THEY SAY THAT WHEN ONE SIBLING IS FUN LOVING, THE OTHER IS USUALLY SERIOUS.
THINGS GENERALLY BALANCE OUT.

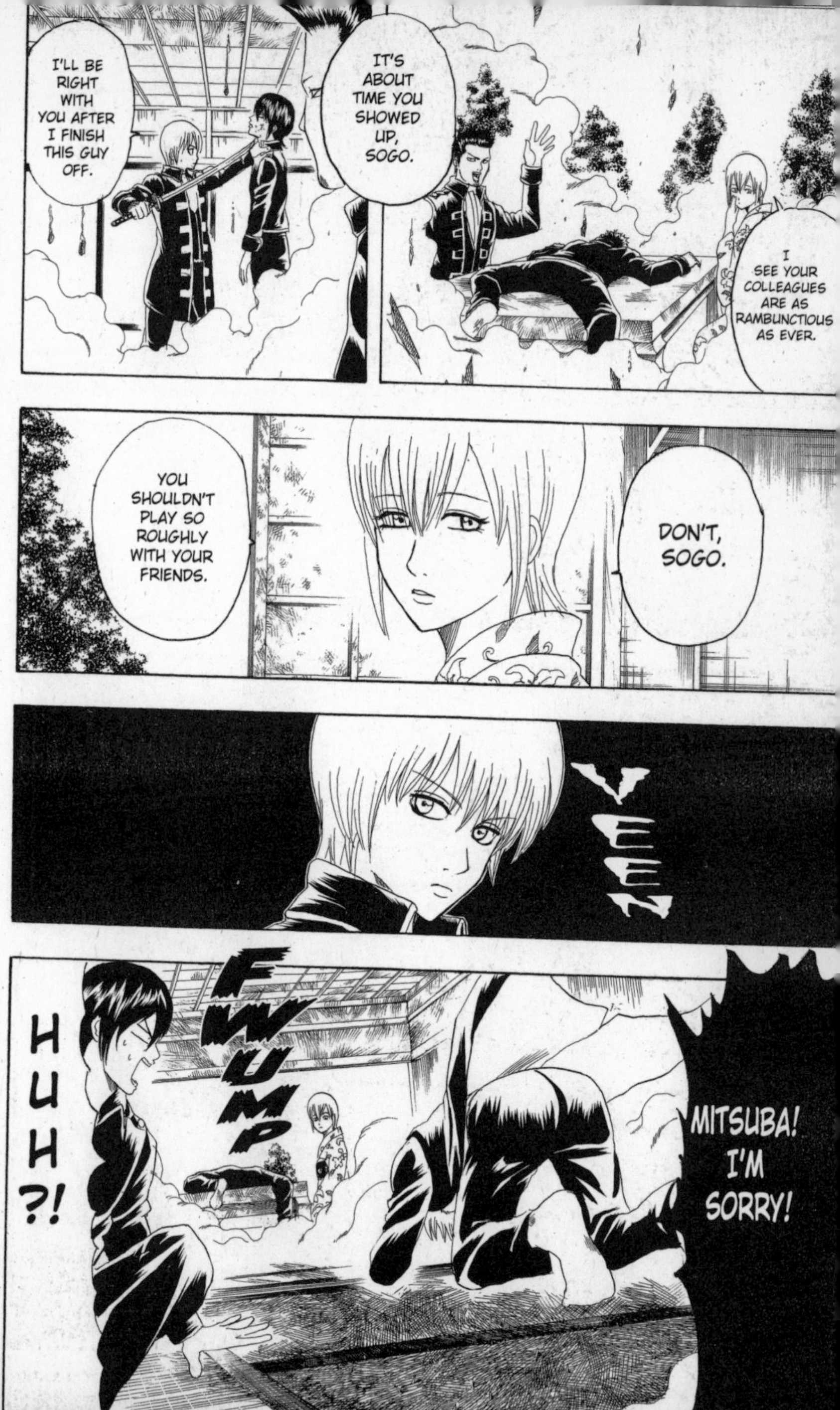
I SEE YOUR COLLEAGUES ARE AS RAMBUNCTIOUS AS EVER.
IT'S ABOUT TIME YOU SHOWED UP, SOGO.
I'LL BE RIGHT WITH YOU AFTER I FINISH THIS GUY OFF.
DON'T, SOGO.
YOU SHOULDN'T PLAY SO ROUGHLY WITH YOUR FRIENDS.
YEEN
MITSUBA! I'M SORRY!
FWUMP
HUH?!

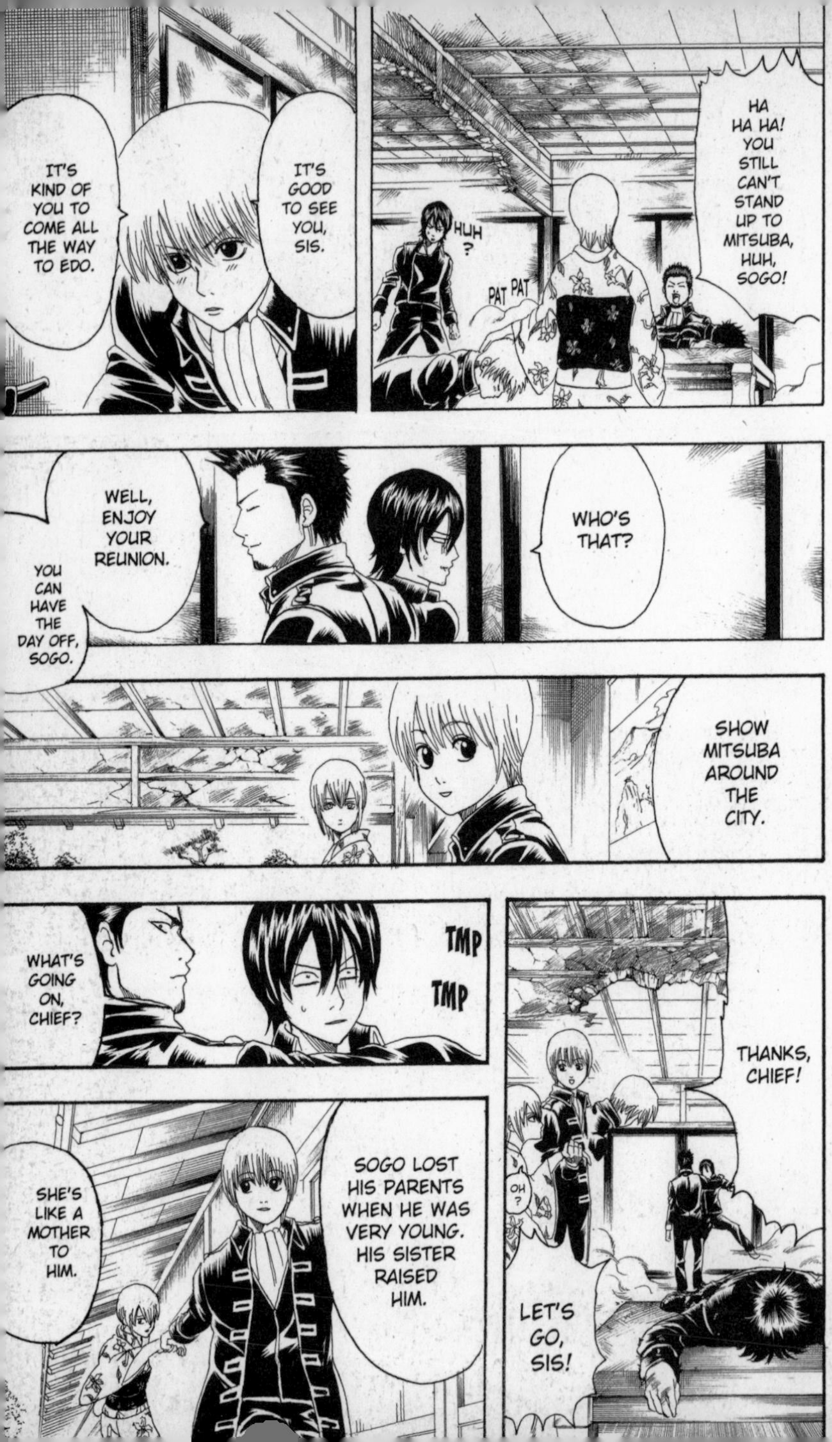
HA HA HA! YOU STILL CAN'T STAND UP TO MITSUBA, HUH, SOGO!
HUH ?
PAT PAT
IT'S GOOD TO SEE YOU, SIS.
IT'S KIND OF YOU TO COME ALL THE WAY TO EDO.
WHO'S THAT?
WELL, ENJOY YOUR REUNION.
YOU CAN HAVE THE DAY OFF, SOGO.
SHOW MITSUBA AROUND THE CITY.
THANKS, CHIEF!
OH ?
LET'S GO, SIS!
TMP
TMP
WHAT'S GOING ON, CHIEF?
SOGO LOST HIS PARENTS WHEN HE WAS VERY YOUNG. HIS SISTER RAISED HIM.
SHE'S LIKE A MOTHER TO HIM.

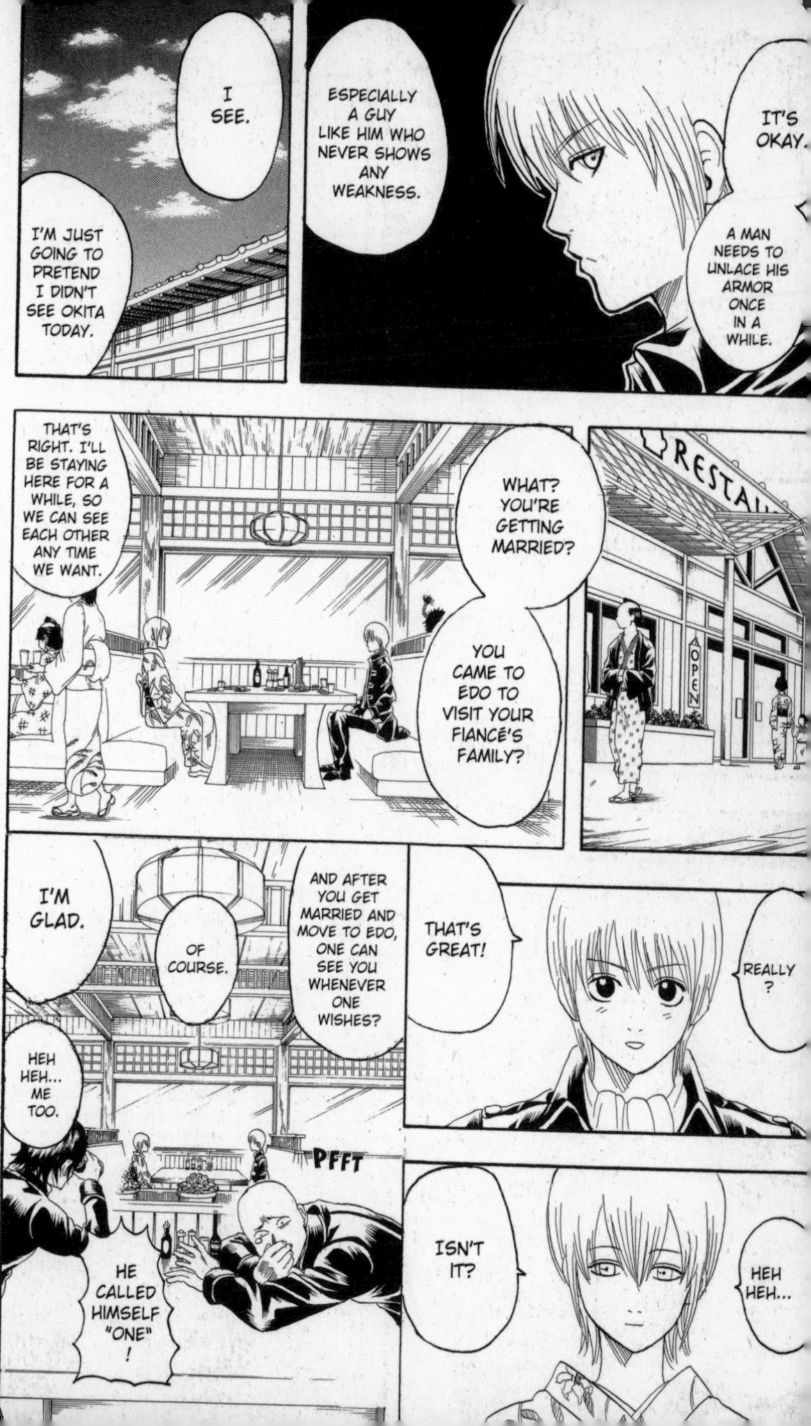
IT'S OKAY.
A MAN NEEDS TO UNLACE HIS ARMOR ONCE IN A WHILE.
ESPECIALLY A GUY LIKE HIM WHO NEVER SHOWS ANY WEAKNESS.
I SEE.
I'M JUST GOING TO PRETEND I DIDN'T SEE OKITA TODAY.
RESTAU
OPEN
WHAT? YOU'RE GETTING MARRIED?
YOU CAME TO EDO TO VISIT YOUR FIANCÉ'S FAMILY?
THAT'S RIGHT. I'LL BE STAYING HERE FOR A WHILE, SO WE CAN SEE EACH OTHER ANY TIME WE WANT.
REALLY?
THAT'S GREAT!
HEH HEH...
ISN'T IT?
AND AFTER YOU GET MARRIED AND MOVE TO EDO, ONE CAN SEE YOU WHENEVER ONE WISHES?
OF COURSE.
I'M GLAD.
HEH HEH... ME TOO.
PFFT
HE CALLED HIMSELF "ONE"!

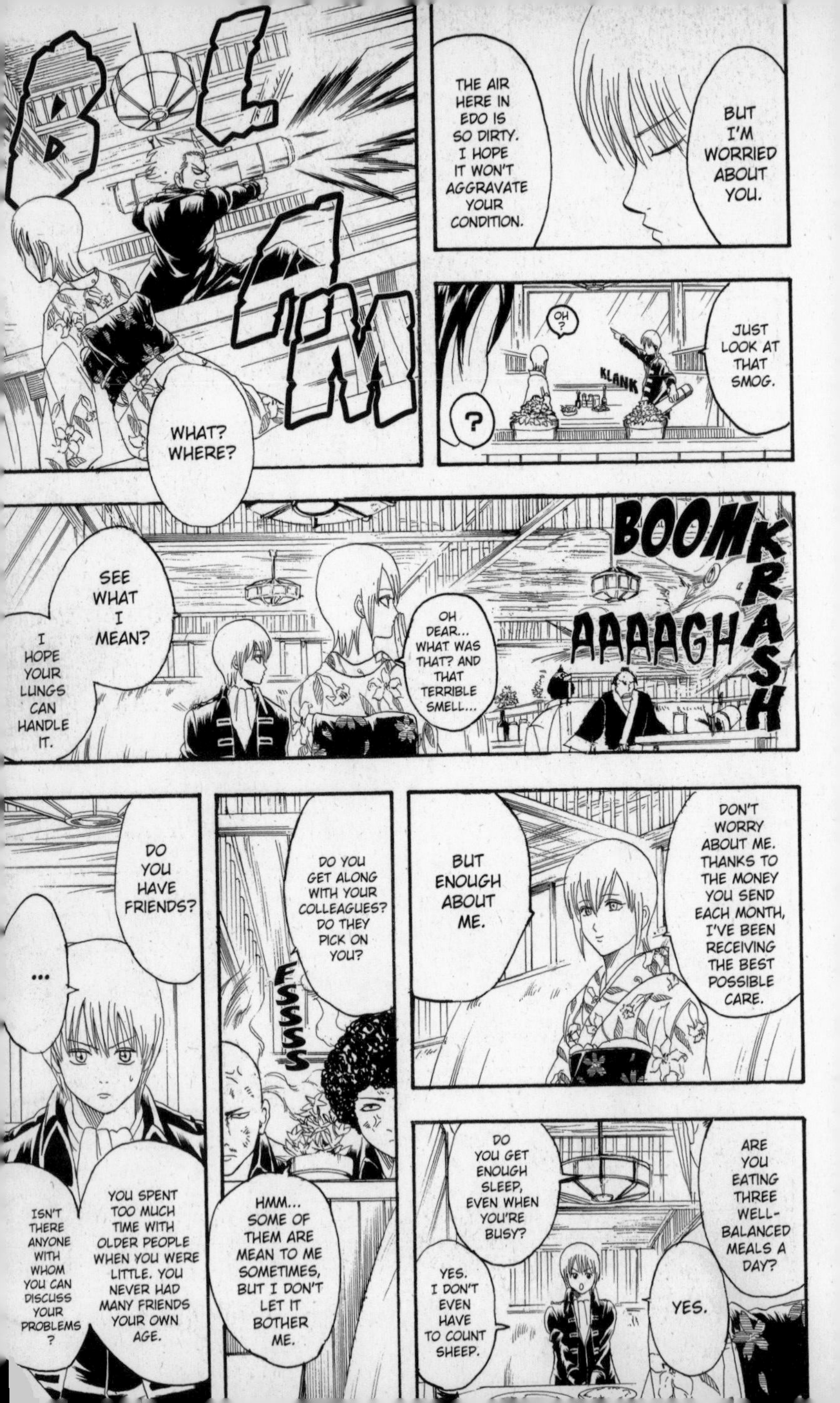
BUT I'M WORRIED ABOUT YOU.
THE AIR HERE IN EDO IS SO DIRTY. I HOPE IT WON'T AGGRAVATE YOUR CONDITION.
JUST LOOK AT THAT SMOG.
OH ?
KLANK
?
BLAM
WHAT? WHERE?
BOOM
KRASH
AAAAGH
OH DEAR... WHAT WAS THAT? AND THAT TERRIBLE SMELL...
SEE WHAT I MEAN?
I HOPE YOUR LUNGS CAN HANDLE IT.
DON'T WORRY ABOUT ME. THANKS TO THE MONEY YOU SEND EACH MONTH, I'VE BEEN RECEIVING THE BEST POSSIBLE CARE.
BUT ENOUGH ABOUT ME.
ARE YOU EATING THREE WELL-BALANCED MEALS A DAY?
YES.
DO YOU GET ENOUGH SLEEP, EVEN WHEN YOU'RE BUSY?
YES. I DON'T EVEN HAVE TO COUNT SHEEP.
DO YOU GET ALONG WITH YOUR COLLEAGUES? DO THEY PICK ON YOU?
HMM... SOME OF THEM ARE MEAN TO ME SOMETIMES, BUT I DON'T LET IT BOTHER ME.
DO YOU HAVE FRIENDS?
...
YOU SPENT TOO MUCH TIME WITH OLDER PEOPLE WHEN YOU WERE LITTLE. YOU NEVER HAD MANY FRIENDS YOUR OWN AGE.
ISN'T THERE ANYONE WITH WHOM YOU CAN DISCUSS YOUR PROBLEMS ?

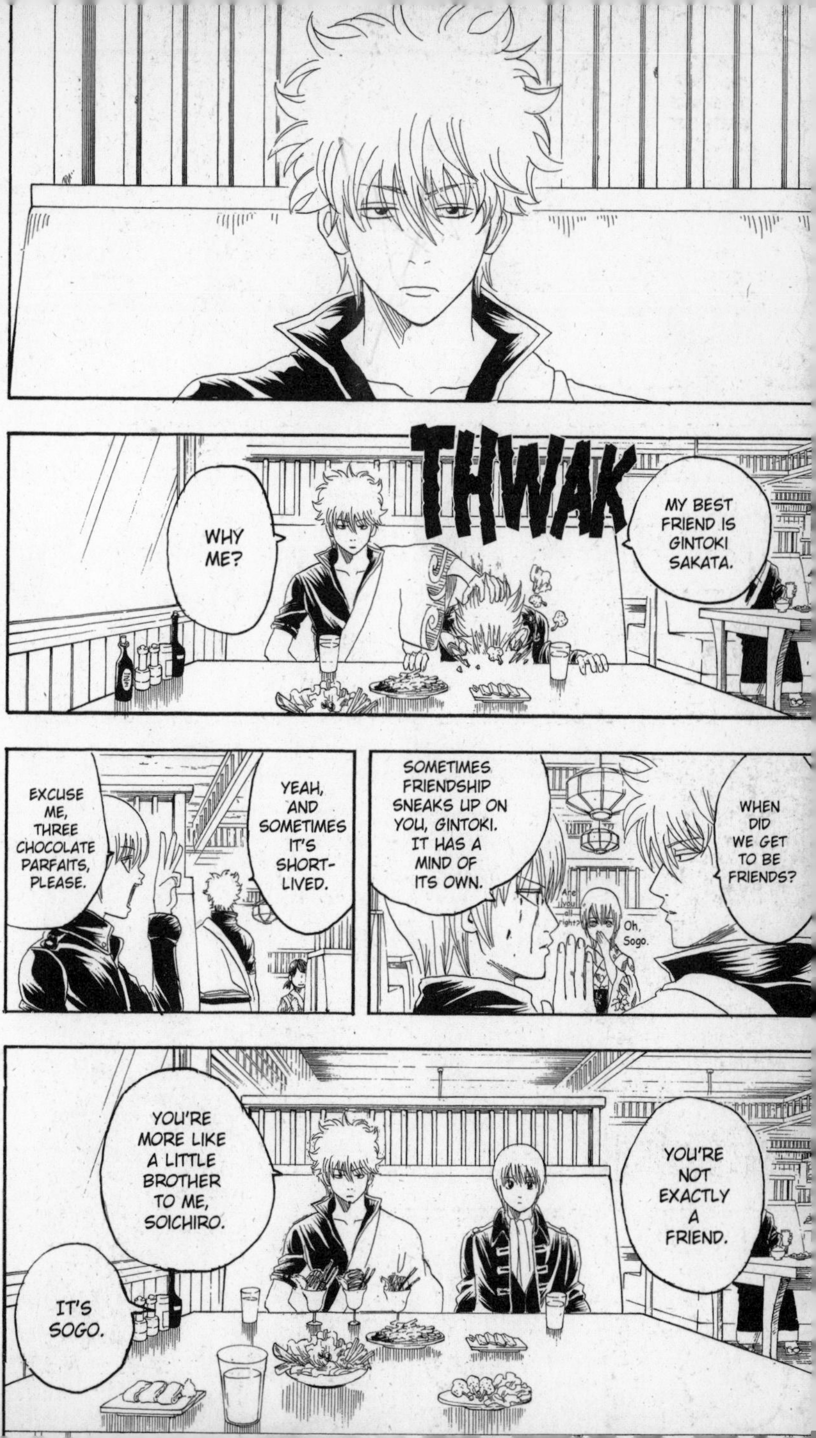
MY BEST FRIEND IS GINTOKI SAKATA.
THWAK
WHY ME?
WHEN DID WE GET TO BE FRIENDS?
SOMETIMES FRIENDSHIP SNEAKS UP ON YOU, GINTOKI. IT HAS A MIND OF ITS OWN.
Are you all right?
Oh, Sogo.
YEAH, AND SOMETIMES IT'S SHORT-LIVED.
EXCUSE ME, THREE CHOCOLATE PARFAITS, PLEASE.
YOU'RE NOT EXACTLY A FRIEND.
YOU'RE MORE LIKE A LITTLE BROTHER TO ME, SOICHIRO.
IT'S SOGO.

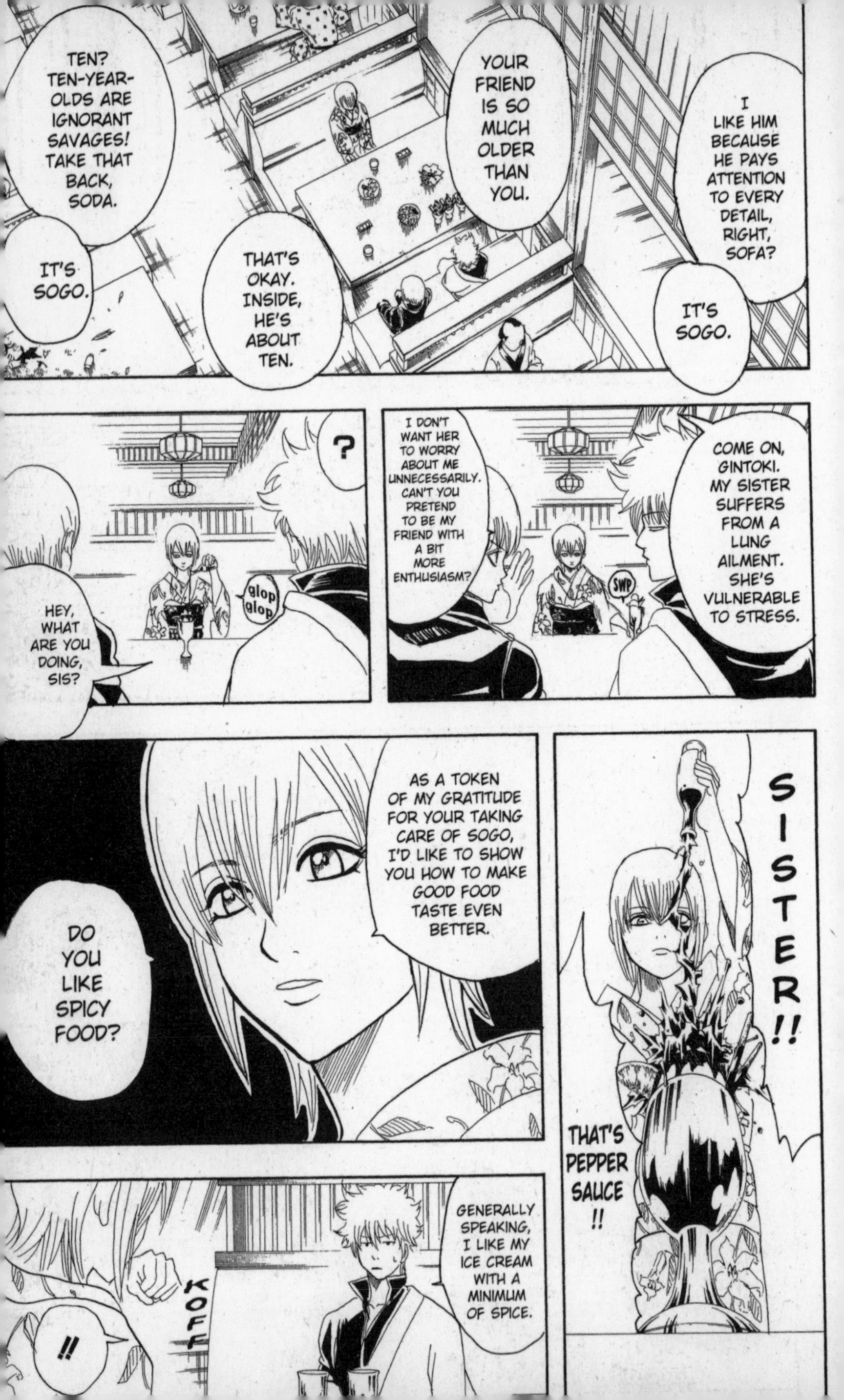

I LIKE HIM BECAUSE HE PAYS ATTENTION TO EVERY DETAIL, RIGHT, SOFA?
IT'S SOGO.
YOUR FRIEND IS SO MUCH OLDER THAN YOU.
THAT'S OKAY. INSIDE, HE'S ABOUT TEN.
TEN? TEN-YEAR-OLDS ARE IGNORANT SAVAGES! TAKE THAT BACK, SODA.
IT'S SOGO.
COME ON, GINTOKI. MY SISTER SUFFERS FROM A LUNG AILMENT. SHE'S VULNERABLE TO STRESS.
SWP
I DON'T WANT HER TO WORRY ABOUT ME UNNECESSARILY. CAN'T YOU PRETEND TO BE MY FRIEND WITH A BIT MORE ENTHUSIASM?
?
glop glop
HEY, WHAT ARE YOU DOING, SIS?
SISTER!!
THAT'S PEPPER SAUCE!!
AS A TOKEN OF MY GRATITUDE FOR YOUR TAKING CARE OF SOGO, I'D LIKE TO SHOW YOU HOW TO MAKE GOOD FOOD TASTE EVEN BETTER.
DO YOU LIKE SPICY FOOD?
GENERALLY SPEAKING, I LIKE MY ICE CREAM WITH A MINIMUM OF SPICE.
KOFF
!!

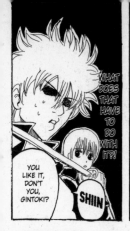

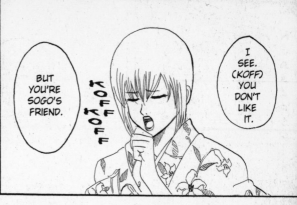

I SEE. (KOFF) YOU DON'T LIKE IT.
KOFF KOFF
BUT YOU'RE SOGO'S FRIEND.
WHAT DOES THAT HAVE TO DO WITH IT?!
YOU LIKE IT, DON'T YOU, GINTOKI?
SHIIN
I'VE NEVER KNOWN ANYONE TO TAKE SEASONING SO PERSONALLY.
HEH... UM, MAYBE I DO LIKE IT. YEAH, NOW I REMEMBER.
I LOVE HOT PEPPERY PARFAITS.
IT STIMULATES THE APPETITE. IT'S HELPED ME MANY TIMES WHEN I DIDN'T FEEL LIKE EATING.
ONE WRONG STEP AND...
KOFF
KOFF
BUT I'VE ALREADY EATEN TWO PARFAITS, SO I'M PRETTY FULL NOW.
KOFF
GACK
KOFF
KOFF
KOFF
HACK
BLEGH
GINTOKI!!
G...
SHAKE
GET SOME WATER!!

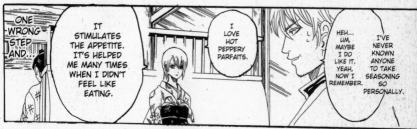

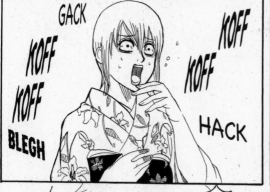

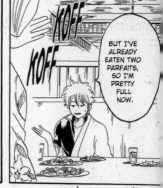

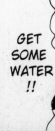

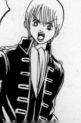

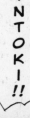

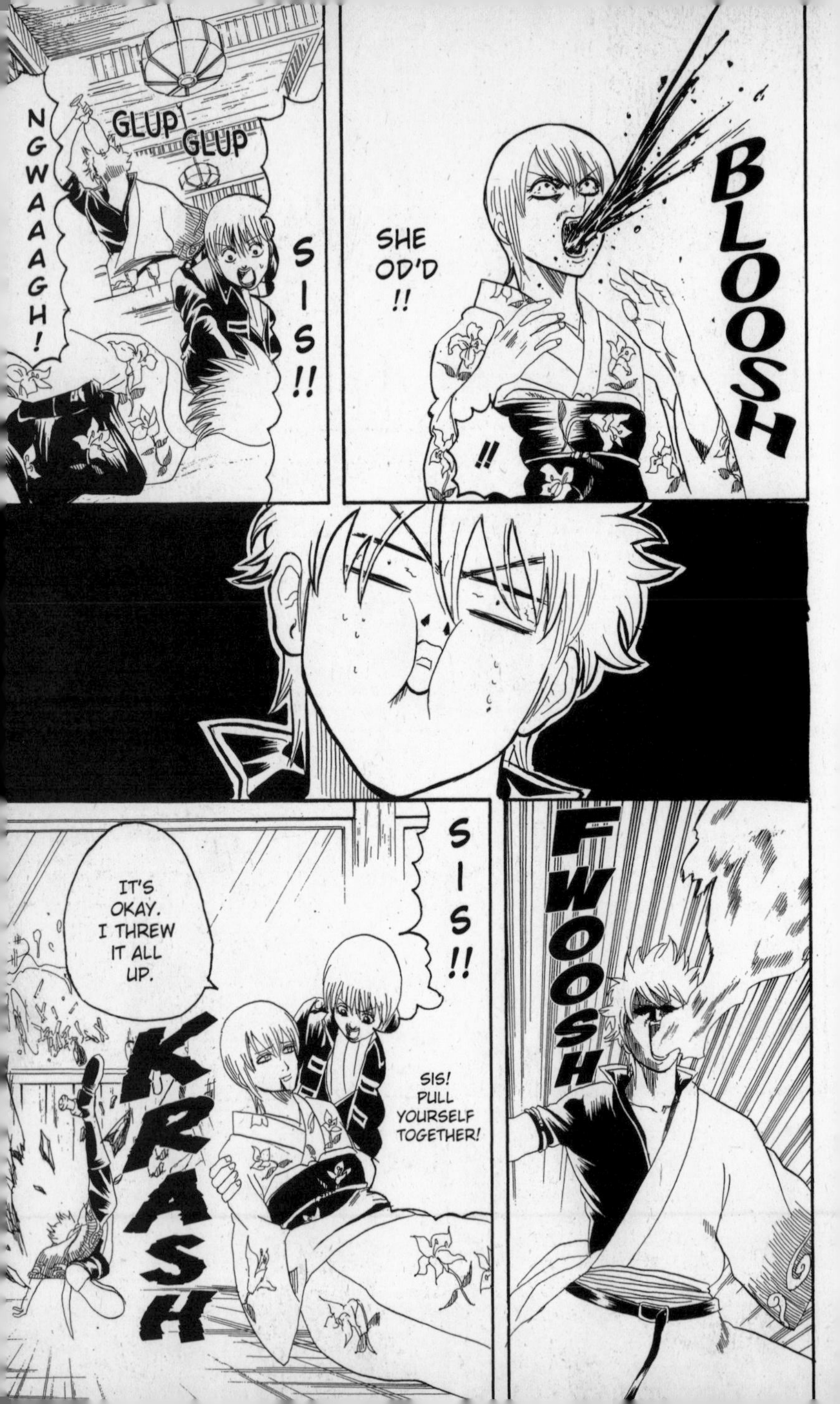
BLOOSH
SHE OD'D!!
!!
GLUP GLUP
SIS!!
NGWAAAAGH!
FWOOOSH
SIS!!
IT'S OKAY. I THREW IT ALL UP.
SIS! PULL YOURSELF TOGETHER!
KRASH

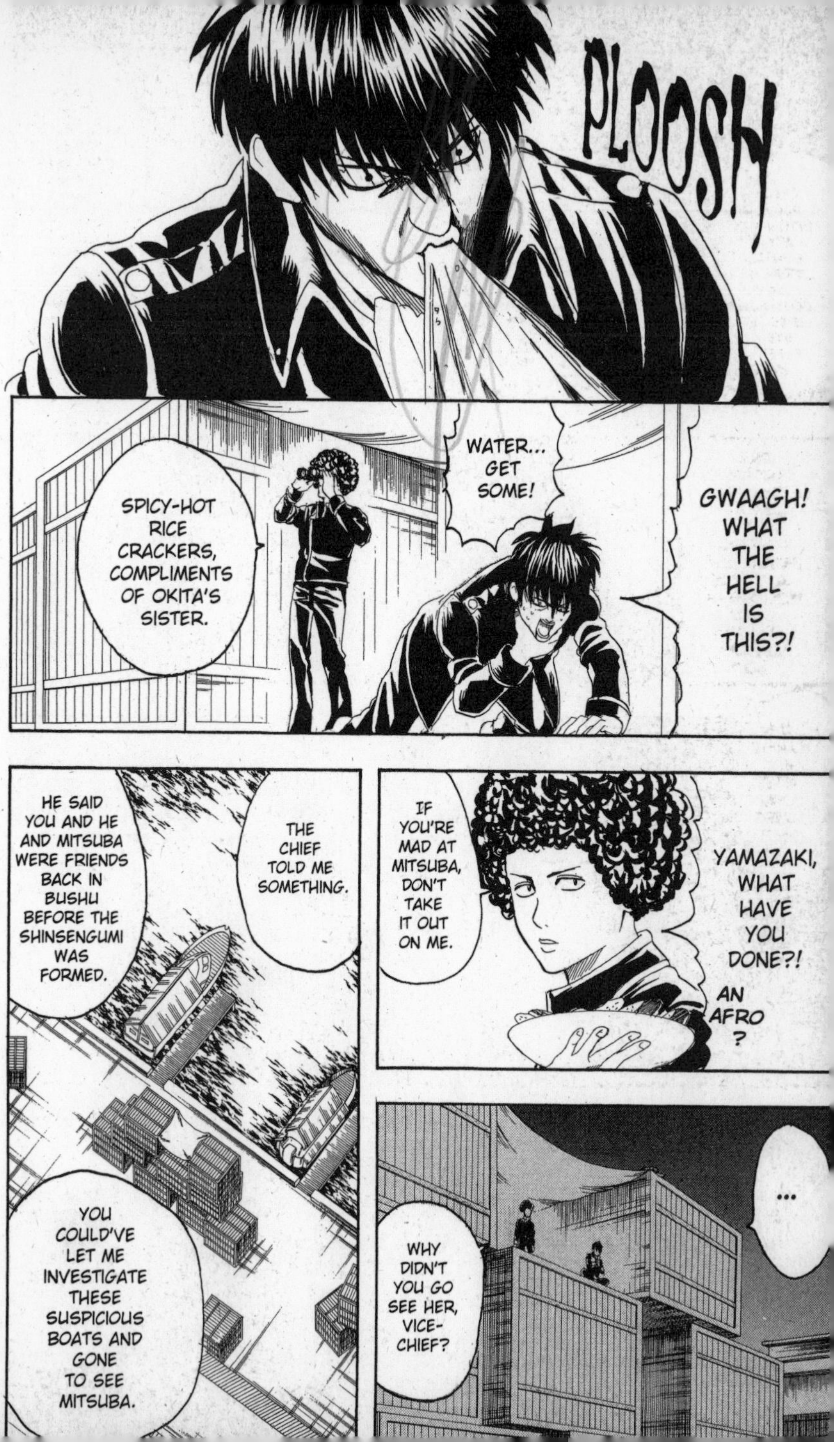
PLOOSH
GWAAGH! WHAT THE HELL IS THIS?!
WATER... GET SOME!
SPICY-HOT RICE CRACKERS, COMPLIMENTS OF OKITA'S SISTER.
YAMAZAKI, WHAT HAVE YOU DONE?!
AN AFRO?
IF YOU'RE MAD AT MITSUBA, DON'T TAKE IT OUT ON ME.
...
WHY DIDN'T YOU GO SEE HER, VICE-CHIEF?
THE CHIEF TOLD ME SOMETHING.
HE SAID YOU AND HE AND MITSUBA WERE FRIENDS BACK IN BUSHU BEFORE THE SHINSENGUMI WAS FORMED.
YOU COULD'VE LET ME INVESTIGATE THESE SUSPICIOUS BOATS AND GONE TO SEE MITSUBA.

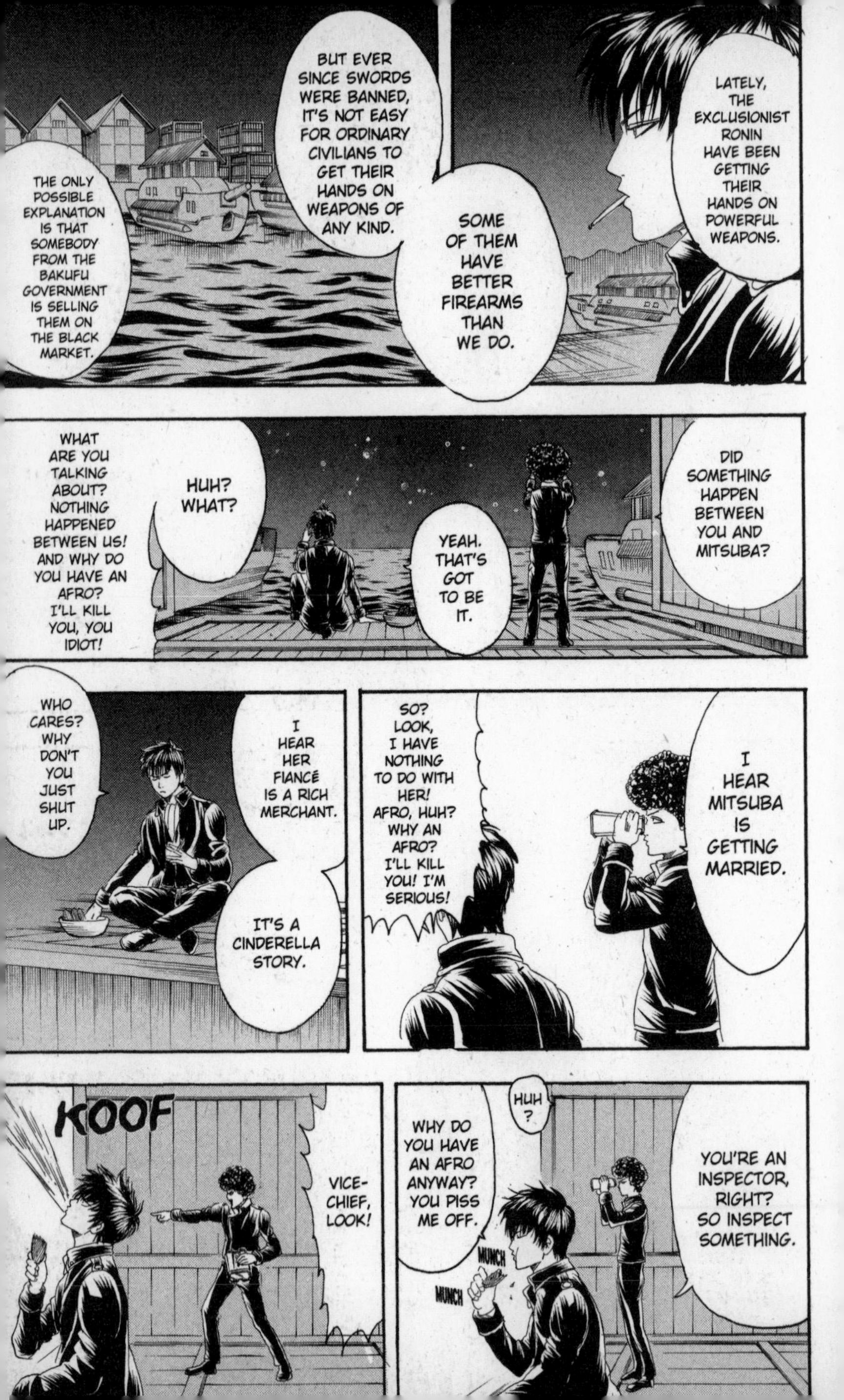
LATELY, THE EXCLUSIONIST RONIN HAVE BEEN GETTING THEIR HANDS ON POWERFUL WEAPONS.
SOME OF THEM HAVE BETTER FIREARMS THAN WE DO.
BUT EVER SINCE SWORDS WERE BANNED, IT'S NOT EASY FOR ORDINARY CIVILIANS TO GET THEIR HANDS ON WEAPONS OF ANY KIND.
THE ONLY POSSIBLE EXPLANATION IS THAT SOMEBODY FROM THE BAKUFU GOVERNMENT IS SELLING THEM ON THE BLACK MARKET.
DID SOMETHING HAPPEN BETWEEN YOU AND MITSUBA?
YEAH. THAT'S GOT TO BE IT.
HUH? WHAT?
WHAT ARE YOU TALKING ABOUT? NOTHING HAPPENED BETWEEN US! AND WHY DO YOU HAVE AN AFRO? I'LL KILL YOU, YOU IDIOT!
I HEAR MITSUBA IS GETTING MARRIED.
SO? LOOK, I HAVE NOTHING TO DO WITH HER! AFRO, HUH? WHY AN AFRO? I'LL KILL YOU! I'M SERIOUS!
I HEAR HER FIANCÉ IS A RICH MERCHANT.
IT'S A CINDERELLA STORY.
WHO CARES? WHY DON'T YOU JUST SHUT UP.
YOU'RE AN INSPECTOR, RIGHT? SO INSPECT SOMETHING.
HUH?
WHY DO YOU HAVE AN AFRO ANYWAY? YOU PISS ME OFF.
MUNCH
MUNCH
VICE-CHIEF, LOOK!
KOOF

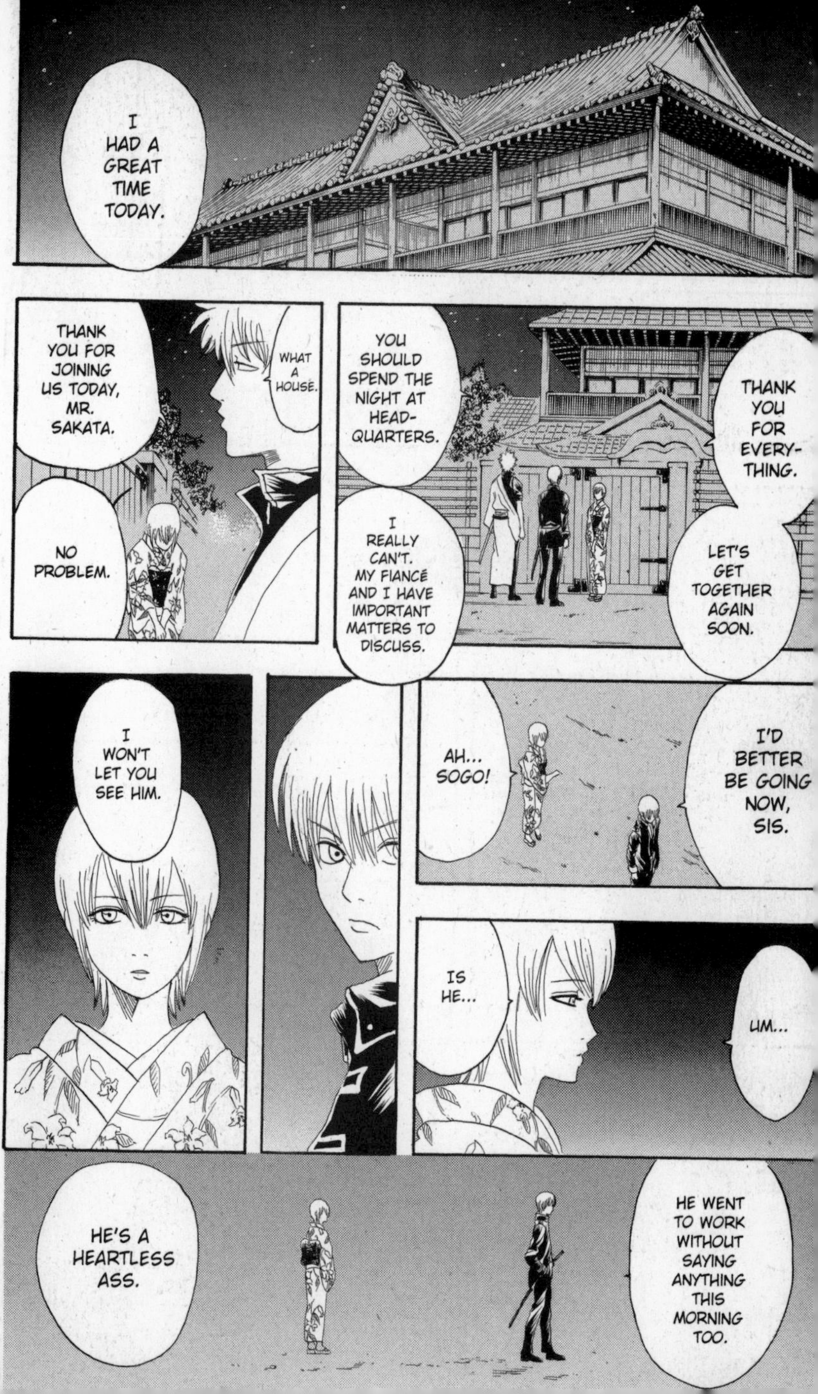

I HAD A GREAT TIME TODAY.
THANK YOU FOR EVERYTHING.
LET'S GET TOGETHER AGAIN SOON.
YOU SHOULD SPEND THE NIGHT AT HEADQUARTERS.
I REALLY CAN'T. MY FIANCE AND I HAVE IMPORTANT MATTERS TO DISCUSS.
WHAT A HOUSE.
THANK YOU FOR JOINING US TODAY, MR. SAKATA.
NO PROBLEM.
I'D BETTER BE GOING NOW, SIS.
AH... SOGO!
UM...
IS HE...
I WON'T LET YOU SEE HIM.
HE WENT TO WORK WITHOUT SAYING ANYTHING THIS MORNING TOO.
HE'S A HEARTLESS ASS.

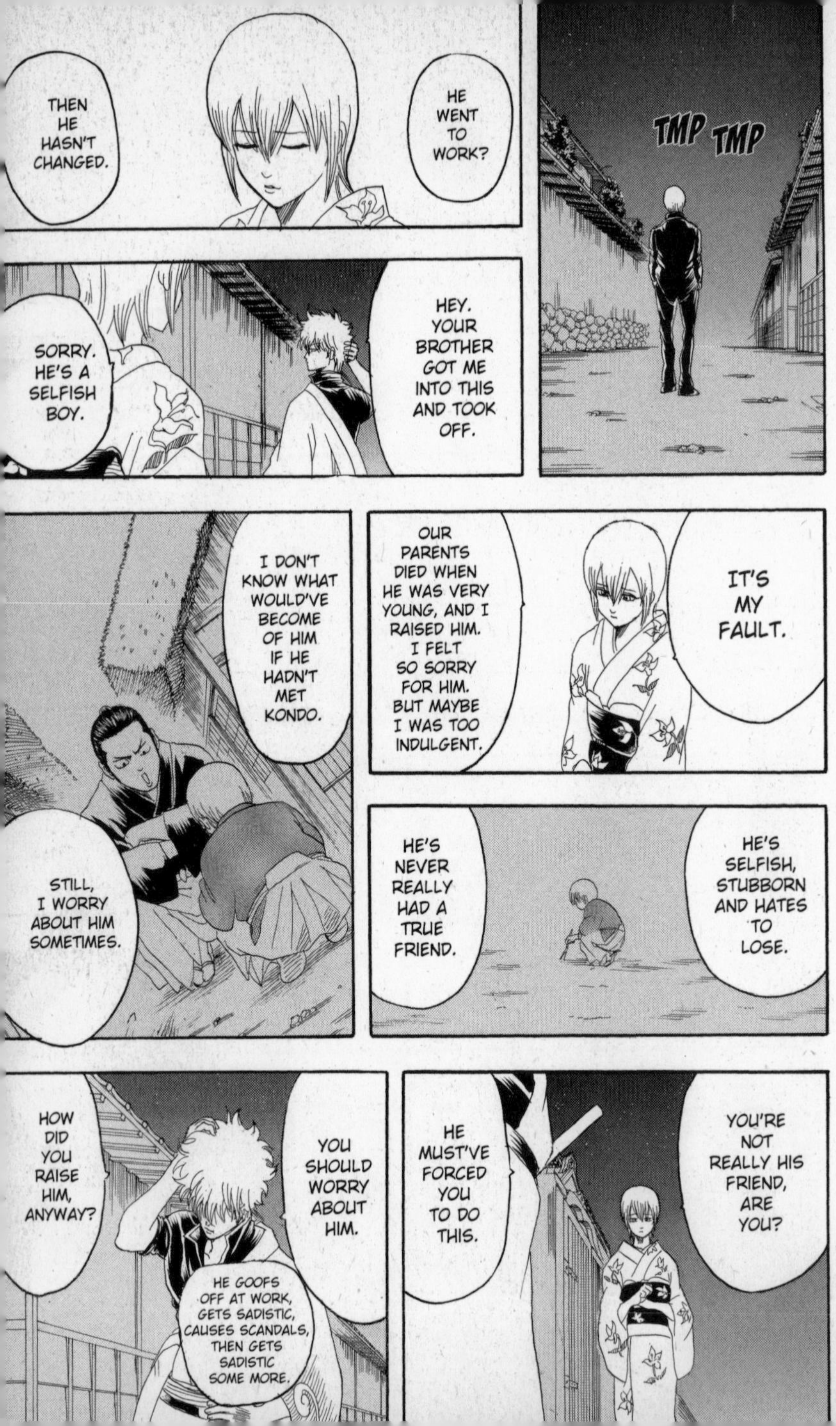
TMP TMP
HE WENT TO WORK?
THEN HE HASN'T CHANGED.
HEY. YOUR BROTHER GOT ME INTO THIS AND TOOK OFF.
SORRY. HE'S A SELFISH BOY.
IT'S MY FAULT.
OUR PARENTS DIED WHEN HE WAS VERY YOUNG, AND I RAISED HIM. I FELT SO SORRY FOR HIM. BUT MAYBE I WAS TOO INDULGENT.
HE'S SELFISH, STUBBORN AND HATES TO LOSE.
HE'S NEVER REALLY HAD A TRUE FRIEND.
I DON'T KNOW WHAT WOULD'VE BECOME OF HIM IF HE HADN'T MET KONDO.
STILL, I WORRY ABOUT HIM SOMETIMES.
YOU'RE NOT REALLY HIS FRIEND, ARE YOU?
HE MUST'VE FORCED YOU TO DO THIS.
YOU SHOULD WORRY ABOUT HIM.
HOW DID YOU RAISE HIM, ANYWAY?
HE GOOFS OFF AT WORK, GETS SADISTIC, CAUSES SCANDALS, THEN GETS SADISTIC SOME MORE.

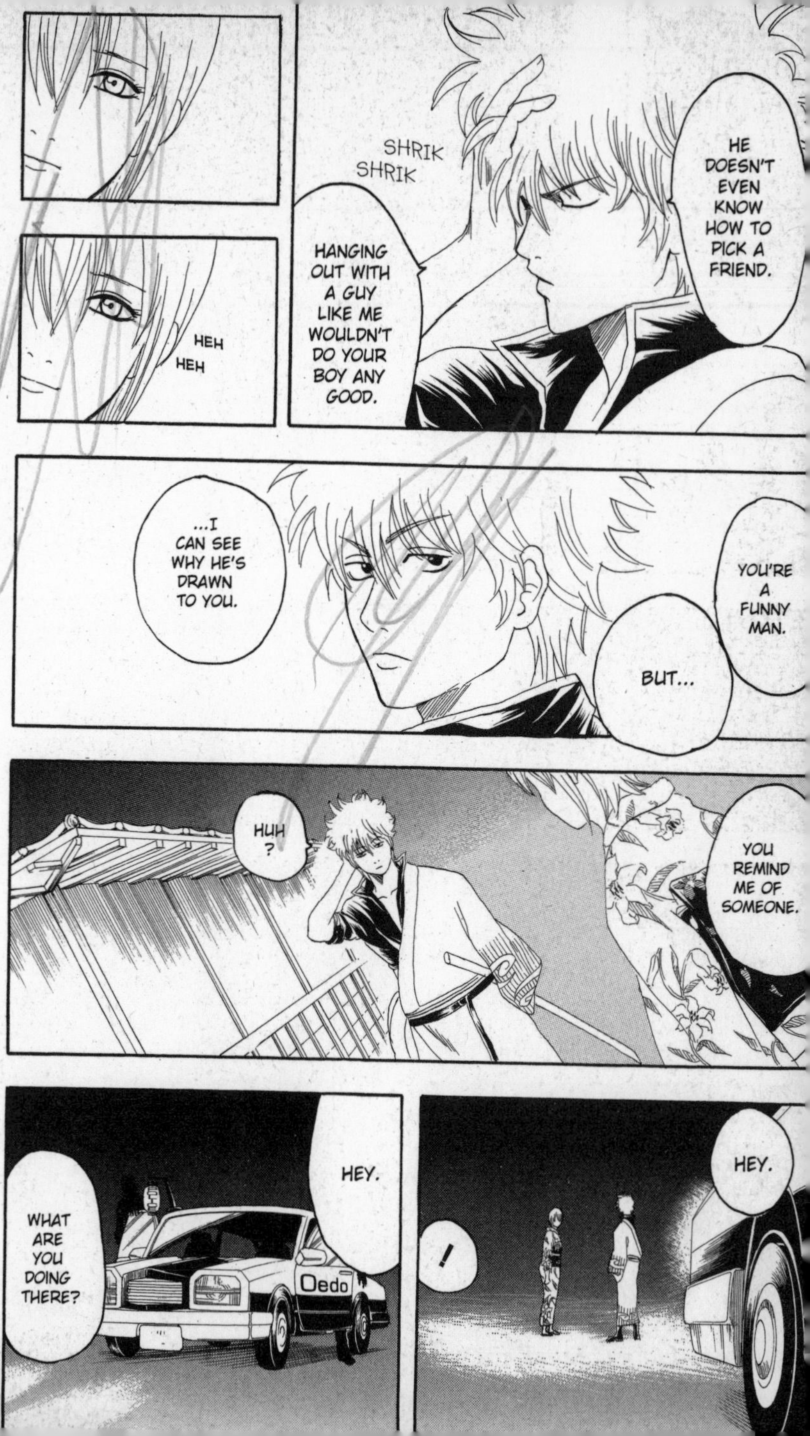
HE DOESN'T EVEN KNOW HOW TO PICK A FRIEND.
SHRIK SHRIK
HANGING OUT WITH A GUY LIKE ME WOULDN'T DO YOUR BOY ANY GOOD.
HEH HEH
YOU'RE A FUNNY MAN.
BUT...
...I CAN SEE WHY HE'S DRAWN TO YOU.
YOU REMIND ME OF SOMEONE.
HUH ?
HEY.
!
HEY.
WHAT ARE YOU DOING THERE?
Oedo

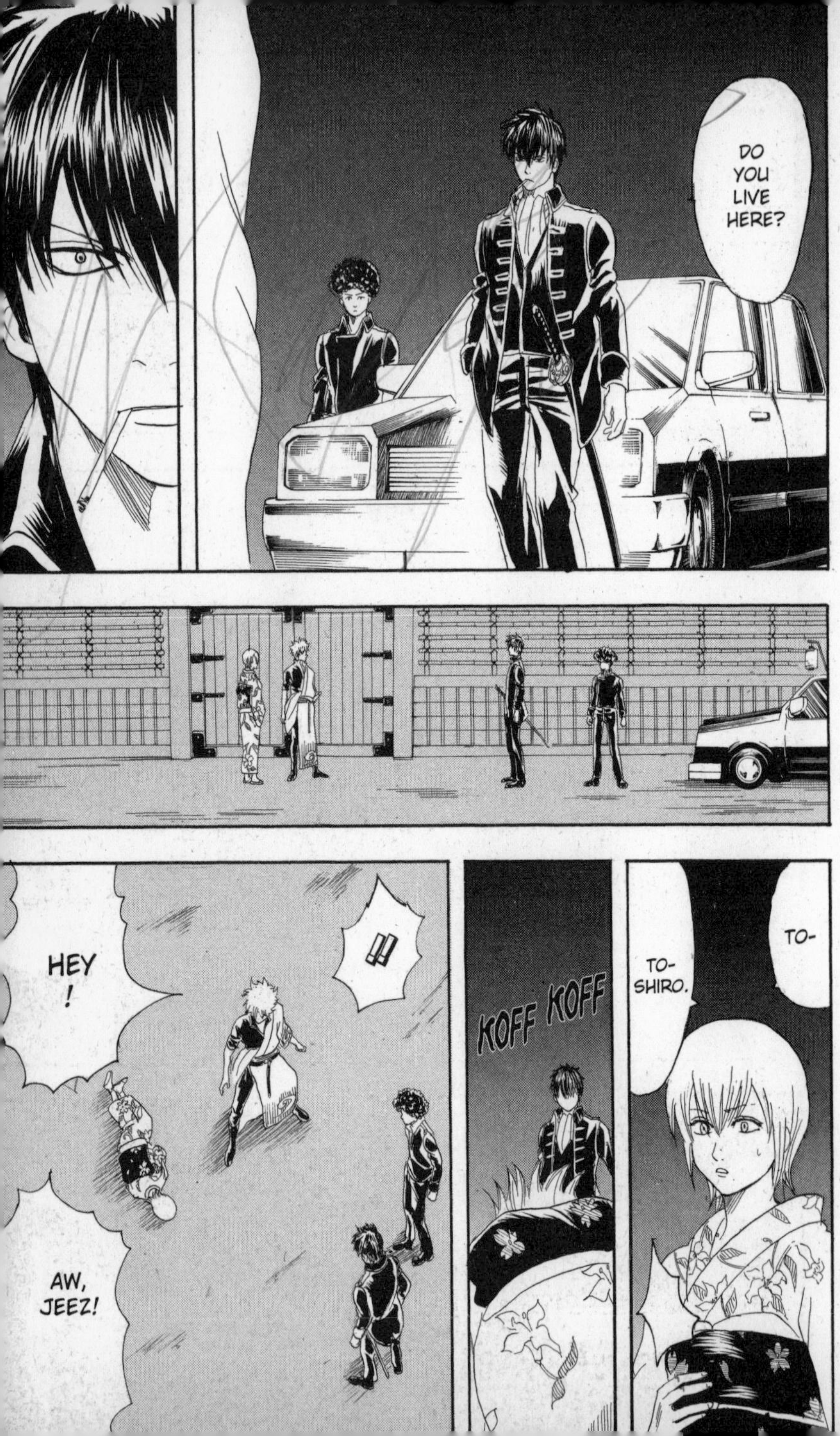
DO YOU LIVE HERE?
TO-
TO-SHIRO.
KOFF KOFF
!!
HEY!
AW, JEEZ!

Sorachi's Q&A
Hanging with the Readers #46

<Question from Kobayashi from Chiba Prefecture>

Were you behind those bogus previews in *JUMP* like "Gin invents a new way of swimming" and "Gin becomes a rapper"? And what does bogus mean, anyway?

<Answer>

My editor, Chimpanzee Onishi, arbitrarily predicts the next episode and writes the previews. Because the storyline of Gin Tama changes all the time, and I often write a totally different story without telling my editor or even discussing it with him beforehand, it's hard to write the previews. So my editor has given up and just writes whatever comes into his head. So it goes. Still, when he writes a preview called "The Kabukicho marathon" when I'm writing a serious story, it's frustrating.

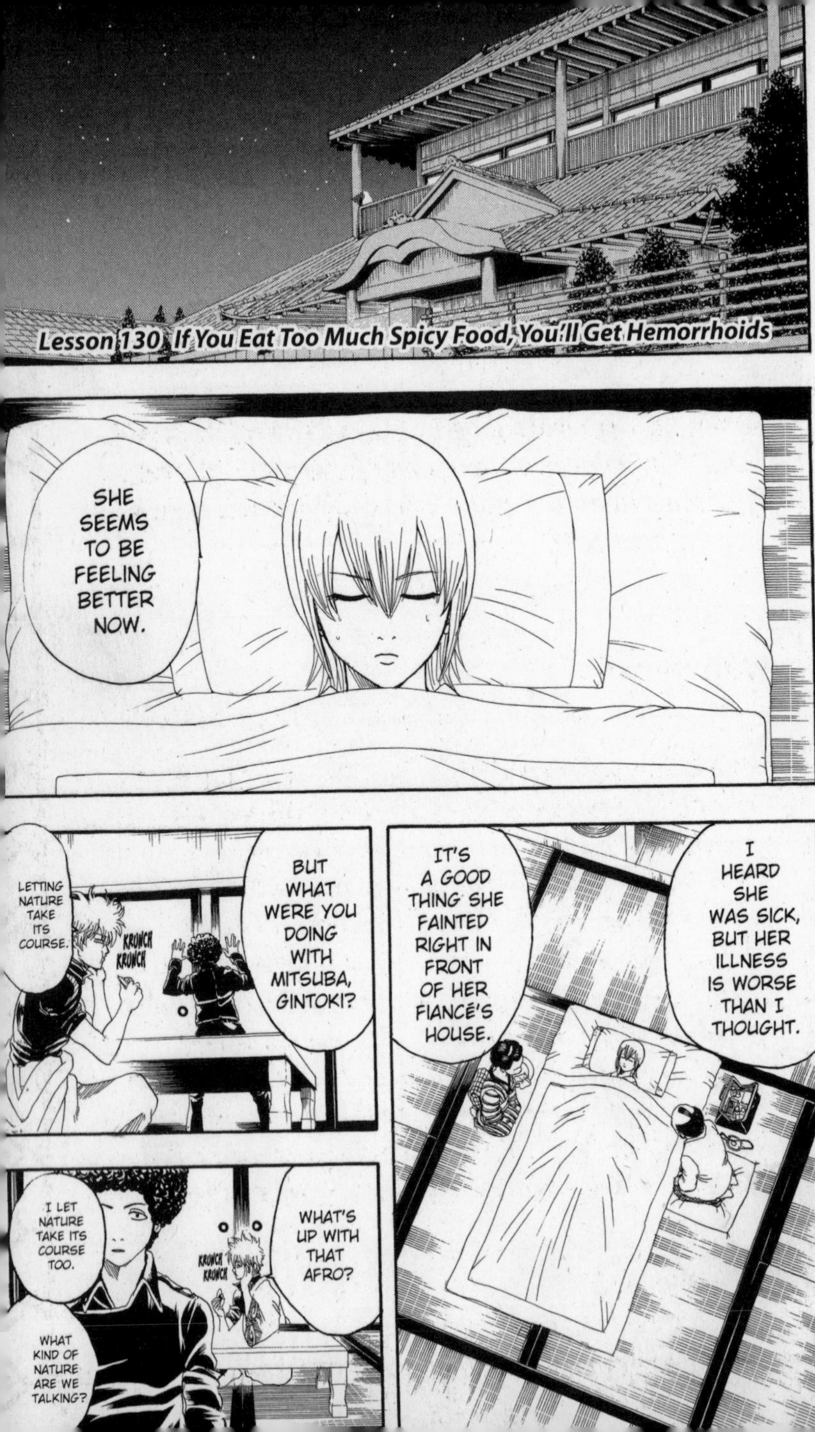
Lesson 130 If You Eat Too Much Spicy Food, You'll Get Hemorrhoids
SHE SEEMS TO BE FEELING BETTER NOW.
I HEARD SHE WAS SICK, BUT HER ILLNESS IS WORSE THAN I THOUGHT.
IT'S A GOOD THING SHE FAINTED RIGHT IN FRONT OF HER FIANCÉ'S HOUSE.
BUT WHAT WERE YOU DOING WITH MITSUBA, GINTOKI?
KRONCH KRONCH
LETTING NATURE TAKE ITS COURSE.
WHAT'S UP WITH THAT AFRO?
KRONCH KRONCH
I LET NATURE TAKE ITS COURSE TOO.
WHAT KIND OF NATURE ARE WE TALKING?

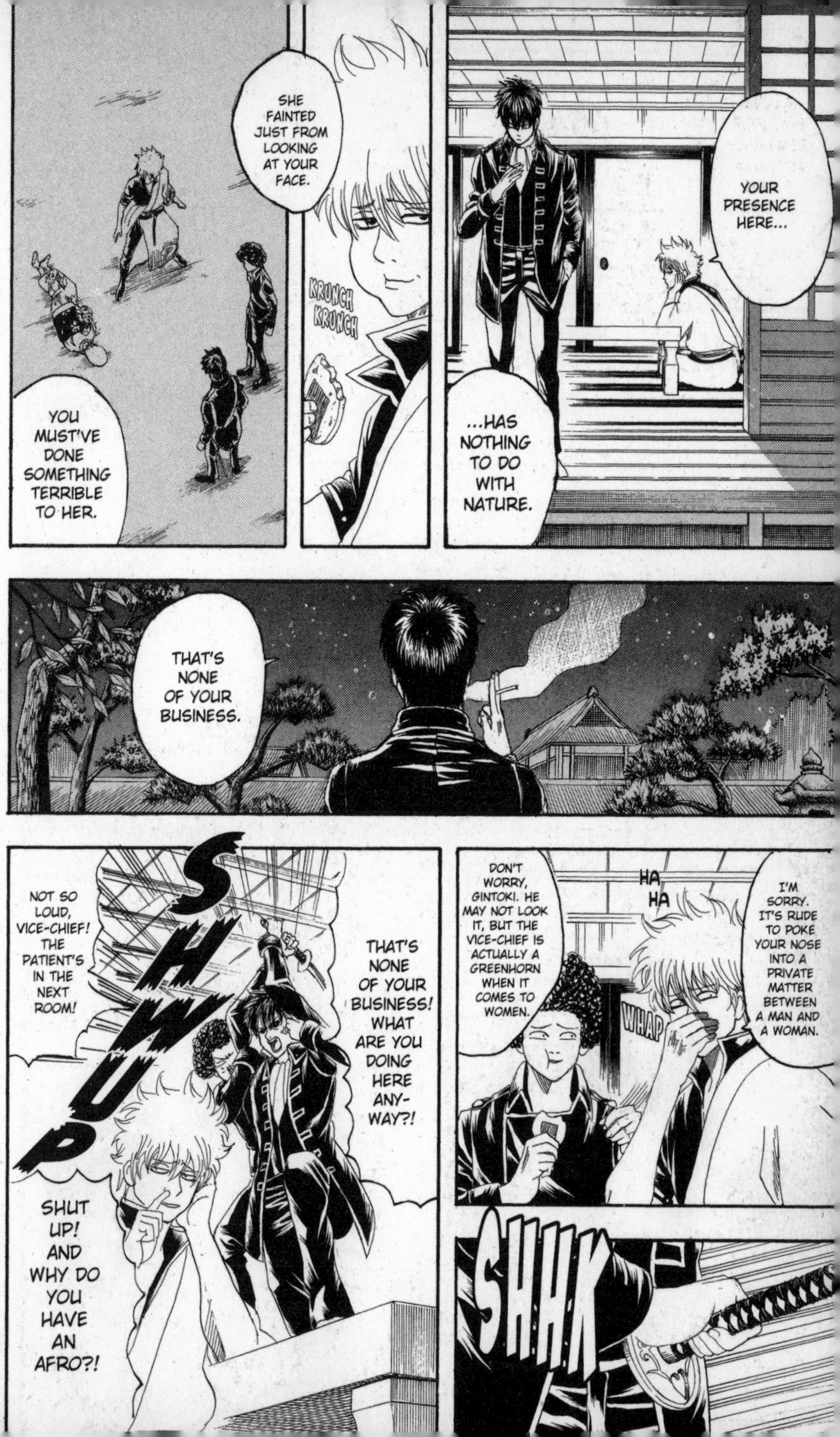
YOUR PRESENCE HERE...
...HAS NOTHING TO DO WITH NATURE.
SHE FAINTED JUST FROM LOOKING AT YOUR FACE.
KRUNCH KRUNCH
YOU MUST'VE DONE SOMETHING TERRIBLE TO HER.
THAT'S NONE OF YOUR BUSINESS.
I'M SORRY. IT'S RUDE TO POKE YOUR NOSE INTO A PRIVATE MATTER BETWEEN A MAN AND A WOMAN.
HA HA
WHAP
DON'T WORRY, GINTOKI. HE MAY NOT LOOK IT, BUT THE VICE-CHIEF IS ACTUALLY A GREENHORN WHEN IT COMES TO WOMEN.
SHHK
THAT'S NONE OF YOUR BUSINESS! WHAT ARE YOU DOING HERE ANY-WAY?!
SHWUP
NOT SO LOUD, VICE-CHIEF! THE PATIENT'S IN THE NEXT ROOM!
SHUT UP! AND WHY DO YOU HAVE AN AFRO?!

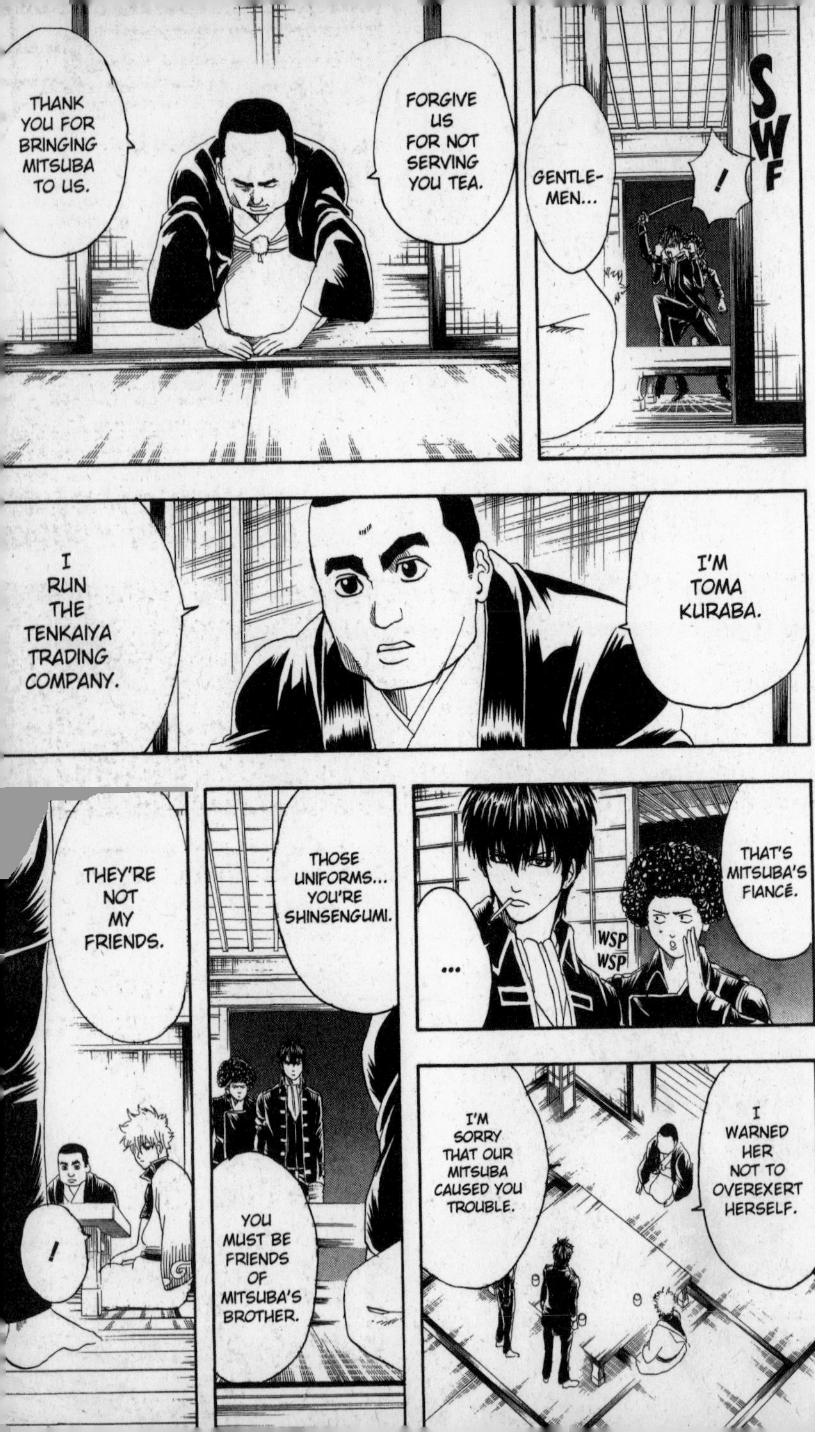

SWF
!
GENTLE-MEN...
FORGIVE US FOR NOT SERVING YOU TEA.
THANK YOU FOR BRINGING MITSUBA TO US.
I'M TOMA KURABA.
I RUN THE TENKAIYA TRADING COMPANY.
THAT'S MITSUBA'S FIANCÉ.
WSP WSP
...
I WARNED HER NOT TO OVEREXERT HERSELF.
I'M SORRY THAT OUR MITSUBA CAUSED YOU TROUBLE.
THOSE UNIFORMS... YOU'RE SHINSENGUMI.
YOU MUST BE FRIENDS OF MITSUBA'S BROTHER.
THEY'RE NOT MY FRIENDS.
!

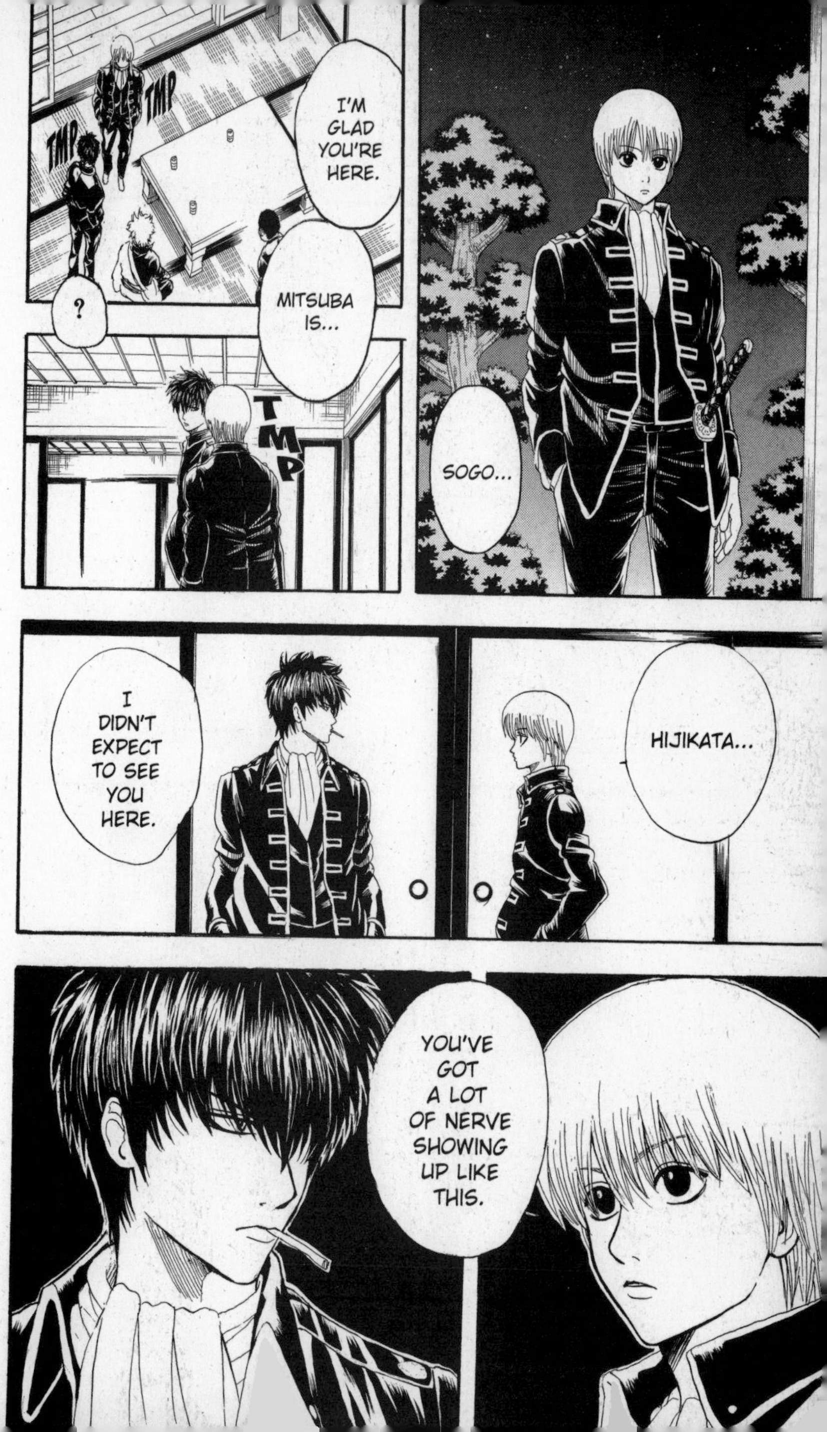
SOGO...
I'M GLAD YOU'RE HERE.
TMP
TMP
TMP
?
MITSUBA IS...
TMP
TMP
HIJIKATA...
I DIDN'T EXPECT TO SEE YOU HERE.
YOU'VE GOT A LOT OF NERVE SHOWING UP LIKE THIS.

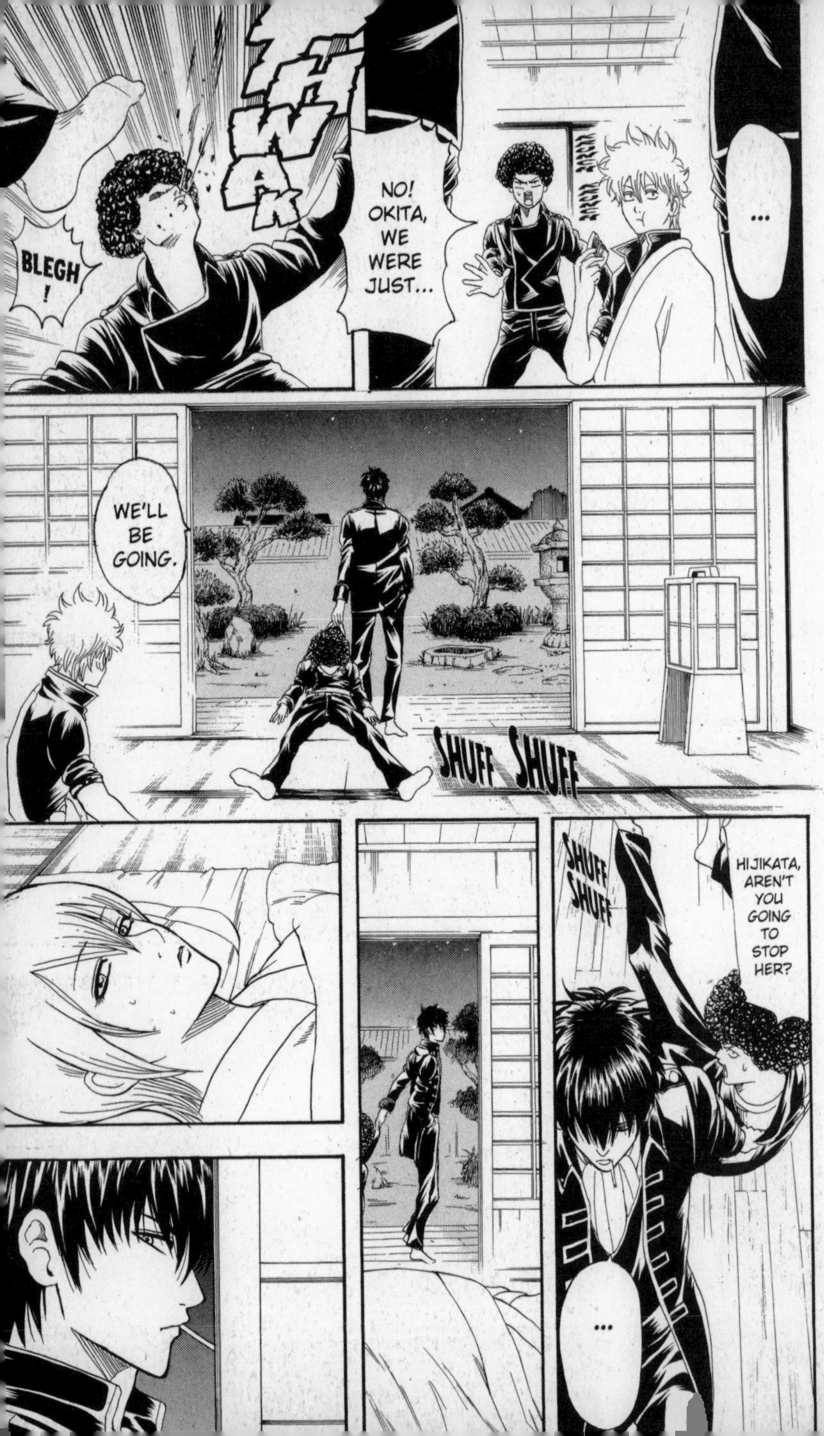
...
MUNCH MUNCH
NO! OKITA, WE WERE JUST...
THWAK
BLEGH!
WE'LL BE GOING.
SHUFF SHUFF
SHUFF SHUFF
HIJIKATA, AREN'T YOU GOING TO STOP HER?
...

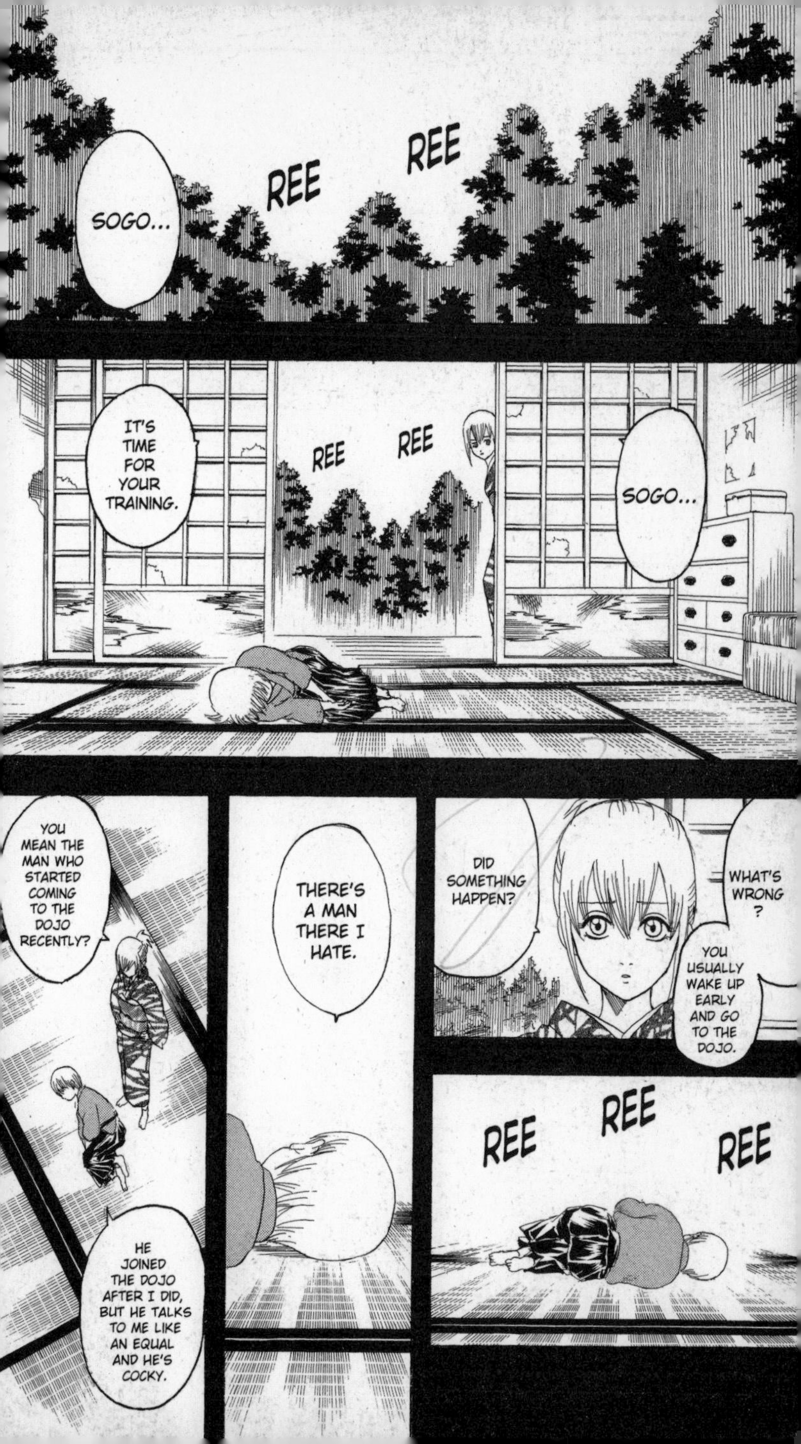
SOGO...
REE
REE
SOGO...
REE
REE
IT'S TIME FOR YOUR TRAINING.
WHAT'S WRONG?
DID SOMETHING HAPPEN?
YOU USUALLY WAKE UP EARLY AND GO TO THE DOJO.
REE
REE
REE
THERE'S A MAN THERE I HATE.
YOU MEAN THE MAN WHO STARTED COMING TO THE DOJO RECENTLY?
HE JOINED THE DOJO AFTER I DID, BUT HE TALKS TO ME LIKE AN EQUAL AND HE'S COCKY.

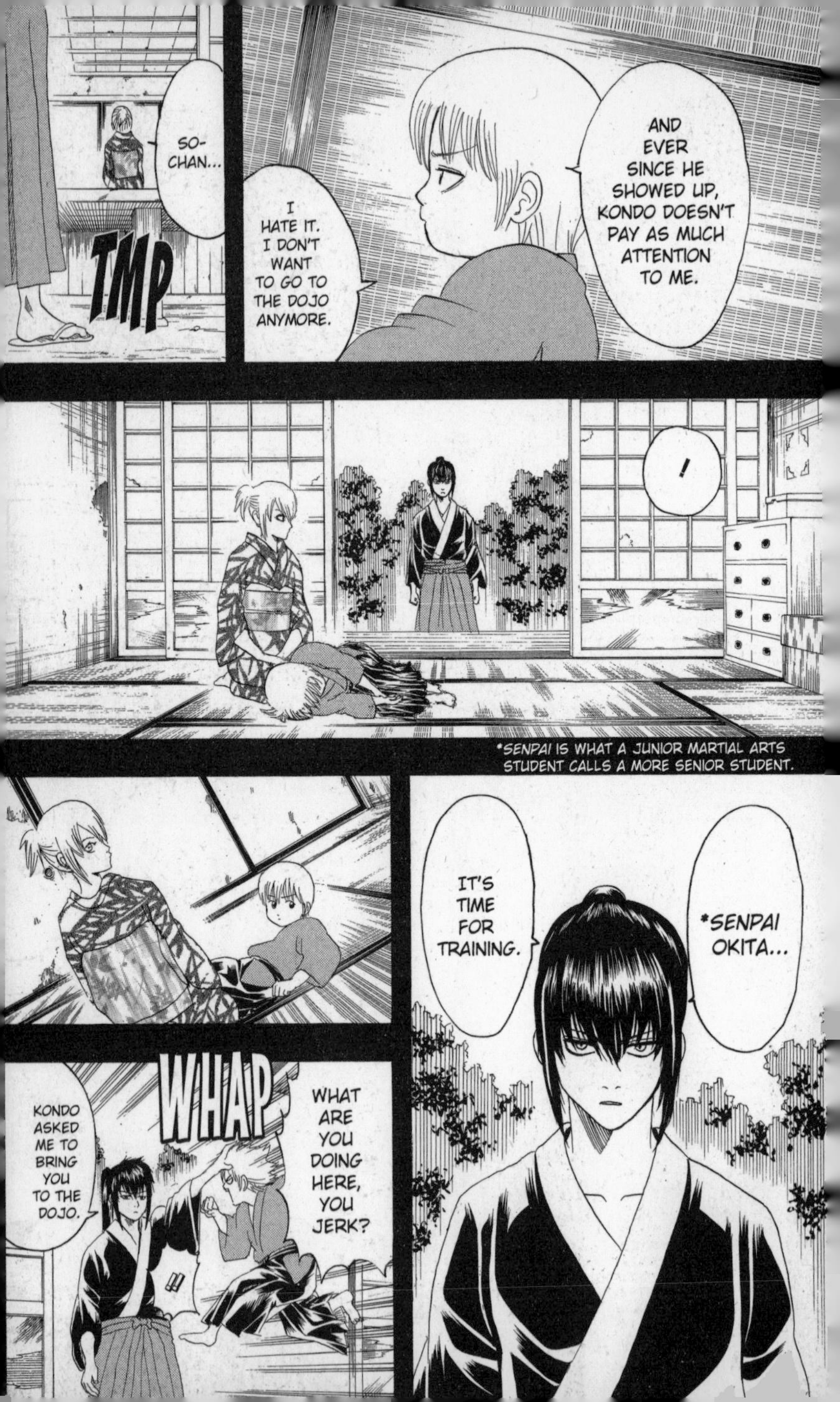
AND EVER SINCE HE SHOWED UP, KONDO DOESN'T PAY AS MUCH ATTENTION TO ME.
I HATE IT. I DON'T WANT TO GO TO THE DOJO ANYMORE.
SO-CHAN...
TMP
!
*SENPAI OKITA...
IT'S TIME FOR TRAINING.
WHAT ARE YOU DOING HERE, YOU JERK?
WHAP
KONDO ASKED ME TO BRING YOU TO THE DOJO.

*SENPAI IS WHAT A JUNIOR MARTIAL ARTS STUDENT CALLS A MORE SENIOR STUDENT.

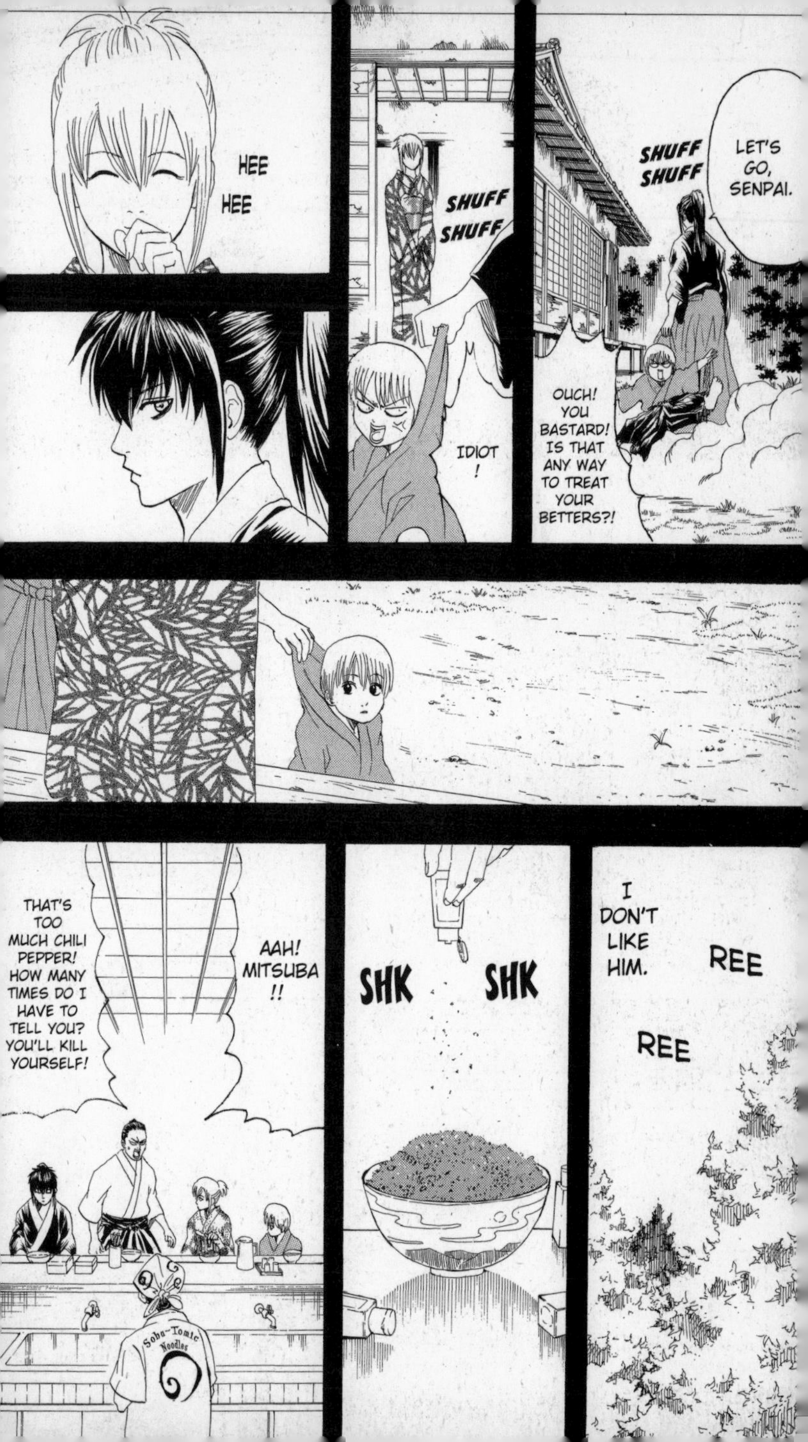
LET'S GO, SENPAI.
SHUFF SHUFF
OUCH! YOU BASTARD! IS THAT ANY WAY TO TREAT YOUR BETTERS?!
SHUFF SHUFF
IDIOT!
HEE HEE
I DON'T LIKE HIM.
REE
REE
SHK
SHK
AAH! MITSUBA!!
THAT'S TOO MUCH CHILI PEPPER! HOW MANY TIMES DO I HAVE TO TELL YOU? YOU'LL KILL YOURSELF!

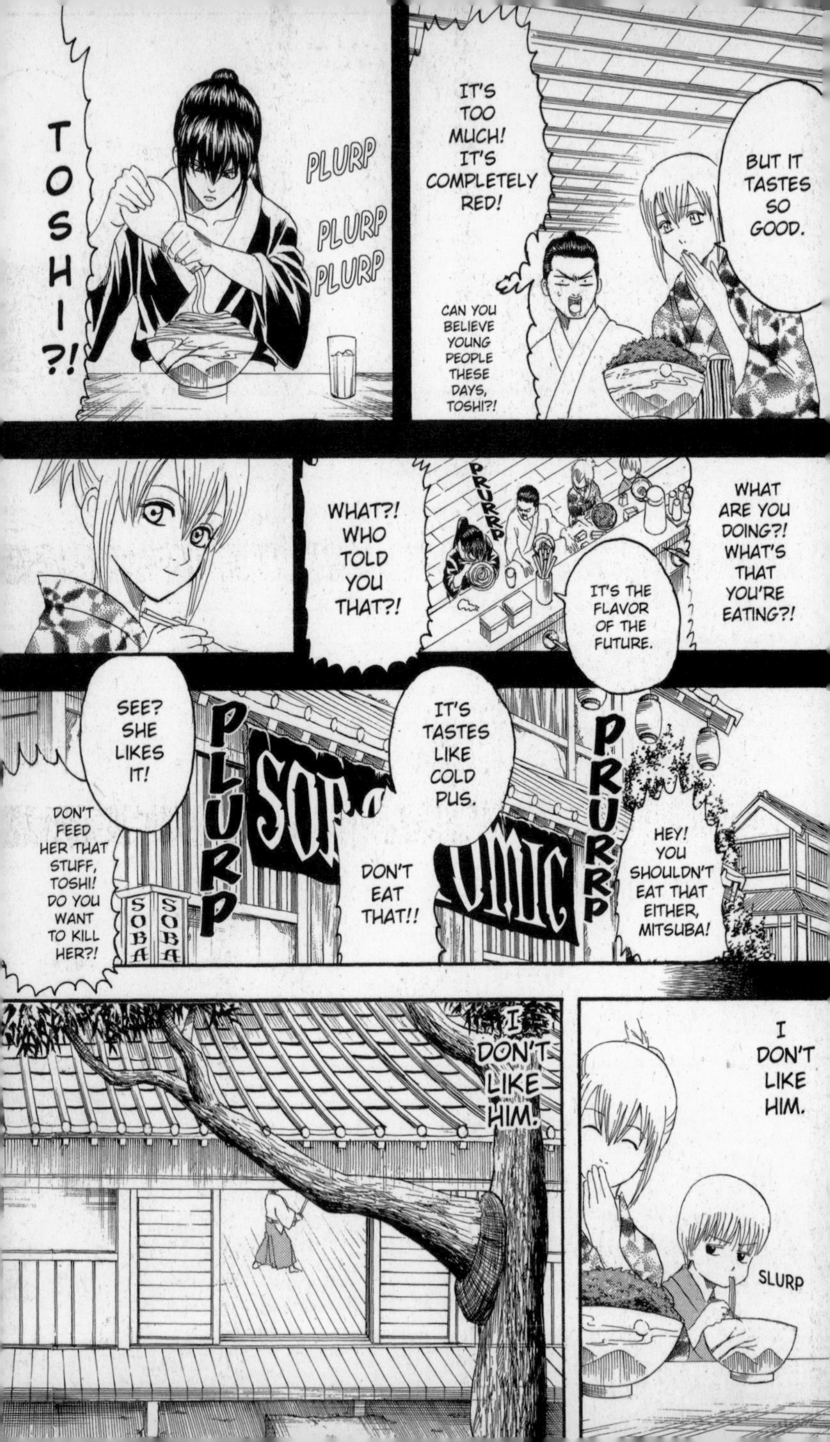
BUT IT TASTES SO GOOD.
IT'S TOO MUCH! IT'S COMPLETELY RED!
CAN YOU BELIEVE YOUNG PEOPLE THESE DAYS, TOSHI?!
PLURP
PLURP
PLURP
TOSHI?!
WHAT ARE YOU DOING?! WHAT'S THAT YOU'RE EATING?!
IT'S THE FLAVOR OF THE FUTURE.
PRURRP
WHAT?! WHO TOLD YOU THAT?!
HEY! YOU SHOULDN'T EAT THAT EITHER, MITSUBA!
PRURRP
IT'S TASTES LIKE COLD PUS.
DON'T EAT THAT!!
SEE? SHE LIKES IT!
PLURP
DON'T FEED HER THAT STUFF, TOSHI! DO YOU WANT TO KILL HER?!
SOBA
SOBA
I DON'T LIKE HIM.
SLURP
I DON'T LIKE HIM.

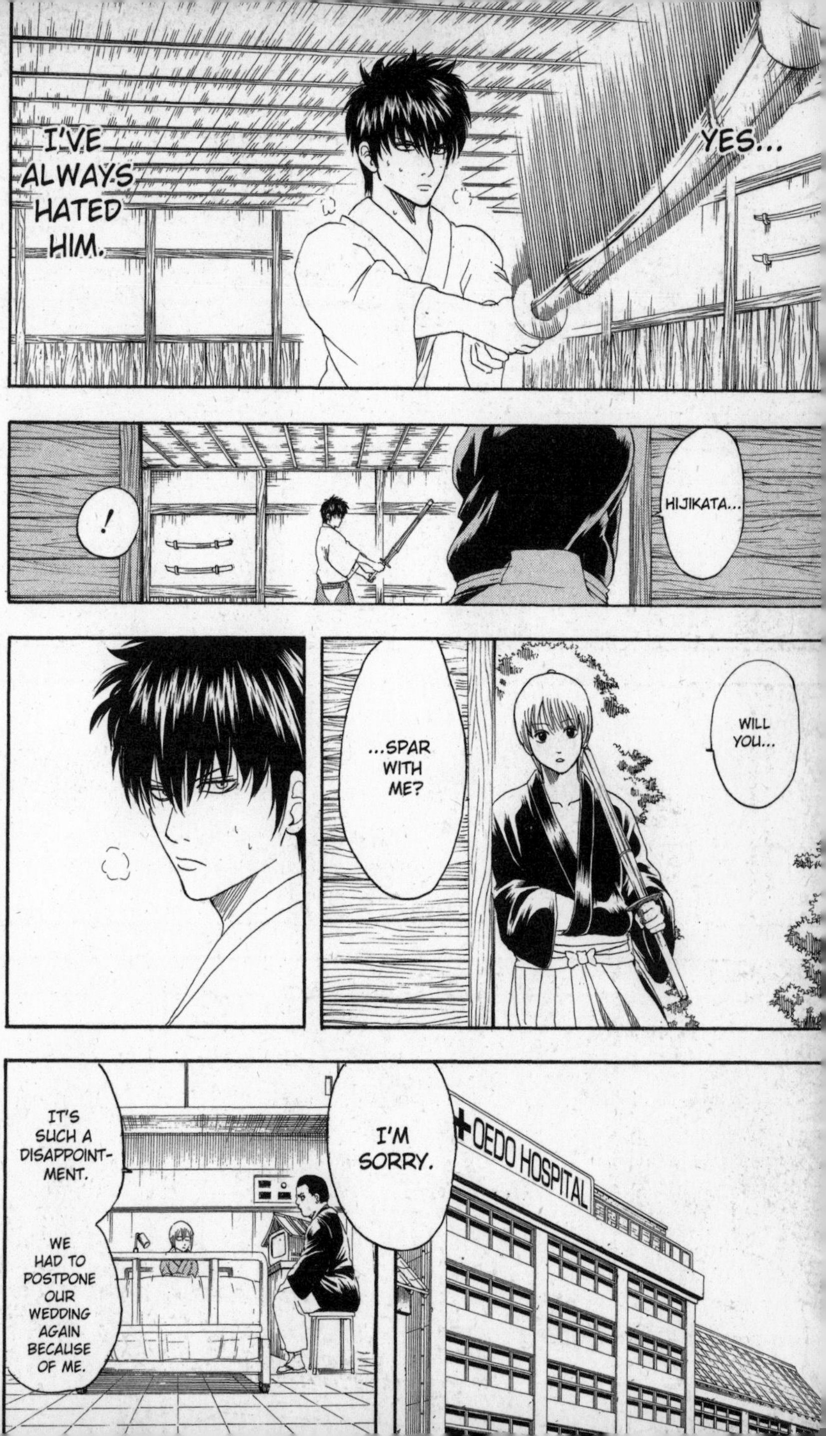
YES...
I'VE ALWAYS HATED HIM.
HIJIKATA...
!
WILL YOU...
...SPAR WITH ME?
I'M SORRY.
OEDO HOSPITAL
IT'S SUCH A DISAPPOINTMENT.
WE HAD TO POSTPONE OUR WEDDING AGAIN BECAUSE OF ME.

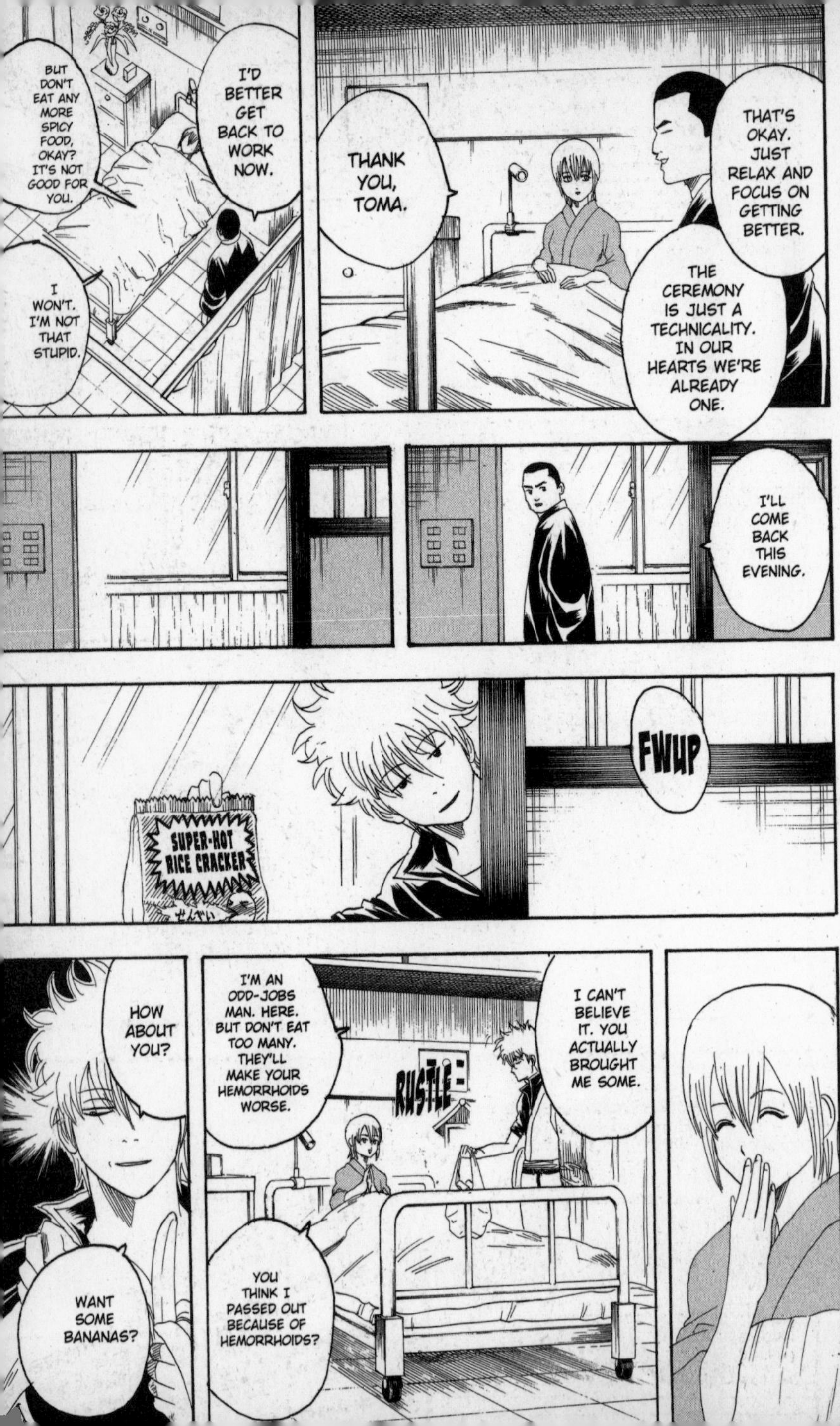
THAT'S OKAY. JUST RELAX AND FOCUS ON GETTING BETTER.
THE CEREMONY IS JUST A TECHNICALITY. IN OUR HEARTS WE'RE ALREADY ONE.
THANK YOU, TOMA.
I'D BETTER GET BACK TO WORK NOW.
BUT DON'T EAT ANY MORE SPICY FOOD, OKAY? IT'S NOT GOOD FOR YOU.
I WON'T. I'M NOT THAT STUPID.
I'LL COME BACK THIS EVENING.
FWUP
SUPER-HOT RICE CRACKER
I CAN'T BELIEVE IT. YOU ACTUALLY BROUGHT ME SOME.
RUSTLE
I'M AN ODD-JOBS MAN. HERE. BUT DON'T EAT TOO MANY. THEY'LL MAKE YOUR HEMORRHOIDS WORSE.
YOU THINK I PASSED OUT BECAUSE OF HEMORRHOIDS?
HOW ABOUT YOU?
WANT SOME BANANAS?

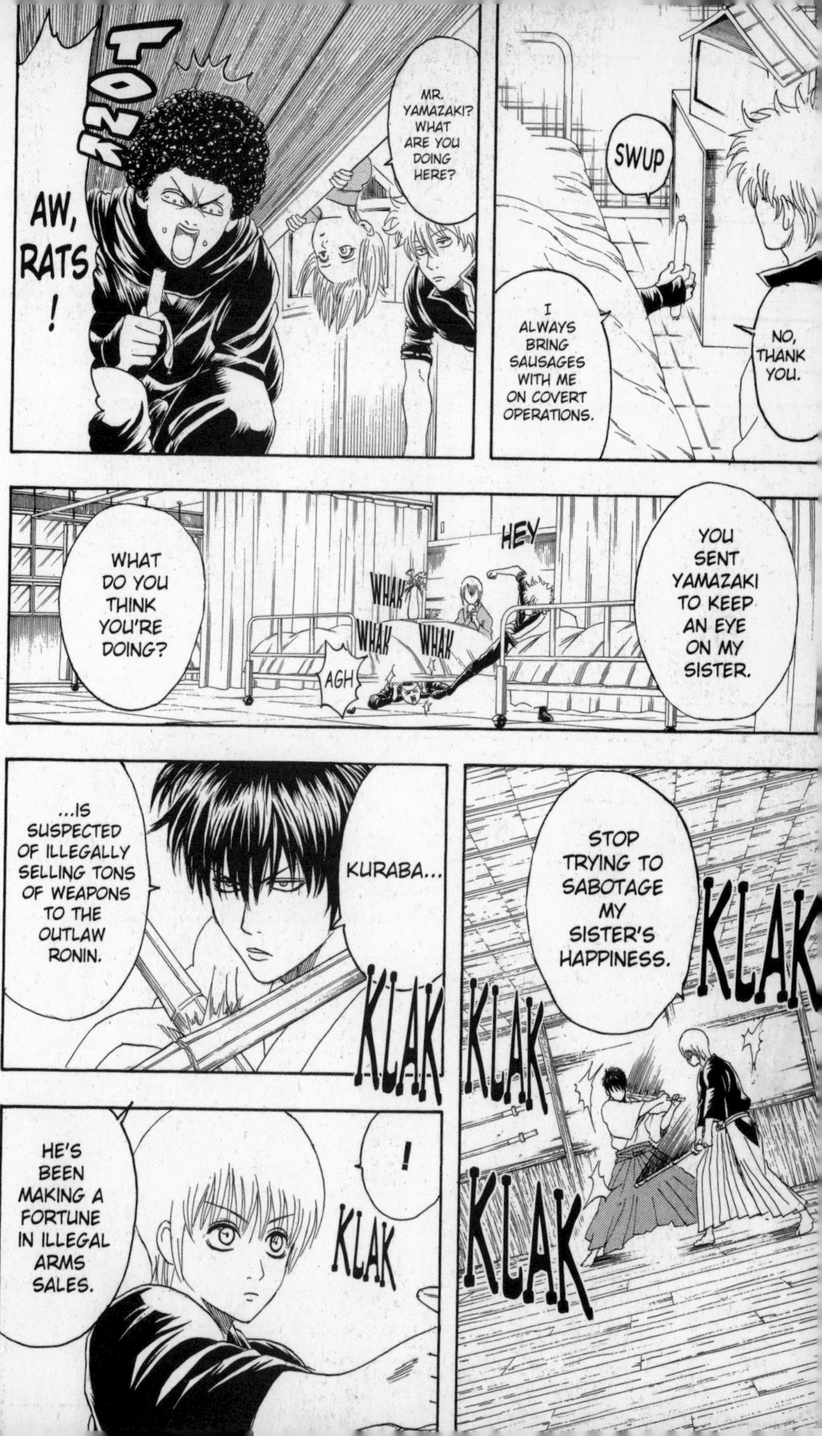
SWUP
I ALWAYS BRING SAUSAGES WITH ME ON COVERT OPERATIONS.
NO, THANK YOU.
MR. YAMAZAKI? WHAT ARE YOU DOING HERE?
TONK
AW, RATS!
YOU SENT YAMAZAKI TO KEEP AN EYE ON MY SISTER.
HEY
WHAK
WHAK
WHAK
AGH
WHAT DO YOU THINK YOU'RE DOING?
STOP TRYING TO SABOTAGE MY SISTER'S HAPPINESS.
KLAK
KLAK
KLAK
KURABA...
...IS SUSPECTED OF ILLEGALLY SELLING TONS OF WEAPONS TO THE OUTLAW RONIN.
KLAK
!
HE'S BEEN MAKING A FORTUNE IN ILLEGAL ARMS SALES.
KLAK

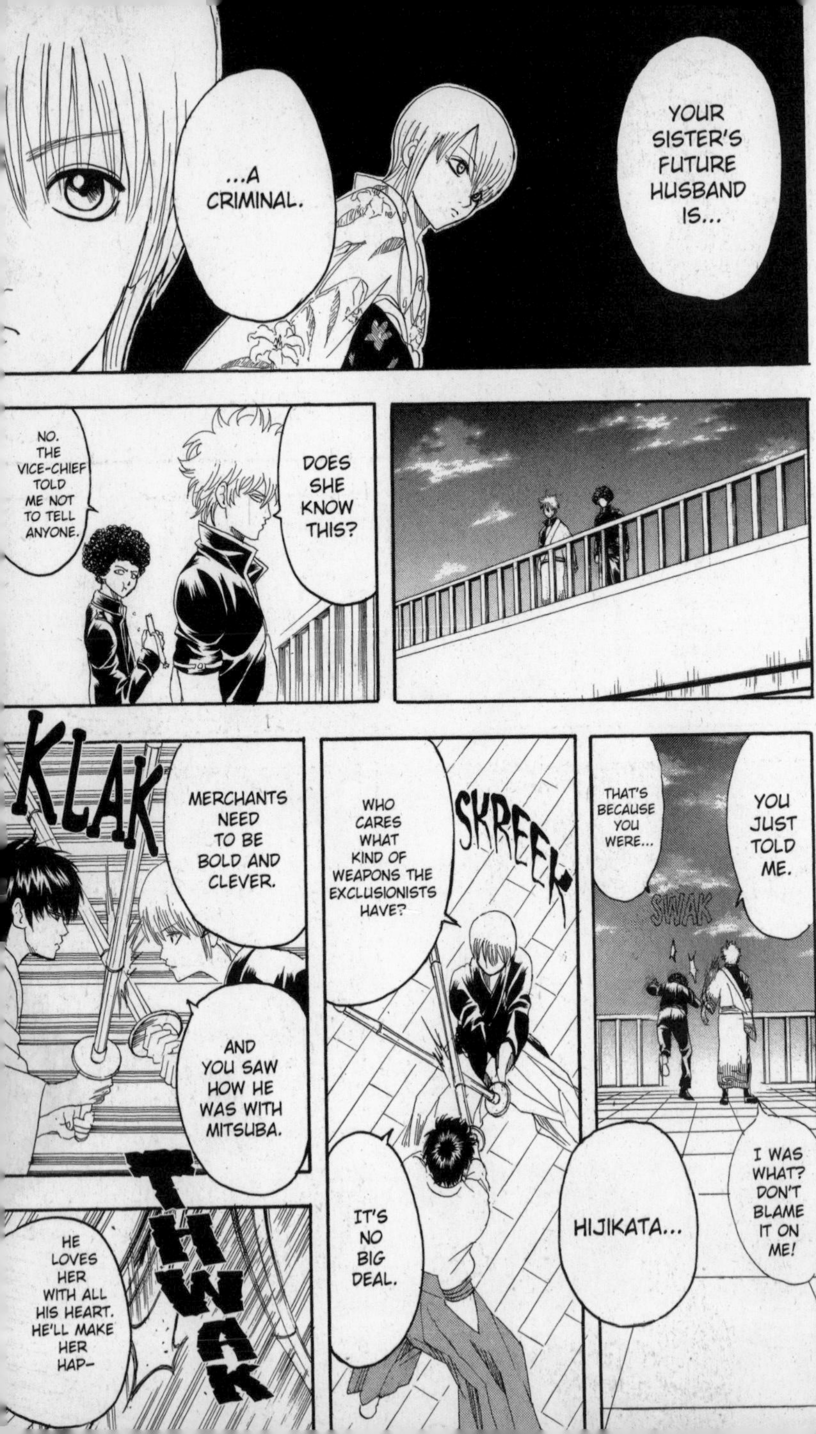
YOUR SISTER'S FUTURE HUSBAND IS...
...A CRIMINAL.
DOES SHE KNOW THIS?
NO. THE VICE-CHIEF TOLD ME NOT TO TELL ANYONE.
YOU JUST TOLD ME.
THAT'S BECAUSE YOU WERE...
SWAK
I WAS WHAT? DON'T BLAME IT ON ME!
HIJIKATA...
SKREEK
WHO CARES WHAT KIND OF WEAPONS THE EXCLUSIONISTS HAVE?
IT'S NO BIG DEAL.
KLAK
MERCHANTS NEED TO BE BOLD AND CLEVER.
AND YOU SAW HOW HE WAS WITH MITSUBA.
THWAK
HE LOVES HER WITH ALL HIS HEART. HE'LL MAKE HER HAP-

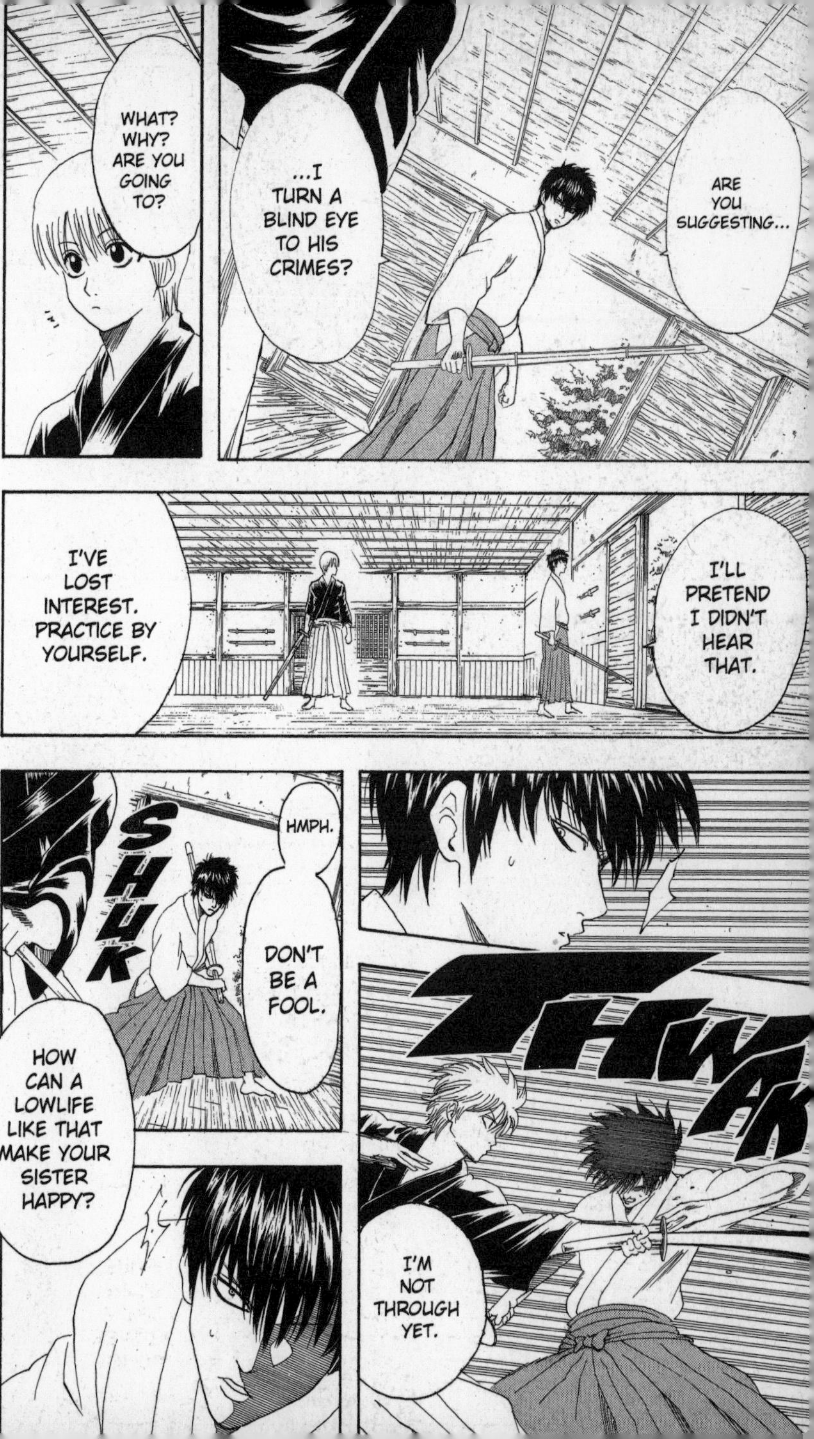
ARE YOU SUGGESTING...
...I TURN A BLIND EYE TO HIS CRIMES?
WHAT? WHY? ARE YOU GOING TO?
I'LL PRETEND I DIDN'T HEAR THAT.
I'VE LOST INTEREST. PRACTICE BY YOURSELF.
SHUK
HMPH.
DON'T BE A FOOL.
HOW CAN A LOWLIFE LIKE THAT MAKE YOUR SISTER HAPPY?
ZHWAK
I'M NOT THROUGH YET.

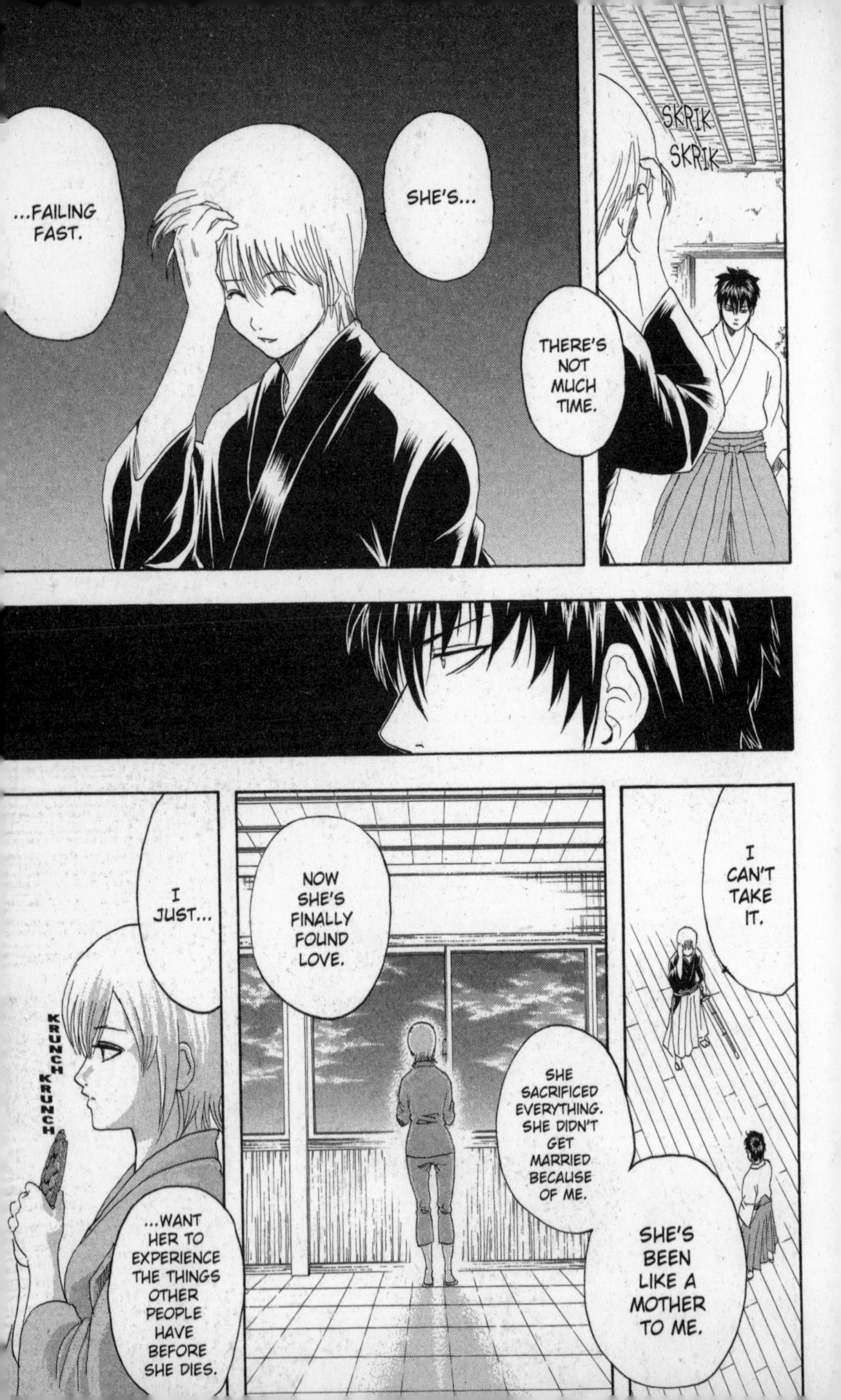
SKRIK
SKRIK
THERE'S NOT MUCH TIME.
SHE'S...
...FAILING FAST.
I CAN'T TAKE IT.
SHE'S BEEN LIKE A MOTHER TO ME.
SHE SACRIFICED EVERYTHING. SHE DIDN'T GET MARRIED BECAUSE OF ME.
NOW SHE'S FINALLY FOUND LOVE.
I JUST...
KRUNCH
KRUNCH
...WANT HER TO EXPERIENCE THE THINGS OTHER PEOPLE HAVE BEFORE SHE DIES.

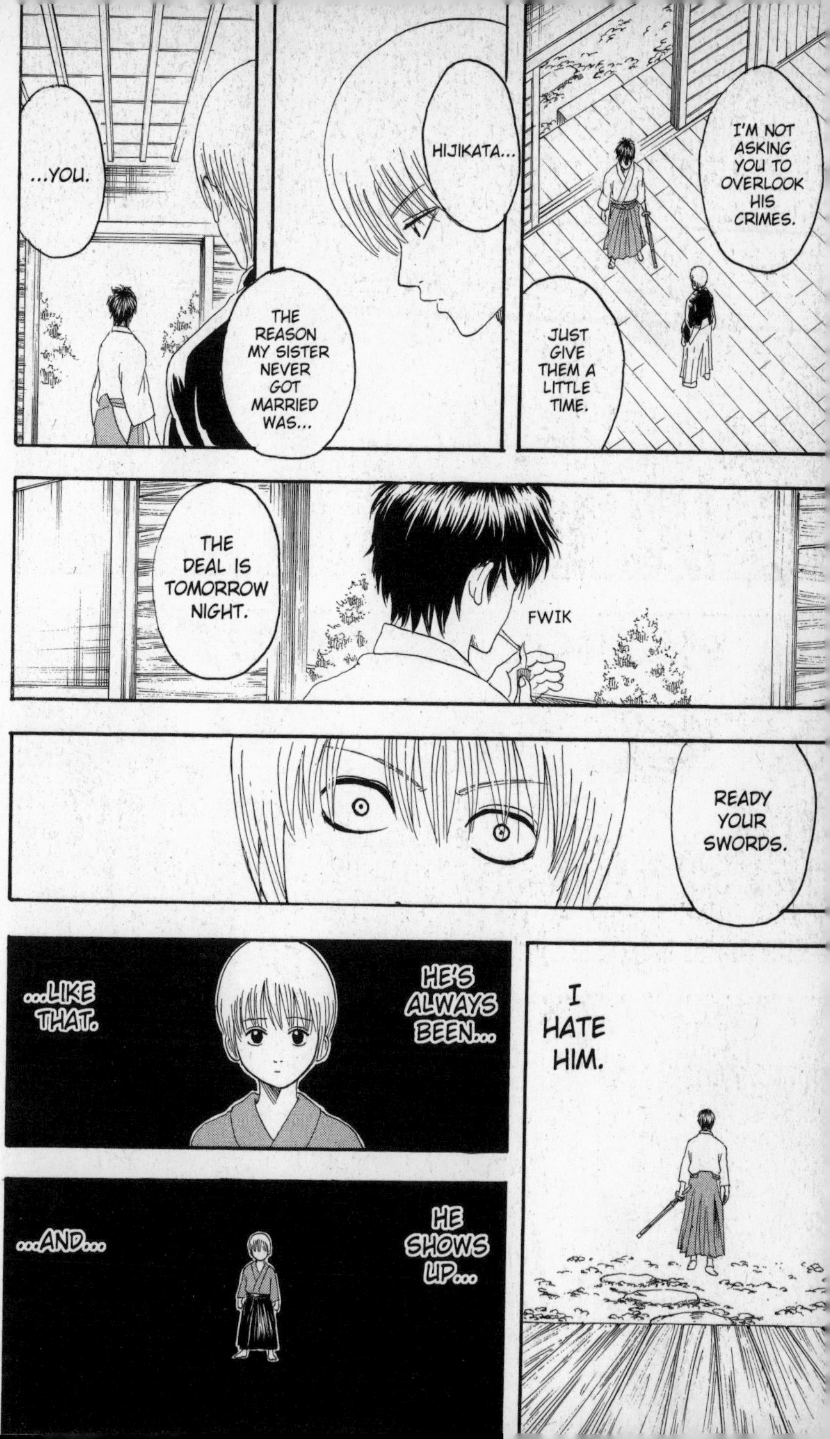
I'M NOT ASKING YOU TO OVERLOOK HIS CRIMES.
JUST GIVE THEM A LITTLE TIME.
HIJIKATA...
THE REASON MY SISTER NEVER GOT MARRIED WAS...
...YOU.
THE DEAL IS TOMORROW NIGHT.
FWIK
READY YOUR SWORDS.
I HATE HIM.
HE'S ALWAYS BEEN...
...LIKE THAT.
HE SHOWS UP...
...AND...

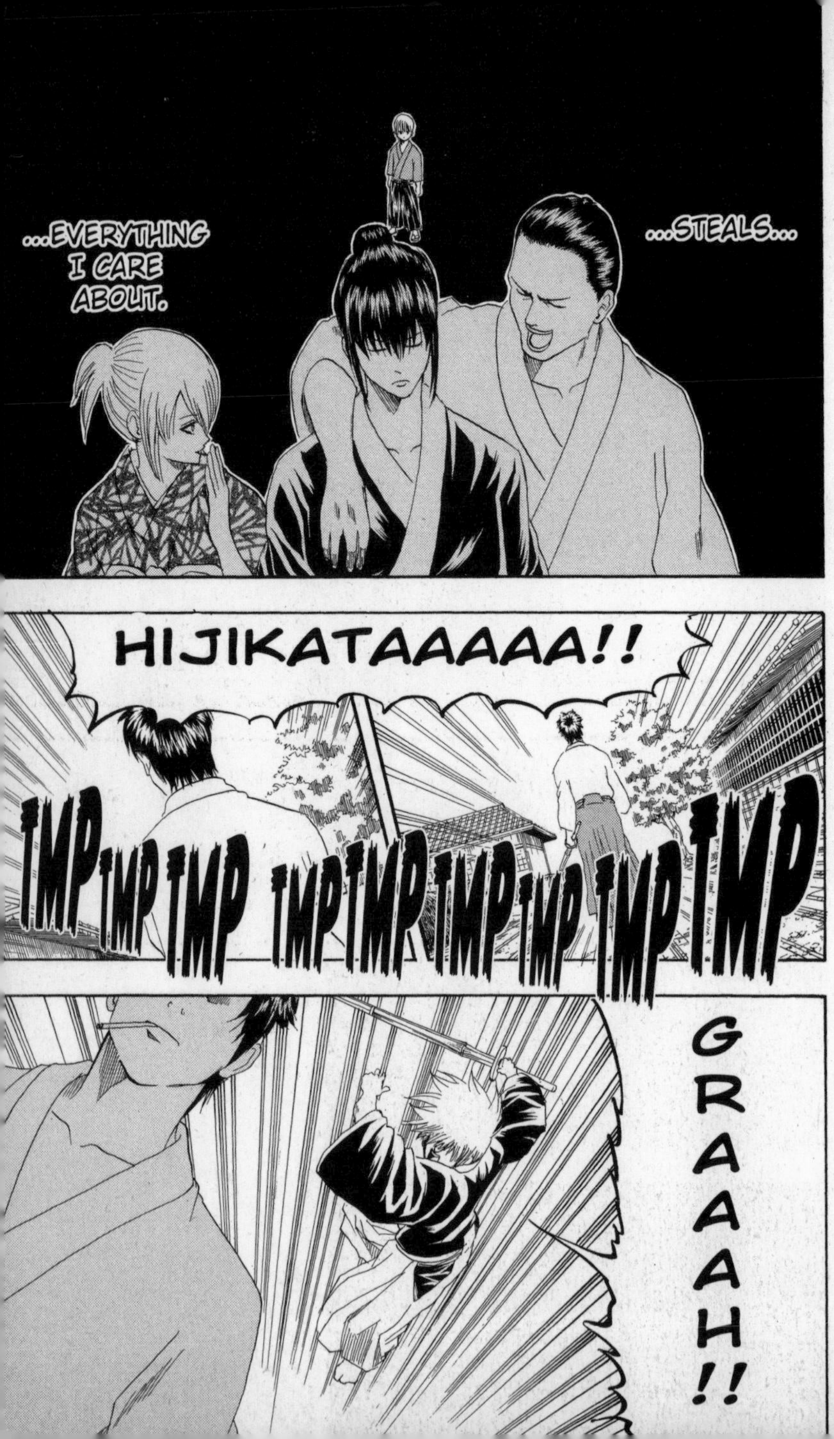
...STEALS...
...EVERYTHING I CARE ABOUT.
HIJIKATAAAAAA!!
TMP TMP TMP TMP TMP TMP TMP TMP TMP
GRAAAH!!

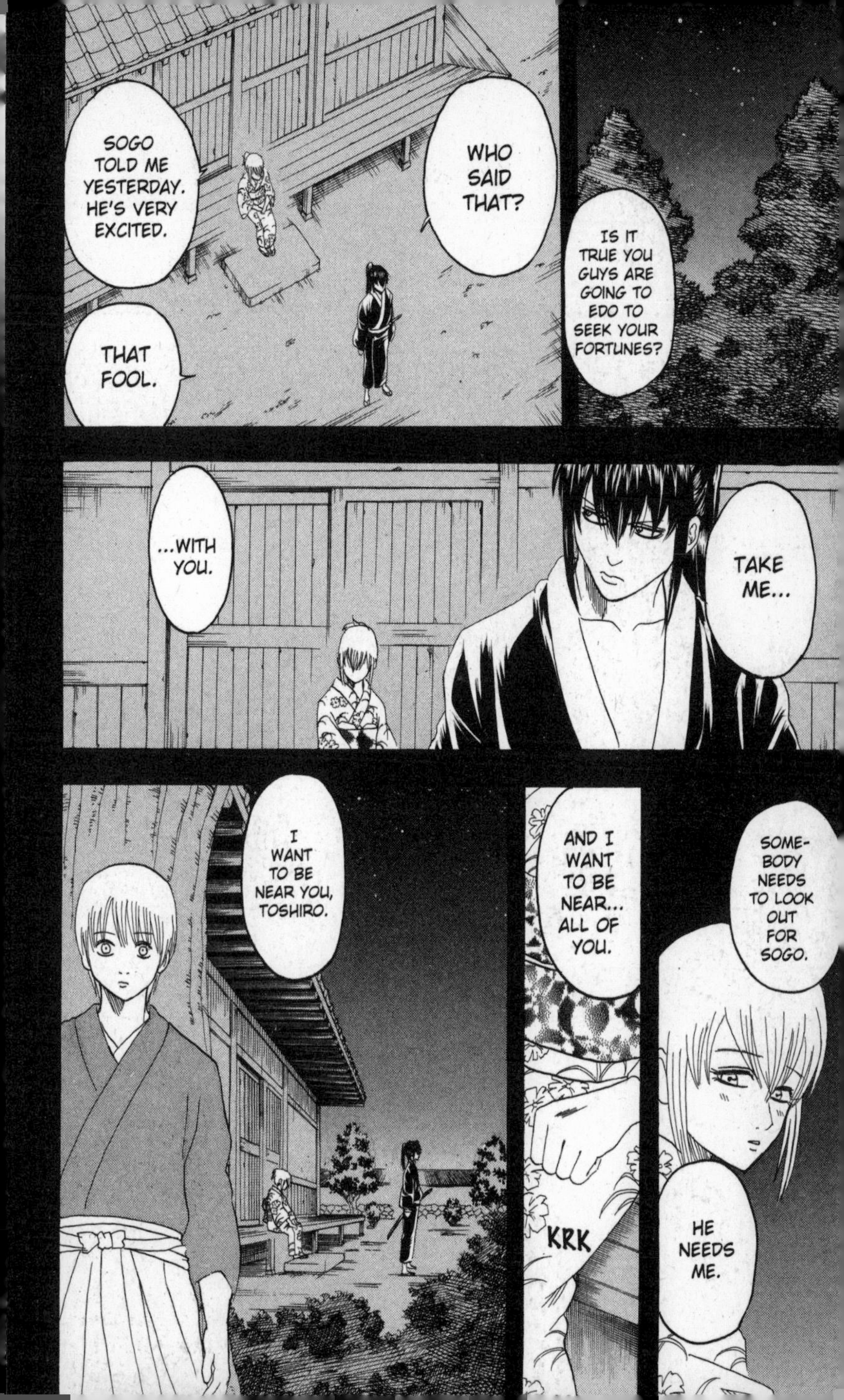
IS IT TRUE YOU GUYS ARE GOING TO EDO TO SEEK YOUR FORTUNES?
WHO SAID THAT?
SOGO TOLD ME YESTERDAY. HE'S VERY EXCITED.
THAT FOOL.
TAKE ME...
...WITH YOU.
SOME-BODY NEEDS TO LOOK OUT FOR SOGO.
HE NEEDS ME.
AND I WANT TO BE NEAR... ALL OF YOU.
KRK
I WANT TO BE NEAR YOU, TOSHIRO.

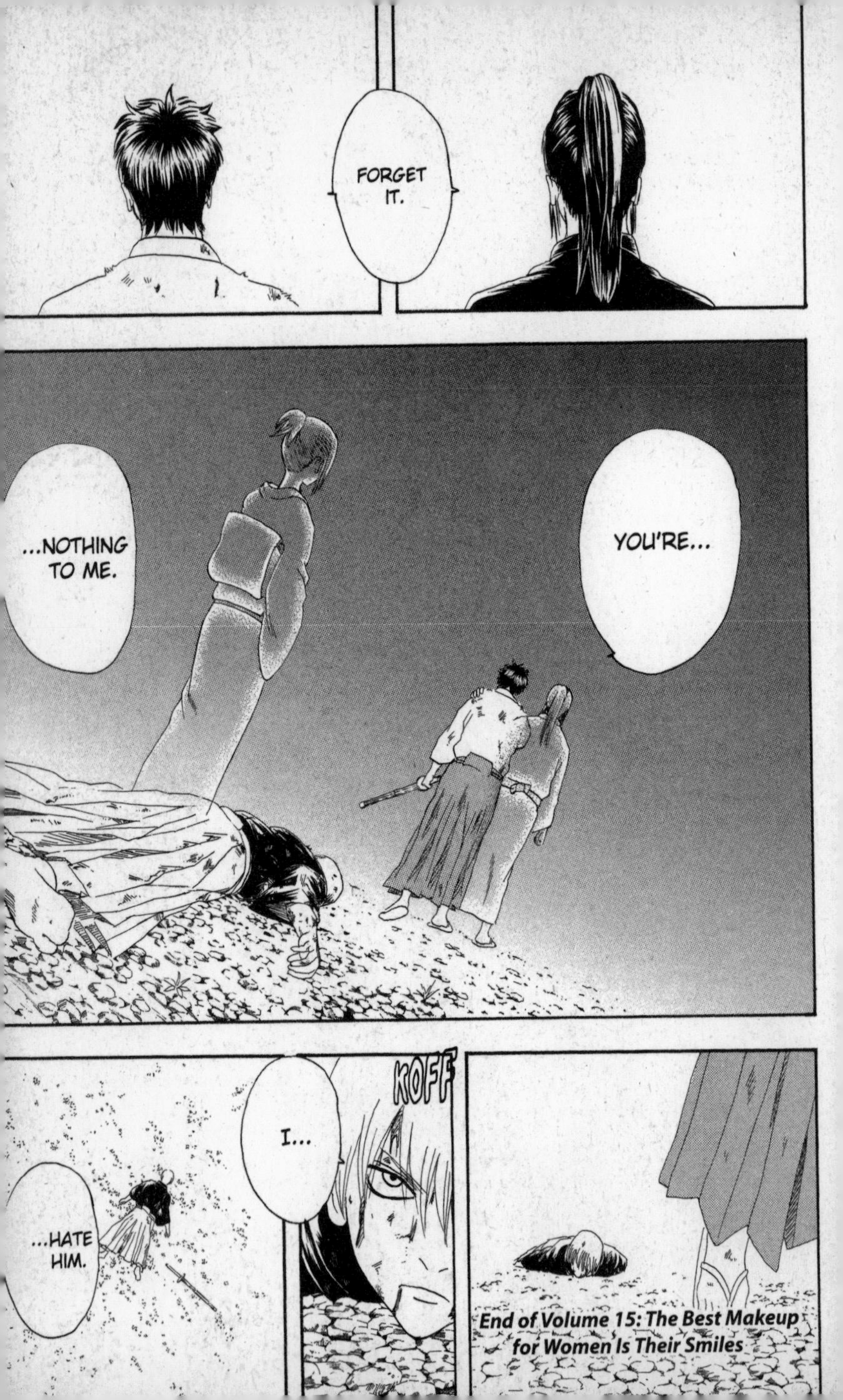
FORGET IT.
YOU'RE...
...NOTHING TO ME.
End of Volume 15: The Best Makeup for Women Is Their Smiles
KOFF
I...
...HATE HIM.

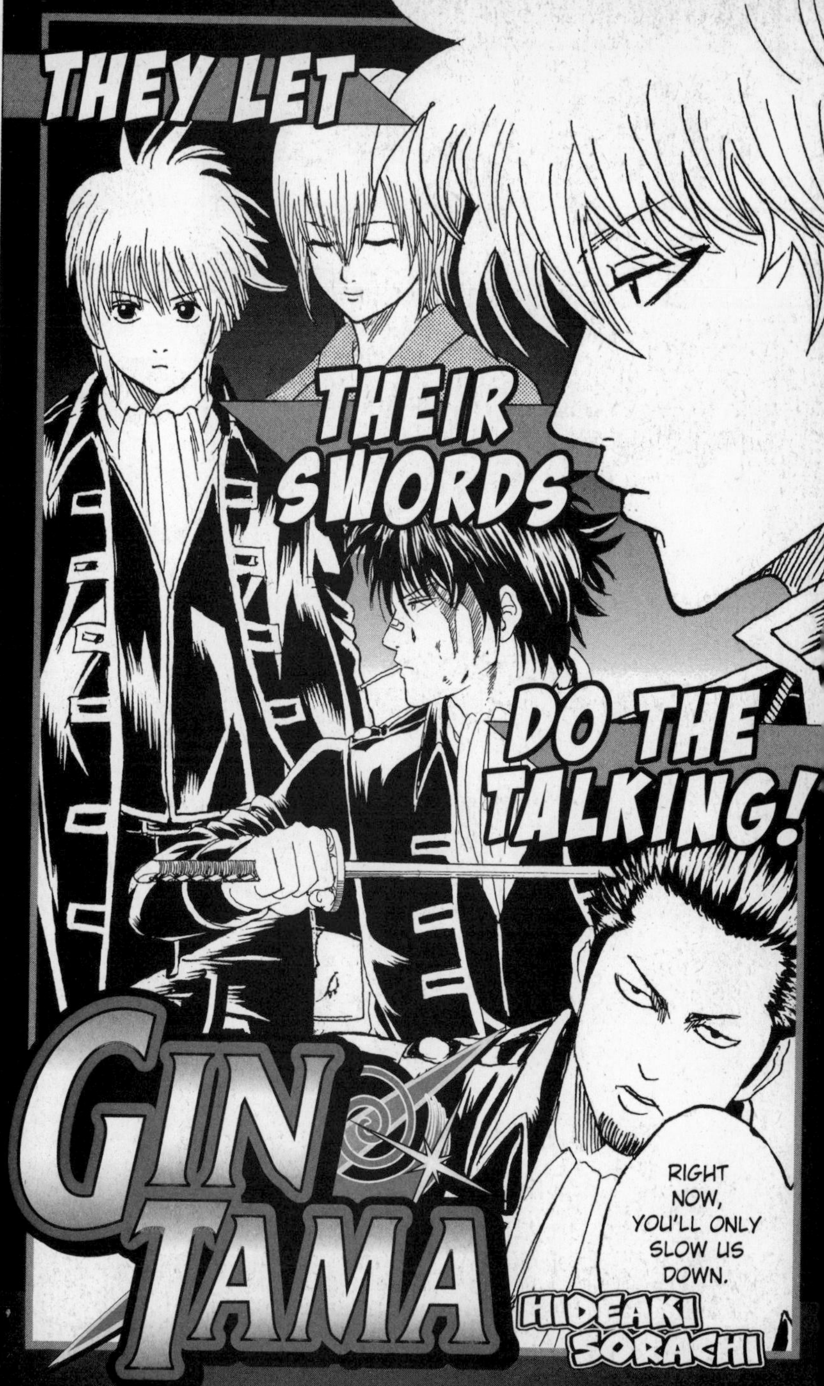
THEY LET
THEIR SWORDS
DO THE TALKING!
GIN TAMA
RIGHT NOW, YOU'LL ONLY SLOW US DOWN.
HIDEAKI SORACHI

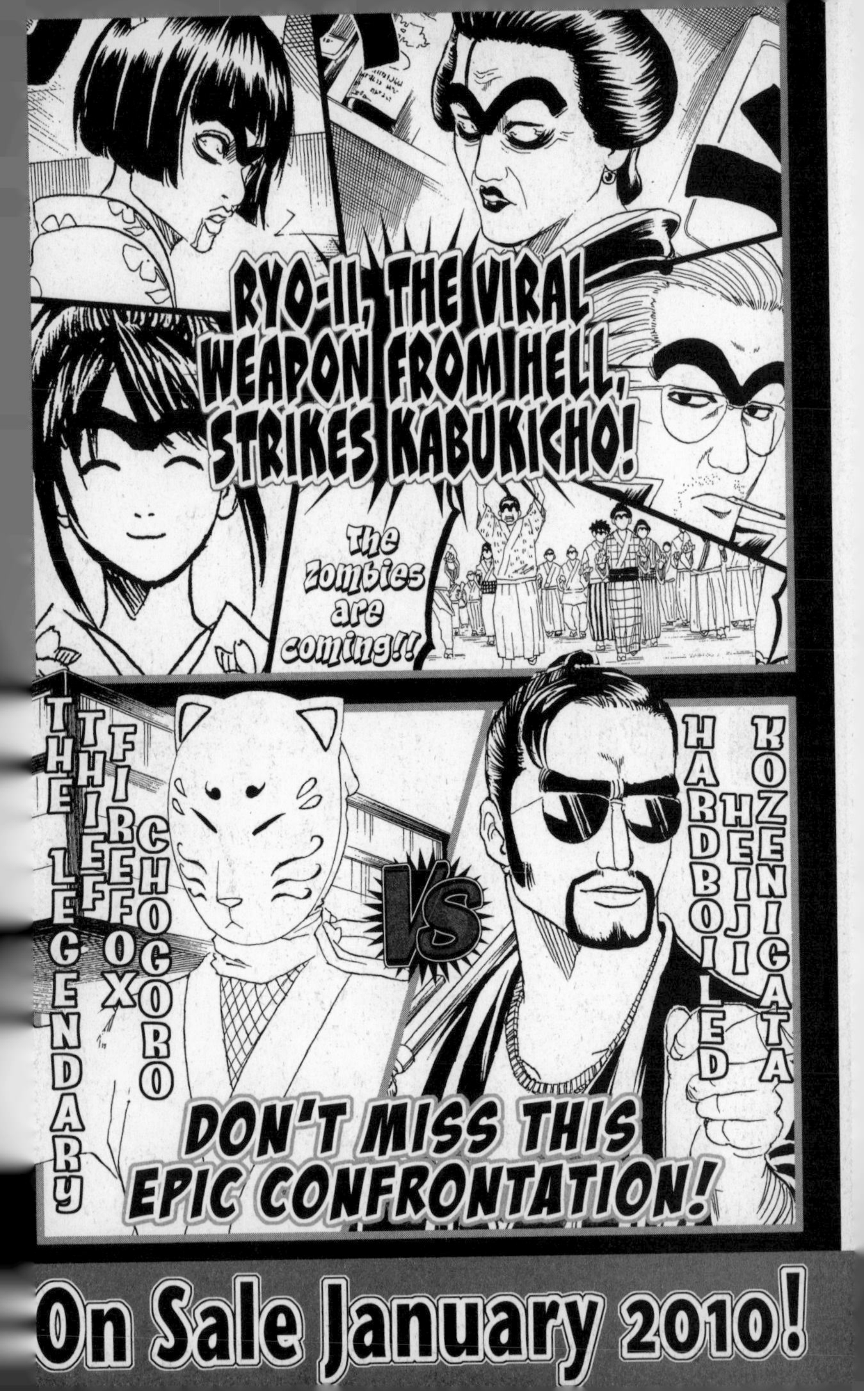
RYO-II, THE VIRAL WEAPON FROM HELL, STRIKES KABUKICHO!
The zombies are coming!!
HARDBOILED HEIJI KOZENIGATA
VS
THE LEGENDARY THIEF FIREFOX CHOGORO
DON'T MISS THIS EPIC CONFRONTATION!

Send us your Fan Art!

We'd like to give you, our loyal *Gin Tama* readers, a chance to show off your artistic talents! Send us your drawings of the Yorozuya crew or your other favorite characters from *Gin Tama*! If they're good enough to impress Granny Otose (which ain't easy), you just might see them in the pages of future VIZ Media volumes of *Gin Tama*!

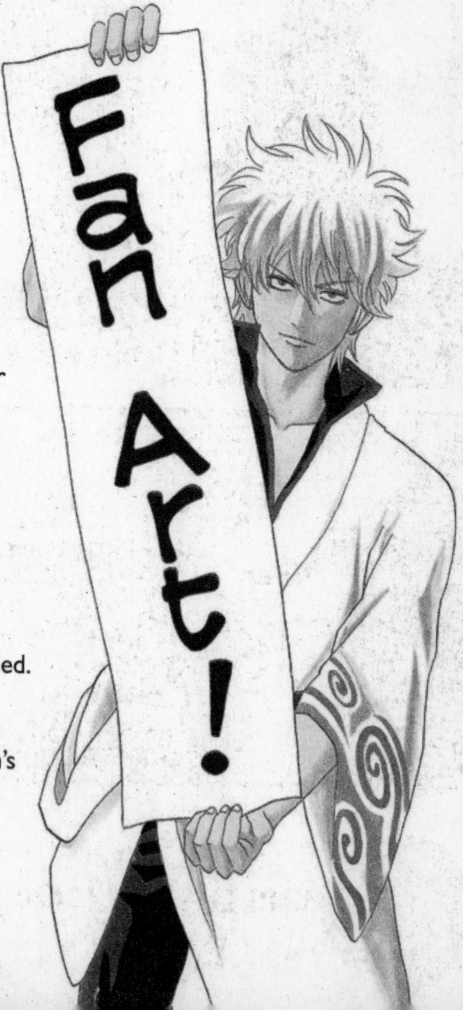

Fan Art!

Send your fan art to:

VIZ Media
Attn: Alexis Kirsch, Editor
295 Bay St.
San Francisco, CA 94133

Be sure to include the signed release form available here: http://www.shonenjump.com/fanart/Fan_Art_Release.pdf
Submissions will not be returned.
Submissions without a signed release form will be fed to the Amanto sea lions at Fisherman's Wharf…

Step on It!

Top 5 Things I'll Change When I'm Shogun (by Shinpachi)

1. Mandatory driving classes for Shinsengumi officers
2. Unibrows for everyone!
3. Zero-tolerance policy for cheesy "hard-boiled" dialogue
4. Lock up all the pervy architects
5. I get in free to speed-dating parties

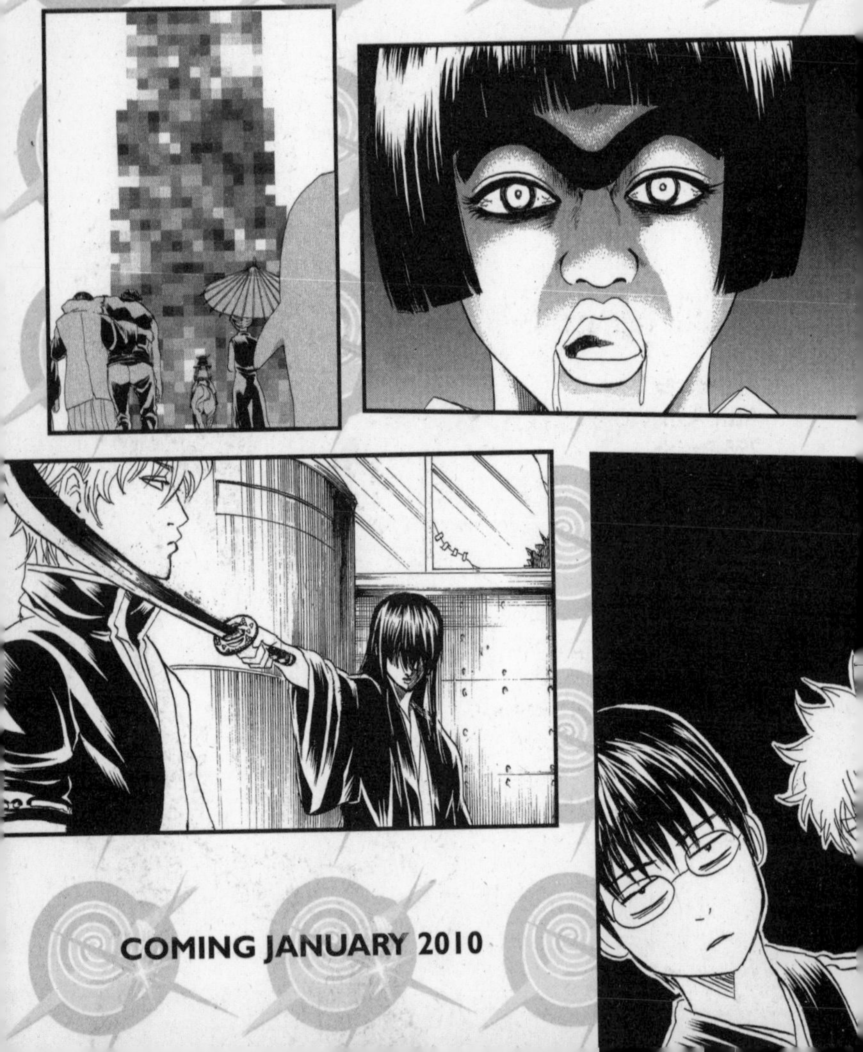

COMING JANUARY 2010

Tell us what you think about SHONEN JUMP manga!